Metaphor in Foreign Language Instruction

Applications of Cognitive Linguistics

Editors
Gitte Kristiansen
Francisco J. Ruiz de Mendoza Ibáñez

Honorary editor
René Dirven

Volume 42

Metaphor in Foreign Language Instruction

Edited by
Ana María Piquer-Píriz
Rafael Alejo-González

DE GRUYTER
MOUTON

ISBN 978-3-11-062673-5
e-ISBN (PDF) 978-3-11-063036-7
e-ISBN (EPUB) 978-3-11-062687-2
ISSN 1861-4078

Library of Congress Control Number: 2019947565

Bibliographic information published by the Deutsche Nationalbibliothek
The Deutsche Nationalbibliothek lists this publication in the Deutsche Nationalbibliografie;
detailed bibliographic data are available on the Internet at http://dnb.dnb.de.

© 2020 Walter de Gruyter GmbH, Berlin/Boston
Typesetting: Integra Software Services Pvt. Ltd.
Printing and binding: CPI books GmbH, Leck

www.degruyter.com

Acknowledgments

First and foremost, this book is a message of gratitude to Fiona MacArthur for her substantial contribution to the study of metaphor in second language learning and for her generous work as an academic and a university lecturer. Without her inspiration, the field would not be what it is now. We would also like to thank the authors of the different chapters included in this volume for their excellent articles and for having attended our call to contribute to the volume while at the same time complying with the deadlines as well as accepting to go through a serious review process. We are also grateful to all the reviewers of the chapters and especially to Frank Boers, who commented on the pre-final manuscript thus contributing to improve the final result. Finally, we are thankful to the series editors and to the editors of Mouton de Gruyter, who have made the whole process of publication easier.

https://doi.org/10.1515/9783110630367-202

Contents

Introduction

Part I. **Theoretical Considerations: Reviews and Perspectives**

Part II. **New Empirical Studies**

Part II. 1. **Learners' Use and Knowledge of L2 Figurative language**

Part II. 2. **Fostering Knowledge of L2 Figurative Language**

Introduction

Ana M. Piquer-Píriz and Rafael Alejo-González
Metaphor in L2 Instruction: Key Issues

1 Rationale

Since the publication of *Metaphors We Live By* (Lakoff and Johnson 1980) and the subsequent development and consolidation of Cognitive Linguistics (CL) as a well-established theory in Linguistics, exploring the role that metaphor, in particular, and figurative language, in general, play in our linguistic and conceptual systems has attracted a great deal of attention from scholars of different disciplines.

One of the areas in which applications of the theoretical tenets of CL have been particularly fruitful is foreign language instruction (Bielak 2011; Boers and Lindstromberg 2006; De Knop, Boers and De Rycker 2010; Littlemore and Low 2006; Piquer-Píriz and Alejo-González 2016; Piquer-Píriz and Boers 2019). A ground-breaking contribution to how to approach metaphor when teaching an L2 was Low's seminal article published in *Applied Linguistics* in 1988 (which is revisited by the author in Chapter 2 of this volume). This was followed in the 1990s by several journal articles introducing CL-oriented teaching proposals (Boers and Demecheleer 1998; Deignan, Gabryś and Solska 1997; Kövecses and Szabó 1996; Lazar 1996, Lindstromberg 1996; MacLennan 1994; Ponterotto 1994). In the 2000s, several monographs and collective volumes further defined what has become known as Applied Cognitive Linguistics (ACL) (Achard and Niemeier 2004; Boers and Lindstromberg 2008; De Knop, Boers and De Rycker 2010; Holme 2009; Littlemore 2009, 2017; Littlemore and Juchem-Grundmann 2010; Littlemore and Low 2006; Nacey 2017; Pütz, Niemeier and Dirven 2001a, 2001b, Pütz and Sicola 2010; Robinson and Ellis 2008). While some of these volumes included mostly contributions of a rather theoretical or exploratory nature, they have been complemented by an ever growing number of empirical studies demonstrating that the application of CL tenets can have a positive influence on instructed L2 acquisition (Alejo 2010; Alejo, Piquer Píriz and Reveriego 2010; Boers 2000, 2004; Boers, Eyckmans and Stengers 2007; Boers, Piquer-Píriz, Stengers and Eyckmans 2009; Condon 2008; Dirven 2001; Lindstromberg and Boers 2005; Littlemore and MacArthur 2007, 2008; MacArthur and Piquer-Píriz 2007; MacArthur and Littlemore 2008; Piquer-Píriz 2008, 2010; Saaty 2016; Tyler,

Ana M. Piquer-Píriz, English Philology (Faculty of Education), University of Extremadura, Badajoz, Spain, e-mail: anapiriz@unex.es
Rafael Alejo-González, English Philology (Faculty of Education), University of Extremadura, Badajoz, Spain, e-mail: ralejo@unex.es

https://doi.org/10.1515/9783110630367-001

Mueller and Ho 2010). Most of these studies have focused on the notion of motivated polysemy as opposed to semantic arbitrariness and have shown how enhancing the notion of linguistic motivation among L2 learners by means of different techniques (such as identifying conceptual metaphors, raising metaphor awareness in the L1 or using images, etymology, cross-cultural comparisons, or physical enactment to reconnect figurative meanings to their literal underpinnings) may facilitate L2 learners' comprehension and recall of figurative vocabulary. Boers (2011, 2013) reviews CL-inspired studies published between 1996 and 2010 that put the effectiveness of this approach to the test, pointing out the main contributions of these studies to the field but also some of their methodological limitations. In his paper on assessing and integrating Cognitive Linguistic approaches to teaching vocabulary, he concludes that:

> It must be acknowledged, however, that many of these are small-scale, some show only small effect sizes, and some are hard to interpret due to confounding variables. Taken collectively, the reported experiments are nevertheless beginning to constitute a body of evidence in favour of CL-informed instruction that is hard to dismiss, so there is reason to believe that this kind of instruction deserves a niche in second language programmes. (Boers 2013: 208)

However, despite the apparent important insights generated by this body of research in the past three decades, little impact seems to have been made on mainstream teaching materials (Lazar 2003, Rudzka-Ostyn 2003 and Lindstromberg and Boers 2008 are some exceptions) and L2 classroom practice. For example, as MacArthur (2017) states, although it has been shown (Littlemore and Low 2006) that metaphor plays an important role in all four dimensions of communicative competence (linguistic, sociolinguistic, discourse and strategic), it is conspicuously absent in the descriptors established for the Common European Framework of Reference for Languages (CEFRL) and "is still regarded as somewhat marginal in the materials published for English as S/FL." (MacArthur 2017: 418). Thus, despite the continued and fruitful effort to give metaphor its well-deserved place in foreign language instruction, there are still many gaps to be filled.

Exploring the role of figurative language in L2 instruction and cross-cultural communication have been the two main foci of Dr. Fiona MacArthur, the scholar to whom we dedicate the present collective volume (e.g., MacArthur 2005, 2010, 2016a, 2016b, 2016c, 2017; MacArthur et al. 2012; MacArthur, Krennmayr and Littlemore 2015; Musolff, MacArthur and Pagani 2014). The opening chapter of this volume, by Gibbs, reviews a selection of MacArthur's publications and emphasises how "by recognizing the limitations of our methods and the constant need for broader contextualization of how we study real-life metaphor use [...] she offers us a distinctive, ideal model on how to best study metaphor." (Gibbs, this volume: 35). Throughout her academic career, she has not only shown an endless interest in metaphor but she has been, and is still, able to instil this enthusiasm also in her students and colleagues. A group of close colleagues, some of whom are also eminent scholars in the field, have got together in this volume to offer an overview of the study of metaphor in L2 instruction, including identification of areas that need further research, as well as to illustrate new developments in empirical Applied Cognitive Linguistics research using diverse methods (such as analyses of learner corpora and classroom interventions). The findings demonstrate the relevance of the basic premises of CL for L2 acquisition research and provide insights into how CL can be applied in real instructional contexts.

This volume consists of two main parts. Part I comprises four review articles that touch upon issues of continuing relevance to the discipline (e.g. why metaphor is relevant for L2 learners and how it can be taught) and identify areas in need of further research (such as metaphor in the instruction of languages other than English or how metaphorical competence can be fostered with young L2 learners). These conceptual reviews of specific bodies of research will hopefully help readers to interpret and appreciate the value of the empirical studies reported in the second part of the book. Part II consists of eight new empirical studies that illustrate both methodological challenges and promising practices, lighting various paths that can be followed when analysing the role that metaphorical language plays in L2 instruction in real contexts. These eight original studies belong to two different broad areas: The first five explore L2 learners' knowledge of L2 figurative language and how they use it while the last three chapters evaluate different possibilities for enhancing knowledge of non-literal language in the foreign language classroom.

2 Part I. Theoretical Considerations: Reviews and Perspectives

Gibbs opens the first part of the volume with a review of what he considers the most influential contributions by Fiona MacArthur to the study of metaphor. He shows how her work on metaphor in classroom discourse, metaphor in interaction between native and non-native speakers of a language, and metaphor use in various socio-cultural contexts is directly relevant to some of the general topics that have been raised in metaphor studies such as: (1) the understanding of primary metaphors, (2) the role of metaphorical reasoning in an L2, (3) how not only linguistic but also historical, cultural and social factors underlie metaphorical language, (4) how speakers of more than one language 'mix' metaphors and (5) metaphor identification. According to Gibbs, one of MacArthur's greatest contributions to our discipline is that she keeps reminding us of the complexities of studying metaphor, the interconnection between language, culture and thought and the particularities of metaphor use in situated discourse, where metaphor should be viewed as a resource to meet individual and collective adaptive needs.

The chapter by Low is a review of one of the most influential (and most cited) publications on metaphor and foreign language instruction, written by the author over thirty years ago. Low identifies the issues that remain relevant in relation to the importance of metaphor for L2 learners such as his 'treatment' definition of metaphor, its 'core' functions and the importance of metaphorical competence, and he also summarises a number of notable new developments in the field in the past thirty years, including the outcomes from corpus research, studies into learner language and learning strategies, and empirical studies of teaching metaphor as part of foreign language training.

The last two chapters in this first part tackle under-explored issues in the field of metaphor and foreign language instruction. Piquer-Píriz addresses the topic of metaphor and young L2 learners, and connects the findings from child language studies into children's understanding and production of figurative language in their L1 with the insights from metaphor research studies on the pedagogical potential of enhancing learners' appreciation of motivated polysemy already with L2 learners at a young age.

Finally, Suárez-Campos, Hijazo-Gascón and Ibarretxe-Antuñano focus on metaphor in L2 instruction in a language other than English, in this case, Spanish. They point out that although English has been the predominant language to which CL-oriented pedagogies have been applied, other languages, such as Chinese or Spanish have also been explored. Focusing mainly on the notions of 'conceptual metaphor' and 'metaphorical competence' and their importance for L2 instruction, they review the available studies that use metaphor in the acquisition of Spanish as an L2, thus illustrating how the pedagogical applications of metaphor theory as a tool are also applicable to Spanish as a second language.

3 Part II. New Empirical Studies

Part II of the book offers a selection of new empirical studies which expand and continue the research carried out following an Applied Cognitive Linguistic perspective, as cited above. More specifically, the chapters included here examine broad areas organised in two different sections. In the first section, five chapters deal with L2 learners' knowledge and use of metaphorical language while in the second part, three chapters evaluate pedagogic procedures for fostering L2 metaphorical competence in diverse instructional contexts.

The first chapter included in section 1 is authored by Littlemore, Pérez-Sobrino, Julich and Leung, who present the results of a large-scale question-naire-based project on word-colour associations. Respondents were speakers of two of the most widely used languages in the world: English and Cantonese. One of the aims of the study was to determine to what extent the level of em-bodiment perceived in word-colour associations influences the likelihood that L2 learners will gradually adopt typical L2 associations in their interlanguage.

The presence of metaphor in Higher Education is dealt with in the following chapter, where Philip analyses the problems posed by the metaphors that appear in a translation course (English-Italian) at an Italian university. The more basic challenge has to do with the recognition of metaphors in the text-task at which most students are successful but also with choosing the translation that best fits the context and is compatible with the lexis of the source domain of the meta-phor in the target language. Sometimes, students are unable to find the appropri-ate term but the fact that in most cases they are willing to risk a metaphorically less optimal translation in the target language is already an indication that they are becoming aware of its importance in translation. Philip also finds that lower-proficiency students tend to be less successful at translating metaphors and are more prone to misinterpreting metaphorical language as literal. So, again, the profile of the learner matters, even within a population of students sharing the same interest and aspiration (in this case, becoming professional translators).

Krennmayr, who has already published an article with Fiona MacArthur on a similar topic before (MacArthur et al. 2015), pays attention to yet another edu-cational context where metaphor is common: office hours' consultations by Spanish Erasmus students on their year abroad. These consultations are carried out in English and provide a good opportunity for exploring the use of meta-phor in academic dialogue between novice and expert users, when the typical context for oral academic communication, lectures, is mostly monologic and unidirectional. In this way, it provides the perfect testing ground to analyse how interlocutors use and reuse the same conceptual metaphor to achieve alignment, a feature of oral interaction that allows the conversation to flow. In her article, she focuses on SIGHT metaphors and explores the use of the WMatrix semantic annotation tools to carry out her analysis.

The following chapter, authored by Nacey, also deals with metaphorical competence, although this time the connection is established with general profi-ciency. Reminiscent of earlier work by Littlemore et al. (2014), a corpus of written English (TraWL) serves to examine metaphor use by Norwegian school learners belonging to different age groups. The greater metaphor density found in the more advanced school grades –grade being used as a proxy of proficiency- is interpreted as a natural progression in L2 acquisition, not only because of the development in metaphorical competence by the learners but also because of the more abstract nature of the topics they are asked to write about. This progression is not only shown quantitatively but also qualitatively in the selection of functions that metaphors perform.

The relationship between lexical and metaphorical competence in L2 acquisition, a connection seldom dealt with in the literature, is explored by Castellano-Risco and Piquer-Píriz. To do so, they analyse the extent to which the learners' knowledge of the metaphors identified in two standard vocabulary tests (VLT and PVLT) correlate with their global scores on these tests, research complemented by an analysis of the success rate of the individual metaphor items in comparison to the other lexical items in the tests. The results are preliminary but point to the possibility that including metaphorical items in the tests may imply an added degree of difficulty not captured by word frequency in a corpus (i.e., the main selection principle behind these vocabulary tests).

The second section of part II begins with a chapter by Wang, Boers and Warren, who give continuation to the research emphasizing the importance of providing meaning motivation in the teaching of L2 vocabulary. In this case, the authors study to what extent students at different levels of proficiency benefit from the explanations provided about the origin or motivation of idiomatic expressions. The results show that more advanced students do not need the motivation to be convincing to remember the idioms they have been taught, while less advanced students did not profit as much from explanations that they found far-fetched. In this way, the authors highlight the importance of the other part of the equation in teaching contexts: the learners. Not all methods or approaches are created equal when it comes to metaphor teaching.

The need to raise metaphor awareness in another educational context, CLIL (Content and Language Integrated Learning), is emphasized in the chapter by Alejo-González and García-Bermejo, who analyse the metaphor density of two textbooks (Social and Natural Science) used to teach these subjects in bilingual schools in Spain. The study shows that, in spite of being designed for non-native speakers of English, these books contain a high number of open class metaphors, although not as many as in 'real' academic prose. At the same time, the analysis shows that metaphor density is not evenly spread. For one, the lessons belonging to Natural Science show a greater use of metaphorical language. For another, within each lesson unit, some sections show a greater metaphor density than others, and this can be accounted for by the pedagogic functions they fulfil.

Finally, the chapter by Saaty explores the importance of metaphor awareness in vocabulary teaching and performs a comparative analysis of three different techniques used in the teaching of vocabulary to L2 learners: 1) the use of bodily enactment as a way of connecting figurative uses of expressions to their literal meanings, 2) the use of verbal discussions to help students appreciate the conceptual metaphor underlying the figurative expressions, and 3) activities involving the same figurative expressions but without explicit attention to the connections with their literal meanings. The results show an advantage of the first technique, which not only enhances comprehension but also longer-term retention of the target expressions.

4 Conclusion and Outlook

As pointed out above, despite the continued and fruitful efforts to give metaphor its well-deserved place in foreign language instruction for the past thirty years, there are still many gaps to be filled.

In the first place, it has been largely acknowledged that the concept (and measures) of 'metaphorical competence' needs to be further developed. Five of the chapters included in this volume (those by Low; Piquer-Píriz; Suárez-Campos, Hijazo-Gascón and Ibarretxe-Antuñano; Nacey; and Castellano-Risco and Piquer-Píriz) approach this issue from different perspectives.

Secondly, very few attempts have been made to develop CL-oriented specific teaching materials and the main findings from this line of research do not seem to have reached mainstream textbooks and classroom practice (Boers, 2014, MacArthur 2017). The chapters by Saaty; Alejo-González and García-Bermejo; and Wang, Boers and Warren offer some suggestions for either specific teaching techniques or general ways to enhance metaphor awareness in the English as an L2 classroom.

Thirdly, there is a clear need to extend the applications of CL to L2 instruction in languages other than English. Suárez-Campos, Hijazo-Gascón and Ibarretxe-Antuñano's chapter offers relevant insights for the case of Spanish as an L2.

And fourthly, there is also an evident need to be sensitive to the specific profiles of different learners groups (and individual learners within seemingly homogenous groups). Four of the chapters illustrate this issue, by looking at young L2 learners (in the chapters by Nacey and Piquer-Píriz), learners specialising in a particular area (students of Translation, in the chapter by Philip), and learners with different levels of L2 achievement (in the chapters by Nacey and Wang, Boers and Warren).

Both the more theoretical accounts and the new empirical studies presented in these pages also indicate promising avenues for future research and possible pedagogical applications of metaphor in L2 classrooms. We indeed hope that the information presented in the different chapters of this volume will inspire further research into the fascinating, multifaceted issue of metaphor in L2 instruction.

References

Achard, Michel & Susanne Niemeier. 2004. *Cognitive linguistics, second language acquisition, and foreign language teaching (Vol. 18)*. Berlin/New York: Mouton de Gruyter.

Alejo, Rafael. 2010. Where does the money go? An analysis of the container metaphor in economics: The market and the economy. *Journal of Pragmatics* 42(4).1137–1150.

Alejo, Rafael, Ana M. Piquer-Píriz & Guadalupe Reveriego. 2010. Phrasal verbs in EFL coursebooks. In Sabine De Knop, Frank Boers & Antoon De Rycker (eds.), *Fostering language teaching efficiency through cognitive linguistics*, 59–78. Berlin: Mouton de Gruyter.

Bielak, Jakub. 2011. Cognitive linguistics and foreign anguage pedagogy: An overview of recent trends and developments. In Miroslaw Pawlak (eds.), *Extending the boundaries of research on second language learning and teaching*, 241–262. Berlin, Heidelberg: Springer Berlin Heidelberg.

Boers, Frank. 2000. Metaphor awareness and vocabulary retention. *Applied Linguistics* 21. 553–571.

Boers, Frank. 2004. Expanding learners' vocabulary through metaphor awareness: What expansion, what learners, what vocabulary? In Susanne Niemeier & Michel Achard (eds.), *Cognitive linguistics, second language acquisition, and foreign language teaching*, 211–232. Berlin: Mouton de Gruyter.

Boers, Frank. 2011. Cognitive semantic ways of teaching figurative phrases: An assessment. *Review of Cognitive Linguistics* 9. 227–261.

Boers, Frank. 2013. Cognitive linguistic approaches to teaching vocabulary: Assessment and integration. *Language Teaching* 46. 208–224.

Boers, Frank. 2014. Cognitive linguistics and language pedagogy: Finding ways forward. Paper presented at the 9th AELCO International conference, Badajoz, Spain.

Boers, Frank & Murielle Demecheleer. 1998. A few metaphorical models in (western) economic discourse. In Wolf A. Liebert, Gisela Redeker & Linda R. Waugh (eds.), *Discourse and perspective in cognitive linguistics*, 115–131. Amsterdam: John Benjamins.

Boers, Frank, June Eyckmans & Hélène Stengers. 2007. Presenting figurative idioms with a touch of etymology: More than mere mnemonics? *Language Teaching Research* 11(1). 43–62.

Boers, Frank & Seth Lindstromberg. 2006. Cognitive linguistic approaches to second or foreign language instruction: Rationale, proposals and evaluation. In Gitte Kristaensen, René Dirven, Michel Achard & Francisco J. Ruiz-Mendoza (eds.), *Cognitive linguistics: Current applications and future perspectives*, 305–358. Berlin: Mouton de Gruyter.

Boers, Frank & Seth Lindstromberg (eds.). 2008. *Cognitive linguistic approach to teaching vocabulary and phraseology*. Berlin: Mouton de Gruyter.

Boers, Frank & Seth Lindstromberg. 2008. How cognitive linguistics can foster effective vocabulary teaching. In Frank Boers & Seth Lindstromberg, *Cognitive linguistic approach to teaching vocabulary and phraseology*, 1–65. Berlin: Mouton de Gruyter.

Boers, Frank & Seth Lindstromberg. 2009. *Optimizing a lexical approach to instructed second language Acquisition*. Basingstoke: Palgrave Macmillan.

Boers, Frank Ana M. Piquer-Píriz, Hélène Stengers & June Eyckmans. 2009. Does pictorial elucidation foster recollection of idioms? *Language Teaching Research* 13. 267–382.

Condon, Nora. 2008. How cognitive linguistic motivations influence the learning of phrasal verbs. In Frank Boers & Seth Lindstromberg (eds.), *Cognitive linguistic approaches to teaching vocabulary and phraseology*. 133–158. Berlin: Mouton de Gruyter.

De Knop, Sabine, Frank Boers & Antoon De Rycker. 2010. *Fostering language teaching efficiency through cognitive linguistics* (Vol. 17). Berlin: Mouton de Gruyter.

Deignan, Alice, Danuta Gabryś & Agnieszka Solska. 1997. Teaching English metaphors using cross-linguistic awareness-raising activities. *ELT journal* 51(4). 352–360.

Dirven, René. 2001. English phrasal verbs: Theory and didactic application. In Martin Pütz, Susanne Niemeier & René Dirven (Eds.), *Applied cognitive linguistics II: Language pedagogy*, 3–27. Berlin: Mouton de Gruyter.

Holme, Randal. 2009. *Cognitive linguistics and language teaching*. Berlin: Springer Berlin Heidelberg.

Kövecses, Zoltán & Péter Szabó. 1996. Idioms: A view from cognitive semantics. *Applied Linguistics*, 17(3). 326–355.

Lakoff, George & Mark Johnson. 1980. *Metaphors we live by*. Chicago: University of Chicago Press.

Lazar, Gillian. 1996. Using figurative language to expand students' vocabulary. *ELT Journal* 50(1). 43–51.

Lazar, Gillian. 2003. *Meaning and Metaphors: Activities to practise figurative language*. Cambridge: Cambridge University Press.

Lindstromberg, Seth. 1996. Prepositions: Meaning and method. *ELT Journal* 50(3). 225–236.

Lindstromberg, Seth & Frank Boers. 2005. From movement to metaphor with manner-of-movement verbs. *Applied Linguistics* 26(2). 241–26.

Lindstromberg, Seth & Frank Boers. 2008. *Teaching chunks of language: From noticing to remembering*. London: Helbling Languages.

Littlemore, Jeannette. 2009. *Applying cognitive linguistics to second language learning and teaching*. Berlin Heidelberg: Springer Berlin Heidelberg.

Littlemore, Jeannette. 2017. Metaphor use in educational contexts: Functions and variations. In Elena Semino & Zsófia Demjén (eds.), *The Routledge handbook of metaphor and language*, 283–295. London: Routledge.

Littlemore, Jeannette & Constanze Juchem-Grundmann. 2010. Introduction to the interplay between cognitive linguistics and second language learning and teaching. *AILA Review* 23(1). 1–6.

Littlemore, Jeannette, Tina Krennmayr, James Turner & Sara Turner. 2014. An investigation into metaphor use at different levels of second language writing. *Applied Linguistics* 35(2). 117–144.

Littlemore, Jeannette & Graham D. Low. 2006. *Figurative thinking and foreign language learning*. Basingstoke: Palgrave Macmillan.

Littlemore, Jeannette & Fiona MacArthur. 2007. What do learners need to know about the figurative extensions of target langauge words? A contrastive corpus-based analysis of thread, hilar, wing and aletear. In Ignasi Navarro i Fernando, José L. Otal Campo & Antonio J. Silvestre López (eds.), *Metaphor and discourse, a special edition of culture, language and representation: Cultural studies journal of universitat Jaume I* 5. 131–149.

Littlemore, Jeannette & Fiona MacArthur. 2012. Figurative extensions of word meaning: How do corpus data and intuition match up? In Dagmar Divjak & Stefan T. Gries (eds.), *Frequency effects in language representation*, 195–233. Berlin: Mouton de Gruyter.

Low, Graham D. 1988. On teaching metaphor. *Applied Linguistics* 9(2). 125–147.

MacArthur, Fiona. 2005. The competent horseman in a horseless world: Observations on a conventional metaphor in Spanish and English. *Metaphor and Symbol 20*. 71–94.

MacArthur, Fiona. 2010. Metaphorical competence in EFL. Where are we and where should be going? A view from the language classroom. *AILA Review 23* (1). 155–173.

MacArthur, Fiona. 2016a. Beyond engaged listenership: Assessing Spanish undergraduates' active participation in academic mentoring sessions in English as academic lingua franca. In Jesús Romero-Trillo (ed.), *Yearbook of Corpus Linguistics and Pragmatics 2016. Global Implications for Society and Education in the Networked Age*, 153–178. Cham: Springer.

MacArthur, Fiona. 2016b. Overt and covert uses of metaphor in the academic mentoring in English of Spanish undergraduate students at five European universities. *Review of Cognitive Linguistics* 41(1). 23–50.

MacArthur, Fiona. 2016c. When languages and cultures meet: Mixed metaphors in the discourse of Spanish speakers of English. In Raymond W. Gibbs (Ed.), *Mixing metaphor*, 133–154. Amsterdam: John Benjamins.

MacArthur, Fiona. 2017. Using metaphor in the teaching of second/foreign languages. In Elena Semino & Zsófia Demjén (eds.), *The Routledge handbook of metaphor and language*, 413–424. London: Routledge.

MacArthur, Fiona, Tina Krennmayr & Jeannette Littlemore. 2015. How basic is UNDERSTANDING IS SEEING when reasoning about knowledge? Asymmetric uses of SIGHT metaphors in office hours' consultations in English as academic lingua franca. *Metaphor and Symbol* 30(3). 184–217.

MacArthur, Fiona & Jeannette Littlemore. 2008. A discovery approach using corpora in the foreign language classroom. In Frank Boers & Seth Lindstromberg (eds.), *Cognitive linguistic approaches to teaching vocabulary and phraseology*, 159–188. Berlin: Mouton de Gruyter.

MacArthur, Fiona, José L. Oncins-Martínez, Manuel Sánchez-García & Ana M. Piquer-Píriz. 2012. *Metaphor in use: Context, culture and communication*. Amsterdam: John Benjamins.

MacArthur, Fiona & Ana M. Piquer-Píriz. 2007. Staging the introduction of figurative extensions of familiar vocabulary items in EFL: Some preliminary considerations. *Ilha de Desterro: a Journal of English Language, Literatures in English and Cultural Studies* 53. 123–134.

MacLennan, Carol H. 1994. Metaphors and prototypes in the learning teaching of grammar and vocabulary. *IRAL-International Review of Applied Linguistics in Language Teaching* 32(2). 97–110.

Mussolf, Andreas, Fiona MacArthur & Giulio Pagani (eds.). 2014. *Metaphor and intercultural communication*. London: Bloomsbury Academic.

Nacey, Susan. 2017. Metaphor comprehension and production in a second language. In Elena Semino & Zsófia Demjén (eds.), *The Routledge handbook of metaphor and language*, 503–515. London: Routledge.

Piquer-Píriz, Ana M. 2008. Reasoning figuratively in early EFL: Some implications for the development of vocabulary. In Frank Boers & Seth Lindstromberg (eds.), *Cognitive linguistics approaches to teaching vocabulary and phraseology*, 219–240. Berlin: Mouton de Gruyter.

Piquer-Píriz, Ana M. 2010. Can people be cold and warm? Developing understanding of figurative meanings of temperature terms in early EFL. In Graham D. Low, Zazie Todd, Alice Deignan & Lynne Cameron (eds.), *Researching and applying metaphor in the real world*, 21–33. Amsterdam: John Benjamins.

Piquer-Píriz, Ana M. & Rafael Alejo-González. 2016. Applying Cognitive Linguistics: Identifying some current research foci (figurative language in use, constructions and typology). *Review of Cognitive Linguistics* 14(1). 1–20.

Piquer-Píriz, Ana M. & Frank Boers. 2019. La lingüística cognitiva y sus aplicaciones a la enseñanza de lenguas extranjeras. In Iraide Ibarretxe-Antuñano, Teresa Cadierno & Alejandro Casteñeda-Castro (eds.), *Lingüística cognitiva y español LE/L2*. London: Routledge.

Ponteretto, Diane. 1994. Metaphors we can learn by: How insights from cognitive linguistic research can improve the teaching/learning of figurative language. *English Teaching Forum* 32(3). 2–7.

Pütz, Martin, René Dirven & Susanne Niemeier. 2001a. *Applied cognitive linguistics I: Theory and Language Acquisition*. Berlin: Mouton de Gruyter.

Pütz, Martin, René Dirven & Susanne Niemeier. 2001b. *Applied cognitive linguistics II: Language pedagogy*. Berlin: Mouton de Gruyter.

Pütz, Martin & Laura Sicola (eds.). 2010. *Cognitive processing in second language acquisition: Inside the learner's mind*. Amsterdam: John Benjamins.

Robinson, Peter & Nick C. Ellis. 2008. *Handbook of cognitive linguistics and second language acquisition*. New York: Routledge.

Rudzka-Ostyn, Brygida. 2003. *Word Power: Phrasal verbs and compounds. A cognitive approach*. Berlin: Mouton de Gruyter.

Saaty, Rawan. 2016. *Teaching L2 Metaphor through awareness-raising activities: Experimental studies with Saudi EFL learners*. Unpublished Doctoral Dissertation. University of Birmingham.

Tyler, Andrea, Charles Mueller & Vu Ho. 2010. Applying cognitive linguistics to instructed L2 learning: The English modals. *AILA Review* 23(1). 30–49.

Part I. **Theoretical Considerations:
Reviews and Perspectives**

Raymond W. Gibbs, Jr.

The Particularities of Metaphorical Experience: An Appreciation of Fiona MacArthur's Metaphor Scholarship

1 The Particularities of Metaphorical Experience

Being a metaphor scholar is really hard work. I recently talked with an old friend, a neurosurgeon, about my own life as a metaphor scholar. He asked pointed questions about what metaphor was, how I studied it as a cognitive scientist, what theories explained metaphor in language and thought, and, finally, why on earth I decided to devote my life to the topic of metaphor in the first place. After hearing my different responses to these questions, my friend commented that metaphor seemed vague, even ethereal, and wondered if any progress in the scientific study of metaphor could ever occur. My old friend even said, and this is an exact quote, "It sounds to me that operating on people's brains is much easier than studying something like metaphor". I laughed at this response, but could not argue with its validity as studying metaphor can often be terribly challenging (even if also quite rewarding).

I admire most of the people in the metaphor community for their courage in the work they do, and have special appreciation for Fiona MacArthur and her scholarship over many years. In my view, she distinguishes herself as a metaphor scholar, par excellence, for approaching metaphor with a keen eye toward the particularities of metaphorical experience in all of its glorious, messy details. Quite a few of us in the multidisciplinary world of metaphor research examine metaphor from a God's eye perspective and aim to capture some of the important generalities about metaphor in broad theoretical terms. Indeed, some of the most famous theories of metaphor have evolved from the consideration of only a few, often literary, examples of metaphor, or from instances noted in dictionaries, or from isolated expressions that arise from our own minds or memories. Others of us look at metaphor as it exists in real discourse, but then scrape the metaphors out of these contexts to draw larger generalizations about metaphor and the presumed people who produce and understand these selected examples. Still others, including myself, study people's understandings of verbal metaphor in scientific experiments, but here too quickly draw inferences from the small group of participants and

Raymond W. Gibbs, Jr., Soquel, CA, USA, e-mail: raymondwgibbs@gmail.com

https://doi.org/10.1515/9783110630367-002

specific verbal metaphors examined to offer grand conclusions about human minds and unconscious, fast-acting processes of metaphor acquisition and interpretation. Finally, other scholars investigate metaphorical discourse in order to draw larger generalizations about how metaphor always emerges from cultural ideas and beliefs. These differing perspectives each offer potentially important insights into the ways metaphor operates in thought, language, and expressive communication. But it is still often the case that these varying approaches to metaphor are seen as competing with one another rather than pointing toward a more harmonious and detailed picture of the adaptive value of metaphor in human life.

Fiona MacArthur has long resisted the temptation to draw facile conclusions about the ways metaphor works in human interaction. She looks at the particularities of how metaphor emerges in discourse and offers a cautionary voice about not ignoring some of the complexities of metaphor use simply because so many of us are primarily interested in grand theories of metaphor. Reading her many publications over the years offers a mosaic, a tapestry of observations about many of the detailed realities of metaphor that are too often ignored in many of the ongoing debates about how people, especially non-native speakers, learn and communicate with metaphorical language. The enduring impression I get from reading each one of her articles is the warning to fellow metaphor research of "Not so fast! Slow down and see how the complexities of metaphorical language use must be a fundamental part of any attempt to theorize about metaphor".

I now review a select few of her scholarly works to both remind us of their important empirical findings and to understand some of the deeper themes that motivate her research as a metaphor scholar. A key focus of my appreciation of her research is that metaphorical language use is always inherently situated in, and emerges from, very particular social, cultural, and environmental circumstances, which make up the "ecology of metaphor". Thinking of metaphor as a resource to meet individual and collective adaptive needs entails certain methodological commitments and attention to the dynamics of how metaphor unfolds.

2 A Case Study of the Primary Metaphor UNDERSTANDING IS SEEING

The introduction of "primary metaphors" within cognitive linguistics added a new dimension for characterizing the relations between bodily experience with metaphorical thought and language (Grady 1997). Primary metaphors reflect strong correlations in everyday embodied experiences, such as the following:

INTIMACY IS CLOSENESS
"We have a close relationship".

DIFFICULTIES ARE BURDENS
"She's weighed down by responsibilities".

AFFECTION IS WARMTH
"They greeted me warmly".

IMPORTANT IS BIG
"Tomorrow is a big day".

MORE IS UP
"Prices are high".

SIMILARITY IS CLOSENESS
"Those colors aren't the same, but they're close".

CHANGE IS MOTION
"My health has gone from bad to worse".

PURPOSES ARE DESTINATIONS
"He'll be successful, but isn't there yet".

CAUSES ARE PHYSICAL FORCES
"They pushed the bill through Congress".

KNOWING IS SEEING
"I see what you mean".

UNDERSTANDING IS GRASPING
"I've never been able to grasp complex math".

These metaphorical correlations arise out of our embodied functioning in the world. In each case, the source domain of the metaphor comes from the body's sensorimotor system. A primary metaphor is a metaphorical mapping for which there is an independent and direct experiential basis that can be expressed within language. Although primary metaphors are often viewed as having a universal character given their roots in embodied correlations, not all languages exhibit the same primary metaphors, such as for example UNDERSTANDING IS SEEING (Ibarretxe-Antuñano 2013).

How do second-language learners of English use and understand a primary metaphor such as UNDERSTANDING IS SEEING? MacArthur, Krennmayr and Littlemore (2015) explored the relevance of UNDERSTANDING IS SEEING in a series of 27 conversations (EuroCoAT corpus) between university instructors of English and their international students at five European universities (i.e., Ireland, England, The Netherlands, Spain, and Sweden). These conversations were all in English while the students were all native Spanish speakers. In general, the UNDERSTANDING IS SEEING metaphor appeared frequently in these conversations, notably because the topics of learning and knowledge were the primary foci of these talk exchanges. Still, there were important variations in the ways that the English instructors and the Spanish students referred to UNDERSTANDING IS SEEING.

The students were asked, prior to the meetings with their instructor, to propose several questions on topics related to the course materials and assignments. The resulting conversations lasted between 7 and 22 minutes, yielding a corpus of over six hours of discourse. About 2/3 of the words were produced by the instructors and 1/3 by the students. An analysis of the talk using corpus analytic tools (Wmatrix) and hand analyses showed that the instructors used terms related to "sight" far more so than did the students. A further analysis using the "metaphor identification procedure" (MIP) (Pragglejaz Group 2007) was attempted to determine which instances of the "sight" terms possibly conveyed metaphorical meaning related to understanding. However, some examples appeared to indicate both metaphorical and non-metaphorical meanings at the same time (e.g., an instructor said, "I have some not so good responses to some questions and you will see what people have done in the past" as he showed the student some examples of what other students had done in the past). For this reason, the analysis revealed three types of "sight" examples (i.e., metaphorical, non-metaphorical, and conflations of both metaphorical and non-metaphorical).[1]

The instructors, furthermore, employed a larger range of "sight" terms (e.g., "see", "look", "focus", "view", "reflect", "observe", "notice", "spot", "visible") than did the students (e.g., ""focus", "look", "see", "watch"). Overall, 40% of all metaphorically used "sight" terms employed the lexical item "see," followed by "look" (33%) and "focus" (12%). Most interestingly, the students used "see" in different ways than did the lecturers. For example, students often used "see" in the passive voice (e.g., "saw" and "have seen"), while the instructors used "see" in the active voice. The instructors also did not typically use "see" to refer to moments of understanding in the past (e.g., "I could see that ….."), but preferred to use "see" metaphorically when talking about current or future actions (e.g., "You're not going to be able to see that they will be analyzed … "). Many of the instructors' uses of "see" were conflations (e.g., "Okay, yeah that fine you can also … as was seen in the – in the film Fresca … "), which mostly reflects cases of understanding that involved visual materials such as films, books, exams, etc. Instructors also signaled their understanding of students' comments through the metaphorical use of "see" (e.g., "right right I see … so will will you use grammar books?"), but the

---

1 The issue of "conflations" is a significant one in metaphor research, but much more attention is needed on this topic.

students rarely employed "see" in this manner. In fact, the one instructor, who was a native speaker of Spanish, also did not employ "see" as a way of signaling understanding of students' questions or comments. This finding suggests that vision may not be a typical way of referring to learning in Spanish, especially in the context of Spanish academics talking with their students.

Students sometimes responded to instructors' uses of sight metaphors by also displaying their learning through similar metaphors (e.g., "I have to be more clear" and "This introduction has to be more focused"). But a further analysis of the discourse contexts in which UNDERSTANDING IS SEEING appeared indicated that English and Spanish speakers think of this metaphor in different ways. In many cases, students failed to pick up on the instructors' use of sight metaphors even when the instructors gestured in metaphorical ways about UNDERSTANDING IS SEEING (e.g., fingers splayed outward as the hand moved downward toward the desk to note what must be focused on).

MacArthur, Krennmayr and Littlemore (2015) offered several conclusions from their analysis of the instructor-student conversations:

> To a certain extent, the mismatch between the lecturers' and the students' metaphorical use of the sight terms can be attributed to the different roles played by the participants in these mentoring sessions. The lecturers see their role as supporting the students' efforts to learn through giving specific advice about how this can be achieved, and as we have seen, sight terms, when used metaphorically, appear to comprise an important means of communicating this advice (MacArthur, Krennmayr and Littlemore 2015: 214)

Most generally, they concluded the following:

> Speakers of Spanish and English do not use the metaphorical expressions motivated by the "UNDERSTANDING IS SEEING" mapping in the same ways: we have noted some overlap but also substantial divergence in terms of the frequency, forms, and meanings of sight metaphors in this corpus" (MacArthur et al. 2015: 214). And, later on, "The experiential base for the metaphor is thus probably very similar in Spain, England, the Netherlands, or Sweden. However, this "primary" metaphor does not surface in the same way among speakers of these different languages, as our data confirm (MacArthur, Krennmayr and Littlemore 2015: 215).

MacArthur, Krennmayr and Littlemore's (2015) examination of UNDERSTANDING IS SEEING illustrates the tremendous context-sensitivity in the way primary metaphors operate in both thinking and speaking about knowing and understanding processes. Even if different primary metaphors have strong embodied roots via correlations between source and target domains, this fact alone does not necessarily imply that all languages will instantiate particular primary metaphors in the same way in regard to people's expressive speaking and writing.

One may dismiss local variance in the ways primary metaphors appear in different languages, or in different facets of discourse, as performance errors on the part of speakers, or claim that primary metaphors are not all that important in a theory of metaphorical thinking and language use. But these variations are critical to understanding the complex ways in which different languages express primary metaphors such that metaphor behavior is always shaped by specific discourse practices, as seen in the particularities of how university instructors interact with the second-language learning students in talk of their writing assignments. The more general lesson here is that important regularities exist between correlations in bodily experience and metaphorical language use. Nonetheless, these regularities do not completely determine how real speakers necessarily link primary metaphors to very specific instances of metaphorical language use in very local discourse contexts. The particularities of the context and discourse practices associated with a topic always matter in terms of when and how speakers use metaphorical language.

3 Learning the Meanings of Body-Part Metaphors

Attention to the specific details of second-language learners' understanding of metaphor is also seen in a study of young learners' of English use and understanding of body part terms (e.g., head, mouth, hand), when these conveyed figurative meanings (e.g., "head of the stairs") (MacArthur and Piquer-Píriz 2007). Although students from ages 5 to 11 understand body part metaphors, they do so using different strategies at different ages. This general finding reveals another particularity in second-language learners' understanding of verbal metaphor.

The children were shown different photographs of scenes depicting a hammer, a flight of stairs, a line of cars, and a bed, and were asked to circle the part of each photo that was identified as the "head". After doing so, the students provided verbal explanations for their choices.

Students were best at identifying the head of a hammer and found it most difficult to circle the head of a line of cars. A closer analysis of the students' explanation showed differences in why they made their "head" identifications. For example, the five- and seven-year-olds clearly associated the metaphorical use of "head" with the top or highest part of an object or scene. One five-year-old circled the top part of the stairs and then explained, "Because it's the highest part and it's got to be the head because it's at the top, the head is at the top of the body." Eleven-year-olds, on the other hand, described "head" as referring to the general idea of importance. Thus, one 11-year-old circled the middle of the stairs as being the "head" and explained his choice in the following way, "The central part because- I don't know- because the head is- because it was the most important thing, so- the staircase- it's the central part".

A closer look at the children's choices and explanations revealed more subtle differences in their metaphorical reasoning. For example, one child explained his circling of the first car in a line of cars by saying, "The first one because the head is at the top". Yet some students, more precisely and also incorrectly, circled only the roofs of the first and second cars as the "head," and they reasoned, "Because it's on top of the first car" or "cos, the head is on top of the human body". Thus, these children relied on the common idea that the head is above the rest of the body. In a different manner, some children explained their choices of the head in a line of cars as being like the head of a snake or worm (e.g., "Because it's like a snake and snakes have their heads at the beginning"). One nine-year-old correctly circled the first car and explained "Because it's the first car and in a line the first car is the one that gives orders- and the head- and our head is the boss".

Overall, the younger children were more successful in identifying the head of a staircase (82%) than the older children (56%). But the older children were better at identifying the head of a line of cars (83%), and explained these choices by referring to the idea that the head has a governing role, compared to only 59% of the seven-year-olds and 42% of the five-year-olds. Even young children exhibited some ability to explain metaphorical extensions of body part terms, but children overall offered different explanations for why they understood these metaphorical uses of words.

One could assume that the children's different metaphorical reasoning about the figurative meaning of body part terms is mostly a matter of their first adopting incorrect understandings of what these terms imply in context. Later on, these students presumably learned the correct reasons for body-part metaphors and performed similar to adults when using these metaphorical terms in discourse. But MacArthur and Piquer-Píriz (2007) recognized important insights in children's incorrect reasoning about why body part terms can express metaphorical meanings. Similar to the writings of the great developmental psychologist Piaget (1923, 1936), who created a theory of cognitive development from the analysis of children's errors in different physical reasoning tasks, MacArthur and Piquer-Píriz concluded that children's so-called "errors" in their explanation of metaphorically used body part terms reveal distinctive metaphorical thinking patterns. Thus, metaphorical thinking comes in many different forms, and adult correct usage of, in this case, body part terms, should not be interpreted as the only form of metaphorical competence. Second-language learners may still be thinking in metaphorical ways, and do so in adaptive ways in certain contexts. The idea that younger second-language learners may think metaphorically when using body part metaphors, even if they do so differently than older children and adults, is important for another reason. Younger children are often thought to use metaphor entirely on the basis of perceptual similarity. As they get older, they presumably acquire an ability to understand relational connections between diverse domains, not just connections based on perceptual resemblances. Yet even younger children learning a new language can relatively quickly infer relational metaphorical mappings. Only by examining the particularities of metaphor experience can scholars recognize the adaptive, communicative value that metaphor has in diverse discourse contexts. This is exactly what MacArthur and Piquer-Píriz (2007) were able to do.

4 A Case Study of Horse Riding Metaphors

In a different study, MacArthur (2005) explored how certain metaphorical themes are used to regulate human action, especially in the context of helping people control potentially damaging events, as seen in the metaphorical idea CONTROL OF AN UNPREDICTABLE/UNDERSIRABLE FORCE IS A RIDER'S CONTROL OF A HORSE. Both Spanish and English have many conventional expressions in which horse and rider serve as the metaphorical source or vehicle. Horses are sometimes difficult to control and, as such, are often identified with other unpredictable or undesirable events that are also difficult to control (e.g., human emotions, sexual passion, disease). Riders exert control over horses through different tack or apparel such as the bridle and reins, the saddle, stirrups, and spurs. These artifacts enable riders to "curb" (i.e., to use the reins to pull the horse's neck in one direction), which can be readily mapped onto distinct target domains as seen in the following metaphorical expressions in both English and Spanish (MacArthur 2005: 79–80):

> "The publishers carefully curbed their comments on the charges".
> [SPEECH]
> "Eating them more often might curb the appetite for fatty foods or confectionery".
> [APPETITE]
> "A promise she had made to curb her temper and her excesses and maintain
> a low profile". [UNDESIRABLE EMOTION-BEHAVIOR]
> "Good diet curbs cancer risk". [DISEASE-DANGER]
> "The government had an income policy of sorts and had curbed the growth
> of public expenditure". [UNDESIRABLE ECONOMIC SITUATION]
> "Children whose instincts are to rebel often get curbed by their teachers".
> [PEOPLE-BEHAVIOR]
> "Poseído por un impulso desbocado, se puso en pie". [UNDESIRABLE
> EMOTION-BEHAVIOR]

"Su política expansionista de déficit público desbocado" [UNDESIRABLE
ECONOMIC SITUATION]
"Se siente fuera de control, desbocado". [PEOPLE-UNDESIRABLE
EMOTION-BEHAVIOR]
*"Sudoroso y satisfecho, víctima del magnetismo febril de sus jóvenes fans,
entre los que se encontraba algún que otro adulto* desbocado, *puso punto
final al recital".* [PEOPLE-BEHAVIOR]
"El mito del progreso desbocado *que pusieron en boga los ilustrados"*
[GROWTH-DEVELOPMENT]

These examples demonstrate how horse riding behaviors can be extended to
understand the control (or lack of control in the examples in Spanish) of different, sometimes abstract, events (e.g., DISEASE-DANGER and GROWTH-
DEVELOPMENT). Note also that the above English and Spanish conventional
expressions with "curb" convey a specific evaluative stance regarding the target
domain, namely concern with uncontrolled, "runaway", progress/development
or disease. Some of the processes in need of control refer to external forces (e.g.,
people, economic situations, and disease), while others relate to the control of
internal forces (e.g., appetite, desires, and passions within an individual).

Other horse riding metaphors express how the rider controls the horse by
being "in the saddle" or "riding high in the saddle" or having "firm control of
the reins" (e.g., a boss in control of a company). Many conventional horse riding metaphors describe the undesirable or difficult to control aspects of some
force, again in terms of controlling a horse, as seen in the following examples
(MacArthur 2005: 82):

"A man must decide to either curb *his appetites or to surrender to them"*
"I am holding *my thoughts* on a tight rein *and refusing to think ahead"*
"I took myself *in* hand *about a year ago and lost weight".*
"A partir de entonces, ella tuvo que sujetar las riendas *de su hogar".*

If one is unable to control a horse, usually through the failure to use proper
riding apparatus or a rider's improper use of that equipment, this can result in
several negative metaphorical events, such as seen in the following statements
(MacArthur 2005: 82–83):

"It is sheer, unbridled *greed,"*
"A return to the pagan ways of unbridled *pleasure and carnal gratification".*
"They let *their emotions* run away *with them".*
"He lets *his imagination* run away *with him".*
"Kenneth's aggressive nature has got a bit out of hand".
"The Kremlin felt things were rapidly getting out of hand".
"Es verdad: he perdido los estribos *y he dicho tonterías".*
"¿Quieres tranquilizarte, por favor? ¡Estás perdiendo los estribos!"
"Se le fue la lengua".

> "Soltando las riendas *al temperamento racial*".
> "*En aquel desierto de sentimentalismo en el que vivía desde hacía meses,
> la carta de Jean de Bornecort* desbocó su corazón y su fantasía".

At the same time, in the expressions seen below, horse riding apparatus can be employed to bring about more forceful and highly desired actions as seen in the following examples (MacArthur 2005: 83):

> "*The shortage of labor acts as a powerful* spur *to more economical methods of production*".
> "*Her approval* spurred *him to enter the poetry contest*".
> "*You need someone to* spur *you on*".
> "*Federico Mayor Zaragoza* espoleó *ayer a la comunidad universitaria*".
> "*La NASA está* espoleada *por el hallazgo de indicios de vida en Marte*"
> "Espolea *su imaginación*".

Out of control horses, nonetheless, still need to be brought under the rider's control, suggesting that some forces may be difficult to control through human action (MacArthur 2005: 83):

> "*Dying of* galloping *consumption*"
> "*The* galloping *inflation of the previous two years seemed to have been brought under control*".
> "*In just six months, the country's* runaway *inflation has been brought under control*".
> "*Una anciana con artritis* galopante".
> "*Tisis/cáncer* galopante".
> "*Paralizados en el seno de una verbosidad* galopante".
> "*Parecía imposible atajar una inflación* galopante".
> "*La insipidez del Barça se convirtió en apatía* galopante".

In this study, the entrenchment of many conventional metaphors regarding horse riding results in aspects of the target domains being more easily understood than aspects of the source domain (something that seems contrary to the common belief that source domains are typically more familiar and concretely understood than are target domains. Thus, some dictionaries offer no purely literal definitions of words such as "unbridled" in English, or detail the literal meaning of "spur" further down on the list of the word's senses. Many figurative senses related to horse riding may have been part of English, for example, for such a long time that these have become fossilized.[2]

---

2 Contrary to MacArthur, I would maintain that these fossilizations are not necessarily "dead" metaphors given how productive these horse riding metaphors still appear to be in many discourse contexts.

Another interesting observation is that horse riding may still be relevant to aspects of contemporary life in Spain and Britain, yet it is not highly salient in everyday experience anymore. Deignan (2003), in fact, showed that cars are far more salient for English speakers than are horses, but horse riding appeared to motivate the creation, and continued use, of many metaphors, far more so than is the case with cars. This imbalance suggests to Deignan that the link between metaphor and culture is only indirect as many metaphors "allude to knowledge shared as part of our cultural repository, but is no longer directly experienced" (Deignan 2003: 220). MacArthur (2005: 88) further suggested, along this same line of argument, that "Physical experience or embodiment cannot, thus, account for its general acceptance as an apt way of reasoning about control either now or in earlier times. Rather, the widespread use of this (horse riding) metaphor in language implies that, for some reason or other".

MacArthur speculated that the persistent salience of horse riding metaphors in Spanish and English may be partly due to the fact that these inherit part of the more general conceptual metaphor LIFE IS A JOURNEY even if people mostly do not have direct experience with horses or horse riding. Thus, "commonsense knowledge of some domain cannot always, in these cases, be taken to arise from first-hand experience, but must be a product of cultural mechanisms of some kind" (MacArthur 2005: 89). Indeed, language itself enables speakers to be aware of different conceptual representations rather than conceptual representations emerging from bottom-up embodied experiences. But the language that persisted over time through "high-density social networks" may come from social groups with prestige or power, such as the horse riding aristocracy within certain European countries. "Seen in this light, social processes, rather than shared experience may have been responsible for the spread of not only this (horse riding) but also other entrenched metaphorical themes, such as those often mentioned in the literature on conceptual metaphor" (MacArthur 2005: 91).

This work on horse riding metaphors offers a valuable contemporary lesson for scholars whenever they aim to discern the motivation for any metaphorical concept or theme. As much as many scholars often immediately seek out embodied experiences (e.g., horse riding) as the motivating foundations for conventional metaphorical language, care must be taken to explore the importance of historical, cultural, social and linguistic influences on why people speak in the particular metaphorical ways they do. More generally, the motivation for why many metaphorical words and phrases have the meanings they do is a complex, interacting set of constraints, ranging from historical and cultural forces down to faster-acting cognitive and linguistic ones (Gibbs 2017). Once again, explaining the particularities of metaphorical language means that scholars should resist the temptation to correlate patterns, including errors in metaphor usage, with a single level of analysis (e.g., embodiment alone).

5 Mixing Metaphors in Instructor-Second Language Learner Discourse

Mixing metaphor is something speakers do all the time, mostly without any awareness that they are doing so. As argued in MacArthur (2016a), people who speak more than one language also mix metaphors, especially when speaking to individuals who are also bilingual. Yet this mixing of metaphor is not at all an indication of mental confusion or misunderstanding about what is to be said. Instead, mixed metaphors often emerge from speech and writing given various cognitive constraints and rhetorical considerations that individuals face in different situations. Thus, mixed metaphors are not production errors and are actually created for several possible reasons.

As MacArthur (2016a) emphasized, English is now an international language or lingua franca, which means that the idea that native speakers adopt "native-speaker norms" is now on very shaky grounds. Similarly, thinking of any metaphor production as an error (i.e., the mixing of metaphors) is also mistaken given the ubiquity of metaphor in language as an incredibly adaptive rhetorical device. On top of the emerging belief that much of everyday abstract thought is metaphorical, it makes little sense to see metaphor variations as violations of cognitive or communicative maxims. After all, the context in which variations of verbal metaphors appear also makes metaphorical language use of all sorts generally easy to produce and interpret (Gibbs 1994).

MacArthur (2016a) examined several instances of metaphors being employed by speakers using English who were all native speakers of other languages, including Spanish. She has argued from this work that metaphor must always be examined as a discourse phenomenon and not just as a cognitive realization or a simple linguistic instantiation of underlying conventional metaphorical thinking.

A number of scholars have argued that effective communication in a second language greatly depends on adapting the specific linguistic and conceptual practices of native speakers of the target language. However, MacArthur (2016a) argued that variations in metaphor use are both critical to native and non-native speakers' use of language. The fact that native speakers often create novel metaphorical forms, or even mix their metaphors together, offers evidence against the common belief that standardization and conventional use of metaphor are the rule in both speech and writing. Being metaphorically fluent requires much more than simple acquisition of only the conventional forms of metaphor. Once again, context enables speakers to express metaphorical ideas in a variety of ways. Variation is particularly likely to arise in cases in which non-native speakers are far removed from the places and situations in which a specific target language first originated (MacArthur 2016a).

MacArthur (2016a) further explored these ideas through an examination of the ways non-native speakers of English talk with one another in English. A good example of this is seen in a conversation between three non-native speakers of English, all of whom were business students. The conversation focused on one student (S1), a male from Venezuela, talking about his reluctance to go out on a date given a recent haircut he got. Two other speakers (S2, a Dutch woman, and S3, a man from Indonesia) commented on S1's reluctance, partly through discussion of the metaphor employed to describe how S1 believed he now appeared (MacArthur 2016a: 139):

S2: And just have a good night's sleep go on your DATE or whatever you want to do tonight=
S1: =no: i'm not going to cos i gotta ma:n i've shaved i look like a puppy (.)
S2: \<imitating\> so maybe she likes pu:ppies \</imitating≥
S2 =oh man no but this \<1\>\<fast\> you're a woman \</fast\> \</1\>
S3 \<1\> is that \</1\> what's bothering you? \<2\> \<@\> your shaving \</@\> @ \</2\> @@@
S1 \<2\> @@@@\</2\>
S2 i don't MIND a puppy look from time to time?
S1 \<soft\> from time to time \</soft\>
S3 it's a ritual \<@\> man @ @ man's shaving \</@\> (.)
S2: yeah (1)
S1: i haven't shaved in the longest time (2) like ALL of it. like it's all gone (2)
S2: puppy (2)
S1: and they're probably thinking something else \<to S4\> no it's my fa:ce we're talking about \</to S4\> (1)

S1 describes his facial appearance as being "like a puppy" because he was recently shaved. S2 repeats "puppy" three times (e.g., "maybe she'd like puppies," "puppy like," and "puppy"). Note, however, that "I look like a puppy" in this case is unusual given S1's negative appraisal of this possibility. English speakers do not typically refer to "puppy" or looking "like a puppy" in this negative way. These non-native speakers of English have created a very local understanding of "look like a puppy," which reflects what others have referred to as a "conceptual pact" within conversation. Brennan and Clark (1996) describe conceptual pacts as cases where speakers frequently refer to some referent in a novel manner for temporary purposes of that conversation. Once these conceptual pacts are established, they can quickly, yet temporarily, become conventionalized with a specific talk exchange such that "I look like a puppy" later on in the brief conversation becomes "puppy like" and later just "puppy". In general, these non-native speakers of English were able to quite efficiently use a metaphor to communicate their ideas even when the metaphor was not employed with its most conventional meaning. As MacArthur (2016a: 150) claimed,

> the choice of a specific metaphor in a particular communicative context is often the result of local factors (for example, the topic under discussion) and arises precisely because individuals and groups of people have different experiences of all kinds –of physical environments, of prior experience of discourse events, of concerns and interests, among many others – that affect the kind of metaphors they employ in different circumstances.

She also suggested that this evidence of contextual variation in second language learners' metaphor use has pedagogical implications. Second language learners should not merely aim to acquire native-speaker norms, such as in the use of conventional English metaphors. Instead, novel or hybrid metaphors enable second-language learners from different cultural and linguistic backgrounds to effectively communicate in ways that simply parroting conventional metaphor may be unable to do.

6 Determining the Basic Meaning of Words

My last appreciation of Fiona MacArthur's work here focuses on the specifics of metaphor identification. Several methods have been proposed for identifying metaphorically used words in discourse such as MIP (Pragglejaz Group 2007) and MIPVU (Steen et al. 2010), These methods first ask analysts to determine the basic meanings of words before drawing inferences about whether their contextual meanings differed from their basic meanings in terms of similarity. Dictionaries are often employed to determine the basic mean meanings of words. As a member of Pragglejaz, I easily recall the many debates the group had over which dictionaries may be most appropriate to use when running MIP, as we observed significant differences in the ways dictionaries listed and articulated their varying definitions, or senses, of lexical items. MacArthur more fully considered the utility of "Macmillan English Dictionary for Advanced Learners" (MEDAL) for identifying basic senses of potential metaphorical words in a corpus of English conversations between university instructors and students who were non-native speakers of English (MacArthur 2015).

These 27 conversations focused on general academic topics, including students' assignments and difficulties in understanding the course contents. Presented below is one segment from the dialogues where the instructor was speaking. Note the different "say" verbs (these are presented in boldface):

> FL er and there (.) we want you to introduce each paragraph <fast> with what we call a topic sentence </fast> and that topic sentence should then (.) **say** what the main idea (.) in the paragraph is about (.) erm (.) Oscar Wilde **contradicts** himself yet again when he **says** da da da (.) then you **say** that (.) this is (.) that that first sentence **tells** us that (.) this is what you will *talk* about in the paragraph (.) which means that a topic sentence can never be (.) just a statement (.) Oscar Wilde (.) came from Ireland (.) that is a bad (.) topic sentence because it's just a statement you you cannot (.) prove it or disprove it it's just a fact (.) what you do is that you pick out something that you want to (.) **argue** for or against or (.) prove or (.) develop (.) that is the that is the topic sentence (MacArthur 2015: 125).

As Fiona summarized, "In this extract, it is clear that the lecturer is metaphorically framing the topic of successful communication in an academic essay, by inviting the student to 'see' the writing process as one of guiding the reader through the text". For example, the instructor noted that the student essay was "difficult to follow" and that the student should "pick/lift out" the main idea to "make it clear," in order to "lead the reader into the world of [the] essay". Thus, the instructor guided the students by commenting, "we want to see you, we want to see Oscar Wilde, and we want to see other critics also". (MacArthur 2015: 129).

Many of the "saying" verbs in the above extract appear to express metaphorical meaning by framing the students' take on a journey which leads to the writer guiding readers to a particular place, or understanding of Oscar Wilde. Overall, the participants used the verb "saying" 16 times, "contradict" 9 times, "talk" three times, "tell" once, and "argue" once. Yet not all of these related instances of "say" are necessarily used metaphorically and so Fiona looked up their meanings in MEDAL to see if she could identify a basic sense for each one that may vary in some way from how the words were used in context. This proved to be a difficult task.

For instance, what is the basic sense of the verb "say"? The first entry for "say" stated that the verb means "to express something in words". This makes some intuitive sense, perhaps, but what is really meant by "express" or even "words"? "Express" is defined as "to tell someone about a feeling, opinion by speaking or writing about it". "Word" is "a single unit of written or spoken language". Taken together, the meanings of most uses of "say" in the instructor and student conversation did not appear to be metaphorical.

When Fiona focused on "contradict" she found it defined as "to say the opposite of what someone has said is true". Herein lies the famous circularity problem in dictionaries, namely that one has to first define "say" in order to understand the basic sense of "contradict".

To "tell" someone something is defined as "to give information to someone," which suggests a physical transfer of something about (information) to another person. This contrasts with the real physical giving of a material object to another person, which suggests that it is used metaphorically in the context of the instructor and student conversations. However, note that the dictionary definition of "tell" is ambiguous because much depends on what is understood by "give". The dictionary definition seems to assume that one can "give" something to another without any real physical transfer. But "give" may be vague enough to allow nonphysical transfer in which case "tell" is not really metaphorical in the instructor and student exchange.

The meaning of "talk" was also found to be problematic given its dictionary definition of "to communicate using words," which may or may not indicate the use of words to communicate in written language, not just oral discourse. Nonetheless, the examples also "Can the baby talk yet?" and "Am I talking too much?" were also presented by the dictionary. For these reasons, the use of "talk" in the instructor-student conversations which refer to the student's written communication appears to contrast with the more basic oral model of communicating sense of "talk". Thus, the three uses of "talk" in the student feedback conversations should, perhaps, be marked as potentially conveying metaphorical meanings.

The meaning of "argue" is defined in two senses that are somewhat different: "if people argue, they speak to each other in a challenging way because they disagree," and "to give reason why you believe that something is right or true". Dictionaries often give multiple senses for words and it is not always clear which of these is assumed to be most "basic," if there is even any assumption that some senses are more basic than others in the construction of dictionaries. In this case, the first definition explicitly refers to spoken language, while the second, once more, uses the ambiguous "give," which has a metaphorical flavor. Should definitions that are metaphorical be seen as actually providing a word's "basic" sense?

As MacArthur (2015) pointed out, both MIP and MIPVU state the basic meanings are typically "more concrete" and are "related to body action". But these additional specifying criteria do not really help matters much given that both definitions of "argue" involve human agents engaging in body actions. We are left, then, being uncertain as to how to classify "argue" in the context of the instructor and student conversations.

Finally, "speak" is defined as "to talk to someone about something," and secondarily as "to use your voice to talk". If these senses were "basic," then the student's statement "but when I speak," in reference to something she actually wrote, appears to convey metaphorical meaning. Fiona is skeptical of this conclusion.

Overall, her analysis resulted in two words (e.g., "say" and "contradict") being judged as not metaphorical, two words (e.g., "talk" and "argue") being marked as potentially metaphorical, while other words (e.g., "speak") were metaphorical framings of the writer's task. If these results were valid, the instructor "was – confusingly – continually – switching from the literal to the figurative in his talk about good academic writing. Or at least, this is what the dictionary tells us he was doing" (MacArthur 2015: 134). But she noted that she "perceives no such incoherence in the discourse" to really assert that the instructor was confused in this way (MacArthur 2015: 134).

In the end, she suggested that "one might simply conclude that going through the painstaking procedure of identifying the basic meaning of each and every word in some discourse with a dictionary in hand is simply silly (and, incidentally, very time consuming)". On the other hand, MacArthur seems to believe that, "it might simply be that our basic resource (the dictionary recommended) is to blame, because the definitions it provides do not help us as researchers decide with any confidence if the contextual meaning of the words being used can be understood in comparison or contrast with the basic senses of those words – for the simple reason that in some cases we are not provided with any 'basic' sense of those words, but rather with metaphorically-expressed, pedagogically-oriented definitions, aimed at nonnative speakers of English" (MacArthur 2015: 134).

This detailed analysis of using a dictionary reveals several difficulties in applying standard identification procedures to identify metaphor in context. I do not believe MacArthur aims to discredit attempts to systematize metaphor identification for different research purposes. Nonetheless, there is perhaps too much of an emphasis in metaphor studies in applying identification procedures to large corpora, where analysts then quickly draw generalizations about how metaphors appear in some discourse topic or genre. Doing so may overlook many of the real complexities of metaphor use in very local contexts. Once again, Fiona's work offers a cautionary warning to scholars to always attend to the particularities of metaphor, which gives appropriate consideration to the real speakers (e.g., non-native speakers of English) in specific discourse situations.

7 Conclusion

This appreciation of Fiona MacArthur's metaphor scholarship has examined some of the important empirical findings and theoretical conclusions seen in several of her research articles. My lasting impression of her research is the detailed manner in which she explores metaphor use in context, paying close attention to some of the particularities of metaphor experience. This attention to the details of exactly how specific groups of people (e.g., second-language learners' of English) learn to use metaphor in particular discourse contexts (e.g., educational discourse) reveals a complex portrait of the interplay between generalities and variations in the ecology of metaphor.

Metaphor scholars, as seen across many academic disciplines, often struggle in balancing the desire of offering broad theories of metaphor, possibly relevant to all people in all contexts, with the need to be completely accurate in spelling out the nuances of metaphorical experience. Many of us in the metaphor business choose to embrace one side of this generality and variation divide. However, Fiona MacArthur's work is constantly striving to see generalities in the detailed particularities of real people using metaphor in different circumstances. She is not just a metaphor scholar, but more importantly, someone with a deep interest in how people communicate across cultures and languages while using metaphor for adaptive purposes. For example, she has a keen eye for detecting how metaphor is a tool for intercultural communication even when the metaphors employed are novel or vary from what is often thought to be accepted use. Yet this emphasis is not merely a matter of characterizing the students' learning of metaphor in terms of schematic systems of metaphor (e.g., primary metaphors, conventional patterns of metaphor within a target language). Instead, the larger lesson here is that all metaphor use is inherently contextualized, situated, and particular to individuals and specific discursive practices. In this manner, the particularities of metaphor experience help us understand the true generalities, and richness, of why metaphor is such an important conceptual and linguistic tool.

Her scholarship makes us stop and think more closely about what we are doing in our scientific and applied studies of metaphor. She pushes us to see the interconnectedness between language, culture, and minds and to have a greater appreciation for the humanity of metaphor as a fully human endeavor, not just an abstract topic that is examined from different disciplinary perspectives. Reading her many articles, book chapters, and edited collections also give us a strong sense of her personal and scholarly commitment to "getting metaphor right" by recognizing the limitations of our methods and the constant need for broader contextualization of how we study real-life metaphor use.

I salute Fiona for her diverse scholarly achievements and for what she has taught many of us about the complex realities in studying metaphor in all of its glorious, messy, and all so beautiful details. She offers us a distinctive, ideal model on how to best study metaphor.

References

Brennan, Susan and Herbert Clark, 1996. Lexical choice and conceptual pacts in conversation. *Journal of Experimental Psychology: Learning, Memory, and Cognition* 22, 1482–1493.

Deignan, Alice. 2003. Metaphorical expressions and culture: An indirect link. *Metaphor and Symbol* 18. 255–271.

Gibbs, Raymond W. 1994. *The poetics of mind: Figurative thought, language, and understanding*. New York: Cambridge University Press.

Gibbs, Raymond W. 2017. *Metaphor wars: Conceptual metaphor in human life*. New York: Cambridge University Press.

Grady, Joseph. 1997. Theories are buildings revisited. *Cognitive Linguistics* 8. 267–290.

Ibarretxe-Antuñano, Iraide. 2013. The relationship between conceptual metaphor and culture. *Intercultural Pragmatics* 10. 315–339.

MacArthur, Fiona. 2005. The competent horseman in a horseless world: Observations on a conventional metaphor in Spanish and English. *Metaphor and Symbol* 20. 71–94.

MacArthur, Fiona. 2015. On using a dictionary to identify the basic senses of words. *Metaphor and the Social World* 5. 124–136.

MacArthur, Fiona. 2016a. When languages and cultures meet: Mixed metaphors in the discourse of Spanish speakers of English. In Raymond W. Gibbs (ed.), *Mixing metaphor*, 133–154. Amsterdam: John Benjamins.

MacArthur, Fiona. 2016b. Overt and covert uses of metaphor in academic mentoring in English and Spanish undergraduate students at five European universities. *Review of Cognitive Linguistics* 14. 23–50.

MacArthur, Fiona, Tina Krenmayr & Jeannette Littlemore. 2015. How basic is UNDERSTANDING IS SEEING when reasoning about knowledge? Asymmetric uses of sight metaphor in office hours's consultations in English as academic lingua franca. *Metaphor and Symbol* 30. 184–217.

MacArthur, Fiona & Ana M. Piquer-Píriz. 2007. Staging the introduction of figurative extensions of familiar vocabulary items in EFL: Some preliminary considerations. *Ilha do desterro: A Journal of English Language, Literatures in English and Cultural Studies 53*. 123–135.

Pragglejaz Group. 2007. MIP: A method for identifying metaphorically-used words in discourse. *Metaphor and Symbol* 22. 1–40.

Steen, Gerard J., Aletta G. Dorst, Berenike Herrmann, Anna A. Kaal, Tina Krennmayr & Trijntje Pasma. 2010. *A Method for Linguistic Metaphor Identification: From MIP to MIPVU*. Amsterdam: John Benjamins.

Graham Low

Taking Stock after Three Decades: "On Teaching Metaphor" Revisited

1 Introduction

In the early 1980s, I read R. J. Alexander's seminal (1983) paper on the importance of helping English as a Foreign Language (EFL) learners come to terms with metaphors, connotations and allusions, as well as early work on conceptual metaphor, like Lakoff and Johnson's (1980) *Metaphors we live by*, Lakoff's (1982) *Categories and cognitive models*, and Lakoff and Kövecses's (1983) *The cognitive model of anger inherent in American English*. This, plus some research I was doing at the time on metaphorical expressions of anger in English, led me to the realisations (a) that metaphor was a more important component of English use and lexis than EFL theories, courses and tests were at that time acknowledging, (b) that metaphor was surprisingly complex, (c) that most applied linguists seemed to have little idea, or interest in, what to do about it, and (d) that some ideas from conceptual metaphor theory seemed potentially very relevant to foreign language teaching, but the theory did not seem to explain all metaphoric use, and even in its early stages conceptual metaphor theory and terminology seemed to need simplifying or reinterpreting for use in the language classroom.

I therefore decided to have a first stab at formulating a number of points that I felt were important in foreign language teaching and learning. These were divided into four topic areas: What is metaphor? What functions does metaphor have? What do we want a skilled L2[1] user to be able to do with metaphor? How might L2 metaphor usefully be taught (and to a lesser degree, tested)? The result was published in 1988 in the paper *On teaching metaphor*. It has been much cited in the intervening years, and I reviewed my position on metaphor and education generally in 2008, but until recently (e.g., O'Reilly 2017), many of the ideas in it were not empirically tested or developed. Thirty something years on (2019), thus seems like a good point to look back at the 1988 paper and ask whether I still agree with it, and to try to establish if there were any major gaps or gaffes. I shall

---

1 I shall use the acronyms L1 and L2 conventionally to mean first language and target language. Similarly I will use FL adjectivally to mean foreign language. The label "native speaker" will be avoided.

Graham Low, Selby, North Yorkshire, UK, e-mail: grahamlow018@gmail.com

https://doi.org/10.1515/9783110630367-003

treat the points using the same topic areas used in 1988, but limit the viewpoint taken and examples in the main to EFL learners. I should perhaps add as a proviso that in this sort of reflection on one's previous work, however objective one tries to be, there remains an inevitable element of subjectivity.

2 What Is Metaphor?

The 1988 paper was written for applied linguists not metaphor specialists, so it adopted a definition, designed to be easily comprehensible, that more or less covered various theoretical positions: "Treating X as if it were, in some ways, Y (where X and Y can show varying degrees of difference)" (1988: 126).

It seems reasonable to wonder whether this definition is adequate, allowing for some lexical reinterpretation, as a foreign-language (FL) classroom or coursebook explanation, for older learners (meaning older teenagers and adults) at least.

On the positive side, it allows for metaphoricity to be a cline (the greater the apparent difference between X and Y, the greater, or at least clearer, the metaphoricity), for metaphor to be treated selectively on the "surface" or in terms of underlying X IS Y propositions, for metaphor to be primarily unidirectional (TIME IS MONEY being different from MONEY IS TIME) and for metaphor to be expressed visually, gesturally, or auditorily, as well as linguistically. The use of "in some ways" also encompasses the need, stressed later by both Cameron (2003) and the Pragglejaz group (2007), that to be metaphorically used, some plausible account of the basic sense/literal-to-figurative change (implying one or more connection or correspondence) needs to be specifiable, such that the randomly named particle labels in Physics, like *colour* and *charm*, for example, remain non-metaphoric. Lastly, where subsidiary clauses continue to treat X as Y (as in "Anne seemed a rose, that bloomed in June and faded later in the same year"), the reader can choose to see the clauses as "inheriting" (as Steen 1999 put it) the metaphoricity of the main clause, or identify *rose, bloomed*, and *faded* as independently metaphorically used.

With hindsight, a treatment definition has the added advantages that it allows for expressions such as "John is (the new) Fred" to be metaphoric or not, depending on how one thinks of Fred, and it allows for multimodal realisations where X is in one modality and Y is in another (as in many cartoons, advertisements and graffiti). There is also no requirement for the speaker/writer and the hearer/reader to agree on the meaning of an utterance, leaving the hearer/reader to guess on the basis of the available contextual evidence whether a metaphor is involved or was intended, and if so, how.[2] It would seem to also cover the ideological position where a believer sees, say, heaven as literally in the sky, but a non-believer sees the same link not as truth but as metaphorical (to the non-believer, the "as if it were Y" applies).

Neither blending theory (e.g., Fauconnier and Turner 2008) nor primary metaphor (Grady 1998; Grady and Johnson 2002) were around in the early 1980s. To take blending theory first, while some lexis that FL learners are likely to encounter represents clear examples of figurative + non-figurative blending (like *frogman* for example), these can be easily explained as a man treated as if he were in some ways a frog. I would argue that the complex and abstract terminology involved in blending theory and the difficulties with specifying "generic space" in particular, rule out its use in the majority of FL situations.

Primary metaphor constitutes a different 'problem', as several primary metaphors (or variations on them) are highly relevant to FL contexts and easily understandable. Thus PSYCHOLOGICAL (DISTANCE) IS PHYSICAL DISTANCE and SOCIAL (DISTANCE) IS PHYSICAL DISTANCE are frequently involved in common interaction expressions, explaining why *"This* is John" (vs *"It's* John", or *"That's* John") works as a social introduction – making John not just visible but a member, even if temporary, of the interaction group – and a worried listener might answer the phone with "Who's *that?"* or "Is *that* John?" (rather than "Is *this* John?" "Is *it* John?", or *"Are you* John?"). Many primary metaphors may well be grounded in metonymic relations, as Grady claims, but for practical purposes they can still be described as "treating X as if it were Y" even if one has to hunt around and look "under the surface" to isolate appropriate Xs and Ys. There would seem no need, however, to introduce either of the labels "primary metaphor" or "primary scene" to FL learners. In short, primary metaphor can be dealt with in FL contexts using the 1988 treatment definition.

Sharifian (2017: 18 and elsewhere), arguing from a Culture Linguistics stance, again developed after 1988, has argued that it is preferable to formulate X IS Y as X AS Y, to emphasise the partial and culturally-constructed linking of the two (e.g., rephrasing Yu's [2007: 27] wording to HEART AS RULER OF THE BODY in Chinese) – something which again dovetails neatly with the "treatment as Y" definition.

Cameron's (2003 and elsewhere) use of complexity theory to explain how texts have different layers or narratives, with metaphors relating to different layers and resonating with current and earlier contexts to differing degrees, fits

---

2 The notion of "deliberate metaphor" (Steen 2011a, 2011b) remains controversial. I am here simply suggesting (with Deignan, Littlemore and Semino 2012: 22) that there are times when the author's aims and intentions are worth hypothesising.

the "treatment as Y" definition. Moreover, the idea of a metaphoric expression, for example, *chivalrous*, reflecting, say, a cultural context from the past, while at the same time having a role, such as "old-fashioned, geriatric" behaviour, in the present discourse needs to be covered in FL situations. The hearer/reader may well, of course, be guessing whether a link with the past is intended and whether the speaker is trying to make a point or not about the present.

While the 1988 definition thus has some advantages and covers several situations that are likely to recur in FL contexts, including ideas developed post-1988, there are a number of problems. The main one is that it excludes simile. "Treating X as if it were in some ways Y" implies the identification (albeit partial[3]) of Y with X. Simile, however, involves comparison (e.g., *Teaching is like cooking*), not identification (e.g., *Teaching is cooking*). There is good reason to keep metaphor separate from simile, in that (1) not all similes are best treated as figurative – *Your house is like mine* is most likely to be seen as a non-figurative, or literal, comparison – (2) "X is Y" and "X is like Y" can have different meanings – examples can be found in Littlemore and Low (2006: 42–43), including *Life is a joke* (definitely not funny, on a par with *You're having a laugh!*) versus *Life is like a joke* (where it could well be) – and (3) the X-Y relationship is clearer with simile than the corresponding metaphor (thus I suggested in Low (2015: 22) that research prompts in elicited metaphor studies could reduce confusion by using *X is like Y* format).

However, at the same time, it is often desirable to ally simile with metaphor, and to be able to see a simile such as *Teaching is like cooking* as close in meaning to *Teaching is cooking*. The justification is that (1) it is not always easy to establish whether markers like 'kind of' are flagging metaphor, simile or literal subcategorisation (Low 2010: 293) and (2) speakers/writers often mix the two, either in stretches of discourse/text involving expansion or development of a figurative link, or in repair sequences. An example of the latter comes from a UK university lecture on business strategy (the numbering represents tone groups):

1721   the I mean organisations *are like sort of*
1722   er you know
1723   *have huge buffering* power
1724   to actually stop any change
                (from Low 2010: 298, example 4)[4]

---

3 Veale (2012: 335) calls the identification "absolute", but this would seem to imply more than "in some ways" and imply a sameness between X and Y.
4 The source is the British Academic Spoken English (BASE) corpus. My thanks to Hilary Nesi for permission to cite extracts for research purposes. The BASE corpus was developed at the Universities of Warwick and Reading under the directorship of Hilary Nesi and Paul Thompson.

So, with hindsight, the 1988 paper could usefully have linked simile and metaphor better, and in a more detailed way. In self-defence, I can only say that when I wrote the paper I had not examined the complex roles that the two play in discourse.

The second main problem with the treatment definition is that it appears to cover numerous examples of metonymy. Thus in *The sandwich lunches sit at the back of the room* or *Put the tools in the Ford* it could be argued that the eaters are being treated as the prototypical objects eaten, or that the vehicle/product is being treated as the manufacturer/ producer. While the close connections between metonymy and metaphor became abundantly clear with primary metaphor, and there are (other) cases where it is not clear which of the two is involved, it was not my intention in 1988 to conflate them. Perhaps a compromise position would be to apply the treatment definition to both, but to regard part-whole examples as metonymy. Close association examples could be metonymic or metaphorical depending on the degree of closeness, or whether the hearer/reader felt that connection or discrepancy/difference was being emphasised. One could then explain *This firm needs some new blood* (= we need new people, and we need new ideas) as treating both people and ideas as blood, with people as blood being part-whole metonymy and ideas as blood being either metaphor or (populist) close association metonymy (greater blood flow to the brain generates more ideas).[5]

A third potential problem, and one highly relevant to FL learners, is the variable metaphoricity of technical terminology, where a specialist author may begin by treating a technical term as metaphoric, but in subsequent mentions treat it as literal or minimally metaphoric, whereas a non-specialist reader sees it throughout as highly metaphorical. Deignan, Littlemore and Semino (2013: 8) would treat this an example of the more general topic of "insider discourse". I do not think this is a genuine problem for the "treatment" definition, however, as individual words and phrases can be resubjected to it at different points in the text, and it can be applied using the viewpoints of different protagonists. Thus slang or jargon can at times be seen as talking to insiders, while excluding outsiders.

Lastly, one might wonder if proverbs, which were not dealt with in the 1988 paper, represent another problem area for the treatment definition. I shall take

---

Corpus development was assisted by funding from BALEAP, EURALEX, the British Academy and the Arts and Humanities Research Council. The URL is http://www2.warwick.ac.uk/fac/soc/al/re search/collect/base/.
5 This is not to disagree with the point made by Steen (2007: 59) that when identifying examples of figurative use in research exercises, it is preferable to identify metaphor and metonymy separately.

"a rolling stone gathers no moss" and "it's the early bird that catches the worm" as examples. In the first, a person who does not settle in a job/community is treated as a stone that rolls (in a wood? Or where?). In the second, a person who gets up early, or starts a task before others have committed to it, is treated as an early-rising bird. Like most English proverbs, they have two parts and involve an action > result storyline (or scenario[6]), so treating a job, home and/or family as moss and a reward/payoff as a worm seems adequate for most FL purposes. In practice, the FL learner may additionally be faced with having to identify the proverb, as only the first half is often explicit, as well as establishing the moral force of the utterance (eating worms may always be a good practice, but do we want stones to have moss?), but neither of these tasks affects the viability of the definition. Lakoff and Turner (1989: 162–166) suggest a complex creation/interpretation pathway for proverbs via the conceptual metaphor generic is specific. However, I would argue that most adult and teenage FL learners will know at a general level how to interpret a proverb (equivalents seem to exist in most languages); what they need is to know is if a proverb is being referred to, and if so which one, what its 'dictionary' sense is, how this relates to the current situation and whether irony is involved. A treatment definition, plus explanations of the scenario involved, is likely to be adequate for most FL purposes; recourse to complex generic and specific logic may well confuse rather than help.[7]

3 What Core Functions Does Metaphor Have?

The 1988 paper isolated half a dozen core functions, likely to be encountered by many learners. However, there are many types of learner, with differing wants and needs concerning the L2, so the functions of metaphor that are most likely to be relevant to learners does not constitute a fixed set (making it hard to list functions as part of a general L2 proficiency profile). The 1988 set is nevertheless worth briefly reviewing.

---

6 I use "scenario" for narratives at lexical level and "story" for narratives created at discourse level. With proverbs, the two are more or less equivalent.

7 Sullivan and Sweetser (2010) argue that a blending theory approach can provide a better explanation than conceptual metaphor theory, accounting for both more- and less-metaphorical linguistic examples in a principled way. While I take their point, I would still argue that the terminological complexity of blending theory and the difficulties with mapping generic spaces rule it out for any but the most linguistics-oriented FL learners.

To Enable People to Talk at All about X

Abstract concepts like emotions, the mind, time, colour hue, saturation and luminosity, life and death, friendship are all heavily metaphorised, often viewed in terms of containers, journeys, locations, or rivers/seas/fluids. Many of these topics have exponents that come into L2 courses early (e.g., a *dark* blue, vs a *deep* blue, or a *rich* blue etc) and recur at all levels.

To Relate or Structure X

Clearly the famous conceptual metaphors with large amounts of transferred structure, such as ARGUMENT AS WAR or LIFE AS A JOURNEY can be seen as structuring aspects of argument or life reports; similarly, treating the mind as a computer, a building or a person can help people develop (or reflect) mental models of the mind. Less obviously, perhaps, there is the way vertical UP-DOWN scales are used for so many concepts, or how scenarios involving actors, actions and events are used. One "problem" with structuring via metaphor is the inconsistencies, or structural gaps, which show up in the collocational tendencies of conventional metaphorical expressions. Thus I can "*put* my mind to a problem", "*apply* it to a problem" or "*get* my brain onto a problem", but I cannot conventionally *move* it (mind or brain), *push* it, *place* it, or *put* it *back*. Again, a bank account is fairly consistently a boxlike container in English: you *open/close* an account, pay *into* it, have money *in* it, and *take* money *out* of it (though you don't open it immediately prior to paying into it), but it sounds very odd to talk about a balance being calculated *inside* an account. And "put it *on* my account" represents a different type of account (one which is a list of money owing) and seemingly a different underlying metaphor (a two-dimensional "slate"). Collocational inconsistency is so widespread in English and such a minefield for FL learners, that creating sets of what you can and cannot say seems well worth the effort.

To Extend Thought

Extending thought is perhaps only relevant for some learners, such as those following university courses in the L2, who are exposed to analogies for technical concepts or different theories in lectures and readings, and for whom learning about critical thinking via metaphors is important. But even elementary-level learners can usefully extend conventional English via playing with

"Love is ... ", or "Anger is ... "; and the use of direct elicited metaphor ("Learning English is ... "[8]) to help learners think about their own learning (e.g., the papers in Wan and Low 2015; or the evaluation in Low 2017) seems to be successful if appropriate methodological precautions are taken.

To Dramatise X

Metaphor is often used in discourse, in genres like verbal reports, or advertisements, along with hyperbole, to dramatise an event, by exaggerating it positively or negatively. Sometimes this involves the creation of metaphor-based stories, (something not considered in the 1988 paper). Dramatisation occurs at both discourse and lexical levels, and learners need to be able to cope with both.

Dramatisation can be achieved lexically by use of markers or "flags" such as *literally*: e.g., "*At this point she literally hit the roof*". This sort of dramatization is easy for FL learners to achieve, as long as they can cope with *literally* having two very different senses!

Dramatisation at discourse level seems less frequently taught on EFL courses. As a brief illustration of creating a metaphor-based story, which relies on combining conventional metaphoric phraseology with discourse, the following anecdote about whale meat is embedded inside a longer anecdote in the previously cited UK university lecture on business strategy. The speaker is part of a group in an Icelandic restaurant:

1347   in this actual room
1348   two two Norwegians
1349   and said the wonderful classic phrase (.)
1350   what is so wrong
1351   about killing minky whales
1352   and and to see the sort of head of Greenpeace
1353   *virtually go through the ceiling*
1354   *before coming down* (.)
1355   *and sort of killing all in his path* (.)
　　　　　　　　　　(from Cameron, Low and Maslen 2010)

---

8 As argued Sec. 2, a teacher might well generate a clearer prompt here by using a simile (*Learning English is like ...*).

The speaker creates a small three-event story involving the head of Greenpeace getting angry, via a conventional idiom (*go through the ceiling*), plus an intensifier (*virtually*) flagging that the idiom is metaphoric as well as forceful, and then acting wildly (*killing all in his path*). The metaphoric idiom and the relatively fixed rampaging animal phrase are connected narratively by inserting a bridge, *coming down* (which creatively extends the metaphor in the idiom), and the three events are held together rhetorically by being framed between two polysemous uses of *killing* (lines 1351, 1355).

To Prevaricate, Avoid Clarity, Not Actually Commit Oneself

The example in the 1988 paper came from Lerman's (1985) study of a US presidential speech and journalists' reactions to it, whereby, having said nothing literal the speaker is not committed to, or responsible for anything concrete. While this function may not be appropriate for many younger and/or lower-proficiency learners, it seems highly useful as regards both comprehension and production for upper intermediate and advanced learners, especially those studying politics.

To Allow/Facilitate Discussion of Emotionally Charged Topics

There is abundant evidence that writers/speakers often use more (though not necessarily more creative) metaphors, leading to short bursts or clusters, when showing emotions, and/or at "emotional centres" of discourse (Lerman 1983: 3). A good recent example comes from the editor of a photography magazine enthusiastically introducing the issue; the opening sentence has seven or eight metaphorical words or phrases, but the rate then declines fast:

Have I got hues for you
Vivid images *infused* with *rich* hues *sit alongside striking* archive photography in an *issue* that *showcases* the best of both *worlds*.
As he prepares for a headline appearance at The Photography Show, Miles Aldridge explains the role of colour in his work. . ..

(K. Morgan, *The RPS Journal*, March 2018: 161)[9]

---

9 My thanks to Kathleen Morgan for permission to cite the extract from her editorial.

EFL learners seem to be increasingly faced with tasks requiring subjective or emotive responses of various sorts. Littlemore et al. (2014) in their study of 200 written exam scripts by German and Greek EFL learners found a qualitative difference at B2 (upper intermediate) level. Below B2, metaphors primarily involved function words like prepositions, but at and above B2 they involved open class words more. As MacArthur (2010: 419) put it, this seemed to be a task effect, inasmuch as at/from elementary level, "in response to tasks requiring that they state their personal opinions on certain issues or highlight their personal significance, learners needed to use metaphorical language."

It is also worth reiterating the research and/or therapy use of metaphor. Wan (2011, 2012), Fisher (2013) and others have, as noted above, used direct elicited metaphor with reasonable success to aid feedback on courses, both academic and foreign language.

Other Functions

The 1988 paper briefly mentioned the use of metaphor to summarise, and/or disengage with a topic, and with hindsight, two related aspects of this function seem worth stressing as useful to L2 learners. First there is the finding by Drew and Holt (1995) that British and American speakers wanting to change topic in a conversation (or end the conversation) frequently add a summarising idiom or metaphor, which the listener can accept or reject. Secondly, there is the finding (Low 1997) that written texts such as editorials, novels or book reviews not infrequently add metaphoric expressions near the start and end of text units like sections and paragraphs, thereby creating metaphoric borders or frames, some of which mark changes of topic. The *RPS Journal* extract above is an example of an initial text border.

One last core function not mentioned in the 1988 paper is that of reassuring the listener/reader and relating unfamiliar topics to familiar ones. In one sense this relates to vast amounts of conventional metaphor, where abstract Xs are associated with concrete, familiar Ys often based round the human body and common bodily events. But an aspect of reassurance/familiarisation to which listeners and readers of "authentic" English are likely to be frequently exposed, but which is not commonly dealt with on EFL (or FL) courses with any degree of systematicity, is the use of animacy or personification. As an example, in Low (2005) I showed how even a fairly formal popular science article explaining research in Darwinian evolution repeatedly (and ironically given the topic) animated/personified elements undergoing change, seemingly allowing them intentions. The moral is that animacy is a common instructional device, and its use can override the logic of the topic being instructed. A second genre, to which EFL learners are likely to be exposed, and which, in the UK at least, involves repeated animacy, is TV weather forecasting, as in:

> "the (cold) front *nudges its way* across (the UK) before it *makes itself at home* (+ location)"
>
> (O. W. Evans, BBC1, Late *Look North*, 20 Feb 2018)

In both the popular science and the weather forecasting cases, the aim seems to be the opposite of "insider language" ("outsider language"?), or rather to give outsiders non-threatening access to insider concepts, processes or argumentation.

It should be added that metaphor can serve the reverse function, via what Halliday (1985/1994; see also Steen 2007: 85–88) called grammatical metaphor, where, say, an action, process or event is treated as an object. To the extent that this involves a change of syntactic class, like nominalisation, the label seems valid. The example below contrasts three (imagined) utterances:

(a) *He left*. Then the family had breakfast. >
(b) *After he left*, the family had breakfast. >
(c) *After his departure*, the family had breakfast.

The effect of (a) > (b) > (c) is to increasingly background the action of leaving, and to increase the implication that the reader already knew he would leave, or had left (thereby emphasising familiarity with the action by *in*creasing, rather than *de*creasing, abstraction). Grammatical metaphor would thus seem to cover academic arguing via abstract nouns, a practice FL teachers might want to encourage or discourage depending on the situation of the learners and purpose of the course.

To sum up, with a couple of additions, the core function list seems as valid today for foreign language learning as it did in 1988.

4 Metaphoric Competence

"Competence" can be envisaged in several ways, from the social to the psychological, focussing on the process or the result, and from abilities directly related to the action/result to ones underlying it and only indirectly related to it. The 1988 paper took an approach based round a range of discourse-based skills, which could in theory at least be directly tested, though how test scores could be combined to form an overall index remained (and still remains) unclear.

Indeed, the whole topic of how a notion called metaphoric competence fitted into general language competence (i.e. via proficiency testing, rather than testing what had been taught) was not elaborated on. The important question of L2 identity was also overlooked in 1988; how far particular learners see themselves as the sort of person who uses a lot of metaphor and plays with ideas/words in the L2 may well influence the discourse they produce, as well as how they interact (which will in turn affect their proficiency test scores); while there has been research into differing identities in L1 and L2, I have not seen studies relating this specifically to metaphor teaching, learning or use.

Metaphoric competence probably needs to be seen as encompassing more than discourse (even though the skills envisaged in the 1988 paper had implications for grammar and lexis too). Indeed, when Littlemore and Low (2006a, 2006b) explored general models of communicative competence commonly used in foreign language teaching/learning at the time, especially that of Bachman (1990) and Bachman and Palmer (1996), it became clear that aspects of metaphor in lexis or discourse needed to be addressed by learners at all stages of proficiency and in all four dimensions of competence (linguistic, sociolinguistic, discourse and strategic).

Littlemore (2001) took a different approach to testing metaphoric competence from Low (1988) and developed a series of psychologically-based tests, some of which tested underlying skills thought to correlate with metaphoric competence. Apart from test sets by Azuma (2003, 2005) and a discursive review of metaphoric competence by MacArthur (2010), little research has been published at the time of writing to reconcile and compare empirically the social and psychological approaches to metaphoric competence.

Until it is, I think that listing things that learners need to be able to do in and with the L2 represents a valid, if not comprehensive, approach to teaching metaphoric competence, and for general purpose FL contexts (rather than specific purposes contexts) I would endorse the general summary I gave in Low (2008: 221)[10]:

> Productively, speakers need to know how to use non-specific metaphor to "decouple" from a narrative or conversational topic, in order to summarise it, evaluate it, withdraw gracefully from the argument, or simply change topic. Receptively, listeners need to be able to pick up on the previous speaker's metaphor, use their knowledge of the target culture and discourse practices to guess what the speaker is implying, and choose to "run with" the metaphor, extend it or even close it down. They need moreover to be aware of the implications of the strategy they themselves adopt. They need to recognise where style jumps take place, where speakers and writers stop being metaphoric. They need to recognise where the speaker is extending or elaborating beyond conventional

---

10 My thanks to Cambridge University Press for permission to cite this extract.

language and why – are they being friendly, humorous, sarcastic or even addressing a third party? Learners need to recognise where the speaker is avoiding a topic, or refusing to take responsibility (Lerman, 1983). Lastly, they need to recognise when texts or speakers are operating simultaneously on multiple levels (as in many, possibly most, jokes, advertisements and banter) and to establish what effects and messages are being hinted at on each level.

To the above one could add the need to understand euphemisms (like conventional and mildly creative expressions for lavatory) and their appropriate contexts of use, and to know how to intensify (or tone down) a metaphoric utterance (e.g., by using *really, seriously, literally, kind of* etc.).

5 Teaching and Learning Implications

I begin this section by noting the stark conclusions drawn by MacArthur (2017) that after all the years of work by linguists of various sorts, there has been little attempt to integrate metaphoric competence into national FL syllabuses, examination profiles, or textbooks. Despite the existence of a few standalone materials and activity books/sets, metaphor (and especially its use in discourse/pragmatics) is "still marginal" (*ibid.*: 418) to mainline FL language teaching and testing.

Limiting FL metaphor teaching to vocabulary, with a concomitant lack of focus on teaching metaphor use in discourse, is clearly worrying, given the list of skills and the examples in the previous two sections. In 1988, I was very interested as an applied linguist in instructional activities that involved multiple texts and multiple tasks, based round one or more "storylines", resulting in a mixture of text types/genres, with jumps of formality, emotion, and mode, and allowing for multimodal products like advertisements (drafts as well as finalised) with pictures and texts. The process and output would be enhanced by small group work, as different participants with different perspectives could be represented.[11] The advantage was that this type of activity covered the metaphor-related skills listed above, but the downside was that they were very time-consuming to create, took up a lot of class time, and did not by themselves explain how the metaphors operated. While task-based learning has over the years developed certain aspects of multi-text, multi-task activities, I have rarely seen tasks that foreground metaphor-related skills. The possibility of creating them, even shortish ones, as part of mainline instructional packages remains, though.

---

11 Outlines of several possible multi-text, multi-task activities were given in (1988: 139–141).

Both the 1988 and 2008 papers touched on the key pedagogical question of whether the fact that you can treat, say *in horror* as metaphorical (PSYCHOLOGICAL STATE AS CONTAINER) means that you should necessarily teach it as such. My experience with talking to language teachers has shown that there is still considerable unwillingness to teach much prepositional use or tenses as metaphorical. There is likely to be no ideal solution to this problem, but one might suggest that there are advantages to showing learners where multiple structural details apply ("I told you not to let him get *into danger*; he's *in danger* now, so it's your job to get him *out of danger*") and where they do not (*in haste, in anger, in horror*).

In Low (2008) I emphasised a related problem that simply teaching learners about metaphor does not *per se* guarantee that the form or meaning will be remembered for long, or that productive use of them will improve. Having said that, much of the research into metaphor teaching has involved recommending (e.g., Golden 2010) or giving explanations of conceptual metaphor structure and/or etymology and continues to do so. While pictures and etymology discussions can add a degree of critical engagement by learners, MacArthur (2017), commenting on Boers et al. (2008), Boers et al. (2009), MacArthur (2006) and Szczepaniak and Lew (2011), notes that pictures do not seem good at cueing the exact wording, or appropriate use, of new (= to the learner) metaphorical phrases; indeed there is the danger that what is remembered is the picture not the phrase.

I shall base the last half of this section around two recently published studies: the first qualitative, the second quantitative, both on teaching vocabulary/conventional phraseology. In the first study, Niemeier (2017) asked 26 German pre-intermediate level EFL students aged 13 to 15 years about colour idioms involving seven expressions each for blue, red, green and yellow. Learners were first asked to collect colour idioms from memory, dictionaries, or a previous school project on colour symbolism. In lesson 2 they brainstormed in groups which objects were literally blue etc, which of the 7x4 given idioms were the same in German and English and which were English only. Then in lesson 3 they reported on the earlier tasks, speculated on the motivations/etymologies involved and thought up contexts for using the idioms. There was lastly a homework writing task which had to include four of the taught idioms. Finally, after three weeks, learners completed a gap-fill post-test. Despite the seeming absence of a pretest or control group, Niemeier reported that the learners remained motivated and their vocabulary knowledge "improved noticeably" (ibid.: 280). It is hard from the report to isolate specific factors contributing to success, but one might speculate, based on research into the value of reflection and dialogic approaches on learning generally (e.g., Willis (1996) on reflection and Pontefract and Hardman, or Hardman (2008) on dialogic approaches) that the group negotiation/discussion (student-student and student-teacher), limited input data per colour, making the main task one of actively placing idioms with and without L1 equivalents on diagrams (as if playing a board game), and the creation of a coherent narrative production task, may have helped.

Niemeier also raised the vexed question of whether to use pictures, but decided against using them. The problem was not so much recall of exact wording, but that posed by confusing and inaccurate details – a difficulty earlier raised briefly by Low (2008, re diagrams of the movement of time) and far more seriously by Boers and MacArthur (2009) and MacArthur (2010), so if comprehensive pretesting of pictures was not possible, Niemeier's solution was probably the right one.

The second study, Pan (2019), was again small scale, but involved a more rigorous research design, with pre-test, control group, and immediate and delayed post-tests. The aim was to test out the viability of the "conceptual metaphor approach" (CMA) with young learners and to teach 43 elementary-level EFL learners in China (aged 10 to 12 years) anger expressions relating to ANGER IS A HOT FLUID IN A CONTAINER. This involved explaining the details of the conceptual metaphor to the metaphor/experimental group, consistently teaching literal senses before metaphoric ones (thus *steam* before *steam up*), creating paired associates (following Boers and Lindstromberg 2009), so that seeing *steam* should cue *steamed up* as well as vice versa. The delayed post-test showed that the metaphor group and the higher proficiency students (i.e. in the metaphor group and the control group) did significantly better than the non-CMA/control group and lower proficiency students, so the conclusion was that a conceptual metaphor approach to teaching could work successfully with elementary level students. As in Niemeyer's study, the metaphor group students were keen and interested. Unlike in Niemeier's study, no attempt was made to establish how Chinese expressions for anger differed from English ones.

One needs to be careful before generalising about the success of CMA teaching. Firstly, age may be a significant factor; CMA may cause problems, or require different teaching methods, with some young learners (MacArthur 2006; MacArthur and Piquer-Píriz 2007), who interpret FL expressions via metonymy rather than metaphor – though Pan's lower age limit was 10 years. Secondly, most research studies apart from those by Boers and colleagues have been small scale, involving small numbers of students, few teaching sessions (Niemeyer had but three, Pan had just one, and even Boers did not integrate the idiom teaching into a whole EFL course curriculum), unmotivating control group activities (frequently emphasising rote-learning of lists [MacArthur 2017: 420]), small numbers of expressions taught (indeed Pan reported some surprise at just how little content could be taught per session), and a focus on learning lexical items rather than discourse-level skills. Pan also reported, and this is an important point, that the regular teacher who actually taught the class found the CM method exerted a heavy toll on her (something which matches my anecdotal finding above, that multi-text, multi-task activities are hard and time-consuming to create). The "effort and tiredness" problem can affect students as well as teachers. While Pan's and Niermeier's learners appear to have remained motivated, Condon's (2008: 249) experimental group students were reportedly very tired when asked to engage with metaphorical verbs at the end of the teaching day. The implication is that it would be hard for teachers to integrate CM (or indeed non-CM) metaphor teaching into a regular or full syllabus/curriculum, unless publishers created extensive course materials using it, with explanations for teachers.

How far FL metaphor teaching should focus on explicit comparisons with the first language remains unclear. Nacey and Jensen (2017: 284) noted that Norwegian EFL learners' main problem with selecting prepositions was that they tended to go for the equivalent used in Norwegian. One might generalise by concluding that where first and target languages are close, like English and Norwegian or German, teaching across languages is useful, as Niemeier found. But it is important to bear in mind Philip's (2010: 75) proviso: "attributing all errors to language interference is somewhat simplistic," so the moral would seem to be to use L1 patterning at times, but not to rely overmuch on it.

Both Niemeier and Pan made sure that basic senses were taught before metaphoric ones were introduced. While this makes logical sense in most cases (MacArthur and Piquer-Píriz 2007), including the two situations considered, the points made in Low (1988) and (2008) remain valid, that the basic sense may be hard to find/agree on, and that there will be numerous contexts where the metaphoric sense is either encountered early on (as with classroom management language (e.g., *write down* vs *write up*, or *sit down* vs *sit up*) see also Low and Littlemore 2009) or before the literal sense (as with technical phrases like *buttress an argument*), assuming the literal sense is ever encountered at all; in these last two situations the "basic/literal sense first" approach will not always be appropriate (a point echoed by MacArthur 2017).

6 Conclusion

The 1988 paper *On teaching metaphor* inevitably omitted approaches like blending theory (for lexis) or Cameron's use of complexity theory (for discourse), details of much corpus research, especially that by (e.g.) Philip, Nacey, or Golden of learner language and strategies, and details of numerous empirical studies of teaching metaphor as part of foreign language training.

However, despite the omissions, the "treatment" definition of metaphor seems usable with (or adaptable to) FL language learners, and the core functions of metaphor remain largely valid: indeed, the point that the skills necessary for using an L2 well involve interactional, context-based, ones, and not just the prior learning of conventional lexis, remains something which has not been researched, or integrated into teaching programmes, much in the intervening thirty years. While the notion of generalised "metaphoric competence" can no doubt be refined and revised via the addition of contributory psychological skills, I would argue that for most FL teaching situations, a "concrete" approach based round what a learner needs to be able to do with the L2 when hearing/reading it or producing it remains useful. As does the suggestion that multi-text, multi-task, storyline activities can aid the learning of interactional and discourse (spoken and written) aspects of L2 metaphor.

In short, *On teaching metaphor*, together with the 2008 update *Metaphor and education* are still valid sources of ideas for teaching and learning, as well as for future applied research. There is little excuse for the continuing marginality, as MacArthur (2017) put it, of metaphor to EFL teaching or FL teaching in general.

References

Alexander, Richard. 1983. *Metaphors, connotations, allusions: Thoughts on the language-culture connexion in learning English as a foreign language*. Trier: University of Trier, L. A. U. T. Papers, Series B, No. 91.

Azuma, Masumi. 2003. Metaphorical competence in an EFL context. Paper presented at the 5th International Conference of Researching and Applying Metaphor (RAAM V), Paris September 3–5. Program and Abstracts 54.

Azuma, Masumi. 2005. Metaphorical competence in an EFL context. Tokyo: Toshindo Publishing.

Bachman, Lyle. 1990. *Fundamental considerations in language testing*. Oxford: Oxford University Press.

Bachman, Lyle F. & Adrian S. Palmer. 1996. *Language testing in practice*. Oxford: Oxford University Press.

Boers, Frank, Seth Lindstromberg, Jeannette Littlemore, Hélène Stengers & June Eyckmans. 2008. Variables in the mnemonic effectiveness of pictorial elucidation. In Frank Boers & Seth Lindstromberg (eds.), *Cognitive linguistic approaches to teaching vocabulary and phraseology*, 189–216. Berlin: Mouton de Gruyter.

Boers, Frank, Ana Piquer-Píriz, Hélène Stengers & June Eyckmans. 2009. Does pictorial elucidation foster recollection of figurative idioms? *Language Teaching Research* 13(4). 367–388.

Boers, Frank & Seth Lindstromberg. 2009. *Optimising a lexical approach to instructed second language acquisition*. Basingstoke: Palgrave Macmillan.

Boers, Frank & Fiona MacArthur. 2009. The use of pictorial and gestural modes in fostering the learning of idioms and conventional metaphors in instructed second language acquisition: An overview. Paper presented at RaAM 2009 Workshop 'Metaphor, metonymy and multimodality, University of Amsterdam, June 4 –5.

Cameron, Lynne. 2003. *Metaphor in educational discourse*. London: Continuum.

Cameron, Lynne, Graham Low & Robert Maslen. 2010. Finding systematicity in metaphor use. In Lynne Cameron & Robert Maslen (eds.), *Metaphor analysis: Research practice in applied linguistics, social sciences and the humanities*, 116–146. London: Equinox.

Deignan, Alice, Jeannette Littlemore & Elena Semino. 2013. *Figurative language, genre and register*. Cambridge: Cambridge University Press.

Drew, Paul & Elizabeth Holt. 1995. Idiomatic expressions and their role in the organisation of topic transition in conversation. In Martin Everaert, Erik-Jan van der Linden, André Schenk & Rob Schreuder (eds.), *Idioms: Structural and psychological perspectives*, 117–131. Hillsdale, NJ: L. Erlbaum.

Fauconnier, Gilles & Mark Turner. 2008. Rethinking metaphor. In Raymond Gibbs, Jr (ed.), *The Cambridge handbook of metaphor and thought*, 53–66. Cambridge, UK & New York: Cambridge University Press.

Fisher, Linda. 2013. *Constructing beliefs in the foreign language classroom using metaphor as a sociocultural tool*. Cambridge: University of Cambridge, PhD dissertation.

Golden, Anne. 2010. Grasping the point: A study of 15-year-old students' comprehension of metaphorical expressions in schoolbooks. In Graham Low, Zazie Todd, Alice Deignan & Lynne Cameron (eds.), *Researching and applying metaphor in the real world*, 35–62. Amsterdam: John Benjamins.

Grady, Joseph. 1998. The Conduit Metaphor revisited: A reassessment of metaphors for communication. In Jean-Pierre Koenig (ed.), *Conceptual structure, discourse and language 2*, 205–218. Stanford, CA: CSLI Publications.

Grady, Joseph & Christopher Johnson. 2002. Converging evidence for the notions of *subscene* and *primary scene*. In René Dirven & Ralf Pörings (eds.) *Metaphor and metonymy in comparison and contrast*, 533–554. Berlin: Mouton de Gruyter.

Halliday, Michael. 1985/1994. *An introduction to functional grammar* (2nd ed.). London: Edward Arnold.

Hardman, Frank. 2008. Promoting human capital: The importance of dialogic teaching in higher education. *Asian Journal of University Education* 3(1). 31–48.

Lakoff, George. 1982. *Categories and cognitive models*. Trier: University of Trier, L. A. U. T. Papers, Series A, No. 96.

Lakoff, George & Mark Johnson. 1980. *Metaphors we live by*. Chicago, IL: Chicago University Press.

Lakoff, George & Zoltán Kövecses. 1983. The cognitive model of anger inherent in American English. (Mimeo). Berkeley, CA: University of California at Berkeley, Cognitive Science Program, Institute of Human Learning.

Lakoff, George & Mark Turner. 1989. *More than cool reason: A field guide to poetic metaphor*. Chicago, IL: Chicago University Press.

Lerman, Claire. 1983. The functions of metaphor in discourse: Masking metaphor in the Nixon conversations. Paper presented at the 1983 Whim Conference "Metaphors be with you: Humour and metaphor." (Mimeo.) English Department, Arizona State University. (Short version published in Don L. F. Nilsen (ed.), *Whimsy* 2. 133–148.)

Lerman, Claire. 1985. Media analysis of a presidential speech: Impersonal identity forms in discourse. In Teun van Dijk (ed.), *Discourse and communication: New approaches to the analysis of mass media discourse and communication*, 185–215. New York: Walter de Gruyter.

Littlemore, Jeannette. 2001. Metaphoric competence: A language learning strength of students with a holistic cognitive style? *TESOL Quarterly* 35(3). 459–491.

Littlemore, Jeannette, Tina Krennmayr, James Turner & Sarah Turner. 2014. Investigating figurative proficiency at different levels of second language writing. *Applied Linguistics* 35(2). 117–144.

Littlemore, Jeannette & Graham Low. 2006a. Metaphoric competence and communicative language ability. *Applied Linguistics* 27(2). 268–294.

Littlemore, Jeannette & Graham Low. 2006b. *Figurative thinking and foreign language learning*. Basingstoke: Palgrave Macmillan.

Low, Graham. 1988. On teaching metaphor. *Applied Linguistics* 9(2). 125–146.

Low, Graham. 1997. Figurative boundary frames in written text. (Mimeo).

Low, Graham. 2005. Explaining evolution: The use of animacy in an example of semi-formal science writing. *Language and Literature* 14(2). 129–148.

Low, Graham. 2008. Metaphor and education. In Raymond W. Gibbs, Jr (ed.), *The Cambridge handbook of metaphor and thought*, 212–231. Cambridge, UK & New York: Cambridge University Press.

Low, Graham. 2010. Wot no similes? The curious absence of simile in university lectures. In Graham Low, Zazie Todd, Alice Deignan & Lynne Cameron (eds.), *Researching and applying metaphor in the real world*, 291–308. Amsterdam: John Benjamins.

Low, Graham. 2015. A practical validation model for researching elicited metaphor. In Wan Wan & Graham Low (eds.), *Elicited metaphor analysis in educational discourse*, 15–37. Amsterdam: John Benjamins.

Low, Graham. 2017. Eliciting metaphor in education research: Is it really worth the effort? In Francesca Ervas, Elisabetta Gola & Maria-Grazia Rossi (eds.), *Metaphor in communication, science and education*, 249–266. Berlin: de Gruyter.

Low, Graham & Jeannette Littlemore. 2009. The relationship between conceptual metaphors and classroom management language: Reactions by native and non-native speakers of English. *Iberica*, 17 (Special issue on metaphor and language for specific purposes). 25–44.

MacArthur, Fiona. 2006. The effects of pictorial representations on the learning of imageable idioms in EFL. Paper presented at the 6th International Conference on Researching and Applying Metaphor (RaAM6), Leeds, April.

MacArthur, Fiona. 2010. Metaphorical competence in EFL: Where are we and where should we be going? A view from the language classroom. *AILA Review* 23. 155–173.

MacArthur, Fiona. 2017. Using metaphor in the teaching of second/foreign languages. In Elena Semino & Zsófia Demjén (eds.), *The Routledge handbook of metaphor and language*, 413–425. Abingdon & New York: Routledge.

MacArthur, Fiona & Ana M. Piquer-Píriz. 2007. Staging the introduction of figurative extensions of familiar vocabulary items in EFL: Some preliminary considerations. *Ilha do Desterro* 53. 123–136.

Nacey, Susan & Bård U. Jensen. 2017. Metaphoricity in English L2 learners' prepositions. In Francesca Ervas, Elisabetta Gola & Maria-Grazia Rossi (eds.), *Metaphor in communication, science and education*, 283–304. Berlin: de Gruyter.

Niemeyer, Susanne. 2017. Teaching (in) metaphors. In Francesca Ervas, Elisabetta Gola & Maria-Grazia Rossi (eds.), *Metaphor in communication, science and education*, 267–282. Berlin: de Gruyter.

O'Reilly, David. 2017. *An investigation into metaphoric competence in the L2: A linguistic approach*. University of York, PhD dissertation.

Pan, Molly Xie. 2019. The effectiveness of the Conceptual Metaphor Approach to English idiom acquisition by young Chinese learners. *Metaphor & the Social World* 9(1). 59–82

Philip, Gill. 2010. "Drugs, traffic and many other dirty interests": Metaphor and the language learner. In Graham Low, Zazie Todd, Alice Deignan & Lynne Cameron (eds.), *Researching and applying metaphor in the real world*, 63–80. Amsterdam: John Benjamins.

Pontefract, Caroline & Frank Hardman. 2005. The discourse of classroom interaction in Kenyan primary schools. *Comparative Education* 42(1). 87–106.

Pragglejaz group. 2007. MIP: A method for identifying metaphorically used words in discourse. *Metaphor and Symbol* 22(1). 1–40.

Sharifian, Farzad. 2017. *Cultural linguistics*. Amsterdam: John Benjamins.

Skehan, Peter. 1998. *A Cognitive approach to language learning*. Oxford: Oxford University Press.

Steen, Gerard. 1999. From linguistic to conceptual metaphor in five steps. In Raymond W. Gibbs & Gerard Steen (eds.), *Metaphor in cognitive linguistics*, 55–77. Amsterdam: John Benjamins.

Steen, Gerard. 2007. *Finding metaphor in grammar and usage*. Amsterdam: John Benjamins.

Steen, Gerard. 2011a. When is metaphor deliberate? In Nils-Lennart Johannesson, David C. Minugh & Christina Alm-Arvius, (eds.), *Selected papers from the 2008 Metaphor Festival, Stockholm*, 43–63. Stockholm: Acta Universitatis Stockholmiensis.

Steen, Gerard. 2011b. What does 'really deliberate' really mean? More thoughts on metaphor and consciousness. *Metaphor and the Social World* 1(1). 53–56.

Sullivan, Karen & Eve Sweetser. 2010. Is "generic is specific" a metaphor? In Fey Parril, Vera Tobin & Mark Turner (eds.), *Meaning, form and body*, 309–328. Stanford, CA: CSLI Publications.

Szczepaniak, Renata & Robert Lew. 2011. The role of imagery in dictionaries of idioms. *Applied Linguistics* 32(3). 323–347.

Veale, Tony 2012. A computational exploration of creative similes. In F. MacArthur, José Luis Oncins-Martínez, Manuel Sánchez-García & Ana María Piquer-Píriz (eds.), *Metaphor in use: Context, culture, and communication*, 329–343. Amsterdam: John Benjamins.

Wan, Wan. 2011. An examination of the validity of metaphor analysis studies: Problems with metaphor elicitation techniques. *Metaphor and the Social World* 1(2). 261–288.

Wan, Wan. 2012. *Using metaphorical conceptualisation to construct and develop ESL students' writing: An exploratory study*. University of York, PhD dissertation.

Wan, Wan & Graham Low. (Eds.). 2015. *Elicited metaphor analysis in educational discourse*. Amsterdam: John Benjamins.

Willis, Jane. 1996. *A framework for task-based learning*. Harlow: Longman.

Yu, Ning. 2007. Heart and cognition in ancient Chinese philosophy. *Journal of Cognition and Culture* 7(1). 27–47.

Ana M. Piquer-Píriz
Figurative Language and Young L2 Learners

1 Introduction

For a long time figurative language was considered one the highest achievements of cognitive development and not available to young children (Piaget and Inhelder 1969). Nowadays, however, there seems to be a general consensus among linguists, psychologists and psycholinguists (Cameron 1996, 2003; Johnson 1999; Özçalışkan 2011, 2014; Nerlich, Clarke and Todd 1999; Stites and Özçalışkan 2013; Vosniadou 1987; Winner 1988; Zurer Pearson 1990) that figurative language is part of our communicative system from early childhood (for some recent reviews, see Özçalışkan 2011, 2014). It is common to listen to children using, for instance, metaphors (e.g. *it's a flying unicorn*, referring to a moving, horse-shaped cloud) or personifications (*it's having a wee*, referring to a plant that has just been watered) from a very early age.

It has also been shown that children are able to cope with figurative meanings in a second language (L2). When confronted with non-literal, semantic extensions of words that are commonly employed in a literal sense in the L2 classroom (e.g. *give me a hand*), young L2 learners were able not only to understand these meanings but also to explain verbally the connections between the literal and figurative senses (Piquer-Píriz 2005, 2008a, 2008b and 2010), showing that they are also ready to benefit from a CL-oriented approach to L2 vocabulary learning in the way that has been advocated for older learners (cf. Boers and Lindstromberg 2008).

This chapter aims to explore how children's figurative competence may facilitate their systematic building of connections among the semantic extensions of core meanings in an L2. In order to do so, section 2 presents a brief definition of the theoretical notions of figurative competence and linguistic motivation focusing on how they are interrelated and may have an impact on the acquisition of vocabulary in an L2. The rest of the chapter develops these two notions. Section 3 focuses on the former and is divided into two parts: The first part offers a brief overview of the existing research into children's figurative thinking in their L1 and the second part reports on my own research into children's understanding of L2 meanings.

Ana M. Piquer-Píriz, English Philology (Faculty of Education), University of Extremadura, Badajoz, Spain, e-mail: anapiriz@unex.es

https://doi.org/10.1515/9783110630367-004

Section 4 is devoted to the notions of linguistic motivation and motivated polysemy and analyses their potential in young learners' development of vocabulary in an L2.

2 Defining Figurative Competence and Linguistic Motivation

Researchers from different areas have taken great interest in exploring what has been termed 'children's figurative competence' (for a complete definition, see Levorato and Cacciari 1992), which, in this chapter, is broadly understood as children's ability to understand and produce non-literal meanings of words and phrases. It should be noted that the term 'figurative' is used here to denote all kinds of non-literal expressions since, as will be seen in the next section, it has been shown that children's ability to deal with non-literal forms is not restricted to metaphor but it also covers other forms such as metonymy, personification or irony that are also present in children's language and thought.

The concept of 'figurative competence' can be equated to the more widely used notion of 'metaphorical competence' (Gardner and Winner 1978, Danesi 1986, 1992, 2008, 2016; Littlemore 2001, Littlemore and Low 2006a; Low 1988). The emergence of this idea can be traced back to the 1970s in the work carried out by psychologists such as Gardner and Winner (1978) and has, since then, been analysed in the development of the L1 and other languages (see Nacey 2017 for an overview of the literature on metaphorical competence; Littlemore and Low 2006a, 2006b and MacArthur 2010 for insightful discussions of the importance of this competence in L2 learning; or Littlemore 2010 for a study that explores the relationship between metaphor interpretation and production behaviour in L1 and L2). As can be seen, this construct and, particularly, the role that it plays in L2 acquisition has attracted a great deal of interest among researchers and, in fact, several chapters included in the present volume explore this issue from different perspectives (see the chapters by Low; Suárez Campos, Hijazo-Gascón and Ibarretxe-Antuñano; Nacey; or Castellano-Risco and Piquer-Píriz).

At the same time, cognitive linguists have been emphasising the importance of linguistic 'motivation'. For them, language use is a reflection of general cognitive processes, grounded in experiential correlations and mediated by culture and, instead of treating linguistic manifestations as arbitrary, they look for plausible explanations for their characteristics, highlighting how the different meanings of a word are motivated and interrelated. This gave rise to a new conception of polysemy which, according to Lakoff (1987: 13), "arises from the fact that there are systematic relationships between different cognitive models and between elements of the same model. The same word is often used for elements that stand in such cognitive relations to one another". This notion of motivated polysemy has inspired applied cognitive linguists to try out new methods to present new L2 vocabulary to learners as well as to explore how effective these CL-oriented practices may be on the basis that "learners who are aware that an L2 is much more than a system of arbitrary form-meaning connections may be relatively likely to adopt mnemonically fruitful practices of insightful learning rather than less effective ones associated with blind memorisation" (Boers and Lindstromberg 2008: 18).

In my view, the two notions of figurative competence and motivated polysemy are intrinsically connected and this can have very important implications in the process of learning an L2 even at very early ages. Most definitions of 'metaphorical competence' generally describe it as the ability to understand and produce metaphor (Danesi 1986, 1992, 2008, 2016; Littlemore 2001; Low 1988; Nacey 2013) and, in the specific case of the role it may play in the process of learning an L2, some authors relate it to a more global capacity that has been labelled 'conceptual fluency' (Danesi 1992) or 'figurative reasoning' (Littlemore and Low 2006a). And this is precisely where the connection lies. The ability to use our concrete knowledge to understand abstract concepts on the basis of our embodied and cultural experiences and our interaction with the world corresponds to the basis of the Cognitive Linguistic paradigm (Lakoff and Johnson 1980, 1999). It is quite simple to put this tenet to the test informally. When I have tried to explain this idea to my university students, colleagues and even friends I have tended to use a very simple example. Depending on whether they are Spanish, English or Portuguese L1 speakers, I ask them why they think that we use *cabecero-a / head /cabeceira* to refer to *el/la cabecero/a de la cama / the head of the bed / a cabeceira da cama*. There are always two main answers that seem to reflect, on the one hand, associative (metonymically-based) reasoning, e.g. because that is the part where we lay our head on; and analogical (metaphorically-based) processing, e.g. because it is the top of the bed. This little test is certainly very unscientific but quite revealing: there seems to be a natural, spontaneous ability that allows us to connect concrete and abstract meanings in the way that cognitive linguists have advocated and this capacity has been shown to be part of the human reasoning abilities from early infancy (Özçalışkan 2011, 2014) and also available to children with L2 figurative uses (Piquer-Píriz 2005, 2008a, 2008b, 2010).

Thus, this natural capacity to understand abstract concepts by relating them in different ways to more concrete ones would be conceptual (see Gibbs' [1999] for a discussion on the difference between the mental process and the linguistic products) and, therefore, not restricted to the way we reason in our native language but would also be applicable to any additional languages we may speak. Some more rigorous explorations have been carried out with L2 learners of different ages: young adults (Piquer-Píriz and Boers 2010), teenagers (Piquer-Píriz, MacArthur and Alejo-González 2010) and children (Piquer-Píriz 2005, 2008a, 2008b, 2010). As will be seen in further detail below, it has been shown that even very young L2 learners (as young as five years of age) establish metaphorical and metonymical connections when asked to explain non-literal L2 meanings. When asked, for instance, to identify and explain the idiomatic expression *give me a hand*, most of the learners, particularly at the younger ages, that took part in Piquer-Píriz's study (2005: 123) employed figurative reasoning (e.g. (1) *"'hand' porque con las manos se puede ayudar"* – 'hand' because you can help with your hands) in preference to other strategies such as interlingual identification (e.g. (2) *" 'hand' porque en español es parecido a 'échame una mano' "* – 'hand' because it's similar to 'échame una mano' in Spanish [2005: 136]). If these young learners are able to establish these connections, it would seem reasonable to think that they would also benefit from an instructional approach that relies on fostering metaphorical competence or, more generally, enhances figurative thought.

3 Figuration and Children

3.1 Children's Figurative Thinking in Their L1

Research, from different perspectives, into the understanding and production of figurative language at the early stages of the development of an L1 (e.g. Cameron 1996, 2003; Johnson 1999; Özçalışkan 2011; Pineda 2015; Stites and Özçalışkan 2013; Vosniadou 1987; Winner 1988; Zurer Pearson 1990) has mostly concluded that children start to produce and understand these linguistic uses shortly after they begin to speak and that their figurative abilities improve with age (Özçalışkan 2011), thus, overcoming the contention that figurative language was one of the highest achievements of cognitive development and not available to an 'immature' mind (Piaget and Inhelder 1969). Children's ability with figurative forms is not restricted to metaphor (Billow 1975; Nippold, Leonard and Kail 1984; Nippold and Sullivan 1987; Vosniadou 1987; Zurer Pearson 1990; Cameron 1996, 2003) and idioms (Gibbs 1987, 1991; Cacciari and Levorato 1989, 1998; Levorato and Cacciari 1992; Abkarian, Jones and West 1992). Metonymy has also been acknowledged to be present in children's language and thought (Nerlich, Clarke and Todd 1999) and children's understanding of irony has also been studied (Winner 1988).

A number of important issues that have emerged from this literature are briefly discussed below.

3.1.1 Developmental psychology: Awareness of a pre-existing similarity between two elements (perceptual vs. psychological links)

From the mid-seventies onwards, developmental psychologists have been rigorously analysing children's figurative capacity and have shown that most of the early ideas about children's inability to understand figurative productions until later childhood were partly a consequence of applying adults' standards to measure and interpret children's capacities (Winner 1988). The results were very different in studies that employed methodological techniques adapted to children such as elicited, verbal repetition (e.g., Zurer Pearson 1990) or the use of stories, sometimes enacted by puppets or toys (e.g., Levorato and Cacciari 1992 or Stites and Özçalışkan 2013).

Establishing criteria that allowed researchers to classify children's utterances as metaphorical and non-metaphorical became central in the field (Vosniadou 1987, Vosniadou and Ortony 1983, Winner 1988). Most of these accounts of the development of children's figurative capacity were based on the idea that there is a pre-existing similarity between two elements and that children should be aware of it in order to classify their productions as metaphorical. The type of relationship existing between the concrete and abstract elements was also considered a key issue. A pioneering study in this regard is Asch and Nerlove's (1960) analysis of children's (aged from three to twelve) understanding of adjectives that refer to both physical properties and psychological traits such as *cold, warm, deep, hard* or *bright*. They found that the physical sense of the term is acquired first, the psychological meaning only comes later and as an independent and, the dual property of the lexeme is realised at last and, in most cases, not spontaneously.

In the eighties, Winner (1988) distinguished between sensory and non-sensory metaphors and claimed that: "What children most often do is find a sensory similarity between topic and vehicle when a nonsensory, relational similarity is at issue" (Winner 1988: 36). She defined non-sensory metaphors as those based on similarity that is not apprehended by our senses. They can be divided into relational and psychological-physical metaphors. The former are based on similarities between objects, situations, or events that are physically dissimilar, but, owing to parallel internal structures, function in a similar way (e.g. clouds and sponges which function to hold and then release water). Psychological-physical metaphors are based on a resemblance between the sensory attributes of a physical object, perceived through any sensory modality, and psychological, non-sensory attributes of a person (e.g. cheerful people are 'sunny', or cranky people are 'sour').

More recently, Özçalışkan (2011, 2014) has also highlighted that, from a very early age, children are able to understand and produce comparisons based on perceptual similarities (e.g. 'The moon is like a balloon') but that they experience more difficulties with comparisons that involve two different domains of experience (e.g. 'a warm person'). A very similar pattern has been observed when children are reasoning in an L2. As will be seen in greater detail in the next section, in a study that explored young Spanish EFL learners' understanding of the figurative meanings of *warm* and *cold* when referring to personality (Piquer-Píriz 2010), the younger children (6- and 8-year-olds) based their answers on the concrete, physical sensations (a person is cold or warm depending on the weather or the clothes they are wearing). In contrast, some of the 10-year-olds could establish the psychological link between the two meanings: coldness was clearly related to unfriendliness and warmth with kindness.

The evidence offered by this body of research suggests that children's perception of properties changes with development, with perceptual or sensory links appearing first, followed by relational or functional links, and finally physical-psychological links. There are two possible explanations for these findings, in relation to children's metaphorical competence. On the one hand, it could be argued that children are not able to perceive the kinds of similarities on which non-sensory metaphors are based and, therefore, their metaphorical competence would not be fully developed until a certain age. On the other, the fact that children are not able to perceive certain types of similarities may not be due to their underdeveloped metaphorical competence but, rather, to their insufficient knowledge of the domains to which the elements that are compared belong, thus limiting the kinds of connections that children perceive. When the child has sufficiently developed knowledge of the elements being linked, they are able to interpret the metaphor even if the ground is non-sensory (Keil 1989). As is shown in the next section, there is some evidence that support this second explanation.

3.1.2 The importance of children's developing knowledge of the world

It seems that children's developing knowledge of the world plays an important role in their understanding and production of figurative language. Several scholars (Carey 1985, Keil 1989, Winner 1988, Vosniadou 1989 or Cameron 1996) have argued that children's 'misunderstanding' of metaphors is not due to their lack of metaphorical capacity but to their developing 'knowledge of the world', particularly, a lack of 'domain knowledge'. These two notions refer to how children's

knowledge of concepts and events and their relations among them become enriched in response to different inputs and experiences (their own social experiences with other people and the world that surrounds them, including the
explanations provided by their parents, teachers, siblings or friends but also stories, cartoons, TV programmes or the Internet, that is, all sort of inputs to which
they are exposed). Children are in the process of developing this knowledge and,
therefore, although even very young children may have the competence to perceive all of the kinds of similarities that adults perceive, they may lack fully developed knowledge of the domains from which either the topic or vehicle is drawn,
and thus fail to see the similarity between them. One cannot know which aspects
of the vehicle domain to map onto the topic domain if little is known about one or
both domains. In order to test this hypothesis, Keil (1989) used metaphors based
on domains that are familiar to children and showed that when children had sufficient knowledge of the two domains involved in the comparison, they demonstrated no difficulty in understanding non-sensory metaphors. Cameron (1996)
argues that discourse context (which, according to her would include situational
context (participants, situation and goals), the immediate linguistic context of the
metaphor, and the textual or interactional context of the metaphor) "can contribute towards accessing and selecting domain knowledge" (Cameron 1996: 54).

3.1.3 Figurative productions as developmental strategies

For other authors, some of the figurative productions uttered by children are products of their language development. In this sense, Clark (1993) described overextensions (e.g. when a child calls a horse 'doggy') as one of the most important
ways that children use to map the meaning that they want to express onto a form
which they have already acquired. In a similar vein, Nerlich, Clarke and Todd
(1999) see overextensions as communicative strategies used by children which can
be based on metaphorical, metonymical and synecdochical relationships. They focused on the analysis of metonymy and found that up to age 2:5, children make
use of what they call 'compelled metonymical overextensions'. They are compelled
because they are based on the fact that at this age children's vocabulary, category
and conceptual systems are still relatively small and unstructured and as soon as
the right word is learned, the use of overextensions stops. These compelled metonymies, which are used by children to fill gaps in their limited lexicons contrast
with creative metonymies used to express something new by not using words already available in their lexicons. At these stages, children's semantic systems, as
well as their systems of concepts and categories, are still incomplete and unstructured and will have to be adjusted and modified in the years to come.

Overextension would be the mechanism used to fill some gaps. As soon as the right word is learnt, it stops. This view raises the controversial issue of what we might call 'unacceptable' vs. 'acceptable' extensions from an adult's point of view. Children's early overextensions are 'unacceptable' from an adult point of view, but as soon as children's categories match the adults', they are not regarded as over-extensions anymore.

3.1.4 Cognitive Linguistics: Johnson's 'constructional grounding'

Johnson's (1999) constructional grounding theory is, in my view, one of the most comprehensive accounts, from a cognitive-linguistic perspective, of the acquisition of figurative language by children which, despite having been published 20 years ago, has unfortunately not been much further developed. Johnson argued that children acquire metaphorical concepts by early conflations of two domains of experience by means of what he calls 'constructional grounding'. This idea is closely related to Grady's (1997) Primary Metaphor Theory, according to which there are some conceptual metaphors – the most basic ones – which arise directly from experiential correlations that are often highly embodied and that happen in our early experience of the world. These metaphors would be unconsciously and automatically incorporated to our understanding of concepts. Thus, the origin of this type of metaphors is not some type of perceived similarity but the notion of co-occurrence (conflation of experiences). One widely quoted example is QUANTITY IS VERTICAL ELEVATION (also expressed as MORE IS UP) which is motivated by "the correlation between quantity and levels in piles, fluids in containers, etc." (Grady 1997: 285).

Johnson's constructional grounding theory is based on constructional and cognitive approaches to language, mainly Tomasello's (2003, 2006) ideas on construction grammar from the point of view of L1 acquisition and Slobin's (1981) notion of the importance of simple scenes experienced by children and the role they play in the process of acquiring their mother tongue. According to Johnson, "a sign that is relatively easy for children to learn serves as the model for another more difficult sign, because it occurs in contexts in which it exemplifies important properties of the more difficult sign in a way that is especially accessible to children" (1999: 1). Two important processes are necessary for constructional grounding to occur: In the first place, there must be some kind of relation between the two signs (co-occurrence or similarity) and they must be frequent utterances in the language input to which children are exposed. All in all, these underlying processes are not very different from those pointed out by developmental psychologists.

3.1.5 Concluding remarks

As can be seen, the development of figurative language in children is a fascinating topic that has attracted the attention of researchers from different fields (mostly psychologists and linguists). Research into it has produced mutually enriching findings that, when considered together, offer a more global (and yet in need of further exploration) picture of this complex phenomenon. From the brief overview of some of the most influential research into figuration and children in their L1 presented above, we can infer that, when analysing children's understanding and production of figurative language, it is important to take into account processing, production and contextual factors. Levorato and Cacciari (1992: 146–147) attempted to define what children's figurative competence may consist of, including the following four abilities that take into account processing (1, 2 and 4), production (4) and contextual (3) factors:

1. The ability to understand the dominant, peripheral and additional related meaning of a word, its position in a given semantic domain and its paradigmatic and syntagmatic relations.
2. The ability to suspend a purely literal-referential strategy. This is a prerequisite not only for figurative language comprehension, but also for most of the linguistic repertoire (for instance, polysemous words).
3. The ability to use contextual information in order to construct a coherent semantic representation and to integrate it with the lexical and semantic information carried by the figurative expression.
4. The ability to create and understand the figurative uses of a word, a sentence or a given domain as well as to retrieve the conceptual structures involved.

As a conclusion, figurative reasoning and its linguistic products seem to be a continuum in a person's life. In the early stages, some creative figurative uses may be related to the need to fill gaps in the children's growing conceptual and linguistic system, as Nerlich, Clarke and Todd (1999) and Clark (1993) have pointed out. These productions, strange by adults' standards, seem to be common to children, who might simply be using a mechanism (seeing something in terms of something else) which appears to be available to them from a very early age. This mechanism will be used throughout their lives as a fundamental tool for recognition, classification, learning, and even scientific discovery and creativity (Vosniadou and Ortony 1989, Gentner 2003) and, consequently, when enriching vocabulary in both their mother tongue and a second language. At the same time, not only the ability to perceive something in terms of something else but also the co-occurrence of highly embodied, experiential correlations of concrete and abstract notions accompanied by the exposure to the language that expresses those concepts may explain why certain figurative uses are acquired the way they are, as Johnson (1999) explains. Furthermore, children are being exposed to conventional figurative forms through their interaction with adults and peers, education, games, stories, television or the internet. These uses establish the boundaries between accepted, customary, figurative uses of a specific cultural community and creative, sometimes one-shot uses that an individual may employ and that, if congruent with metaphorical usage generally, are very likely to be understood by other language users. Thus, a fundamental characteristic of human figurative competence seems to be continuity: It is present from very early ages and it develops into adult competence as the fundamental ability of analogical reasoning that, in some individuals, might reach its heights, as Gibbs (1994) argues, in the form of scientific discovery or literary production.

3.2 Figurative Language and Young L2 Learners

The role of figurative language and thought at the earliest stages of the second language learning process has been largely unexplored. My own research has focused on children's figurative ability when learning an L2. As stated above, if children are able to interpret and produce non-literal meanings in their L1, they would be expected to behave in a similar way in an L2. In order to analyse this issue, I explored how children understood and reasoned about some figurative meanings in two domains of experience that are very commonly used in the young L2 leaners' classroom: body part terms (Piquer-Píriz 2005, 2008a, 2008b) and temperature terms when applied to colours (Piquer-Píriz 2006) and personality (Piquer-Píriz 2010). A total of 148 children took part in the study that focused on body part terms and 140 participants were involved in the studies that explored temperature terms. Their mean ages ranged from 5:8 to 11:9. They all attended state schools in Extremadura (western Spain) and came from a variety of social and economic backgrounds.

In the case of body part terms, eight semantic extensions of three different body part terms were analysed (Piquer-Píriz 2005): HAND (*give me a hand, the hand of a watch* and *hand it to me*), MOUTH (*not open one's mouth*) and HEAD (*the head of a bed, the head of a hammer, the head of the stairs* and *the head of a line of cars*). The figurative meanings of *warm* and *cold* when applied to colours (red, orange, yellow, light blue, dark blue and green) and personality (*warm* and *cold people*) were also explored.

The main findings were that, first of all, the young (5- to 12-year-old) Spanish learners of EFL that took part were, in general, able to identify different semantic extensions of English body part and temperature terms whose proto-typical meaning they knew from their English lessons. However, not all the extensions were equally transparent for them. Some of the patterns identified in the literature into children's figurative abilities in their L1 reviewed in the previous section were also found in these studies. For example, those comparisons based on perceptual similarities (such as *the head of a hammer*) were more easily identified by learners in all age groups than comparisons that involved two different domains of experience (*cold/warm people*). In the case of the latter, younger children (6- to 8-year-olds) related their interpretations of these figurative meanings to bodily sensations, that is, these children concentrated mainly on the prototypical meaning of *warm* and *cold* as temperature terms and particularly in the bodily sensation of being cold or warm. In the context of the stimuli with which they were provided (i.e., a short story), this was explained in terms of the clothes worn by the dolls used to enact the story:

(3)   C: *"porque tiene más frío – porque lleva menos ropa [se refiere a 'the fat lady']'warm' (R: ésta [thin lady] es 'warm'¿por qué crees?) tiene más calor porque lleva más cosas"*
C: Because she feels colder – because she's got less pieces of clothing on [she refers to the fat lady] warm (R: this one [thin lady] is warm why do you think so?) she feels warmer because she's got more things on.

The youngest children that took part in this specific study (6-year-olds) mainly stayed in the concrete realm and related *cold* and *warm* with their own bodily sensations. This does not mean that they lacked figurative competence but it seems that they had not made the links between temperature terms and personality yet. The 8-year-olds appeared to be on their way to doing so but the process did not seem to be complete yet. In contrast, most of the 10-year-olds related both domains but, in the process of developing their world knowledge, some notions were not clearly conventionalised yet and some of them made their own interpretations (see Piquer-Píriz 2010, for further details).

The figurative uses analysed not only included perceptually-based comparisons but also metonymically-based semantic extensions. In fact, the expressions *give me a hand* and *hand it to me* may well be motivated by experiential correlations, in the sense that Johnson (1999) points out. Interestingly, the results concerning *hand it to me* present the most uniform data across the different age groups, not only in the number of correct responses (over 80%), but also in the interpretation strategy employed in most cases, i.e., the matching of hand with its function of picking up and giving out things, grounded in the children's experiences of manipulating and passing things, in what seems to reflect the importance of Slobin's (1981) notion of simple scenes: children's early experiences manipulating objects. The clearly embodied nature of *hand it to me* seems to have facilitated its comprehension by a very high percentage of children in the three age groups, despite the fact that this particular use involves a shift in part of speech (from noun to verb) which does not happen in Spanish where the possible expressions would be *pásamelo/dámelo (con la mano)* which literally mean *pass it on to me / give it to me (with the hand)*. In fact, 'mano' (hand) is not usually even part of the expression in Spanish. These children focused on the meaning of the figurative extension and not on the linguistic form and successfully interpreted it.

Thus, an important finding from these studies is that children's ability to reason figuratively played a very important role in their interpretation of non-literal uses. In this sense, these results also replicate some of the findings in previous research into the figurative capacity of monolingual children: Analogical reasoning and the transfer of knowledge from a concrete to an abstract domain play a significant role in children's abstract reasoning. Furthermore, they also indicate that this competence operates with linguistic forms in the second language from, at least, the age of five. These children's figurative reasoning was often based on their bodily experiences and their observation of and interaction with the world that surrounds them. The influence of embodiment was especially evident in the study devoted to body parts terms (Piquer-Píriz 2005). For example, many children established metonymical connections of the type HAND FOR FUNCTION to explain different figurative uses of hand. HAND FOR HELPING was used to explain the meaning of *give me a hand*:

(4)   C: " *'hand' porque con las manos se puede ayudar"*
       C: 'hand' because you can help with your hands

And HAND FOR PASSING THINGS in the case of *hand it to me*:

(5)   C: " *'hand' porque normalmente las cosas se dan con la mano"*
       C: 'hand' because you normally use your hand to give things out

Many examples of children's awareness of their environment and the influence of this in their figurative reasoning could be found in the study that dealt with temperature terms when applied to colours (Piquer-Píriz 2006). For instance, when explaining why orange is a warm colour, the following exchange of information took place among three 8-year-old children:

(6) C1: *"porque también cuando está anocheciendo se pone [el sol] algunas*
     veces detrás de las nubes se pone naranja (C2: y morao [morado] – y
     morao [morado] un poquinino [poquito]) (C3: ¿Al amanecer o al ano-
     checer?) (C1: a los dos, a los dos) (C2: una especie de rosa)"
     C1: because at dusk it sometimes hides behind the clouds and gets orange
     (C2: and purple – and a bit purple) (C3: at dawn or at dusk?) (C1: both,
     both) (C2: pinkish)

These findings seem to reveal not only the importance of motivation, i.e., figurative language is not arbitrary but rather grounded in human sensorimotor
and social experiences, but also the fact that young L2 learners can reflect on it.

However, these studies also show that all figurative extensions are not equally
transparent for all children at all ages. It seems that in the process of grasping the
figurative meanings of polysemous words, these young learners go from concrete,
prototypical meanings to abstract senses, a tendency that has also been reported
in their L1 (Winner 1988). Furthermore, as happens in their L1, another key aspect
that influences children's figurative reasoning is the different types of knowledge
children are able to differentiate at different ages, what, as has been mentioned
above, some authors have called 'their developing knowledge of the world' (Keil
1989 or Cameron 1996). The importance of the role played by contextual factors in
this process has also been emphasised by Cameron (1996) who points out that
metaphorical expressions are not used in isolation but within a discourse context.
The children participating in my studies showed the same tendency to refer to a
context which they seem to have closely linked to words and images when, for
example, they referred to *el cabeza del pelotón de la vuelta ciclista o de una carrera*
(the leader of the group of cyclists or the leader in a race) to justify why the first
car in a line is the *head* or when they remembered a similar image or situation in
los dibujos animados (cartoons) or *video juegos* (computer games).

This growing knowledge may lead them, in some cases, to wrong conclusions. For example, for some of the younger learners that took part in the
study, the top part of any of the cars in a line was the head of the line of cars
because that was the highest part and the head is at the top. They were over-
generalising explanations based on the human body schema whereas the older
children, with a better differentiated and more developed knowledge of domains, were more flexible in the use of other schemas and applied the animal
body schema to reason about the head of a line of cars (see MacArthur and
Piquer-Píriz 2007 for further details).

Similarly, most of the participants explained that the head of the stairs is the
top part because it is the part placed at the top of a staircase. They were making a
projection grounded in their knowledge of the human body schema. In this case,

their knowledge of 'stairs' and 'heads' matches that of an adult. However, some of them said that the head of a line of cars was a police car placed in the middle of the line because its lights were slightly above the roofs of the other cars. Here, they were using the same mechanism, but in this case, it does not match the conventional adult link which relates this use of 'head' to the notion of being in first rather than in top place.

Studies on children's development of conceptual domains will therefore clarify the domain differentiations which children are able to establish at different stages. This idea is especially relevant if the problem is approached from a cognitive linguistic perspective. If we accept the cognitive view of metaphor that our abstract reasoning is based on our understanding of concrete concepts via a metaphorical projection from source/concrete to target/abstract domains, then any methodology that aims to enhance this projection needs to take into account what kind of domain differentiation a child is capable of at various ages. For instance, trying to clarify the connection between coldness and unkindness before certain age may not be as efficient as it could be expected.

To sum up, it seems, then, that children are ready and can be helped to make optimal use of a limited lexicon, if guided, to extend meanings through figurative reasoning. This is the question I turn to in the next section.

4 Motivated Meanings, Polysemy and L2 Vocabulary Learning at Early Stages

As has been pointed out above, one of the main tenets of Cognitive Linguistics is that figuration pervades our language and thought and that, in order to understand abstract concepts, we mostly resort to metaphorical or metonymical connections based on our bodily sensations and our interaction with the surrounding environment (Lakoff and Johnson 1980, 1999 or Lakoff 1993 for a detailed description of Conceptual Metaphor Theory). This implies that, for cognitive linguists, language is not arbitrary but mostly motivated. One of the most comprehensive treatments of linguistic motivation in this discipline is Panther and Radden (2004). Starting from some definitions of motivation proposed by both linguists and psychologists, they put forward their own: "a linguistic unit (target) is motivated if some of its properties are shaped by a linguistic source (form and/or content) and language-independent factors. We thus assume that linguistic motivation involves a causal relation. As suggested by the term 'shape' in the above definition, however, the notion of causation is non-deterministic." (2004: 4)

Interestingly they also noted that "traditionally, the term 'motivation' is applied to the form of linguistic units; more recently scholars have also applied it to the extension of senses" (2004: 2).

The understanding of polysemy and semantic extension as motivated by metaphor and metonymy (understood here as mental mechanism) and grounded in experiential correlations of a physical and a social nature has important implications for L2 instruction (for some in-depth analyses of polysemy from a Cognitive Linguistics perspective, see Cuyckens and Zawada 2001, Cuyckens, Dirven and Taylor 2003 or Taylor 2003).

To begin with, it gave rise to models of semantic networks (Lakoff 1987, Langacker 1990) based on the notion that the different meanings of a given lexeme "form a radially structured category, with a central member and links defined by image-schema transformations and metaphors" (Lakoff 1987: 460).

The notion of embodiment (Johnson 1987 or Gibbs 2003) is particularly important in understanding the motivation for polysemy: in this view, human abstract reasoning is embodied, that is, grounded in our sensorimotor experiences and our interaction with the world. According to Johnson, metonymy and metaphor are the means by which it is possible "to ground our conceptual systems experientially and to reason in a constrained but creative fashion" (1992: 351).

Thus, cognitive linguists consider language and its use as a reflection of general cognitive processes, mediated by culture, and, instead of treating language as arbitrary, plausible explanations for its characteristics are sought. The notion, derived from these theoretical tenets, of models for semantic networks (Lakoff 1987 or Langacker 1990) in which the different meanings of a given lexeme form radially structured categories which consist of a central member connected to the others via metonymy, metaphor or image schema implies that whole clusters of lexical items may be linked in systematic, non-arbitrary relations. These ideas have had important implications for L2 instruction. Taking this premise as their starting point, Applied Cognitive Linguists have been exploring, for over two decades, the pedagogical potential of enhancing figurative awareness to facilitate the comprehension and retention of vocabulary in an L2 (see Boers and Lindstromberg 2006 for some theoretical considerations and Boers 2011 for a review of different CL-oriented studies). This research has concentrated mainly on older (intermediate or advanced) learners (Ponterotto 1994; Kövecses and Szabò 1996; Lazar 1996, 2003; Deignan, Gabrys and Solska 1997; Boers and Demecheleer 1998; Boers 2000; Saaty 2016). However, EFL has been expanding and introduced at ever younger ages in the educational systems of many countries and, as shown above, CL has a contribution to make with younger learners.

In an instructed second language setting, learners' grasp of figurative meanings will largely depend on the range of senses which they meet in the graded input of the classroom (MacArthur and Piquer-Píriz 2007) and, therefore, which meanings should be introduced and at what stage of the learning process are important issue to be taken into account when designing L2 syllabi (Piquer-Píriz 2011).

In general terms, MacArthur (2010: 159) describes metaphorical thinking as a great potential for L2 learners to expand their vocabulary:

> Metaphor as a way of thinking about language use is new for most learners and teachers; it is interesting and flexible. Unlike grammar, it has no hard and fast rules: there are no 'correct' or 'incorrect' metaphors, but rather better, communicatively more successful ones in comparison with less successful ones. It is often picturesque and imagistic, favouring the holistic learner over the analytic one (Littlemore 2001). Most important of all, with regard to the learners of English with knowledge of a relative impoverished stock of words, metaphor helps to make meaning from many everyday, highly familiar words, for among all the forces that drive semantic extension, the most powerful is metaphor (Taylor 2003). Metaphor is thus the foreign language learners' best ally in the quest for greater expressive powers … metaphor is used by learners of English, and they can be helped to use it better, but only if it is given a prominent place in classroom discussion.

Metaphor certainly seems to have great potential for L2 learners, including very young learners at the earliest stages of the learning process who have a restricted lexicon. In fact, some of the most effective CL-oriented techniques such as the use of total-physical response (TPR) activities (Lindstromberg and Boers 2005, Saaty 2016) are well-suited for children.

However, the application of CL-oriented pedagogies in the L2 classroom and, particularly, with young learners needs to be cautious. In fact, CL-oriented pedagogies have not reached L2 classrooms as much as might be expected. We need to bear in mind that the fact that figurative meanings are motivated does not mean that they are predictable. But this is, precisely, according to Boers (2013), why enhancing and promoting figurative awareness can be of an aid for L2 learners and why teachers and teaching materials should foster the underlying connections.

This author has suggested that rather than encouraging learners' ability to generate L2 metaphors, it may be more successful to instil a "metaphor awareness" in learners to "organize the steady stream of figurative language they are exposed to" (Boers 2000: 564). In this same line is MacArthur's (2010) paper on metaphorical competence in EFL where she argues for the importance of adding 'metaphor awareness' generally to the experience of learning English in instructed L2 setting: "In this approach, the specific pedagogical techniques employed [...] are seen to be less significant than the general foregrounding of metaphor and the effect(s) this may have on learners' growing awareness of how metaphor permeates language (their own and the L2 to be learnt)." (MacArthur 2010: 157)

The sooner this awareness of metaphor is introduced in the L2 classroom, taking into account all the aspects that have been pointed out above, the better for the learning process.

5 Conclusions

Children, like adults, are endowed with the unique capacity of humans to understand one thing in terms of another, and this ability is also available to them in an L2 and could, therefore, be exploited to help them build their own L2 lexicon in a systematic way. Even very young learners are ready to extend the possibilities of a limited vocabulary in the L2 and benefit from an instructional approach that relies on metaphorical competence or, more generally, figurative thought, in the way applied cognitive linguists have been advocating. In fact, since the L2 lexicon of a beginner is particularly restricted, helping these learners to use their vocabulary as productively as possible will be especially advantageous for them. Furthermore, learning a language is a developmental process and its first stages are fundamental in terms of establishing a solid basis for future development. Encouraging young learners to exploit this capacity and clarifying the prototypical meanings of core lexical items would lay the foundations for later extensions in other areas. Stimulating this capacity alone may not suffice to ensure effective learning and factors such as the children's growing knowledge of the world and their communicative needs at different ages should also be taken into account when selecting what meanings should be taught and when they should be introduced in the young learners' L2 classroom. However, making young learners aware of their own ability to establish connections among the different senses of a word will empower them to build a systematic, rich L2 lexicon.

References

Abkarian, Gene G., Alison Jones & Gretchen West. 1992. Enhancing children's communication skills: idioms 'fill the bill'. *Child Language Teaching and Therapy* 6(3). 246–254.

Asch, Solomon & Harriet Nerlove. 1960. The development of double function terms in children. In Bernard Kaplan & Seymour Wapner, (eds.), *Perspectives in psychological theory*, 47–60. New York: International Universities Press

Billow, Richard. 1975. A cognitive developmental study of metaphor comprehension. *Developmental Psychology* 11(4). 425–423.

Boers, Frank. 2000. Metaphor awareness and vocabulary retention. *Applied Linguistics* 21. 553–571.

Boers, Frank. 2011. Cognitive semantic ways of teaching figurative phrases: An assessment. *Review of Cognitive Linguistics* 9. 227–261.

Boers, Frank. 2013. Cognitive Linguistic approaches to teaching vocabulary: Assessment and integration. *Language Teaching* 46. 208–224.

Boers, Frank & Murielle Demecheleer. 1998. A cognitive semantic approach to teaching prepositions. *English Language Teaching Journal* 53. 197–204.

Boers, Frank & Seth Lindstromberg. 2008. How cognitive linguistics can foster effective vocabulary teaching. In Frank Boers & Seth Lindstromberg (eds.), *Cognitive linguistic approaches to teaching vocabulary and phraseology*, 1–61. Berlin: Mouton de Gruyter.

Boers, Frank & Seth Lindstromberg. 2006. Cognitive linguistic approaches to second or foreign language instruction: Rationale, proposals and evaluation. In Gitte Kristaensen, René Dirven, Michel Achard & Francisco J. Ruiz-Mendoza (eds.), *Cognitive linguistics: current applications and future perspectives*, 305–358. Berlin: Mouton de Gruyter.

Cacciari, Cristina & M. Chiara Levorato. 1989. How children understand idioms in discourse. *Journal of Child Language* 16. 387–405.

Cacciari, Cristina & M. Chiara Levorato. 1998. The effect of semantic analyzability of idioms in metalinguistic Tasks. *Metaphor and Symbol* 13 (3). 159–177.

Cameron, Lynne. 1996. Discourse context and the development of metaphor in children. *Current Issues in Language and Society* 3(1). 49–64.

Cameron, Lynne. 2003. *Metaphor in educational discourse*. London: Continuum.

Carey, S. 1985. *Conceptual changes in childhood*. Cambridge, MA: MIT Press.

Clark, Eve V. 1993. *The lexicon in acquisition*. Cambridge: Cambridge University Press.

Cuyckens Hubert, René Dirven & John R. Taylor. 2003. *Cognitive approaches to lexical Semantics*. Berlin: Mouton de Gruyter.

Cuyckens, Hubert & Britta Zawada (eds.). 2001. *Polysemy in cognitive linguistics*. Amsterdam: John Benjamins.

Danesi, Marcel. 1986. The role of metaphor in second language pedagogy. *Rassegna Italiana di Linguistica Applicata* 18. 1–10.

Danesi, Marcel. 1992. Metaphorical competence in second language acquisition and second language teaching: The neglected dimension. In James E. Alatis (ed.), *Language communication and social meaning* (Georgetown University Round Table on Languages and Linguistics), 489–500. Washington: Georgetown University Press.

Danesi, Marcel. 2008. Conceptual errors in second-language learning. In Sabine De Knop & Antoon De Rycker (eds.), *Cognitive approaches to pedagogical grammar*, 231–256. Berlin: Mouton de Gruyter.

Danesi, Marcel. 2016. Conceptual fluency in second language teaching: An overview of problems, issues, research findings and pedagogy. *International Journal of Applied Linguistics & English Literature* 5(1). 145–153.

Deignan, Alice, Danuta Gabryś & Agnieszka, Solska. 1997. Teaching English metaphors using cross-linguistic awareness-raising activities. *ELT journal* 51(4). 352–360.

Gardner, Howard & Ellen Winner. 1978. The development of metaphoric competence: Implications for humanistic disciplines. *Critical Inquiry* 5(1). 123–141.

Gardner, Howard, Mary Kircher, Ellen Winner & David Perkins. 1975. Children's metaphoric productions and preferences. *Journal of Child Language* 2. 125–141.

Grady, Joseph E. 1997. Foundations of meaning: Primary metaphors and primary scenes. PhD Dissertation, University of California, Berkeley.

Gentner, Dedre. 2003. Why we're so smart. In Dedre Gentner & Susan Goldin-Meadow (eds.), *Language in mind*, 195–235. Cambridge, MA: MIT Press.

Gibbs, Raymond. W. 1987. Linguistic factors in children's understanding of idioms. *Journal of Child Language* 14. 569–586.

Gibbs, Raymond. W. 1991. Semantic analyzability in children's understanding of idioms. *Journal of Speech and Hearing Research* 34. 613–620.

Gibbs, Raymond. W. 1994. *The poetics of mind*. New York: Cambridge University Press.

Gibbs, Raymond W. 1999. *Researching metaphor*. In Graham Low & Lynne Cameron (eds.), Researching and applying metaphor, 29–47. Cambridge: Cambridge University Press.

Gibbs, Raymond W. 2003. Embodied experience and linguistic meaning. *Brain and Language* 84. 1–15.

Johnson, Mark. 1987. *The Body in the mind: The bodily basis of meaning, imagination, and reason*. Chicago: University of Chicago Press.

Johnson, Christopher. 1999. *Constructional grounding: The role of interpretational overlap in lexical and constructional acquisition*. PhD Dissertation, University of California, Berkeley.

Keil, Frank. 1989. *Concepts, kinds and cognitive development*. Cambridge, MA: MIT Press.

Kövecses, Zoltán & Péter Szabò. 1996. Idioms: A view from cognitive semantics. *Applied Linguistics* 17(3). 326–355.

Lakoff, George. 1987. *Women, fire, and dangerous things: What categories reveal about the mind*. Chicago: University of Chicago Press.

Lakoff, George. 1993. The Contemporary theory of metaphor. In Andrew Ortony (ed.), *Metaphor and thought*, 202–251. 2nd edn. Cambridge: Cambridge University Press.

Lakoff, George & Mark Johnson. 1980. *Metaphors we live by*. Chicago: University of Chicago Press.

Lakoff, George & Mark Johnson. 1999. *Philosophy in the flesh: The embodied mind and its challenge to western thought*. New York: Basic Books.

Langacker, Ronald W. 1987. *Foundations of cognitive grammar. Vol. 1, Theoretical prerequisites*. Stanford, CA: Standford University Press.

Langacker. Ronald W. 1990. *Concept, Image and Symbol. The Cognitive Basis of Grammar*. Berlin: Mouton de Gruyter.

Lazar, Gillian. 1996. Using figurative language to expand students' vocabulary. *English Language Teaching Journal* 50(1). 43–51.

Lazar, Gillian. 2003. *Meanings and metaphor: Activities to practise figurative language*. Cambridge: Cambridge University Press.

Levorato, M. Chiara & Cristina Cacciari. 1992. Children comprehension and production of idioms: The role of context and familiarity. *Journal of Child Language* 19. 415–433.

Lindstromberg, Seth & Frank Boers. 2005. From movement to metaphor with manner-of-movement verbs. *Applied Linguistics* 26(2). 241–261.

Littlemore, Jeannette. 2001. Metaphoric competence: a possible language learning strength of students with a holistic cognitive style? *TESOL Quarterly* 35(3). 459–491.

Littlemore, Jeannette. 2010. Metaphoric competence in the first and second language: similarities and differences. In Martin Pütz & Laura Sicola (eds.), *Cognitive processing in second language acquisition: inside the learner's mind*, 293–315. Amsterdam: John Benjamins.

Littlemore, Jeannette & Graham D. Low. 2006a. *Figurative thinking and foreign language learning*. Basingstoke: Palgrave Macmillan.

Littlemore, Jeannette & Graham D. Low. 2006b. Metaphoric competence and communicative language abilities. *Applied Linguistics* 27(2). 268–294.

Low, Graham D. 1988. On teaching metaphor. *Applied Linguistics* 9(2). 125–147.

MacArthur, Fiona. 2006. Metaphor in the real world of EFL: Coursebooks for learners aged 12–18. Paper presented at the RaAM 6 Conference, Researching and Applying Metaphor: Ten Years On, University of Leeds, 10–12 April.

MacArthur, Fiona. 2010. Metaphorical competence in EFL: Where are we and where should we be going? A view from the language classroom. *AILA Review* 23. 155–173.

MacArthur, Fiona & Ana M. Piquer Píriz. 2007. Staging the introduction of figurative extensions of familiar vocabulary items in EFL: Some preliminary considerations. *Ilha do desterro: A Journal of English Language, Literatures in English and Cultural Studies*, 53. 123–134.

Nacey, Susan. 2013. *Metaphors in learner english*. Amsterdam: John Benjamins.

Nacey, Susan. 2017. Metaphor comprehension and production in a second language. In Elena Semino & Zsófia Demjén (eds.), *The Routledge handbook of metaphor and language*, 503–515. Taylor & Francis.

Nerlich, Brigitte, David. D. Clarke & Zazie Todd. 1999. Mummy, I like being a sandwich. In Klaus U Panther, and Günter Radden (eds.), *Metonymy in language and thought*, 361–383. Amsterdam: John Benjamins.

Nerlich, Brigitte, Zazie Todd & David D. Clarke. 2003. Emerging patterns and evolving polysemies: The acquisition of *get* between four and ten years. In Brigitte Nerlich, Zazie Todd, Vimala Herman and David Clarke (eds.), *Flexible patterns of meaning in mind and language*, 333–357. Berlin: Mouton de Gruyter.

Nippold, Marilyn, Laurence B. Leonard & Robert Kail. 1984. Syntactic and conceptual factors in children's understanding of metaphors. *Journal of Speech and Hearing Research* 27. 197–205.

Nippold, Marilyn & Michael Sullivan. 1987. Verbal and perceptual analogical reasoning and proportional metaphor comprehension in young children. *Journal of Speech and Hearing Research* 30. 367–376.

Özçalışkan, Şeyda. 2011. Acquisition of metaphor. In Patrick C. Hogan (ed.), *Cambridge encyclopedia of language sciences*, 486–488. Cambridge: Cambridge University Press.

Özçalışkan, Şeyda. 2014. Development of metaphor. In Patricia Brooks & Vera Kempe (eds.), *Encyclopedia of Language Development*, 374–375. New York: Sage Publishers.

Radden, Günter & Klaus U. Panther. 2004. Introduction: Reflections on motivation. In Günter Radden & Klaus U. Panther (eds.), *Studies in linguistic motivation*, 1–26. Berlin: Mouton de Gruyter.

Piaget, Jean & Bärbel Inhelder, 1969. *Psicología del niño*. Madrid: Ediciones Morata, S.A.

Piaget, Jean. 1962. *Play, dreams and imitation in childhood*. New York: Norton

Pineda, Patricia. 2015. *Looking for and making sense of "special" words. Metaphor recognition and interpretation by school children*. Utrecht: LOT dissertation series.

Piquer-Píriz, Ana M. 2005. *La comprensión de algunas extensiones semánticas de los lexemas "hand", "mouth" y "head" en las primeras etapas del aprendizaje del Inglés*. PhD Dissertation, University of Extremadura. Cáceres: Servicio de publicaciones de la Universidad de Extremadura.

Piquer-Píriz, Ana M. 2006. The embodied and social grounds for figurative meanings: Colour terms in EFL. Paper presented at the II International Workshop on Metaphor and Discourse, University Jaume I, Castellón (Spain).

Piquer-Píriz, Ana M. 2008a. Reasoning figuratively in early EFL: Some implications for the development of vocabulary. In Frank Boers & Seth Lindstromberg (eds.), *Cognitive linguistic approaches to teaching vocabulary and phraseology*, 219–240. Berlin: Mouton de Gruyter

Piquer-Píriz, Ana M. 2008b. Young learners' understanding of figurative language. In Mara S. Zanotto, Lynne Cameron & M. Chiara Calvacanti (eds.), *Confronting metaphor in use: An applied linguistic approach*, 183–198. Amsterdam: John Benjamins.

Piquer-Píriz, Ana M. 2010. Can people be cold and warm?: Developing understanding of some figurative meanings of temperature terms in early EFL. In Graham D. Low, Zazie Todd, Alice Deignan & Lynne Cameron (eds.), *Researching and applying metaphor in the real world*, 21–33. Amsterdam: John Benjamins.

Piquer-Píriz, Ana M. 2011. Motivated word meanings and vocabulary learning: The polysemy of hand in the english for young learners classroom. *Metaphor and the Social World* 1 (2). 154–173.

Piquer-Píriz, Ana M. & Frank Boers. 2010. Individual differences in L2 metaphor processing: A think-aloud experiment. Paper presented at the VII Congreso Internacional de la Asociación Española de Lingüística Cognitiva (AELCO). University of Castilla la Mancha (Spain), 30–2 October.

Piquer Píriz, Ana M., Fiona MacArthur & Rafael Alejo. 2010. Does learning an L2 promote metaphorical thinking? Some preliminary findings from a study of Spanish secondary school learners in CLIL and non-CLIL contexts. Paper presented at the Eighth International Conference on Researching and Applying Metaphor (RaAM 8). VU University (The Netherlands), 30–3 July.

Ponterotto, Diane. 1994. Metaphors we can learn by. *English Teaching Forum* 32 (3). 2–7.

Saaty, Rawan. 2016. *Teaching L2 metaphor through awareness-raising activities: experimental studies with saudi EFL learners*. Unpublished Doctoral Dissertation. University of Birmingham.

Stites, Lauren J. & Şeyda Özçalışkan. 2013. Developmental changes in children's comprehension and explanation of spatial metaphors for time. *Journal of Child Language* 40. 1123–1137.

Taylor, J. R. 2003. Polysemy's Paradoxes. *Language Sciences* 25. 637–655.

Tomasello, Michael. 2003. *Constructing a language: A usage-based theory of language acquisition*. Cambridge, MA: Harvard University Press.

Tomasello, Michael. 2006. Construction Grammar for kids. *Constructions* 1. 1–11.

Vosniadou, Stella. 1987. Children and metaphors. *Child Development* 58. 870–885.

Vosniadou, Stella & Andrew Ortony. 1983. Intelligence of the literal-metaphorical-anomalous distinction in young children. *Child Development* 54. 154–161.

Vosniadou, Stella. 1989. Similarity and analogical reasoning: A synthesis. In Stella Vosniadou and Andrew Ortony, eds., *Similarity and analogical reasoning*, 1–18. Cambridge: Cambridge University Press.

Winner, Ellen. 1988. *The point of words: Children's understanding of metaphor and irony*. Cambridge, MA: Harvard University Press.

Zurer-Pearson, Barbara. 1990. The comprehension of metaphor by preschool children. *Journal of Child Language* 17. 185–203.

Laura Suárez-Campos, Alberto Hijazo-Gascón
and Iraide Ibarretxe-Antuñano
Metaphor and Spanish as a Foreign Language

1 Introduction: Conceptual Metaphor and Metaphorical Competence

Since the publication of Lakoff and Jonson's *Metaphors we live by* (1980), where the basic tenets of Conceptual Metaphor Theory (henceforth, CMT) were established, metaphor stopped being considered just a rhetorical figure and is now recognised as an essential mechanism in the construction of language. A conceptual metaphor is defined as a cognitive mechanism that establishes mappings between a source domain –usually but not necessarily a concrete domain– and a target domain, generally a more abstract domain, e.g. UNDERSTANDING IS SEEING. A metaphorical expression, on the other hand, is characterised as the multimodal linguistic encoding of a conceptual metaphor particular to each language, e.g. *I see what you mean*. The mappings between conceptual domains are not arbitrary, but motivated. This means that they are experientially grounded in the world around us. In other words, the experiential basis of conceptual metaphors is embodied, that is, based on our interaction with the physical, social, and cultural dimensions of our world (see Johnson 1987).

This embodied nature explains why the same conceptual metaphors can be found cross-linguistically. For example, the metaphor UNDERSTANDING IS SEEING

Note: This research has been supported by grants FFI2013-45553-C3-1-P and FFI2017-82460-P from the Spanish Ministry of Economy and Competitiveness and by the Government of Aragon (Psylex H11–17R). Special thanks to the editors for their kind invitation to take part in this volume and to Chris Skedgel for his help. We would like to dedicate this chapter to Fiona, not only for her inspiring work on metaphor and metaphorical competence in different contexts, but also, and above all, for being herself, a truly and fully "competent horsewoman".

Laura Suárez-Campos, Departamento de Lingüística General e Hispánica, Universidad de Zaragoza, Zaragoza, Spain, e-mail: laura.suarez.campos@gmail.com
Alberto Hijazo-Gascón, School of Politics, Philosophy, Language and Communication Studies, University of East Anglia, Norwich, United Kingdom,
e-mail: A.Hijazo-Gascon@uea.ac.uk
Iraide Ibarretxe-Antuñano, Departamento de Lingüística General e Hispánica, Universidad de Zaragoza, Zaragoza, Spain

https://doi.org/10.1515/9783110630367-005

also works in Spanish in metaphorical expressions such as *Ya veo lo que quieres decir* (Lit. [I] already see what [you] want [to] say), *Tienes que echarle otro vistazo* (Lit. [you] must throw it another look), or *El problema estaba bien claro* (Lit. the problem was well clear) (see MacArthur, Krennmayr, and Littlemore 2015).

Over the years since Lakoff and Johnson's publication, CMT has been used to unveil the conceptualisation of a wide variety of domains and fields of knowledge. For instance, CMT has explored the scope of metaphorical source domains such as perception (Speed et al. 2019) or body parts (Maalej and Yu 2011), but also metaphorical target domains such as time (Yu 1998) or emotions (Kövecses 2000). Although English is the predominant language in this type of studies, other languages have also been explored. One example is Yu's research on anger and happiness in Chinese (Yu 1998). There are also some cross-linguistic studies comparing several languages, such as Ogarkova and Soriano (2018). As far as Spanish is concerned, work on conceptual metaphor is long and well-established in some areas such as emotions (Barcelona and Soriano 2004; Soriano 2003; Soriano and Valenzuela 2009), but still incipient in other areas such as, for instance, body parts (but see, Gutiérrez Pérez 2010; López Rodríguez 2009; Olza 2011).

Another important contribution of CMT has been to offer plausible solutions and explanations to traditional problems and long standing issues such as the question about how and when figurative (abstract) concepts are acquired, i.e. metaphoric competence in the L1 (Cometa and Eson 1978). Danesi (1988) coins the term metaphorical competence for the specific acquisition of figurative concepts in an L2. In both cases, the key question is to explain how a language codifies abstract concepts through metaphorical reasoning, but whereas this competence develops naturally and unconsciously in an L1, a set of skills need to be learned in an L2 to achieve a good level of metaphorical competence (Danesi 1988).

The L2 skills that learners need to develop in order to acquire this metaphorical competence, however, do not start from scratch. They can be transferred from the learner's L1 (Danesi 1992; Johnson 1991; Littlemore 2010), but they should be also specifically incorporated in foreign language teaching (Danesi 1988, 1992, 2008; Littlemore 2001a, 2001b; Littlemore and Low 2006; Low 1988). As Danesi (1988) points out, L2 learners can use metaphor both as an interaction strategy and as a resource for meaning inference. In order to do so, however, learners need to be aware of how concepts are encoded and reflected in language through metaphorical reasoning. This is what Boers (2000) calls metaphorical awareness; that is, the ability to recognise the non-arbitrary relationship between the form of a metaphorical expression and its meaning, as well as the acceptance of cultural and linguistic differences in metaphorical expressions (Boers, Demecheleer, and Eyckmans 2004). Metaphorical awareness is not just crucial to help learners improve their metaphorical competence, and hence, their linguistic skills in an L2, it will also improve their memorising (Boers and Lindstromberg 2008).

The acquisition of metaphorical competence and its implementation in the foreign language class is becoming a hot topic in second language acquisition (see MacArthur 2017 for a review). Although most of the earlier studies focused on the acquisition and teaching of English as a foreign language (henceforth EFL), nowadays there is a growing body of research that pays attention to other languages. The goal of this chapter is to offer an overview of the research carried out around the role of conceptual metaphor and metaphorical competence in Spanish as a foreign language (henceforth, SFL). Section 2 summarises some of the main studies on the acquisition, both comprehension and production, of metaphorical competence in SFL. Section 3 presents some of the pedagogical implementations of CMT in SFL and discusses how and to what extent this practice could be beneficial for second language learners.

2 The Acquisition of Metaphorical Competence in SFL

As mentioned above, there is a growing interest in the development of metaphorical competence in L2 acquisition and its practical application in the classroom, and SFL is no exception (see Suárez-Campos and Hijazo-Gascón 2019, for an overview). Recent research on metaphor in SFL shows that metaphor reasoning brings benefits to the acquisition of linguistic patterns, such as the verbal system (Nieto and Martínez Vázquez 2014; Real Espinosa 2009), verbal morphology (Ruiz Campillo 2014), and the use of prepositions (Llopis-García 2015; Mendo Murillo 2019). Most of the studies on metaphor and SFL focus on vocabulary learning and on fostering metaphorical competence, following previous studies in EFL (Boers 2000, 2006, 2013; Danesi 1992, 2008; Littlemore 2001a, 2001b, 2010; Littlemore et al. 2012, 2013; Low 1988; MacArthur 2010).

The main findings of the studies on metaphor in SFL will be discussed in this section. First, studies dealing with comprehension will be presented and, second, those focused on metaphor production in SFL. Finally, we will review the studies that propose pedagogical materials using metaphors to be applied in SFL instruction.

2.1 Comprehending Metaphors in Spanish

Learners' comprehension of the different elements that are involved in a metaphorical expression is crucial to achieve metaphorical competence. Studies in EFL show that metaphorical comprehension depends on the strategy used by the student to infer the meaning of the expressions (Azuma 2009; Littlemore 2004). This choice of strategy is related to students' cognitive style (Boers and Littlemore 2000). While analogical learners focus on the correspondences between the source and the target domain, holistic learners understand both domains as a whole. However, L2 learners can also adapt their strategies to the situation, by using different cognitive processes, such as associative thinking, analogical reasoning, image formation, and metaphoric extension (Littlemore 2008; Littlemore and Low 2006).

There are several strategies used to infer meaning in an L2. They can be based on linguistic knowledge (about the L2 in general or in relation to its similarities with the L1) or on cognitive reasoning (Polisse 1990). One of the most frequent non-linguistic strategies used by L2 students is finding metaphorical motivations. In Ferreira's study (2008), participants used this strategy even in cases where they could rely on the context to infer meaning. Students can also search for conceptual similarities between the L1 and the L2. However, this is a more challenging strategy as they lack awareness about these similarities between languages (Chen and Lai 2013).

The studies focused on strategies to infer metaphorical expressions in SFL are consistent with previous research in EFL (De Cock and Suñer 2018; García Caballero 2017; Mayo Martín 2017). Their results also point out that the influence of the learning styles of the students is crucial for the choice of the strategies. They also show that the importance of context is minimal and that strategies based on conceptual similarities are not straightforward for L2 learners.

García Caballero (2017) notes that the students' cognitive styles and the type of metaphor are conditioning factors for the comprehension of metaphors in SFL. In her study, she checked the ability of a group of SFL students to identify metaphors in a text. The SFL students had a high level of proficiency (B2–C1) and different L1s. Taking into account their cognitive style, students were classified according to two axes: visual/verbal and intuitive/perceptive. Learners with a visual cognitive style are better at interpreting metaphors with an external image structure, as in *en las penumbras del amor* (Lit. in the shadows of the love) 'in the dark hours of love' while verbal cognitive style learners find it easier to process metaphors with a simile structure, as in *como Pedro por su casa* (Lit. like Pedro around his house) 'like he owned the place'. Perceptive learners prefer metaphors that are also lexicalised in the L1 whereas intuitive learners favour novel metaphors.

Mayo Martín (2017) focuses on colloquial language and on the role of context and cultural distance to infer metaphorical meaning. Her results show that the conceptual distance between the languages seems to affect the comprehension of metaphorical expressions. L2 learners could infer more easily the meaning of expressions that belong to conceptual metaphors shared in the L1 and the L2. For example, they were presented with two euphemistic metaphorical expressions meaning 'to die', one with a counterpart in their L1s, *no estar* ('not be'), and one without, *palmarla* (Lit. print the palm of the hand). Students were able to infer the meaning of the former but not the latter. Context was not always used as a strategy to infer the meaning of these expressions, which is consistent with Ferreira's (2008) results for EFL.

A similar methodology is used by De Cock and Suñer's (2018) study. French-speaking Belgian learners of Spanish had to explain the meaning of sexual taboo metaphorical expressions that were presented to them with and without context. The expressions chosen present some similarities with the L1, but also some conceptual and sociocultural differences. For instance, the Spanish term *los huevos* (Lit. the eggs) referring to the testicles and the expression *la tiene morcillona* (Lit. he has it like a blood sausage) to indicate the state before an erection are not shared with French and their comprehension needs some cultural knowledge.

Interestingly, the level of proficiency (B2 and C1) in De Cock and Suñer's study did not play a role in the comprehension of metaphorical expressions. In fact, the variable that proved to be determinant was whether participants had an immersion experience in a Spanish-speaking country, as learners who had lived in a Spanish-speaking country had better results. Since these are taboo expressions related to sex, they are rarely treated in an L2 class, and therefore they can only be acquired through frequent exposure to different registers and types of discourse.

These studies identify some of the difficulties that SFL students face when they have to infer the meaning of Spanish metaphorical expressions. For example, their lack of awareness of conceptual similarities between languages seems to be a problematic area that hinders the correct comprehension of metaphorical expressions. These studies also highlight some of the determining factors for meaning comprehension, such as the cognitive style of the students and their exposure to the target language. They also show that, interestingly enough, the level of proficiency does not seem to be particularly relevant when students have to interpret the meaning of metaphorical expressions. It is also very revealing to find that learners do not tend to rely on context to infer these meanings. More studies on metaphor comprehension in SFL are needed (on different registers and contexts) to achieve a better understanding on how metaphorical meanings are inferred in SFL.

2.2 Producing Metaphors in L2 Spanish

The production of metaphors has been mostly studied in relation to written discourse in EFL (Littlemore et al. 2012, 2013; Nacey 2013; MacArthur 2010; Paris 2014a, 2014b), although there are a few studies in other L2s, such as Norwegian (Golden 2012) and Spanish (Gómez Vicente 2013, 2019; Masid 2014). There is nevertheless a growing interest in oral production, mainly in EFL (MacArthur 2011, 2016a, 2016b; MacArthur, Krennmayr, and Littlemore 2015; Paris 2014a).

These studies show differences in the use of figurative language in the L1 and in the L2. As one would assume, native speakers use more metaphorical expressions than L2 learners. As Nacey (2013) explains, however, it is important to clarify that this difference in frequency is related to the different types of metaphors that native and non-native speakers produce. L1 speakers tend to use more conventional metaphors, while L2 speakers use novel metaphors with more frequency. These novel metaphors in the L2 are in many cases transferred from their L1 and consequently they tend to be considered inappropriate for the L2. It is also noted that metaphors in the L2 are more frequently used by learners with higher levels of proficiency (Golden 2012; Littlemore et al. 2012, 2013).

Results in these studies in SFL are consistent with the findings for EFL. Gómez Vicente (2013, 2019) explores how emotions are expressed through metaphor in SFL by L1 French students. Her results confirm that metaphor is very frequently used in the expression of emotions. As expected, metaphor is more used by native speakers. However, it is important to note that non-figurative language is preferred in both groups. Literal statements are more used than metaphorical expressions, even in the case of native speakers' narratives. When looking into the use of metaphors, native speakers use more figurative language than L2 speakers and, consequently, a lower metaphorical density is found in L2 texts. The results also show that the vast majority of metaphorical expressions used are related to the spatial domain, closely linked with embodied motivation (Gómez Vicente 2013). This study shows the importance of metaphor to express abstract concepts such as emotions, and its benefits to L2 learners to improve their written performances.

The number of studies in metaphorical language production in L2 is still limited, in relation to both written and oral discourse. However, production is crucial to understand the acquisition of metaphors in an L2. It seems clear that L2 learners need to understand and produce metaphors in their written texts and in their oral expression. Future research is needed to shed more light on how learners use figurative language in Spanish L2 and into what strategies they use during these processes, especially in the understudied area of oral production.

2.3 Metaphor in Language Instruction

There are a number of studies that include both comprehension and production of metaphor in Spanish L2. Their aim is to assess the impact of pedagogical intervention in the production and comprehension of metaphors at different proficiency levels (Acquaroni 2008; Acquaroni and Suárez-Campos 2019; Lavín Carrera 2016; Masid 2014, 2017). Participants in these studies completed a pretest before receiving instruction on metaphor, and a post-test following the instruction. The results of both tests are contrasted in order to find whether there is an improvement in the metaphorical competence of the students, independent of their cognitive styles or their level of proficiency.

In Acquaroni's (2008) longitudinal study, SFL learners with mixed levels of proficiency (from B1 to C2), enrolled in a creative writing course during a full term. These students were trained in understanding and producing metaphors in Spanish. During this course, they had different tasks, individually or in groups, with the aim of improving their writing skills. Their level of metaphorical competence was compared to a control group of SFL students. Results show that students who prefer a visual cognitive style have better results in the pre-test. However, the increase in metaphorical density is similar for all the students in the post-test, regardless of their cognitive style. Therefore, the pedagogical intervention is beneficial for all the students.

Masid's research (2014, 2017) tests the efficiency of a pedagogical intervention designed to develop metaphorical competence with the aid of a website. There were two groups of informants: one group had informants from Slovakia and received online training whereas the other group had German informants who followed the instruction as part of their on-site Spanish classes. Results show a positive effect of pedagogical intervention in both production and comprehension regardless of the informants' level of proficiency (levels A2 to B2). Masid concludes that the explicit treatment of metaphor in the classroom improves both the comprehension and the production of the metaphorical expressions in SFL at any level. Consequently, the introduction of activities with metaphor in the SFL classes is beneficial and complements the learning of the L2.

Similarly, Lavín Carrera (2016) argues for the benefits of introducing metaphors in classroom instruction. In this study, students' metaphor awareness improves after being exposed to a corpus of metaphorical expressions compiled from a sample of textbooks and classified on the basis of the domains involved in their underlying mappings.

The abovementioned studies show the benefits of metaphor instruction to SFL students. These are relevant to all levels of proficiency and independent of the student's learning style. Future research should include replications of these studies comparing these learning gains with non-metaphor-oriented interventions. It is also necessary to carry out studies with metaphors in the teaching of Spanish in lower levels of proficiency and in child second language acquisition.

3 Pedagogical Proposals for Teaching Metaphor in SFL

Previous studies in English and Spanish show that introducing metaphors in language instruction is beneficial for all types of learners, at any age (MacArthur and Piquer-Píriz 2007; Piquer-Píriz 2008a, 2008b, 2011) and at any level of proficiency (Littlemore et al. 2012, 2013). However, these findings on the benefits of metaphorical competence are not reflected in language teaching instruction and metaphors are still considered a difficult area of language in relation to literary skills.

This absence of metaphorical competence in second language instruction is probably caused by the fact that the use of metaphor has not been systematised in the descriptors in the CEFRL (*Common European Framework of Reference for Languages* 2001). Consequently, there are only minimal references to metaphor in the descriptors of the CPCI (*Curriculum Plan of the Cervantes Institute* 2006), which specifies CEFRL descriptors for the teaching of Spanish. The CPCI includes metaphorical expressions only from a B2 level onwards.[1] As a result, explicit treatment of metaphors is absent in SFL materials and textbooks or, if they are included, they are always in relation to literary texts for higher levels of proficiency.

There are, however, some signs of change in language teachers' views on metaphor and an increasing awareness of the potential of metaphor in SFL learning process. In a survey carried out by Rivera León (2016), more than 80% of the SFL teachers surveyed agreed or strongly agreed with the idea that metaphor plays a major role in the compensatory and interactive aspects of strategic

---

[1] The CEFRL levels have been compared to the levels established by the American Council for the Teaching of Foreign Languages (ACTFL). The B2 Level of the CEFRL can correspond to an Advanced Mid, following Vandergrift (no date). Martínez Baztán (2008) considers that the oral evaluation of B2 corresponds to an Intermediate High/Advanced Low of the ACTFL. For the equivalences of CEFRL levels with other institutions see Vandergrift (no date).

competence. More than 67% were interested in integrating metaphor in their SFL classes. However, most teachers believed that explicit exposure to metaphor in the classroom is insufficient. They perceived that the use of metaphor in class tends to be restricted to high level groups (from B2). Only 10% of SFL teachers claimed to integrate activities involving metaphor in the classes for lower proficiency levels. In addition, the vast majority of them considered that the resources they can find to integrate this practice into the classroom are scarce.

The reviews of SFL textbooks made by Masid (2014) and Mayo Martín (2017) confirm this lack of metaphor-related content in textbooks and pedagogical materials. Therefore, most publications on metaphor in SFL aim at investigating the practical application of CMT in SFL class, and to apply the findings of research on the acquisition of metaphorical competence to pedagogical proposals that can be used in SFL instruction.

3.1 Metaphor in the Classroom

As mentioned above, one of the main difficulties faced by students when they deal with metaphorical expressions in an L2 is the lack of awareness of the cultural similarities and differences that often underlie the meaning of a metaphorical expression (Danesi 1992). Boers (2000, 2006, 2013) argues that metaphorical awareness by L2 students can be fostered if both the context of use and the origin of metaphorical expressions are explained. He also suggests focusing students' attention on the source domain in order to establish a system of meanings associated with this source domain. Other authors in the field of L2 metaphor acquisition have also claimed the need for metaphors to be explicitly taught in the classroom (Boers and Lindstromberg 2008; Kalyuga and Kalyuga 2008), and the need to develop specific pedagogical proposals based on thematic groupings, the promotion of metaphorical extensions, and analogical reasoning (Littlemore 2001b). In some cases, the relevance of using photographs and audiovisual materials is also highlighted (Littlemore and Low 2006).

Some of the studies on Spanish provide guidelines for the introduction of metaphor in the teaching of SFL (Bandera-Nápoles 2016; Gómez Vicente 2013; Guillén Solano 2012; Hijazo-Gascón 2011; Lantolf and Bobrova 2014; Masid 2014). These are concerned with the appropriate choice of the metaphorical expressions and suggest how to introduce them in the class. They also agree with Boers (2000, 2006) in presenting metaphors explicitly, paying attention to the context and their motivation. Finally, they are also systematic in the activities with metaphor in the class. Let us review some of these studies.

Hijazo-Gascón (2011) argues for the importance of metaphors to develop learning and communication strategies. He focuses on metaphors for emotions and considers that the use of metaphor in class benefits analogical reasoning, awareness of the differences between L1 and L2, and fosters strategic competences. He proposes the use of conceptual metaphors to talk about emotions and in relation to other linguistic content such as verbs of change *ponerse* 'get', *volverse* 'turn', and *quedarse* 'remain', vocabulary for emotions as well as pragmatic and discourse-related strategies.

Based on teaching observations of SFL classes, Guillén Solano (2012) singles out three factors in the use of metaphorical expressions in class. First, the need to take into account whether the metaphorical expression is frequent in all varieties of Spanish or whether it is specific to one dialectal area. Second, the type of discourse in which the metaphorical expression occurs so that it can be contextualised and analysed in relation to style. Finally, the potential morphosyntactic combinations in which metaphorical expressions occur since sometimes these expressions cannot be modified. For example, in an expression such as *tomar el pelo* (Lit. take the hair) 'to mock someone', it is not possible to change the definite for an indefinite article (**tomar un pelo* (Lit. take one hair)) or in the expression *por si las moscas* (Lit. for if the flies) 'just in case', the noun *moscas* 'flies' must take the plural form and not the singular one (**por si la mosca* (Lit. for if the fly)). Guillén Solano also identifies the three most successful strategies to favour metaphor comprehension: (i) to group phraseological units by their domains; (ii) to make explicit the relationship between form, meaning, and function; and (iii) to contextualise metaphorical expressions.

Gómez Vicente (2013) presents a series of pedagogical units to apply metaphor to SFL teaching. Her activities include the metalinguistic, the conceptual, and the linguistic dimensions in pedagogical progression. This means that it is necessary to reflect on the concept of metaphor, and then to explain the conceptual structures that underlie the expressions. Gómez Vicente also argues that it is crucial to teach the linguistic elements that convey these conceptual schemes. Among her recommendations, she proposes some complementary techniques to integrate the teaching of the vocabulary of emotions. One of those recommendations is to replace random lists of expressions for thematically-grouped sets of expressions. Following this procedure, students have to search for the motivation of a given expression with the help of their own intuition and to establish comparisons with the students' own L1.

Masid (2014) suggests choosing the expressions and vocabulary items to be taught in class in relation to their frequency and productivity. According to this author, the most productive and general expressions should be selected. They should be gradually integrated into the teaching activities, until reaching the most complex meanings. Masid also recommends introducing metaphor in class from the beginning of the learning process and in a systematic way.

Similarly, Lantolf and Bobrova (2014) also agree with a gradual introduction of metaphors in the SFL classroom. Students should be familiarised with metaphorical structures first and should be aware of the presence of metaphor in everyday language. After that, teachers should explain its underlying conceptual structure, which can be done by comparing the metaphorical expressions found in Spanish and their counterparts in the learners' L1.

With the aim of specifying how to gradually introduce metaphors and systematise their practice in the SFL class, Bandera-Nápoles (2016) recommends encouraging the student to engage in independent work. This practice needs to be integrated within the task-based approach, since this methodology is believed to foster different skills and competences simultaneously. Metaphorical competence will therefore be developed through associated learning tasks, which will both consolidate previous knowledge and prepare the student to deal with new metaphorical content.

3.2 Practical Activities with Metaphor for the SFL Class

Many scholars in the field of SFL acquisition and teaching argue for the positive aspects of introducing metaphor explicitly in the L2 Spanish classes (Gómez Vicente 2013; Hijazo-Gascón 2009, 2011; Kaitian 2011; Lamartí 2011; Masid 2013; Rivera León 2016). In some cases, they also develop specific teaching materials to develop metaphorical competence and to raise awareness of metaphors. These pedagogical proposals also provide students with strategies to prepare them to understand and produce metaphors in Spanish. In order to achieve this goal, it is necessary for students to be familiarised with conceptual metaphors and to be able to carry out activities in which they relate these conceptual metaphors with their corresponding metaphorical expressions.

Different types of activities are proposed with this goal in mind. For instance, identifying conceptual metaphors and metaphorical expressions in a text, asking the students to find different metaphorical expressions corresponding to conceptual metaphors in their L1 and L2, and translating the Spanish metaphorical expressions into the students' L1. In other cases, activities are based on the crosslinguistic comparison of metaphorical expressions (Lamartí 2011; Pérez Bernal 2004). This type of activity is argued to help students (i) to understand the metaphorical expressions, (ii) to be aware of conceptual differences among languages, and (iii) to achieve a better understanding of the cultural framework in the target language. In this sense, as Encina and Franco

(2010) explain, metaphors encapsulate a great amount of cultural content that should also be explored in the SFL class.

Another crucial factor for the teaching of metaphor is to present metaphorical expressions in real discourse contexts. For instance, Bandera-Nápoles' (2016) pedagogical proposal focuses on the use of metaphors in real audiovisual productions. By a series of pre- and post-activities related to a documentary, students are induced to reflect not only on the metaphorical expressions used in the documentary but also on thematically-related metaphors.

Visual productions are not the only means to introduce the student metaphorical expressions. Any kind of material such as images, music, pieces of art or recreational activities can also be used with the same purpose. Metaphors, which can be found in all of these contexts, will foster students' creativity and analogical reasoning (Rodríguez Santos and Foncubierta 2016). Some pedagogical proposals also include work with dictionaries (Gutiérrez Pérez 2004), online corpora (Oster 2010), and poetry (Acquaroni 2011).

Another possibility is to work with creative metaphors in Spanish L2. Acquaroni (2008), for instance, focuses on these metaphors mainly in relation to creative writing workshops. Students have to use figurative language consciously, individually or in groups, to create their own texts in Spanish. They also acquire knowledge of the metaphorical conceptualisation through the analysis of Spanish literary texts, where they identify and relate conceptual metaphors with their corresponding expressions. However, it is important to note that metaphors are not exclusive to literature and poetry. Metaphor can be found in all kinds of discourse, as explained in Section 2.1. in relation to taboo metaphors in colloquial language.

One of the semantic domains that often turns up in L2 classroom interventions is that of emotions. There are several converging reasons that explain why this semantic domain is popular in this context. One reason is that emotions tend to be expressed through metaphor, and therefore, metaphorical expressions for emotion are easily found. Another reason relates to the students' own experience. They need to communicate what they feel in different contexts, and metaphors are excellent evaluative mechanisms to encapsulate emotions, attitudes along with any additional semantic and pragmatic meaning. There are different pedagogical proposals in relation to certain emotions such as lust (Hijazo-Gascón 2009), pride (Oster 2010), happiness and sadness (Acquaroni 2011), love (Rivera León 2016), and to feelings in general (Gómez Vicente 2013; Hijazo-Gascón 2011).

Activities and pedagogical proposals to work with metaphors in SFL are mostly aimed at adult learners at intermediate and high proficiency levels (usually B2). However, metaphor is neither restricted to adult population nor B2 levels. Studies on metaphorical competence by young learners of L2 English

(Piquer-Píriz 2008a, 2008b, 2011) and on metaphor use at lower proficiency levels of the CEFRL (Littlemore et al. 2012, 2013) have shown that metaphor is present in both child and adult learners at all proficiency levels. These studies in English make clear the current need for pedagogical proposals to address the use of metaphors in class with young learners and at beginner levels in SFL. Martínez Franco (2015) is a pioneering study where metaphor activities related to topics covered at initial levels of proficiency (daily routines, cooking recipes, describing the house, talking about the weather, etc.) are developed.

4 Conclusions

This chapter has offered an overview of how Conceptual Metaphor Theory has been applied to the acquisition and teaching of Spanish as a Foreign Language. Similar to previous results in EFL, studies on metaphor comprehension in SFL have revealed the importance to encourage the use of different strategies to infer meaning from metaphorical expressions, since comprehension depends on many variables such as the cognitive style of the students, their exposure to the language, and the conceptual distance between languages. Studies on metaphor writing production, on the other hand, have evidenced the need to use metaphor and, therefore, have argued that it is crucial to make students be aware of the embodied motivation that grounds the conceptual metaphor, since it can be used as a compensatory strategy. Research on the implementation of metaphor in the SFL class has demonstrated that it is beneficial for students to teach metaphor in class because it improves the students' metaphorical competence as well as their communication skills. Despite the importance of metaphor in all these SFL contexts, the number of studies devoted to investigate the impact of metaphor on the acquisition and teaching of SFL is still limited. There are areas such as the role of metaphor in oral comprehension and production or the role of age (young learners) and proficiency level (beyond B2) that remain yet untouched.

Research reviewed in this chapter (Hijazo-Gascón 2009, 2011; Gómez 2013; Lantolf and Bobrova 2014; Masid 2014; Acquaroni and Suárez-Campos 2019) has claimed that a systematic teaching of metaphor will provide students with a coherent framework to acquire figurative language, avoiding traditional learning by memorisation. Researchers in this field are increasingly aware of the potential benefits of introducing the teaching of metaphor right from the beginning of the learning process. Metaphor helps students developing their cognitive skills and enhancing their autonomy in their future learning of figurative language. As a result, the number of pedagogical proposals related to metaphor in SFL is increasing but not quickly enough. At the moment, and probably (but not only) due to the lack of metaphorical descriptors in the CEFRL and the CPCI, the body of materials available to systematically teach metaphor in the SFL classroom is scanty.

In conclusion, conceptual metaphor in SFL is an area of study with an enormous potential, with multiple didactic applications, and, in short, with endless paths for future research.

References

Acquaroni, Rosana. 2008. *La incorporación de la competencia metafórica a la enseñanza-aprendizaje del español como segunda lengua a través de un taller de escritura creativa: estudio experimental*. Madrid: Universidad Complutense de Madrid dissertation.

Acquaroni, Rosana. 2011. Metáfora y poesía como instrumento para la comunicación intercultural en el aula de ELE: la conceptualización de la tristeza y de la alegría a través de un poema de Miguel Hernández. Paper presented at FIAPE IV International Conference, University of Santiago de Compostela, 17–20 April 2011.

Acquaroni, Rosana & Laura Suárez-Campos. 2019. El desarrollo de la competencia metafórica en la enseñanza del español LE/L2. In Iraide Ibarretxe-Antuñano, Teresa Cadierno & Alejandro Castañeda Castro (eds.), *Lingüística cognitiva y español LE/L2*, 371–391. London: Routledge.

Azuma, Masumi. 2009. Positive and negative effects of mother-tongue knowledge on the interpretation of figurative expressions. *Papers in Linguistic Science* 15. 165–192.

Bandera-Nápoles, Aneyansis. 2016. La metáfora cognitiva y la conversación en la clase de ELE. [Special issue] *Maestro y Sociedad* 2. 169–180.

Barcelona, Antonio & Cristina Soriano. 2004. Metaphorical conceptualization in English and Spanish. *European Journal of English Studies* 8(3). 295–307.

Boers, Frank. 2000. Metaphor awareness and vocabulary retention. *Applied Linguistics* 21(4). 553–571.

Boers, Frank. 2006. Expanding learners' vocabulary through metaphor awareness: What expansion, what learners, what vocabulary. In Gitte Kristiansen, Michel Achard, René Dirven & Francisco J. Ruiz de Mendoza Ibáñez (eds.), *Cognitive linguistics: Current applications and future perspectives*, 211–232. Berlin: Mouton de Gruyter.

Boers, Frank. 2013. Cognitive linguistics approaches to teaching vocabulary: Assessment and integration. *Language Teaching* 46(2). 208–224.

Boers, Frank & Seth Lindstromberg. 2008. *Cognitive linguistic approaches to teaching vocabulary and phraseology*. Berlin: Mouton de Gruyter.

Boers, Frank & Jeannette Littlemore. 2000. Cognitive style variables in participants' explanations of conceptual metaphors. *Metaphor and Symbol* 15(3). 177–187.

Boers, Frank, Murielle Demecheleer & June Eyckmans. 2004. Cross-cultural variation as a variable in comprehending and remembering figurative idioms. *European Journal of English Studies* 8(3). 375–388.

Chen, Yi-Chen & Huei-Ling Lai. 2013. The influence of cultural universality and specificity on EFL learners' comprehension of metaphor and metonymy. *International Journal of Applied Linguistics* 23. 312–336.

Cometa, Michael S. & Morris E. Eson. 1978. Logical operations and metaphor interpretation: A Piagetian interpretation. *Developmental Psychology* 49. 649–659.

Danesi, Marcel. 1988. The development of metaphorical competence: A neglected dimension in second language pedagogy. In Albert N. Mancini, Paolo Giordano & Pier Raimondo Baldini (eds.), *Selected papers from the Proceedings of the Third Annual Conference of the American Association of Teachers of Italian*, 1–10. River Forest, IL: Rosary College.

Danesi, Marcel. 1992. Metaphorical competence in second language acquisition and second language teaching: the neglected dimension. In James E. Alatis (ed.), *Georgetown University round table on languages and linguistics*, 489–500. Washington, D.C.: Georgetown University Press.

Danesi, Marcel. 2008. Conceptual errors in second-language learning. In Sabine De Knop & Teun De Rycker (eds.), *Cognitive approaches to pedagogical grammar*, 231–256. Berlin: Mouton de Gruyter.

De Cock, Barbara & Ferrán Suñer. 2018. The influence of conceptual differences of processing taboo metaphors in the foreign language. In Andrea Pizarro Pedraza (ed.), *Linguistic taboo revisited. Novel insights from cognitive perspectives*, 201–222. Berlin: Mouton de Gruyter.

Encina, Pablo & Penélope Franco. 2010. Metáfora y metonimia en las clases de L2 en China. III Jornadas de formación de profesores de ELE en China. *Suplementos SinoEle* 3. 1–15.

Ferreira, Luciane. 2008. A psycholinguistic study on metaphor comprehension in a foreign language. *Revista Virtual de Estudos da Linguagem*. ReVEL 6(11). 1–23.

García Caballero, Ana. 2017. La importancia del componente metafórico en el aprendizaje de E/2L. Acercamiento pragmático. *RedELE* 29. https://www.mecd.gob.es/dam/jcr:98e9dc4f-06ec-42c0-b660-389a1917bf5c/redele-2017-29-7-garcia-caballero-ana.pdf (accessed 10 February 2018).

Golden, Anne. 2012. Metaphorical expression in L2 production. The importance of the text topic in the corpus research. In Fiona MacArthur, José Luis Oncins-Martínez, Manuel Sánchez-García & Ana María Piquer-Píriz. (eds.), *Metaphor in use. Context, culture and communication*, 136–148. Amsterdam: John Benjamins.

Gómez Vicente, Lucía. 2013. L'expression métaphorique de l'évènement émotionel en français (L1) et en espagnol (L1/L2): Les images schéma *haut/bas* et *dedans/dehors*. Analyse descriptive et proposition didactique. *Recherches en didactique des langues et des cultures* 10(1). 81–102.

Gómez Vicente, Lucía. 2019. La expresión de las emociones en la enseñanza de español LE/L2. In Iraide Ibarretxe-Antuñano, Teresa Cadierno & Alejandro Castañeda Castro (eds.), *Lingüística cognitiva y español LE/L2*, 340–370. London: Routledge.

Guillén Solano, Patricia. 2012. La incorporación del léxico coloquial en la clase de español como segunda lengua: estrategias para el estudio de metáforas lexicalizadas. *Revista Kariña* XXXVI. 93–100.

Gutiérrez Pérez, Regina. 2004. La metáfora en la enseñanza de español como segunda lengua. In Mª Auxiliadora Castillo Carballo, Olga Cruz Moya, Manuel García Platero & Juan Pablo Mora Gutiérrez (eds.), *Las gramáticas y los diccionarios en la enseñanza del español como segunda lengua: deseo y realidad. XV Congreso Internacional ASELE*, 444–448. Sevilla: Centro Virtual Cervantes.

Gutiérrez Pérez, Regina. 2010. *Estudio cognitivo-contrastivo de las metáforas del cuerpo. Análisis empírico del corazón como dominio fuente en inglés, francés, español, alemán e italiano*. Frankfurt: Peter Lang.

Hijazo-Gascón, Alberto. 2009. Cross-cultural differences in the conceptualization and their application in L2 instruction. In Reyes Gómez Morón, Manuel Padilla Cruz, Lucía Fernandez Amaya & María de la O Hernández López (eds.), *Pragmatics applied to language teaching and learning*, 42–59. Newcastle: Cambridge Scholars.

Hijazo-Gascón, Alberto. 2011. Las metáforas conceptuales como estrategias comunicativas y de aprendizaje: una aplicación didáctica de la lingüística cognitiva. *Hispania* 94(1). 142–154.

Johnson, Janice. 1991. Developmental versus language-based factors in metaphor interpretation. *Journal of Educational Psychology* 83(4). 470–483.

Johnson, Mark. 1987. *The body in the mind. The bodily basis of meaning, reason and imagination*. Chicago: University of Chicago Press.

Kaitian, Lu. 2011. Metáforas en la enseñanza del español a alumnos chinos: propuestas didácticas para mejorar la conciencia y la competencia metafórica. In Nicolás Arriaga Agrelo, Rocío Blasco García, Ana Mª Ducasse, Santiago González Fernández-Corugedo, Armando Mateo Pérez, Francisco Javier Menéndez Sánchez, Alberto José Sánchez Griñán, Juan Robisco García & José Miguel Blanco (eds.), *Competencias y estrategias docentes en el contexto de Asia-Pacífico. Selección de artículos del II Congreso de Español como Lengua Extranjera en Asia-Pacífico*, 329–346. Manila: Centro Virtual Cervantes.

Kalyuga, Marika & Slava Kalyuga. 2008. Metaphor awareness in teaching vocabulary. *Language Learning Journal* 36(2). 249–257.

Kövecses, Zoltán. 2000. *Metaphor and emotion. Language, culture and body in human feeling*. Cambridge: Cambridge University Press.

Lakoff, George & Mark Johnson. 1980. *Metaphors we live by*. Chicago: University of Chicago.

Lamartí, Rachid. 2011. La metáfora y la competencia conceptual en estudiantes sinófonos de ELE. In Nicolás Arriaga Agrelo, Rocío Blasco García, Ana Mª Ducasse, Santiago González Fernández-Corugedo, Armando Mateo Pérez, Francisco Javier Menéndez Sánchez, Alberto José Sánchez Griñán, Juan Robisco García & José Miguel Blanco (eds.), *Competencias y estrategias docentes en el contexto de Asia-Pacífico. Selección de artículos del II Congreso de Español como Lengua Extranjera en Asia-Pacífico*, 170–181. Manila: Centro Virtual Cervantes.

Lantolf, James & Larysa Bobrova. 2014. Metaphor instruction in the L2 Spanish classroom: Theoretical argument and pedagogical program. *Journal of Spanish Language Teaching* 1(1). 46–61.

Lavín Carrera, Elda. 2016. *La metáfora conceptual: una estrategia para el aprendizaje de vocabulario en E/L2 en el nivel B2*. Santander: Universidad de Cantabria dissertation.

Littlemore, Jeannette. 2001a. Metaphoric competence: a language learning strength of students with a holistic cognitive style? *TESOL Quarterly* 35(3). 459–491.

Littlemore, Jeannette. 2001b. Metaphoric intelligence and foreign language learning. *Humanising Language Teaching* 3 (2). http://www.hltmag.co.uk/mar01/mart1.htm (accessed 3 August 2018).

Littlemore, Jeannette. 2004. Interpreting metaphors in the language classroom. *Les Cahiers de l'APLIUT* 23(2). 57–70.

Littlemore, Jeannette. 2008. The relationship of associative thinking, analogical reasoning, image formation and metaphoric extension strategies. In Mara Sophia Zanotto, Lynne

Cameron & Marilda C. Cavalcanti (eds.), *Confronting metaphor in use: An applied linguistic approach*, 199–222. Amsterdam: John Benjamins.

Littlemore, Jeannette. 2010. Metaphoric competence in the first and second language. Similarities and differences. In Martin Pütz & Laura Sicola (eds.), *Cognitive processing in second language acquisition: Inside the learner's mind*, 293–316. Amsterdam: John Benjamins.

Littlemore, Jeannette, Tina Krennmayr, James Turner & Sarah Turner. 2012. Investigating figurative proficiency at different levels of second language writing. *Research Notes* 47. 14–28.

Littlemore, Jeannette, Tina Krennmayr, James Turner & Sarah Turner. 2013. An investigation into metaphor use at different levels of second language writing. *Applied Linguistics* 35 (2). 117–144.

Littemore, Jeannette & Graham Low. 2006. *Figurative thinking and foreign language learning*. New York: Palgrave Macmillan.

Llopis-García, Reyes. 2015. Las preposiciones y la metáfora del espacio: aportaciones y potencial de la lingüística cognitiva para su enseñanza. *Journal of Spanish Language Teaching* 2(1). 51–68.

López Rodríguez, Irene. 2009. Que no se te vaya la olla. Estudio lingüístico-cognitivo del campo semántico de la "cabeza". *Tonos digital. Revista electrónica de estudios filológicos* 17. http://www.tonosdigital.es/ojs/index.php/tonos/article/view/306/217 (accessed 5 March 2018).

Low, Graham. 1988. On teaching metaphor. *Applied Linguistics* 9(2). 125–147.

Maalej, Zouheir A. & Ning Yu (eds.). 2011. *Embodiment via body parts: Studies from various languages and cultures*. Amsterdam: John Benjamins.

MacArthur, Fiona. 2010. Metaphorical competence in EFL. Where are we and where should be going? A view from the language classroom. *AILA Review* 23(1). 155–173.

MacArthur, Fiona. 2011. On the use of metaphor in office hours' consultations carried out in English between lecturers and students with different first languages. *International Journal of Innovation and Leadership in the Teaching of Humanities* 1(1). 23–44.

MacArthur, Fiona. 2016a. Beyond engaged listenership: Assessing Spanish undergraduates' active participation in academic mentoring sessions in English as academic lingua franca. In Jesús Romero-Trillo (ed.), *Yearbook of Corpus Linguistics and Pragmatics 2016. Global implications for society and education in the networked age*, 153–178. Cham: Springer.

MacArthur, Fiona. 2016b. Overt and covert uses of metaphor in the academic mentoring in English of Spanish undergraduate students at five European universities. *Review of Cognitive Linguistics* 41(1). 23–50.

MacArthur, Fiona. 2017. Using metaphor in the teaching of second/foreign languages. In Elena Semino & Zsófia Demjén (eds.), *The Routledge handbook of metaphor and language*, 413–424. London: Routledge.

MacArthur, Fiona, Tina Krennmayr & Jeannette Littlemore. 2015. How basic is "UNDERSTANDING IS SEEING" when reasoning about knowledge? Asymmetric uses of sight metaphors in office hours consultations in English as academic lingua franca. *Metaphor and Symbol* 30(3). 184–217.

MacArthur, Fiona & Ana María Piquer-Píriz. 2007. Staging the introduction of figurative extensions of familiar vocabulary items in EFL: Some preliminary considerations. *Ilha do Desterro* 53. 123–134.

Martínez Baztán, A. 2008. *Oral evaluation equivalence between the ACTFL guidelines and some of the CEFR scales*. Granada: Universidad de Granada dissertation.

Martínez Franco, Sandra P. 2015. "Hoy mi cerebro no funciona". El uso de las metáforas en la enseñanza del español como lengua extranjera. *4º Encuentro Internacional de Español como Lengua Extranjera*. http://www.spanishincolombia.gov.co/cuartoEncuentroLenguaEspanola/ponencias/Mart%C3%ADnez%20Franco%20Sandra%20Patricia.pdf (accessed 20 January 2018).

Masid, Ocarina. 2013. La metáfora lingüística en el aula de ELE. In Narciso Contreras Izquierdo (ed.), *La enseñanza del español como LE/L2 en el siglo XXI. XXIV Congreso Internacional ASELE*, 895–903. Jaén: Centro Virtual Cervantes.

Masid, Ocarina. 2014. *La metáfora lingüística en el desarrollo de la competencia léxica de ELE. Propuesta semántica y didáctica sobre el léxico somático desde un punto de vista cognitivo*. Madrid: Universidad Complutense de Madrid dissertation.

Masid, Ocarina. 2017. La metáfora lingüística en español como lengua extranjera (ELE): estudio pre-experimental en tres niveles de competencia. *Porta Linguarum: Revista Internacional de Didáctica de las Lenguas Extranjeras* 27. 155–170.

Mayo Martín, Paula. 2017. Estudio sobre expresiones metafóricas tabú de uso frecuente para su aplicación a la enseñanza de Español Lengua Extranjera (ELE). *E-eleando* 5. http://www.meleuah.es/e-eleando/estudio-sobre-expresiones-metaf%C3%B3ricas-tab%C3%BA-de-uso-frecuente-para-su-aplicaci%C3%B3n-la (accessed 20 January 2018).

Mendo Murillo, Susana. 2019. El significado de las preposiciones en la enseñanza del español LE/L2: el caso de *por* y *para*. In Iraide Ibarretxe-Antuñano, Teresa Cadierno & Alejandro Castañeda Castro (eds.), *Lingüística cognitiva y español LE/L2*, 220–234. London: Routledge.

Nacey, Susan. 2013. *Metaphors in learner English*. Amsterdam: John Benjamins.

Nieto, Haydée & Julián Martínez Vázquez. 2014. La metáfora como base de un modelo didáctico. A propósito de 'Fundamento teórico de un modelo para trabajar los verbos *haber*, *ser* y *estar* en el aula de ELE' de Martha Jurado-Salinas. *Revista Nebrija de Lingüística Aplicada a la Enseñanza de Lenguas* 17. 45–78.

Ogarkova, Anna & Cristina Soriano. 2018. Metaphorical and literal profiling in the study of emotions. *Metaphor and Symbol* 33(1). 19–35.

Olza, Inés. 2011. On the (meta) pragmatic value of some Spanish idioms based on terms for body parts. *Journal of Pragmatics* 43. 3049–3067.

Oster, Ulrike. 2010. Pride-Stolz-orgullo: A corpus-based approach to the expression of emotion concepts in a foreign language. In Isabel Moskowich, Begoña Crespo, Inés Lareo & Paula Lojo (eds.), *Language widowing through corpora* II, 593–610. La Coruña: University of La Coruña.

Paris, Justin. 2014a. The expression of emotions by second language learners: Metaphor as a linguistic vehicle. *Poznan Studies in Contemporary Linguistics* 50(1). 99–121.

Paris, Justin. 2014b. Pour une prise ne compte des transferts de la L1 dans l'apprentissage et l'enseignement des expressions figuratives d'une L2. *Mélanges CRAPEL* 35. 135–150.

Pérez Bernal, Marián. 2004. Fraseología y metáfora: materiales para la enseñanza de la fraseología en una L2. In Mª Auxiliadora Castillo Carballo, Olga Cruz Moya, Manuel García Platero & Juan Pablo Mora Gutiérrez (eds.), *Las gramáticas y los diccionarios en la enseñanza del español como segunda lengua: deseo y realidad. XV Congreso Internacional ASELE*, 646–654. Sevilla: Centro Virtual Cervantes.

Piquer-Píriz, Ana M. 2008a. Reasoning figuratively in early EFL: Some implications for the development of vocabulary. In Frank Boers & Seth Lindstromberg (eds.), *Cognitive linguistics approaches to teaching vocabulary and phraseology*, 219–240. Berlin: Mouton de Gruyter.

Piquer-Píriz, Ana M. 2008b. Young learners' understanding of figurative language. In Mara Sophia Zanotto, Lynne Cameron & Marilda Cavalcanti (eds.), *Confronting metaphor in use: An applied linguistic approach*, 183–198. Amsterdam: John Benjamins.

Piquer-Píriz, Ana M. 2011. Motivated word meanings and vocabulary learning: The polysemy of *hand* in the English for young learners' classroom. *Metaphor and the Social World* 1(2). 154–173.

Poulisse, Nanda. 1990. *The use of compensatory strategies by Dutch learners of English*. Berlin: Mouton de Gruyter.

Real Espinosa, Juan Manuel. 2009. Gramática: la metáfora del espacio. *MarcoELE* 8. 1–56.

Rivera León, Lorena. 2016. La metáfora como recurso didáctico en el aula de ELE: un estudio a partir de la lingüística cognitiva. *Boletín de la Asociación para la Enseñanza del Español como Lengua Extranjera (ASELE)* 54. 13–46.

Rodríguez Santos, José María & José Manuel Foncubierta. 2016. Metáforas, símbolos y comunicación en el aula de ELE. *Mosaico* 34. 22–29.

Ruiz Campillo, José Plácido. 2014. La lógica del espacio. Un mapa operativo del sistema verbal en español. *Journal of Spanish Language Teaching* 1(1). 62–85.

Soriano, Cristina. 2003. Some anger metaphors in Spanish and English. A contrastive review. *International Journal of English Studies* 3(2). 107–122.

Soriano, Cristina & Javier Valenzuela 2009. Emotion and colour across languages: implicit associations in Spanish colour terms. *Social Science Information* 48(3). 421–455.

Speed, Laura J., Carolyn O. Meara, Lila San Roque & Asifa Majid (eds.). 2019. *Perception metaphors*. Amsterdam: John Benjamins.

Suárez-Campos, Laura & Alberto Hijazo-Gascón. 2019. La metáfora conceptual y su aplicación a la enseñanza de español LE/L2. In Iraide Ibarretxe-Antuñano, Teresa Cadierno & Alejandro Castañeda Castro (eds.), *Lingüística cognitiva y español LE/L2*, 235–252. London: Routledge.

Vandergrift, Laurens. No date. *Proposal for a Common Framework for Reference for Languages for Canada*. http://elpimplementation.ecml.at/Home/IMPEL/Documents/Canada/ProposalofaCFRforCanada/tabid/122/language/en-GB/Default.aspx#Chapter6 (accessed 03 April 2018).

Yu, Ning. 1998. *The contemporary theory of metaphor: A perspective from Chinese*. Amsterdam: John Benjamin.

Part II. New Empirical Studies

Part II. 1. **Learners' Use and Knowledge of L2 Figurative language**

Jeannette Littlemore, Paula Pérez-Sobrino, Nina Julich
and Danny Leung

Is Comfort Purple or Green?
Word-colour Associations in the First
and Second Language

1 Introduction and Background to the Study

Abstract concepts, in particular emotions, are often associated with particular colours, and many of these associations have a bodily basis. For example, for many speakers of English, anger is red, jealousy is green and purity is white. It has been suggested that there is a degree of universal convergence regarding the associations that people form between abstract concepts, emotions and colours because they are, at some level, bodily-based. At the same time, it has also been argued that culture and language play an important role in determining the associations (see Kövecses 2005 for further discussion of this issue). However, we know very little about the extent to which these associations are bodily-based and how their perceived embodiment relates to their universality.

A number of studies have investigated similarities and differences in the associations that people from different cultures and linguistic backgrounds form with colours, and different reasons have been postulated for these findings. For instance, associations between the colour red and anger have been found in English (Waggoner and Palermo 1989), Hungarian (Kövecses 2005), Chinese (Chen et al. 2014), Japanese (Matsuki 1995) and Polish (Mikolajczuk 1998). However, in Chinese, red has additional connotations. The Chinese word for red, 'hóng', has a number of positive meanings, such as 'hóng shì' (red event) (wedding), 'zõu hóng' (walk red) (become famous), and 'hóng rén' (red) (famous person) (Xing 2008). Other cultures, including English-speaking cultures, have also developed a positive association towards red as it is a symbol of love. Similar sorts of variation have been found for the colour blue (Barchard et al. 2017) and white (Xing 2008).

Jeannette Littlemore, English Language and Linguistics, University of Birmingham, West Midlands, United Kingdom, e-mail: j.m.littlemore@bham.ac.uk
Paula Pérez-Sobrino, Modern Philologies, University of La Rioja, Logroño, Spain, e-mail: paula.perezs@unirioja.es
Nina Julich, Institute for British Studies, Leipzig University, Leipzig, Germany, e-mail: nina.julich@uni-leipzig.de
Danny Leung, Applied Language Studies, The Open University of Hong Kong, Hong Kong, China, e-mail: chleung@ouhk.edu.hk

https://doi.org/10.1515/9783110630367-006

In this chapter, we explore why it is that some word-colour associations are more universal than others, and postulate that one explanatory factor might be the extent to which the associations have a physical basis. Some associations have a clear physical basis, such as the association of the colour red with anger, as this reflects a clear physical response to an emotional experience. Other associations are more easily explained in terms of the interactions that we have through our bodies with the physical environment. This explains, for example, the associations that people in Western societies have with the colour yellow and joy (presumably linked to the warmth of the sun). Associations such as these might also include the association of WHITE/BRIGHT with GOOD/ MORAL, and BLACK/DARK with BAD/IMMORAL as these are based on experiences of self-efficacy in light vs darkness conditions, and experiences of cleanliness vs dirt (Sherman and Palermo 1989). Other associations are very difficult to explain either in terms of the body itself or of its interactions with the environment, such as the association that jealousy has with the colour green for many people living in the Western world.

A second question that is of interest is whether these associations carry over to a second language. We do not know whether when people learn a second language they transfer the word-colour associations from their first language or whether they adopt the associations that are common in the second language, or whether they form associations that are a mixture of L1 and L2 associations. Furthermore, we do not know what specific factors drive language learners to adopt L2 word colour associations rather than retaining their L1 associations, even when speaking the L2. Some associations will be acquired through exposure to the target language, but another way in which they may be acquired is through exposure to the visual culture, particularly through online environments in which the language is encountered. As we will see below, one of the findings made in this study was that Cantonese-speaking people associate the word 'comfortable' with the colour green, whereas English-speaking people do not do this. A Google image search for the Cantonese equivalent of comfortable (自在) results in a screen full of green images, most of which are to do with nature, so we can see immediately that the word has very different connotations in Cantonese than it does in English. If people are exposed to L2 colour contexts on a regular basis they are arguably more likely to internalise them when speaking the target language. One question that has not been addressed is which word-colour associations are most likely to be acquired by second language learners. One possibility is that they are more likely to acquire those which have a strong bodily-based motivation as they make more intuitive sense, whereas those that are more culturally-based will take longer to acquire. In this study we test this hypothesis, investigating whether more bodily-based word-colour associations are (a) more universal and (b) more likely to be acquired by second language learners.

2 Research Questions and Working Hypotheses

In order to address these questions, we conducted a study that compared the colours that are associated with a range of emotions and abstract concepts by participants from two very different cultural backgrounds: English and Cantonese. The study was designed to answer the following research questions:

RQ 1. To what extent do the colours that are associated with abstract concepts vary cross-culturally between speakers of English and Cantonese?
Hypothesis 1: We expect some colour-word pairs to be shared across groups, such as "angry" and "red" due to their strong physical basis but we cannot predict the degree of cross-cultural variation across the two languages.
RQ 2. Does performing a word-colour association task in one's second language engender a move towards second language-type associations?
Hypothesis 2: We expect the speakers to move from typical L1 word-colour associations to those of the L2
RQ 3. To what extent does level of agreement both within and across languages correlate with perceived embodiment?
Hypothesis 3: We expect higher levels of agreement both within and across languages for associations that have a physical basis.
RQ 4. Are physically-based L2 word-colour associations more likely to be adopted by L2 speakers than culturally-based ones?
Hypothesis 4: We expect that physically-based associations will be more likely to be adopted by L2 speakers than culturally-based ones.

3 Methodology

In order to answer the above questions, we conducted a two-part study, which involved the administration of two online Qualtrics questionnaires[1] to native

---

1 All materials including the questionnaires, R-scripts and the raw data are available at https://osf.io/yrbp3/

speakers of English and Cantonese and to Cantonese speakers answering in English. In the first part of the study we sought to answer research questions 1 and 2 by identifying the extent to which the colours that are associated with abstract concepts and emotions vary cross-culturally between speakers of English and Cantonese, and the extent to which performing a word-colour association task in one's second language engenders second language-type associations. We consulted native speakers of English and Cantonese as well as dictionaries and language corpora in an attempt to explain cases of variation. In the second part of the study, we sought to answer research questions 3 and 4 by identifying the extent to which the strength of a particular word-colour association both within and across the two languages correlates with its perceived degree of embodiment and whether bodily-based L2 word-colour associations are more likely to be adopted than culturally-based ones.

3.1 Part 1: Variation In Word-Colour Associations in L1 and L2

3.1.1 Participants

In order to answer research questions 1 and 2, we administered a survey that was designed to identify those colours that are most commonly associated with abstract concepts in English and Cantonese[2]. We distributed the survey to 420 participants divided into three groups. The first group, "English L1", consisted of 99 English participants reading and responding in English (45 female, 54 male). The second group, "Cantonese L1", consisted of 195 bilingual Cantonese/English speakers reading and responding in Cantonese (125 female, 70 male). The third group, "Cantonese/English L2", consisted of 126 bilingual Cantonese/English speakers reading and responding in English (98 female, 28 male). The reason for including this last group was that we were interested in exploring whether the responses provided by bilingual English/Cantonese speakers start to approximate those provided by native speakers of English as an L1. Because the participants were randomly selected we have no reason to expect that their levels of English were different, however we acknowledge that our lack of information about their exact level of English is a potential weakness of the study. All of the Cantonese participants had had at least twelve years of formal

---

2 All analyses were performed in R (R Core Team 2017).

English language education and Hong Kong is a bilingual society.[3] The distributions across age groups are shown in Table 1.

Table 1: Age groups and language backgrounds of the participants in part 1 of the study.

Group/questionnaire language	18–24	25–34	35–44	45–54	55–64	65–74
English L1	7	24	37	17	9	5
Cantonese L1	55	79	40	16	4	1
Cantonese/English L2	42	25	31	20	8	0

3.1.2 Materials and stimuli

Prior to the study, we compiled a list of 41 words that people associate with a particular colour in English. In order to generate this list of words, four informants, all of whom were native speakers of English, were asked to list as many words for non-concrete phenomena that they could think of that were associated with the colours yellow, orange, red, blue, green, purple, brown, black, white and grey. The group then discussed these associations and those that made sense to at least three people were retained for the study. Some of the informants included flavours in their list of associations. After some discussion, we decided to retain these items as they involve cross-sensory metaphor, are relatively abstract and may be susceptible to cross-cultural variation. For the sake of completeness, we decided to include four basic flavours (sweet, sour, salty and bitter) but decided to exclude 'umami' as this would be unfamiliar to many of the English-speaking participants. The resulting list of 41 words consisted of words for abstract concepts (e.g. intelligence), emotions (e.g. anger) and flavours (e.g. sweet). The full list is available at https://osf.io/yrbp3/.

In the study, participants were asked to complete an online questionnaire prepared in Qualtrics. This questionnaire contained the aforementioned 41 words gathered for emotions and abstract concepts in their own language (for the English and Cantonese L1 groups) and in their L2 (English) for the Cantonese/English L2 group. These words were translated by a bilingual speaker of English and Cantonese. Back translations were conducted to confirm that the translations were appropriate. For each word, participants were asked to select from ten

---

3 All of the participants in the study were adults which means that they had all received twelve years of compulsory English Language education in accordance with the country's educational regulations.

different colours (yellow, orange, red, blue, green, purple, brown, black, white, grey), which they felt it was most strongly associated with. The exact wording was:

> You will be shown a number of words, each followed by a list of colours. Please select which colour you associate most strongly with each word you see.

They were given the option to say "I do not associate this word with a colour" if they so wished, as well as "I associate this word with a colour that is not listed here" and "I don't know". The sequence of words was randomised for each participant. The questionnaire was administered via a Snowball sampling technique via social media and email.

3.1.3 Statistical procedures

In order to test whether the differences in word-colour associations across the three language groups were significant, we performed a Cochran-Mantel-Haenszel Test for three-dimensional contingency tables, the three dimensions being abstract concept / emotion, colour, and the three language groups. The distribution was significant ($M^2(480)$=33,385, p<.001), indicating that the language groups preferred different word-colour associations. This analysis was complemented by a within-group analysis as well as an across-group analysis for each of the 41 words.

Within-group analysis: We performed a chi-squared test and Fisher Exact Test[4] for each language group and analysed the residuals to establish which associations were most prominent in each language group.[5]

Across-group analysis: To test whether prominent colour associations differed across the groups, we performed Fisher Exact Tests comparing the distribution of colours selected for each word across the three language groups. For this analysis, we were particularly interested in the behaviour of the Cantonese/English L2 group. We wanted to find out whether this group was more likely to respond in a similar way to the Cantonese L1 group, thus retaining their native culture's

---

4 In the data set, some cells have expected frequencies below 5. For this reason, the p-value was obtained by performing a Fisher Exact Test. Residuals, however, are based on the results of the chi-squared test (see footnote 5).

5 The residuals of a chi-squared test indicate how much an observed value in a cell differs from what would be expected given the overall distribution. The residuals obtained here are Pearson residuals which are calculated by the following formula: observed frequency minus expected frequency divided by the square root of the expected frequency. Residuals above 2 and below -2 are usually interpreted as significant. High positive residuals indicate that a colour is more frequently associated with a particular emotion than expected given the overall distribution. High positive residuals thus indicate strong word-colour associations.

association, or converge with the English L1 group, thereby revealing a move towards the L2 associations in their responses.

3.2 Part 2: The Physical Basis of Word-Colour Associations

3.2.1 Participants

In order to answer research questions 3 and 4 (i.e. to ascertain how 'bodily-based' the most prominent word/colour relations for each of the three groups were perceived to be), we compiled and administered a survey to two new groups of participants. They were contacted via the same social media and email networks as in Part 1 of the study and steps were taken to ensure that the people who had participated in Part 1 of the study did not participate in Part 2. This was done so as to avoid a familiarity effect. The first group, "English L1", consisted of 51 English participants reading and responding in English (29 female, 19 male, 3 unspecified). The second group, "Cantonese L1", consisted of 41 Cantonese speakers reading and responding in Cantonese (28 female, 12 male, 1 unspecified). With this survey we aimed to establish whether or not the degree of perceived embodiment supporting a word-colour association related to the strength of that association within a particular language as well as the tendency of the L2 speakers to adopt the association in their L2. The distributions across age groups are shown in Table 2.

Table 2: Age groups and language backgrounds of participants in part 2 of the study.

Group	18–29	30–39	40–49	50–59	60–69
English L1	20	5	10	11	2
Cantonese L1	9	17	9	5	0

3.2.2 Materials

We selected the most frequently associated colour for each of the concepts from Part 1 in both languages and asked English and Cantonese participants to rate the associations according to their perceived degree of embodiment. For concepts where no colour was strongly associated (e.g. for dishonest in English, are shown in Table 2. We still used the most frequent colour. We excluded 'Angry is Red' because it was used as an introductory item. This yielded 40 items for English and

Cantonese participants each, which were presented to participants in a randomised order. Participants were asked to rate on a sliding scale ranging from 0 ("very weak") to 100 ("very strong") the extent to which they perceived the colour-word pair to have a physical origin. There was also a possibility to rate the pair as "not having a physical origin".

3.2.3 Statistical procedures

We then correlated the perceived embodiment ratings for word-colour associations with their relative frequency of selection in the first study to see whether degree of perceived embodiment was related to the popularity of the responses. Furthermore, for those items where the association in Cantonese and English were different, we were interested in establishing whether Cantonese speakers of English as an L2 would be more likely to adopt bodily-based associations than non-bodily-based ones. In order to do this, we inspected the perceived embodiment ratings in all cases where speakers of the two cultures differed in their associations (which we termed 'culture-specific associations') to establish whether the associations used by Cantonese/English L2 speakers converged to the more bodily-based association.

4 Findings

Our findings are discussed in relation to each of the four research questions listed in Section 2.

4.1 RQ 1. To What Extent Do the Colours That Are Associated with Abstract Concepts Vary Cross-Culturally between Speakers of English and Cantonese?

In order to answer this research question, we identified four types of word-colour association: (1) those words for which the two languages exhibited the same word-colour association; (2) those where the two languages had the same main association, but differed in the rest of choices; (3) those where there was some variation in the order but where the overall choices were broadly similar; and (4) those words where completely different word-colour associations were reported. Here we discuss each of these groups in turn.

Table 3 shows the words where the two languages converged in response patterns (group 1)[6].

Table 3: Cases where Cantonese and English associations were similar.

Word	Cantonese	English	Significance of difference[7]
Angry	red (24.5, 93%)	red (20.1, 91%)	**similar (p=.12)**
Dangerous	red (24.2, 92%)	red (17.2, 80%)	different (p<.001)
Disgusted	brown (13.3, 25%) no colour (7.1, 37%) colour not listed (5.0, 9%)	no colour (5.0, 56%) brown (2.6, 11%) colour not listed (2.2, 5%)	**similar (p=.09)**
Dishonest	no colour (9.8, 45%) don't know (2.2, 4%) grey (2.1, 11%)	no colour (5.9, 61%)	**similar (p=.05)**
Formal	black (19.7, 52%) white (4.4, 12%)	black (19.2, 55%) white (2.0, 8%)	**similar (p=.14)**
Furious	red (21.5, 84%)	red (18.5, 85%)	**similar (p=.86)**
Old	grey (23.7, 53%) brown (13.3, 25%)	grey (16.2, 44%) brown (11.4, 31%)	different (p<.05)
Safe	green (13.8, 32%) white (4.1, 12%) blue (3.8, 17%)	green (8.2, 34%)	**similar (p=.12)**

The associations between the words 'angry' and 'furious' and the colour red might be related to the physical reactions that people have to these emotions or experiences, in that they cause blood to rush to the surface of the skin. The motivation for the association between danger and red relate to the natural world where (for example) red-coloured insects and mushrooms being particularly poisonous or it may derive from the fact that in many cultures the colour red is often used in signs warning of danger because this colour stands out more than other colours. The

---

6 Numbers in brackets indicate residuals and percentages. We only report associations with residuals above a value of 2. The higher the residuals, the stronger the association. Percentages indicate which proportion of the group chose the colour for the given emotion.

7 The last column indicates whether the distributions of selected colours for the emotion were significantly different or not (i.e. similar) across the different language groups, based on a Fisher Exact Test for each emotion.

motivation of the relationship between the word 'disgust' and the colour brown may relate to mud and dirt. With respect to the choice of black for 'formal', it can be argued that it may originate in the wearing of black suits at formal occasions (which is accepted practice in both Hong Kong and in the UK). The association of 'old' with grey may have been due to the fact that colours fade when things grow old, and people's hair turns grey with ageing. In Cantonese people are more likely to talk about hair becoming 'white' (rather than grey), which may explain the difference in English and Cantonese association patterns. Finally, the association of the word 'safe' with the colour green is more difficult to explain. It could be related to nature or to the cultural convention of green lights meaning that it is safe to go ahead when driving. It should be noted however that these explanations are highly speculative, and we address the issue of causal factors in a more systematic way below.

Table 4 displays the cases where the overall distribution was different but the first word-colour association was the same (group 2):

Table 4: Cases where the overall distribution was different but the first word-colour association was the same.

Word	Cantonese	English	Significance of difference
Bored	grey (24.7, 55%)	grey (17.9, 48%) brown (4.3, 15%)	different (p<.05)
Calm	blue (20.9, 53%) white (7.3, 17%)	blue (14.8, 47%) green (6.6, 29%)	different (p<.001)
Corrupt	black (13.5, 38%) brown (7.6, 16%) grey (2.9, 13%)	black (11.1, 34%)	different (p<.001)
Depressed	grey (15.4, 37%) blue (9.1, 28%) purple (3.4, 10%)	grey (9.4, 28%) black (7.9, 26%) blue (5.5, 22%)	different (p<.001)
Dirty	brown (20.9, 37%) black (11.8, 35%) colour not listed (2.4, 6%)	brown (25.9, 65%)	different (p<.001)
Energetic	orange (15.6, 37%) yellow (4.3, 15%) green (3.7, 13%)	orange (9.0, 22%) yellow (4.4, 21%)	different (p<.001)
Evil	black (14.9, 42%) purple (9.9, 21%)	black (13.1, 39%) red (4.7, 32%)	different (p<.001)

Table 4 (continued)

Word	Cantonese	English	Significance of difference
Extrovert	orange (9.2, 25%) yellow (2.4, 12%) don't know (2.2, 4%) green (2.0, 10%)	orange (5.5, 15%) don't know (2.4, 5%)	different (p<.05)
Fresh	green (22.5, 48%)	green (19.5, 69%) white (2.0, 8%)	different (p<.001)
Mysterious	purple (15.2, 29%) black (14.2, 40%) grey (2.9, 13%)	purple (13.7, 27%) black (5.5, 20%)	different (p<.001)
New	white (24.4, 45%)	white (12.4, 28%) green (3.9, 21%)	different (p<.001)
Passionate	red (20.4, 81%)	red (17.2, 80%)	different (p<.01)
Sour	yellow (21.6, 49%) orange (5.1, 17%)	yellow (8.3, 32%)	different (p<.001)
Spontaneous	no colour (14.4, 58%) don't know (6.3, 8%)	no colour (4.4, 52%) orange (2.5, 9%) purple (2.3, 7%)	different (p<.001)
Sweet	colour not listed (11.9, 17%) orange (10.5, 27%)	colour not listed (7.9, 13%) orange (7.5, 18%)	different (p<.05)
Truthful	white (8.9, 19%) no colour (5.0, 31%) blue (3.8, 17%) don't know (3.2, 5%)	white (10.5, 25%) blue (3.3, 16%) no colour (2.3, 41%)	different (p<.05)

It is not easy to find reasons for all of these cases of variation but it is possible to identify possible sources in some cases. For example, the fact that 'depressed' is linked to blue in English but to black in Cantonese could be explained by the idiomatic association between sadness and blue in English (e.g. 'feeling blue'). However, the motivation for this association is unknown. A similar hesitation holds for 'evil': the fact that it is more likely to be associated with red in English than in Cantonese perhaps reflects the fact that this is how the Devil is sometimes portrayed; but, again, we do not know what factors lie behind this association.

Table 5 shows the words for which the same associations were offered, but in a different order of preference (group 3).

Table 5: Cases where the same associations were offered but in a different order of preference.

Word	Cantonese	English	Significance of difference
Cheerful	orange (13.7, 33%) yellow (10.7, 28%)	yellow (16.6, 57%) orange (6.0, 16%) colour not listed (2.2, 5%)	different(p<.001)
Excited	red (13.6, 60%) orange (6.8, 20%)	orange (8.5, 21%) red (2.3, 23%)	different(p<.001)
Happy	orange (9.2, 25%) yellow (7.2, 21%) red (3.4, 29%)	yellow (16.6, 57%) orange (2.0, 8%)	different(p<.001)
Harmonious	green (9.9, 25%) white (9.5, 21%) blue (6.9, 24%) colour not listed (2.4, 6%)	blue (4.8, 20%) green (4.6, 23%) white (2.5, 9%)	different(p<.001)
Joyful	orange (9.7, 26%) red (5.9, 36%) yellow (4.5, 16%)	yellow (9.3, 35%) orange (7.0, 18%)	different(p<.001)
Reliable	blue (10.8, 32%) no colour (3.6, 27%) brown (2.6, 9%)	brown (3.9, 13%) no colour (3.6, 48%) blue (2.5, 14%)	different(p<.001)
Sad	grey (19.4, 45%) blue (6.2, 22%)	blue (13.3, 43%) grey (7.3, 23%)	different(p<.001)

Again, whilst we cannot comment on all the patterns in this table, it is interesting to note that both languages associate orange and yellow with the concepts "happy" and "joyful", but it is only in Cantonese where both concepts are also associated with red. This is in line with the culture-specific association of red with positive things in Chinese culture (Xing 2008). Table 3 also shows a shared connection between "calm" and green and blue (yet with different degrees of saliency in each language), perhaps hinting at the common understanding of nature and the sea as peaceful locations. Finally, it is interesting to note that both languages refer to blue and grey when asked about "sad". We have already mentioned that the choice of blue can be accounted for by the English idiom, but it can also be argued that this connection now has international reach as it refers to a well-known musical style. The choice of grey, in turn, might have a greater physical basis, due to the paleness of the skin in depressed emotional states.

Table 6 shows the words that were associated with completely different colours (group 4).

Table 6: Cases where the words were associated with completely different colours.

Word	Cantonese	English	Significance of difference
Bitter	brown (8.6, 18%) black (5.9, 22%) no colour (2.5, 24%) don't know (2.2, 4%)	yellow (3.0, 17%) brown (2.1, 10%)	different (p<.001)
Comfortable	green (16.0, 36%) blue (6.4, 23%) white (5.7, 14%) purple (2.8, 9%)	purple (4.0, 10%) green (2.9, 18%) blue (2.2, 13%) brown (2.1, 10%)	different (p<.001)
Erotic	yellow (25.9, 57%) purple (2.1, 8%)	red (11.6, 59%) purple (5.7, 13%) colour not listed (2.2, 5%)	different (p<.001)
Fearful	black (17.5, 47%)	no colour (3.6, 48%)	different (p<.001)
Grown	no colour (11.7, 50%)	green (8.2, 34%) no colour (2.9, 44%) don't know (2.4, 5%)	different (p<.001)
Intelligent	blue (5.7, 21%) white (5.7, 14%) purple (5.1, 13%) no colour (4.6, 30%)	no colour (6.3, 63%)	different (p<.001)
Jealous	red (8.1, 43%) purple (8.0, 17%)	green (15.2, 56%) red (2.6, 24%)	different (p<.001)
Salty	no colour (8.2, 40%) brown (7.6, 2%) don't know (3.7, 3%) white (2.9, 4%)	white (13.6, 31%) no colour (2.5, 42%)	different (p<.001)
Shy	colour not listed (8.0, 12%) red (3.3, 28%) no colour (2.3, 23%)	no colour (5.3, 58%) don't know (2.4, 5%)	different (p<.001)
Stable	blue (12.7, 36%)	brown (3.9, 14%) blue (3.7, 17%)	different (p<.001)

Cases of clear divergence are somewhat easier to account for. Some can be explained in very practical terms. For example, for speakers of English, the concept of 'salty' is associated with salt but for speakers of Cantonese it is associated with soy sauce or fish sauce, which are both brown. The same association may also explain why 'bitter' is brown for speakers of Cantonese and yellow for speakers of English; whereas soy sauce is bitter as well as salty, lemons are the most prototypical bitter fruit for English speakers. An interesting case is "comfortable", which is associated with the colour green in Cantonese but purple in English. This might be explained by the fact that the word for 'comfortable' in Cantonese connotes nature, countryside and wellbeing, due to the small size of apartments in Hong Kong. In turn, in English, 'comfortable' is perhaps more likely to be associated with soft furnishing inside the house. The word therefore appears to have a slightly different meaning in the two languages in that in English it implies physical contact with an object (such as an armchair or a bed) whereas in Cantonese it refers to the environment more generally.

We now turn to culture to provide possible explanations for the different colour associations for two of the items: 'jealous' and 'erotic'. The fact that the word 'jealous' is associated with the colour green in English can be explained by the idiom 'green with envy', which does not exist in Cantonese; this might explain why Cantonese rely on a more physical word-colour connection (our faces turn red when we experience a strong emotion such as jealousy). Similarly, the fact that 'erotic' is associated with the word 'yellow' in Cantonese probably relates to the fact that pornographic magazines are referred to as 'yellow magazines', though the origin of this term is unclear. English speakers, on their part, rely on red and thus prime the physical basis of this word colour association. This leaves us with the following items: 'fearful', 'grown', 'intelligent', 'shy' and 'stable'. These items are difficult to explain but will be returned to below.

The similarities and differences observed in Tables 1–4 lead us to retain *Hypothesis 1* insofar as some colour-word pairs appeared to be universal across groups, but there was also a degree of cross-cultural variation across the two languages that will be explored in more detail in the following sections.

4.2 RQ 2. Does Performing a Word-Colour Association Task in One's Second Language Engender a Move towards Second Language-Type Associations?

In order to answer this research question, we looked only at cases where the English and Cantonese native speakers' responses differed significantly from each other (group 4). When this was the case, we were interested to see whether the L2 speakers stuck to the most common L1 associations, according to study 1, or whether they converged towards the L2-type associations. Cases of convergence are highlighted in Table 7 in bold.

Table 7: Word associations provided by L2 speakers shown in comparison with native speaker associations in the two languages.

Word	Cantonese native speakers	Bilingual Cantonese/ English speakers answering in English (referred to here as 'L2')	English native speakers	'L2' vs. Cantonese	'L2' vs. English
Bitter	brown (8.6, 18%)	brown (12.0, 28%)	yellow (3.0, 17%)	**similar (p=.32)**	different (p<.001)
	black (5.9, 22%)	black (6.0, 25%)	brown (2.1, 10%)		
	no colour (2.5, 24%)				
	don't know (2.2, 4%)				
Comfortable	green (16.0, 36%)	green (13.6, 44%)	purple (4.0, 10%)	**similar (p=.24)**	different (p<.001)
	blue (6.4, 23%)	white (5.1, 14%)	green (2.9, 18%)		
	white (5.7, 14%)	blue (2.2, 13%)	blue (2.2, 13%)		
	purple (2.8, 9%)		brown (2.1, 10%)		
Erotic	yellow (25.9, 57%)	purple (5.4, 13%)	red (11.6, 59%)	different (p<.001)	different (p<.001)
	purple (2.1, 8%)	don't know (3.6, 9%)	purple (5.7, 13%)		
		red (3.5, 26%)	colour not listed (2.2, 5%)		
		colour not listed (3.2, 10%)			
		yellow (3.2, 17%)			
Fearful	black (17.5, 47%)	black (2.7, 17%)	no colour (3.6, 48%)	different (p<.001)	different (p<.05)
		purple (2.3, 8%)			
		no colour (2.1, 25%)			

Table 7 (continued)

Word	Cantonese native speakers	Bilingual Cantonese/ English speakers answering in English (referred to here as 'L2')	English native speakers	'L2' vs. Cantonese	'L2' vs. English
Grown	no colour (11.7, 50%)	**green (10.0, 35%)**	**green (8.2, 34%)**	different (p<.001)	different (p<.05)
		no colour (2.5, 26%)	no colour (2.9, 44%)		
		don't know (2.1, 6%)	don't know (2.4, 5%)		
Intelligent	blue (5.7, 21%)	blue (6.7, 25%)	no colour (6.3, 63%)	**similar (p=.15)**	different (p<.001)
	white (5.7, 14%) purple (5.1, 13%) no colour (4.6, 30%)	no colour (3.4, 29%)			
Jealous	red (8.1, 43%)	purple (7.7, 17%)	green (15.2, 56%)	**similar (p=.07)**	different (p<.001)
	purple (8.0, 17%)	red (5.3, 33%)	red (2.6, 24%)		
Salty	no colour (8.2, 40%)	no colour (6.4, 41%)	white (13.6, 31%)	different (p<.01)	**similar (p=.11)**
	brown (7.6, 2%)	white (5.9, 16%)	no colour (2.5, 42%)		
	don't know (3.7, 3%)	blue (3.2, 16%)			
	white (2.9, 4%)				
Shy	colour not listed (8.0, 12%)	no colour (5.1, 36%)	no colour (5.3, 58%)	different (p<.01)	different (p<.05)
	red (3.3, 28%)	colour not listed (2.8, 9%)	don't know (2.4, 5%)		
	no colour (2.3, 23%)				
Stable	blue (12.7, 36%)	blue (7.0, 25%)	brown (3.9, 14%)	**similar (p=.33)**	different (p<.01)
		white (3.9, 12%)	blue (3.7, 17%)		
		black (2.5, 16%) no colour (2.1, 25%)			

These results show that in most cases, the responses given in the second language resemble those that are given in the L1. There was only one case where the L2 association converged towards English: 'salty', where the Cantonese/English group chose white over brown (which was the most prominent choice of the English group). The findings for 'salty' could be explained by the fact that the word contains the word 'salt' itself, thus leading the speakers to think of salt itself in their responses. For this reason, this word might therefore be eliminated from the analysis, allowing us to conclude that the strongest tendency was to retain the L1 association.

There were however some cases where the associations produced in the L2 clearly diverged from Cantonese. These were: 'erotic', 'fearful', 'shy' and 'grown'. In the case of 'shy', there was no strong association with any particular colour. In the case of 'grown', the main association is green as was the case in English. Yet, there was still a significant difference between the overall distribution of colours associated with 'grown' in the L2 and English. This might be interpreted as a weak form of conversion. 'Fearful' behaved in a similar way in that the L2 diverged from Cantonese (black was less strongly associated) and moved towards the English association (where black was not associated at all with fearful). Interestingly, for the word 'erotic', the L2 associations differed significantly from Cantonese but they did not converge towards the English pattern (red) in any significant way. In these cases, the L2 speakers appear to have developed a kind of 'interlanguage' in terms of their associations. Consequently, *Hypothesis 2* is only partly confirmed: speakers move from typical L1 word-colour associations to those of the L2, but they also continue to make use of associations that are used in their L1, as one would expect.

Above we saw that for 'happy' and 'joyful', associations in English and Cantonese are fairly similar. However, Cantonese (in contrast to English) also associates red with these positive concepts. Interestingly, red does not emerge as a significant association for 'happy' and 'joyful' in the Cantonese/English L2 group (see Table 8). This may reflect the cultural rather than bodily-based origin of the association between red and happy / joyful.

So far in our study, we have managed to explain some of the associations in terms of practical considerations (e.g. the colour of soy sauce) or idioms whose etymology is unclear (e.g. 'green with envy'). However, we saw above that it may be the case that some word-colour associations both in the L1 and the L2 can be explained by their levels of perceived embodiment. It is to this issue that we now turn by looking first at the role of perceived embodiment in shaping L1 associations (RQ3) and second at its role in shaping L2 behaviour (RQ4).

Table 8: L2 behaviour for happy and joyful.

Word	Cantonese	Cantonese L2	English	L2 vs. Cantonese	L2 vs. English
happy	orange (9.2, 25%)	yellow (9.6, 33%)	yellow (16.6, 57%)	**different (p<.05)**	different (p<.001)
	yellow (7.2, 21%) red (3.4, 29%)	orange (7.9, 27%)	orange (2.0, 8%)		
joyful	orange (9.7, 26%)	orange (10.4, 33%)	yellow (9.3, 35%)	**different (p<.001)**	different (p<.001)
	red (5.9, 36%) yellow (4.5, 16%)	yellow (9.6, 33%)	orange (7.0, 18%)		

4.3 RQ 3. To What Extent Does Level of Agreement Both within and across Languages Correlate with Perceived Embodiment?

Perceived embodiment ratings and strength of association (operationalised by how frequently a colour was selected for a given word in the first study) were highly correlated for both English and Cantonese (for English: $t = 10.483$, $df = 38$, $r = .86$, $p < .001$; for Cantonese: $t = 5.3159$, $df = 38$, $r = .65$, $p < .001$). This finding suggests that, indeed, strongly associated word-colour pairs are more bodily-based. We thus accept *Hypothesis 3* of the study: the overall trend shows a tight correlation between the most prominent word colour choices and their perceived degree of embodiment. Figure 1 (English) and Figure 2 (Cantonese) plot the correlation between the mean perceived embodiment rating for each association and the strength of the association operationalised by the relative frequency of selection, i.e. percentage of how often the colour was chosen for the given concept (please note that for reasons of display the figures do not present the full range of the rating scale, which was 1 to 100).

It should be noted that the standard deviation for the mean ratings is rather high. The standard deviation indicates how strongly individual ratings for an association differ from the mean rating for the association. If the standard deviation is small, the mean is a good summary for the distribution of ratings for a particular association. The higher the standard deviation, however, the more the data points vary within the distribution. For the English perceived embodiment ratings, the standard deviation on average was 27.8. The smallest standard deviation was

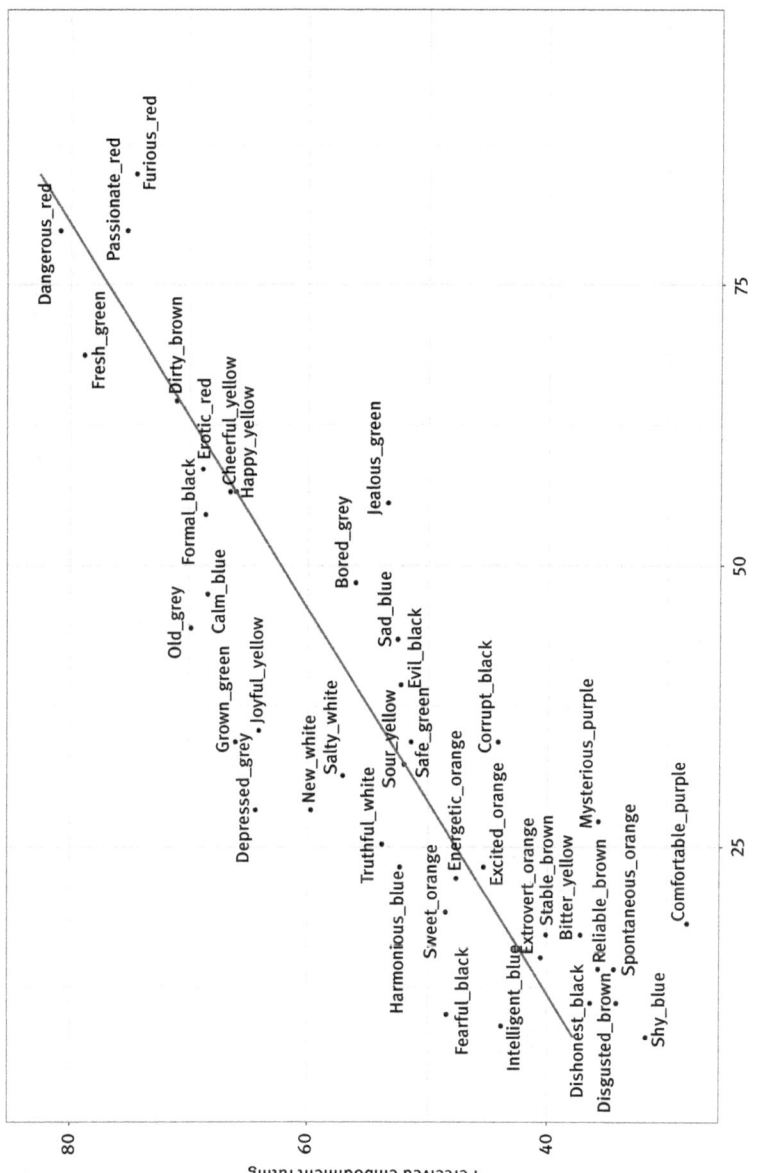

Figure 1: Perceived degree of embodiment for frequently associated word-colour pairs (English).

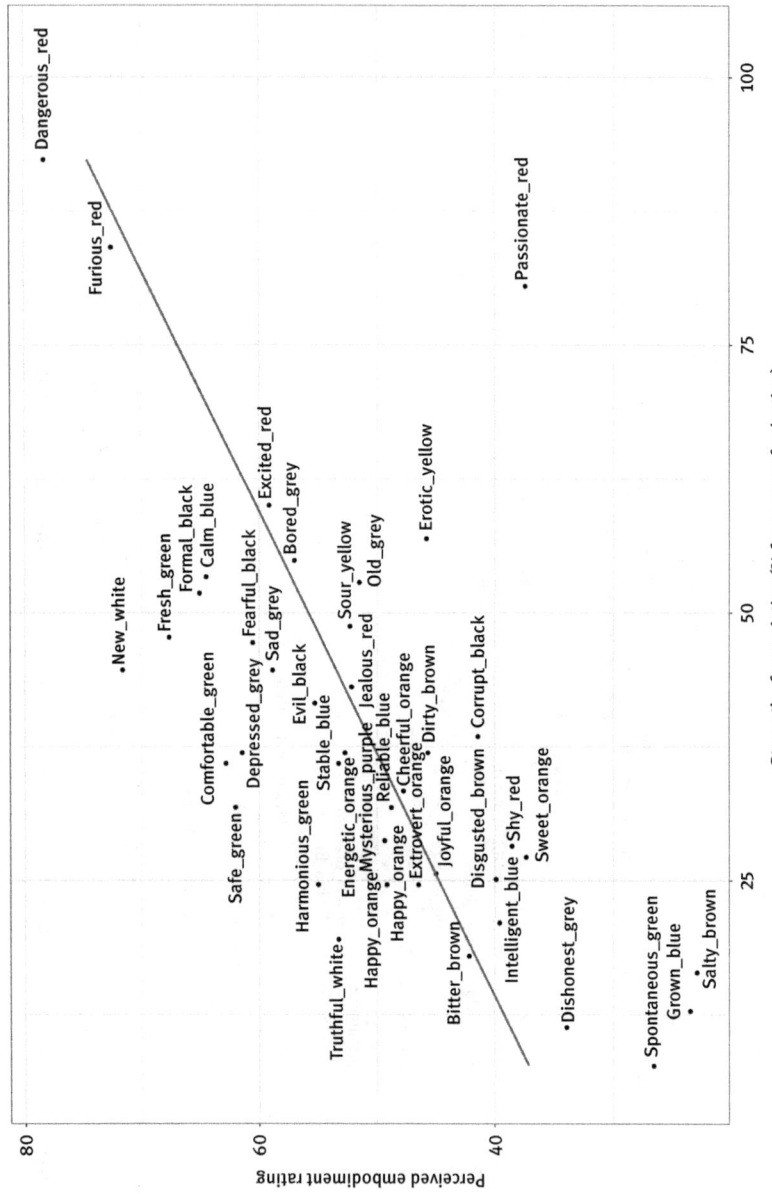

Figure 2: Perceived degree of embodiment for frequently associated word-colour pairs ((Cantonese).

found for 'fresh is green' (SD = 21, variation coefficient 0.27).[8] Thus, this pair exhibited the least amount of variation among participants. The largest standard deviation was found for 'shy is blue' (SD = 29, variation coefficient = 0.91). Thus, this pair exhibited the highest amount of variation, or divergence, among raters.

For the Cantonese perceived embodiment ratings, the standard deviation was equally high. On average, the standard deviation was 27.3, indicating that the individual ratings varied strongly from the mean for a particular association. 'Bitter is brown' showed least variation (variation coefficient = 0.32) and 'salty is white' showed most variation (variation coefficient = 1.54).

Furthermore, it should be noted that when rating the degree of bodily-based motivation for a given word-colour pair, participants also had the option to select "don't associate". It turns out that for some word-colour pairs participants selected this option quite often (e.g. "don't associate" was selected 61% of the times for Jealous is Green in the Cantonese data and even 66.7% for Comfortable is Purple in the English data).[9] The frequency with which this option was selected for a given pair is negatively correlated both with strength of association (t = -6.3435, df = 55, p<.001, r = -.65 for the Cantonese data; t = -8.6991, df = 38, p<.001, r = -.82 for the English data) as well as perceived degree of bodily-based motivation (t = -13.045, df = 55, p<.001, r = -.87 for the Cantonese data; t = -13.464, df = 38, p<0.001, r = -.91 for the English data). This means that participants selected "don't associate" for pairs that were not perceived as being bodily-based and which were not among the most frequent pairings identified in the first study. This finding provides further support for the hypothesis that bodily-based word-colour associations are more universal. We can give two potential explanations for the frequent selection of the "don't associate" option: First, the association might be more cultural than bodily-based, thus "don't associate" was selected; and, second, in the first study, participants may have been pushed to select a colour because there was no "don't associate" option which led to the higher number of "don't associate" answers in the second study for these word-colour pairs.

We also analysed whether perceived embodiment ratings differed significantly between English and Cantonese (Figure 3). Overall, perceived embodiment ratings for shared associations between Cantonese and English (N = 23) were correlated (t = 3.1079, df = 21, p<.01, r = .56). There were only three cases where the mean ratings differed significantly (circled in Figure 3): (1) 'dirty is brown' (t = -4.0264, df = 76.89, p<.001, two-sided, independent samples), (2)

---

8 In order to compare standard deviations, they were normalised by calculating the variation coefficient (Gries 2013: 125).
9 Figures regarding the frequency of the selection of the "don't associate" option can be accessed via the raw data in the online repository.

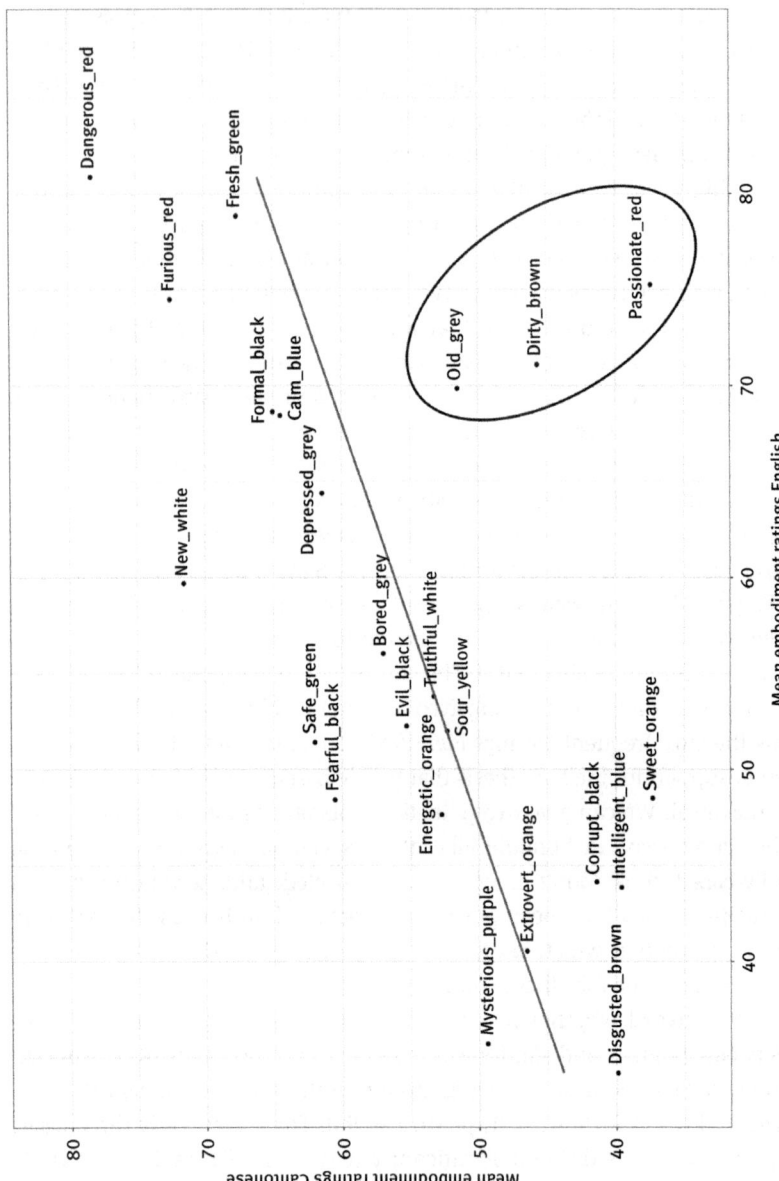

Figure 3: Comparison of perceived embodiment ratings for associations that are shared between English and Cantonese.

'old is grey' (t = -3.3371, df = 76.994, p<.01, two-sided, independent samples), and (3) 'passionate is red' (t = -5.8091, df = 38.72, p<.001, two-sided, independent samples). Our first study showed that in Cantonese, both brown as well as black are almost equally strongly associated with dirty (cf. Table 2). It might be because Cantonese has these two competing colours that dirty and brown were perceived as less bodily-based. With respect to the association between 'old' and 'grey', this was significantly less likely to be perceived as bodily-based in Cantonese than in English. The mean degree of perceived embodiment for 'old is grey' was 51 in Cantonese, and 70 in English. However, the perceived embodiment rating for 'old' and 'grey' in Cantonese was still relatively high. Finally, although 'passionate' and 'red' were strongly associated in Cantonese (actually more so than in English, see Table 2), they were perceived as less bodily-based compared to English. The exceptional character of this word pairing is also clearly noticeable in Figure 3. The reason why the association between 'passionate' and 'red' received such a low degree of perceived embodiment in Cantonese in contrast to its high strength of association requires further research.

In general, this second finding supports the hypothesis that universally shared associations also tend to be more bodily-based, thus confirming *Hypothesis 3*.

4.4 RQ4. Are Bodily-Based L2 Word-Colour Associations More Likely to Be Acquired than Culturally-Based Ones?

In order to find out whether L2 behaviour was driven by degree of perceived embodiment, we considered cases where English and Cantonese differed in their associations (Table 5) and compared these to the perceived embodiment ratings in English and Cantonese. The respective cases were colour associations for 'bitter', 'comfortable', 'erotic', 'fearful', 'grown', 'intelligent', 'jealous', 'salty', 'shy', and 'stable'. See below Figure 4 for exclusive culture-specific associations in English.

We can see that 'grown is green' and 'salty is white' were actually more bodily-based than expected given their frequency of selection. It was for these two pairs that the Cantonese / English L2 group converged towards English. However, even though 'fearful' and 'black' were not significantly associated in English in the first study (cf. Table 5), the association was still perceived as having a relatively high physical basis, as can be seen in Figure 4. The reason why 'fearful' and 'black' were not significantly associated with one another even though there was a great degree of perceived embodiment supporting that connection requires further research. The same applies to 'intelligent is blue', an association which was reported as having a fairly strong physical basis, but which was not found to occur with a high frequency in the first questionnaire.

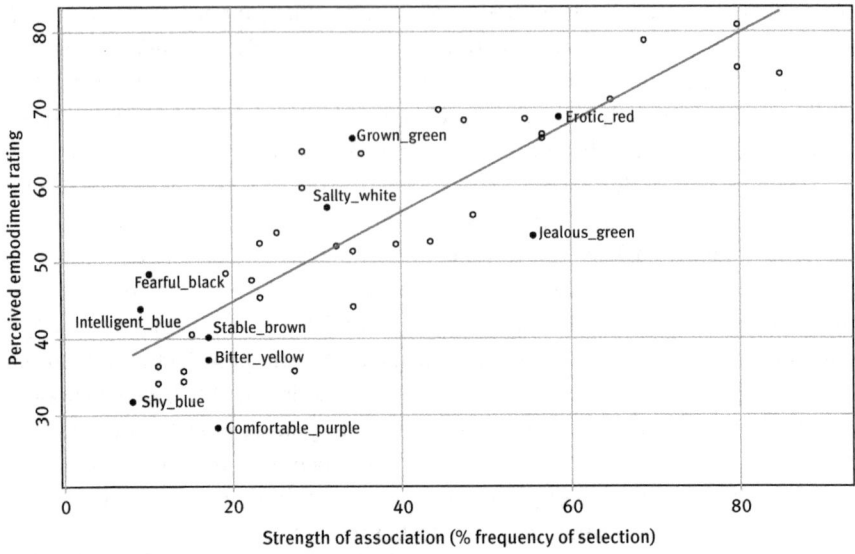

Figure 4: Degree of perceived embodiment for culture-specific associations (English).

The perceived embodiment ratings for associations for 'jealous', 'stable', 'bitter', 'shy' and 'comfortable' were lower than expected given their relatively high frequency of selection. This may explain why we found that the Cantonese / English L2 group did not converge to these specific associations (cf. Table 5).

We now turn our attention to the culture-specific associations for Cantonese (see Figure 5 below). Interestingly, these findings mirror the trends observed for English above. 'Grown is blue' and 'salty is brown' received very low perceived embodiment ratings, and it was for these associations where the Cantonese / English L2 group converged to English. In turn, 'bitter', 'comfortable', 'fearful', 'jealous', and 'stable' received bodily-basis ratings in line with the ratings for the strength of the association (or were even higher), and thus it was in these cases where the Cantonese / English L2 group retained the Cantonese associations.

Two interesting cases that deserve further consideration are 'erotic' and 'shy'. Recall that, for 'erotic', we saw in Table 5 that the Cantonese / English L2 group diverged from the Cantonese associations. This is supported by the fact that 'erotic is yellow' received a comparably low bodily-basis rating. Interestingly, the L2 group still did not converge to the English association, and remained somewhere in between the native and the target language. For 'shy', we can see that in terms of bodily-basis the respective associations received relatively low bodily-basis ratings in both English and Cantonese. This may explain why the L2 did not exhibit any strong preference for shy with any colour.

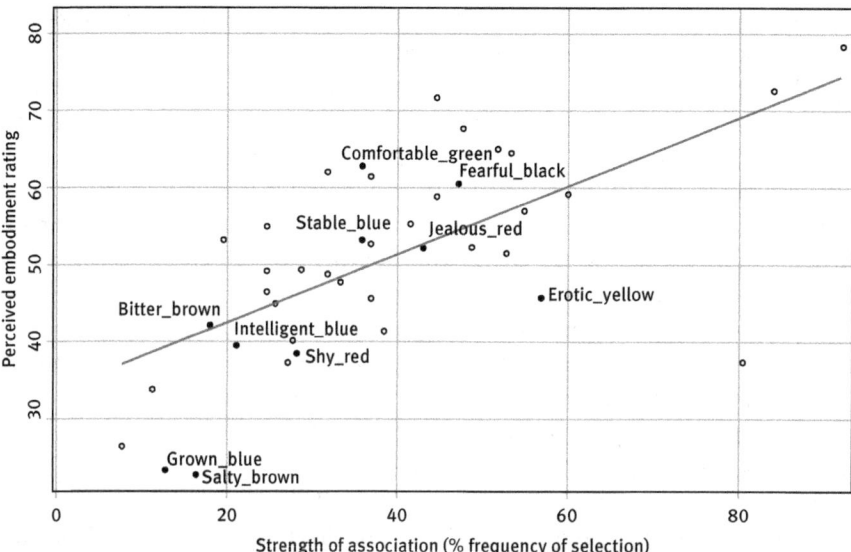

Figure 5: Perceived degree of bodily-basis for culture-specific associations (Cantonese).

Overall, these findings suggest that associations that are formed in the L2 tend to converge to the more bodily-based associations that are present either in the L1 or the L2, much in line with our expectations in *Hypothesis 4*. They also suggest that the less bodily-based an association is in the L1, the less likely it is that a person will remain 'loyal' to that association when they are using their L2.

5 Conclusion

In this chapter we have provided an overview of the most prominent word-colour choices in English and Cantonese. Our data reveals that there is a great degree of convergence between the languages, but more interestingly, a myriad of diverging choices, the study of which has helped to further our knowledge of these two cultures. Whereas some of the diverging choices can be accounted for in terms of cultural differences, the findings from our study suggest that the level of perceived embodiment in the motivation for a particular word-colour association plays a crucial role in determining the level of agreement both within and across languages, as well as the extent to which the association is likely to be adopted by an L2 speaker of the language. These findings provide empirical evidence for the role of perceived embodiment in motivating linguistic and conceptual associations in both the first and second language.

More importantly, our findings have implications for cross-cultural communication, and by extension, the ways in which language teachers deal with implicit meaning, as they suggest that bodily-based associations that have been established in the L1 are more likely to be entrenched than culturally-based associations, and are therefore likely to be difficult to modify when speaking the L2. It would be interesting to investigate whether this pattern also extends to other forms of bodily-based language, such as collocations that are motivated by bodily-based metaphor. For example, Akpinar and Berger (2015) explored the development of collocations over the course of 200 years in a corpus of 5 million books and found that metaphoric collocations that reflect an underlying sensory relationship are significantly more likely to remain in the language than their non-sensory counterparts. Their study revealed that sensory metaphoric collocations were thus 'more culturally successful' than their non-sensory counterparts. For example, the term 'sharp increase' was more likely to remain in the language once it had entered it than the 'severe increase' and the term 'bright future' was more likely to remain than the term 'promising future'. Akpinar and Berger also tested 365 participants on their ability to recall the different terms and found that they were significantly better at recalling the bodily-based metaphorical collocations than their literal equivalents. If these collocations behave in the same way as the bodily-based word-colour associations in our study, then one would expect them to be more entrenched and therefore less resistant to change in cases where the L2 uses a different collocation.

However, a note of caution needs to be sounded as our study was based on correlational analyses and we cannot therefore be sure about the role of causality. Although we have assumed that degree of perceived embodiment explains the frequency of association, it could be that the relationship works in the opposite direction (i.e. where frequent associations lead one to assume that the relationship is bodily-based) or it could be that both frequency of association and perceived embodiment are influenced by a third, as yet unidentified variable.

Other aspects of our data which merit further investigation are those cases where perceived embodiment and strength of association diverge. In other words, it would be useful to conduct an investigation (possibly making use of qualitative methods) into all the cases that appear far from the correlation line in Figures 1 and 2. For example, it would be interesting to explore the idea that 'passionate is red' in Cantonese. This word pair exhibited a strong association in study 1 but received low perceived embodiment scores in study 2. Similarly, the idea that 'fearful is black' was rated as being relatively bodily-based in English and Cantonese but in English it was not at all associated, and in the L2 it was less strongly associated than in Cantonese. Findings such as these are difficult to explain without recourse to interview data.

Finally, other questions that could usefully be explored relate to the range of associations that people make in their first and second language, the reasons that they provide for making these associations, and the role of the participants' idiom knowledge in the first or second language in shaping their responses. In our study, we did not allow for the fact that participants may associate more than one colour with each of the prompts. This is particularly relevant for bilinguals (all of the participants in our study were bilingual speakers of English and Cantonese), who may produce more associations than monolinguals, due to their increased cognitive flexibility and associative networks (Bialystok 2001a, 2001b; Bialystok et al. 2014). Furthermore, we did not ask the participants to provide explanations for their answers. We therefore do not know what motivated their choices. Another consideration is the fact that some L2-type (English) associations may have appeared when participants were performing the task in their first language (Cantonese). More pronounced differences might be found if the study were replicated with inclusion of respondents who were monolingual speakers of a language distant from English. And finally, although we hypothesised that knowledge of idioms may have affected responses to some of the items, we did not explore this systematically. The role played by their explicit knowledge of idioms could be explored through a qualitative examination of the reasons given for their choices and the role played by their implicit knowledge of idioms could be examined through corpus-based frequency studies of the colour-based idioms in each of the two languages. We now intend to conduct a follow-up study in which participants are permitted to provide multiple associations and to motivate their responses. This will be accompanied by a corpus-based analysis of colours and their associated idioms in English and Cantonese, whose findings we will use to help explain some of the variation.

References

Akpinar, Ezgi & Jonah Berger. 2015. Drivers of cultural success: The case of sensory metaphors. *Journal of Personality and Social Psychology* 109(1). 20–34.

Barchard, Kimberley, Kelly Grob, & Matthew Roe. 2017. Is sadness blue? The problem of using figurative language for emotions on psychological tests, *Behavior Research Methods 49* (2).443–456.

Bialystok, Ellen. 2001a. *Bilingualism in development, language, literacy and cognition.* Cambridge: Cambridge University Press.

Bialystok, Ellen. 2001b. Metalinguistic aspects of bilingual processing. *Annual Review of Applied Linguistics* 21. 139–181.

Bialystok, Ellen, Fergus Craik, & Gigi Luk. 2014. Bilingualism: Consequences for mind and brain, *Trends in Cognitive Science* 16. 240–250.

Chen, J., Natalie Kacinik, Yingjun Chen, & Nianyang Wu, N. (2014). Metaphorical color representations of emotional concepts in English and Chinese speakers: Evidence from behavioral data. *Poster session presented at the Society for Personality and Social Psychology conference*, Long Beach, CA.

Gries, Stefan. 2013. *Statistics for linguistics with R. A practical introduction. 2nd edition.* Berlin, Boston: Walter De Gruyter.

Kövecses, Zoltan. 2005. *Metaphor in culture: Universality and variation.* Cambridge, UK: Cambridge University Press.

Kövecses, Zoltan. 2015. *Where metaphors come from: Reconsidering context in metaphor.* Oxford: Oxford University Press.

Matsuki, Keiko. 1995. Metaphors of anger in Japanese. In John R. Taylor & Robert E. MacLaury (Eds.), *Language and the cognitive construal of the world*, 137–151. Berlin: de Gruyter.

Mikolajczuk, Agnieszka. 1998. The metonymic and metaphoric conceptualization of 'anger' in Polish. In Angeliki Athanasjadou & Elzbieta Tabakowska (Eds.), *Speaking of emotions: Conceptualization and expression*, 153–191. Berlin: Mouton.

R Core Team 2017. *R: A language and environment for statistical computing.* R Foundation for Statistical Computing, Vienna, Austria. URL https://www.R-project.org/.

Sherman, Gary & Gerald Clore. 2009. The color of sin: White and black are perceptual symbols of moral purity and pollution, *Psychological Science* 20(8). 1019–1025.

Waggoner, John & David Palermo. 1989. Betty is a bouncing bubble: Children's comprehension of emotion-descriptive metaphors. *Developmental Psychology 25.* 152–163.

Xing, Zhiqun 2008. Semantics and pragmatics of color terms in Chinese. *Journal Of Historical Pragmatics* 9(2). 315–319.

Gill Philip

Metaphorical Reasoning in Comprehension and Translation: An Analysis of Metaphor in Multiple Translations

1 Introduction

Metaphor is routinely said to present a problem in translation (or rather, for translators; see Philip 2016). The evidence to support this hypothesis, however, is pat-
chy. Over recent decades, several scholars have proposed guidelines on how to
tackle the translation problems that metaphor poses, Newmark's (1981) set of procedures being probably the best known (see also van den Broeck 1981; Dobrzyńska
1995; Dickins 2005; Prandi 2010). Such guidelines may suggest ways in which a
translator can deal with metaphor, but remain primarily theoretical. Empirical studies of how translators actually deal with metaphors draw on these, sometimes re-
fining them significantly in the light of their analyses (e.g. Papadoudi 2010;
Shuttleworth 2017). Yet all deal with published or otherwise officially-sanctioned
translations. By the time a translation has reached its definitive version, the strategies used by a translator, and the reasons for doing so, remain opaque. Translation process research offers some insights (see Schäffner and Shuttleworth
2013); equally, we may infer that time constraints or language transfer have influenced translation choices. Ultimately, however, "we cannot retrace the actual
pathways of the translator's decision-making procedures" (Schäffner 2017: 257).

Studying the work of trainee translators offers a different perspective. While it
remains largely impossible to investigate the decision-making process of each individual, the analysis of multiple translations of a given source text offers ample evidence of the strategies that are actually used in translation. It additionally allows
researchers to incorporate aspects of language proficiency into their analysis, a
matter largely taken for granted with professional translations. Both of these issues
are discussed in this chapter, which presents initial findings from ongoing research into trainees' translations, with a particular emphasis on the translation of
figurative language. Section 2 offers an overview of existing research in the field,
and is followed in section 3 with a description of the data and methods used. The
remainder of the chapter is dedicated to matters arising in the translations. Section 4 deals with metaphor comprehension and the role of context in determining

Gill Philip, Department of Humanities, University of Macerata, Macerata, Italy
e-mail: gill.philip@unimc.it

https://doi.org/10.1515/9783110630367-007

translation choices. Section 5 investigates the difficulties posed by creative variants of a conventional metaphor. Finally, Section 6 looks at the interplay between source language proficiency and translation in its examination of a short extract involving metonymy and irony.

2 Student Translation Research

The present research is positioned within a relatively under-explored area of translation studies, one in which novice translator activity is examined by comparing multiple translations. The first attempts to investigate learners' translations began around twenty years ago, Bowker and Bennison's (2003) *Student Translation Archive* (*STA*) probably being the first systematic attempt to compile a computer-readable corpus of learners' translations. The *MeLLANGE* project (Kübler 2008, Castagnoli et al. 2011), drew on this work, expanding the number of languages and including the source texts and some professional translations. An error-tagging inventory was also developed, which forms the backbone of the nascent *Multilingual Student Translation* project (*MUST*, Granger and Lefer 2017), which also features a new query interface designed for the viewing of multiple translations and the original source text.

Other learner translation corpora initiatives have focused on L2 competence rather than translation competence *per se*. These include the Polish-English *PEL-CRA* (Uzar and Waliński 2001) and the Norwegian-English *NEST* (Graedler 2013), which comprise translations into the L2 as a means of examining L2 production. Nacey (2017) investigated aspects of metaphor use in *NEST*, matching translated terms to Newmark's (1981) guidelines for the translation of metaphor and other figurative language. She observes that although different metaphor types seem to incur different strategies, students overwhelmingly prefer to translate (L1) source-language metaphors as metaphors in the (L2) target text rather than paraphrasing or deleting them. However, she does not discuss the quality of the translations, the role of source text interference or the degree to which L2 proficiency *per se* might affect translation choices.

Nacey's (2017) investigation has some points of contact with research conducted into learners' production of figurative language in the L2. Some general trends have emerged and can be summarised as follows. First of all, Nacey (2013) has found that metaphor is at least as frequent in learner writing as it is in native-speaker written production. This is remarkable since many scholars have noted that learners often appear to lack the language awareness necessary to recognize figurative meanings in text (Littlemore 2009) and tend to stick to the core literal meaning of familiar words (Danesi 1994; Littlemore and Low 2006; Littlemore 2009). It is common to find calquing of metaphorical words and phrases (Philip 2006, 2010, 2011a), suggesting that learners assume a connection between word forms and meanings that transcends individual languages. While it would be simplistic to lay the blame entirely on syllabus design, there is a distinct lack of attention paid to metaphorical meaning in the language learning process (see overview in Nacey 2013: 43–61). As a result, learners are ill-equipped to cope with most of the non-literal meanings that they encounter in their foreign language study, with the possible exception of idioms which, despite their apparent prominence, are actually low-frequency vocabulary items (Moon 1998) and are not typical of figurative language in general (Philip 2011b). This chapter intends to investigate whether any of these observations hold true for metaphor comprehension and production in translation.

3 Data and Methods

The data used in this study comprises multiple translations into Italian (L1) of a range of English source texts. The translations were produced by two consecutive cohorts of students studying English and another modern language to advanced (C1–C2) level (mean age 25, native language Italian). The translations were part of a final (5th) year module on metaphor in translation in the Modern Languages and Literatures department of an Italian university, and for this reason the source texts were metaphorically rich, featuring conventional linguistic metaphors, metonymies, metaphorical idioms, analogies, as well as exploitations and creative variants of conventional forms, metaphor clustering, and conceptual metaphor. The initial selection of the source texts was based on their metaphorical content, using an adapted version of MIPVU (Steen et al. 2010) to identify metaphors and other figurative expressions. This analysis informed the sequencing of the texts during the module. Thus texts whose use of metaphor was limited to conventional linguistic and conceptual metaphors were introduced before texts containing creative variants, metaphor clusters and text-structuring metaphor.

Corpus studies of translated texts typically rely on parallel concordances, in which the source text and the target text are aligned at sentence level in order to facilitate querying. By querying a word in the source text, it is possible to view the translation in the equivalent area of the target text. Commercially-available parallel concordancers cannot process multiple target texts, and although some proprietary concordancers can do so, they are restricted to use with corpora which have already been processed and uploaded to the remote server.[1] The current research used *AntConc* (Anthony 2017) to display the concordances via carefully-chosen search terms. These were not hypothetical translations of the source text metaphors, which are expected to vary from translation to translation. Instead, they were unequivocal translation equivalents (e.g. numerals, proper names, technical terms, or words/phrases with only one possible translation) lying in close proximity to the metaphors of interest. By adjusting the viewing settings to show as much context left and right as the software permits, the translations of the metaphors can be viewed by scrolling left or right; they can also be sorted alphabetically to bring out the patterns that emerge. Although the output is not perfectly aligned, it is more than satisfactory for classroom purposes. For more detailed examination, the concordances are extracted and manually aligned, as will be seen below.

4 Comprehension, Context and Translation Choices

Mid-way through *Religion for Atheists*, De Botton deals with the topic of 'Tenderness'. He builds up his argument through a metaphorical framing of Catholicism and Atheism which casts each in stark contrast to the other. The Catholic worldview attracts metaphors of warmth, softness, comfort (particularly with reference to the maternal figure of Mary) as well as negative references to childishness and emotional display; the atheist standpoint is characterised though metaphors of coldness, hardness, sharpness, as well as positively-framed maturity and rationality. This text was presented to cohort 1 in the final lesson, who collectively prepared a definitive version. Cohort 2 tackled the text at an earlier stage (lesson 6).

As a complex persuasive text, many metaphors are present, often occurring in brief bursts. These further reinforce the overriding metaphors mentioned above, and their translation requires not just surface comprehension but also an appreciation of the evaluative stance being conveyed. Here, we will examine the first sentence of paragraph two.

> At its most *withering* and intellectually *pugnacious*, atheism has *attacked* religion for *blinding* itself to its own motives, for being unwilling to acknowledge that it is, at base, nothing more than a glorified response to childhood longings (. . .)
>
> (De Botton 2012: 173, emphasis added)

---

1 Both *NEST* (http://clu.uni.no/humfak/nest/index-e.html) and *MUST* (registered users only) feature such concordancers.

At first blush, the highlighted (italicised) metaphors might be viewed as a sort of mixed metaphor, drawing on three different conceptual source domains. On closer inspection, they can be seen to function together, building up and reinforcing the argument that atheist criticism of Catholicism is powerful and destructive. *Withering* inverts the polarity of the LIFE IS GROWTH metaphor to imply deterioration with little hope of survival. *Pugnacious* (from the Latin word for 'fist', 'punch') and *attacked* appear to exemplify ARGUMENT IS WAR, while *blinding* suggests an extreme interpretation of PHYSICAL INJURY AS IMPEDIMENT, the injury and impediment in this case being permanent and irreversible.

The question arises, with regard to students' translations, as to whether or not this general impression of powerful destructive argument is appreciated (when reading the source text) and adequately conveyed (in the translations). By this stage of the module, students have acquired an initial grounding in the difference between linguistic and conceptual metaphor and are aware that metaphor is not only a literary trope. However, they are only beginning to become familiar with the general principles of the MIP metaphor identification procedure (Pragglejaz group 2007) and its refinement in MIPVU (Steen et al. 2010), and with the different classifications of metaphor in terms of vividness or figurative intensity (Goatly 2007, Hanks 2006). Specific guidelines on how to deal with metaphor in translation, particularly with regard to their deliberate or non-deliberate use (Steen 2014), their conflictual or consistent textual meanings (Prandi 2010), and their power to evoke sensory experience including imagery (Newmark 1981, Shuttleworth 2014, 2017), have yet to be introduced.

Tables 1a–c show the concordances for the first, second, and third parts of the sentence respectively, with the translations of the metaphors highlighted in bold face (duplicates have been removed).

Table 1a: Translations of "At its most *withering* and intellectually *pugnacious*,".

S1	Al più **sferzante**	ed intellettualmente **combattivo**, ...
S2	Al suo massimo **feroce**	e intellettualmente **battagliero**, ...
S3	Nella veste più **spaventosa**	e intellettualmente **combattiva**, ...
S4	Al suo più **spaventoso**	e intellettualmente **pugnante**, ...
S5	All'apice della propria **ferocia**	e intellettualmente **aggressivo**, ...
S6	essendo per la maggior parte **critico**	e intellettualmente **aggressivo**, ...
S7	Nel suo più **profondo**,	e intellettualmente **combattivo**, ...
S8	Al suo massimo **declino**	e intellettualmente **aggressivo**, ...
S9	All'apice della sua **decadenza**	e **aggressività** intellettuale, ...
S10	Al suo massimo **avvizzimento**	e intellettualmente **combattivo**, ...

Table 1b: Translations of "atheism has *attacked* religion ... ".

S1, S3, S4, S6, S8, S10	... l'ateismo ha **attaccato** la religione ...
S2	... l'ateismo ha **criticato** la religione ...
S5, S7	... l'ateismo ha **aggredito** la religione ...
S9	... l'ateismo ha **accusato** la religione ...

Table 1c: Translations of " ... for *blinding* itself to its own motives".

S1	... per **rendere sé stessa cieca** ai suoi motivi ...
S2	... per **eclissarsi** alle sue cause ...
S3	... per **accecare** le proprie ragioni ...
S4	... per il legame stesso alle sue motivazioni ...
S5	... poiché questa **nasconde a sé stessa** i suoi argomenti ...
S6	... per **essersi lasciata abbagliare** dalle sue stesse motivazioni ...
S7	... per **eclissarsi** alle proprie motivazioni ...
S8	... per **aver accecato se stessa** verso le sue proprie motivazioni ...
S9	... di negare l'evidenza ...
S10	... per **abbagliare** i propri motivi ...

The ARGUMENT IS WAR metaphors have, on the whole, been translated well. *Pugnacious*, (Table 1a) for an Italian speaker, bears a clear etymological connection with *pugno* ('fist') which is implied in the cognate *pugnante* and, by extension to the generic domain of fighting, in *combattivo* ('combative') and *aggressivo* ('aggressive') and their derived forms; *battagliero* ('battling') is more explicitly bellicose. *Attacked* (Table 1b) was also translated appropriately, although many of the students fell victim to source-text influence, six choosing the cognate *attaccare* instead of the more appropriate *aggredire*. Although these words are near-synonyms, dictionary definitions indicate that *attaccare* is associated with physical contact (attaching things, and attacking in sports and military attacks) whereas *aggredire* has a well-established figurative sense for verbal attacks (*Oxford-Paravia*). In classroom discussion, it was plain that the students were not aware of these nuanced differences in meaning, yet were it not for the formal similarity with *attack*, it is doubtful that so many of them would have preferred *attaccare* over *aggredire*.

The other two metaphors in the sentence are much more problematic, testified by the far greater variety found in the translations. *Withering* (Table 1a) is conventional but not frequent and is therefore unlikely to have a place in learners' working vocabulary. This makes it an interesting case study as far as translation strategies are concerned, since unfamiliar words prompt students to use dictionaries. However, locating the appropriate meaning in a dictionary is not always straightforward, and much rests on understanding how senses are arranged. The metaphorical sense of *withering* cannot be transferred directly into Italian via the use of the literal equivalent *avvizzire* because it maps onto a different target domain: its metaphorical meaning is "to fade or languish from lack of attention or love" (*Oxford Paravia*).

Of the ten students who produced translations for this text, one (student 10) used the inappropriate literal translation, *avvizzimento*. Two (students 8–9) chose words that are compatible with the Italian metaphorical meanings suggested by *avvizzire* mentioned above, but which are contextually incongruous in this extract, namely *declino* (decline) and *decadenza* (decadence). In other words, the students appreciated that the meaning was metaphorical but failed to recognize the metaphorical meanings of *wither* and *avvizzire* do not correspond. A further individual (student 7) appears to have bypassed the use of dictionaries altogether and guessed the meaning from context alone – no other explanation can account for her translating *At its most withering* with *Nel suo più profondo* ('At its deepest'/ 'at heart'). In all four of these translations (students 7–10), the term chosen is contextually inappropriate and should have been rejected as a result.

Context is all-important, and should be an aid to the translator in ensuring that the choices he or she makes are consistent with the tone as well as the overall meanings being expressed in a text. What *withering* means in this context is reinforced in the lexicogrammar, most obviously through the syntactic coordination of *withering* and *pugnacious* (coordination with *and* normally implies an additional example of the same general idea). More subtle, but essential to the complete understanding of the metaphor, is the point that *withering* is agentive and causative; that is to say, the speaker's words make the hearer *wither*. Six of the translations manage to convey the intended meaning fully, mainly drawing on the source domain of danger: *feroce* ('ferocious'), *spaventoso* ('fearsome'), and *sferzante* ('scathing'). *Critico* ('critical') is the only non-metaphorical translation choice, and is an example of one of Newmark's suggested strategies for dealing with metaphor in translation, namely conversion of metaphor to sense (Newmark 1981: 90). Due to the inappropriateness of using *avvizzire* metaphorically, we can surmise that for the successful translations (students 1–6) students not only recognized that the intended meaning was metaphorical, but also consulted a bilingual dictionary, were able to locate the figurative meaning successfully, and selected words whose meaning were contextually appropriate.

The last metaphor in the sentence, *blinding* (Table 1c) also proved a challenge. In one case (student 4), the metaphor was deleted due to misreading *blind* as *bind* ('legame'). Two students (5 and 9) opted for a literal paraphrase (conversion of metaphor to sense), with *nasconde a sé stesso* ('hide from oneself'), and the more accurate *negare l'evidenza* ('to deny the evidence'). Three other translation options were used, all drawing on the source domain of (lack of) VISION. The first involves derivatives of the verb *accecare* ('to blind') (students 1, 3, and 8). The other two solutions proposed depart from the English word form but are more idiomatically appropriate and convey the intended meaning successfully. They are: *eclissar(si)* (literally, 'to [be] eclipse[d]') chosen by students 2 and 7, and *abbagliare* (literally, 'dazzle') chosen by students 6 and 10. Although the most successful versions (students 2, 3, 7, 9 and 10) adopt different strategies and solutions, they manage to capture the meaning in just a few words. In contrast, the translations that adhere closely to the source text phraseology sound clumsy.

The discussion of the ten translations of De Botton's sentence allows some interim claims to be made regarding the 'problem' of metaphor and how it relates to source text comprehension and target text solutions. In the first place, a source text metaphor has to be recognized as such, because if it is read as literal, the resulting translation will not convey the intended meaning adequately. In some cases the meaning may be radically changed, to the detriment of the translation as a whole. Secondly, it is not enough just to recognise the metaphor, because the translator needs to be able to comprehend its meaning(s) fully. Context helps, but equally important is the lexical environment –the cotext– particularly collocations, grammar, and syntax. Metaphor recognition and comprehension are also identified by Gibbs (1994: 116) as essential for understanding metaphor, although their sequencing appears to be reversed when the stimulus text is in a foreign language (i.e. recognition before comprehension). Finally, conventional linguistic metaphors which co-exist in both source and target languages are on the whole unproblematic in translation, provided the metaphor does not contribute significantly to lexical cohesion, and/or is not involved in word-play. This observation reinforces similar statements made by Steen (2014: 16–17) and Prandi (2010: 318–320) with reference to "non deliberate" and "consistent" metaphor use respectively. Source text influence may, however, lead translators to prefer cognates over more appropriate synonyms.

5 Figurative Thinking and Unfamiliar Lexis in Translation

The translated metaphors in this section feature in an extract from Vance Packard's (1957) *The Hidden Persuaders*, an early text on marketing strategies. The text was presented to two consecutive cohorts of students (a total of 28 translations were submitted). The focus here is on the ways in which the student translators dealt with the author's exploitation of *upper-/ middle- /low-brow* and *brow-wise* in the final sentence of the extract. The exploitations are not codified in monolingual or bilingual dictionaries, making it necessary for students to recognize the metaphors, comprehend them, and then interpret them – this third phase also being listed by Gibbs (1994: 116–117) as essential to the processing of metaphor.

> [Lloyd Warner] defined his social classes not only in terms of wealth and power but in terms of people's consumption and sociability habits. This broader approach to differentiation has received support from other perceptive observers of American society. Russell Lynes, the Harper's editor and writer, in his famous *dissection* of *upper brows, lower brows,* and *middle brows,* used the tossed salad as a more reliable indicator of a person's status *brow-wise* than the size of his bank account.   (Packard 1957: 99, emphasis mine)

Translating anything to do with social class can pose problems due to sociocultural differences in how social status is construed. An extract like this is therefore a real test of comprehension and ability to express an alien concept in a way that is meaningful in the target language. Eleven students translated *upper brows, lower brows, and middle brows* adequately, using words found elsewhere in the extract to bolster their interpretations: seven opted for (social) class, three focused on educational background, and one individual used *strati* ('layers'). The majority, however, found the expression problematic. Five left the English text. Eight used a literal translation equivalent: *fronte* ('brow', 'forehead'), recognising the metonymical connection between high foreheads and intelligence, which is also present in Italian. Four miscued and opted for *sopracciglia* ('eyebrows'). These translations aroused some hilarity in class. One, *delle sopracciglia alzate, delle sopracciglia abbassate, delle sopracciglia al centro* ('of the raised eyebrows, lowered eyebrows and eyebrows in the middle'), evokes eyebrow movement expressing surprise or puzzlement. Another student, having decided upon *eyebrow* as the central translation, translated the expression as *sopracciglia, ciglia inferiori e superiori* ('eyebrows, and upper and lower eyelashes').

These choices had repercussions for the later reference to *brow-wise*. Students who failed to translate *brow* earlier also failed to translate *brow-wise*. Those who had opted for social class or intelligence reiterated this interpretation, as did those who had made reference to foreheads. The 'eyebrow' group produced interesting elaborations on the themes already introduced, adding to the comic relief provided earlier, including a neologism *intelligenza sopracciliare* ('eyebrow intelligence') and a version that suggested that a person's status was determined *in base all'arcata sopraccigliare* ('by their eyebrow shape').

Although the "brow" metaphor was one of the main reasons for selecting this text for inclusion in the course, one of the most problematic features encountered was not a metaphor at all, but a cross-reference to "people's consumption ... habits" (Packard 1957: 99): *tossed salad*. To the native speaker of English, the reference is transparent enough, though its truthfulness might be questioned. The implication is that a preference for salad consisting of iceberg lettuce alone is seen as conservative and culturally impoverished, and is indicative of lower social class. Including more "exotic" leaves such as rocket or lamb's lettuce suggests greater cultural sophistication. The concept was alien to these Italian students, for whom no such cultural stereotype exists: salad is, by definition, mixed.

Twenty students stuck close to the source text's "tossed salad", although several indicated their uncertainty with question marks or set the word apart from the body text with scare quotes. In class discussion, it transpired that they assumed that they were dealing with a metaphorical expression, but since they did not know its intended meaning they decided against deviating from the source text term. This same explanation was given by four students who left a blank at this point in the text. Two students made their figurative interpretation explicit: *l'immagine dell'insalata mista* ('the image of the mixed salad' and *la metafora dell'insalatona* ('the metaphor of the large mixed salad'). A further two students interpreted *tossed salad* metaphorically: as *un modello misto* ('a mixed model') and as *pinzimonio sociale* ('social crutités'[2]), thus preserving the image of the salad within a novel metaphor.

This error –interpreting a literal expression as metaphorical– illustrates a misapplication of *figurative thinking*, defined as "the use of a query routine which assumes that an unknown expression might be figurative" (Littlemore and Low 2006: 6). Here the expression is not unknown, but for these students the literal meaning could not be accommodated into their perceived frame of discourse regarding social class. As we would hope metaphor-aware students might do, they tried to find a way to interpret the intended meaning by matching up their knowledge of salads with plausible contextually-appropriate

---

2 *Pinzimonio* is a selection of raw vegetable sticks to dip in seasoned olive oil or marie-rose sauce.

meanings, as if they were dealing with a metaphor vehicle term. Their efforts were not entirely unsuccessful.

This sentence from Packard's *Hidden Persuaders* raises some additional considerations about the 'problem' of metaphor. As before, it is clear that source text metaphors must first be recognized as being metaphorical, and the meaning in context has to be appreciated in order to find an appropriate candidate term for translation. Source text influence is again seen to lead translators to prefer cognates over more appropriate synonyms. This time, we have seen that this can lead to the coining of new linguistic metaphors (e.g. a new metaphorical use of *fronte* to mirror the English *brow*); it is not clear whether such coinings are a deliberate attempt to adhere closely to the source text or whether the unfamiliar expression creates favourable conditions for an equally unfamiliar expression in the target text. This may therefore be either a deliberate translation strategy (i.e. foreignizing, Venuti 1995) or an interlanguage error, and deserves further investigation. Finally, these students, who are being taught how to identify and interpret metaphorical meanings in text, seem to apply figurative thinking as a general translation strategy for unfamiliar/ incongruous expressions, e.g. in the translations for 'tossed salad'. While the results proved inaccurate in this case, that so many sought a solution outside the realm of the literal can be seen as a vindication of the aims of the module.

6 L2 Language Proficiency and the Successful Translation of Metaphor

During classroom time, when the students' translations were projected on the screen for discussion, it started to become clear that a considerable amount of source text influence was present. This emerged primarily through (over-) adherence to the source text phraseology, syntax, collocations, and lexical choices, and was particularly evident in the second cohort's work. This prompted me to look closer at the grades each of the students had achieved in their C1 language test at the end of the previous academic year and to start matching features in the translations with the five grade bands, A–E. In doing so, what emerged was an immediate confirmation of my suspicions that the first cohort was not simply a 'better' group in terms of translation; their grade point average was indeed a full band higher[3]than that of the second cohort and their Reading/use of English was two bands higher.[4] This suggests that a significant cause of the second cohort's translation problems was, in fact, their lower overall proficiency in English, particularly their ability to fully understand and interpret the source texts.

An overview of each cohort's L2 language proficiency is shown in Table 2. What the grade bands of these students does not immediately suggest is that students' English language proficiency should affect the quality of translations into the L1, Italian. The translations prepared by students with lower L2 proficiency were consistently less sophisticated than those of their peers. In addition to calqued words, collocates and phrases, it is noticeable that the target text lexis often fails to reflect the nuances present in the source text. While it may be misplaced to assume that all students should be equally proficient in their L1 writing skills, there does appear to be a connection between lower L2 comprehension and shortcomings in L1 translation.

Table 2: English language proficiency at level C1, cohorts 1 and 2.

Grade band	Cohort 1	Cohort 2
A (30/ 30 e lode)	4	0
B (27–29)	8	2
C (24–26)	4	7
D (21–23)	1	5
E (18–20)	0	1
Total	17	15

To illustrate how lower overall language proficiency can impact translation, this section focuses on part of a short essay entitled "What Contemporary Art Means to Me", in which the art critic David Lee lambasts the pretentiousness of young contemporary artists. The text was chosen so that students could try their hand at translating irony, contempt and incremental use of invective, and was translated by 28 students in total – 14 from each cohort. The extract discussed here opens the essay.

---

3 Cohort 1's mean overall C1 language proficiency score was 27/30 [B], compared to 24/30 [C] for Cohort 2.
4 Cohort 1's mean reading comprehension and use of English score was 26/30 [C], compared to 20/30 [E] for Cohort 2.

What does 'contemporary art' mean to me, as distinct from plain old 'art'?
First of all, it means an income. Not a very good one, but editing a magazine like Art Review beats working for a living, especially if the alternative requires *kowtowing* to a *suit* with a business studies degree from the University of *South Bacup*.

(Lee 2000: 197, emphasis mine)

Kowtow, a term borrowed from Chinese, is defined in *Collins COBUILD* as follows: "If you say that someone *kowtows* to someone else, you are criticizing them because they are too eager to obey or be polite to someone in authority". Two bilingual dictionaries (*Il Ragazzini, Oxford Paravia*) paraphrase the term as *prostrarsi (davanti a)* ('prostrate oneself [before]') but do not offer an alternative which fully captures the metaphorical and pragmatic nuances. The students overwhelmingly opted for two translations – *prostrarsi* as found in the dictionary (13) and the somewhat more suitable *inchinarsi* ('to bow') (10), or other similar images (*piegarsi* 'bend down/over', and *inginocchiarsi* 'kneel'), as can be seen in Table 3.

Table 3: Translations of *kowtow* and their distribution over the five English proficiency grade bands.

Grade band	bow	prostrate	other
A (30/ 30 *e lode*)	–	prostrarsi (1)	scodinzolare (1)
B (27–29)	inchinarsi (5)	prostrarsi (2)	–
C (24–26)	inchinarsi (5) prostrarsi (1)	prostrarsi (5)	convertire (1)
D (21–23)	piegarsi (1)	prostrarsi (4)	fare salamelecchi (1)
E (18–20)	–	prostrarsi (1)	–
Total	12	13	3

The students who adapted the dictionary definition, interpreting it as more likely to be 'bow' than 'prostrate' can be seen to belong to the grade bands B and C; those who took the dictionary definition at face value come from all levels but there is a concentration at grades C–D. No difference was found between students studying Chinese as their second foreign language (L3) and the others. What did come as a surprise, however, was that only two students –neither of whom knew Chinese– provided idiomatic and pragmatically complete translations. One (L3 French) used *fare salamelecchi*, a borrowing from Arabic which translates literally as 'to do Salaam Aleikums' which captures the deferential attitude in the action and the observer's disapproval; another (L3 Russian) opted for *scodinzolare* ('to wag one's tail'), recalling the behaviour of a dog eager to please its master. The animal metaphor used of a human's behaviour conveys a negative evaluation. There was one anomalous translation (*convertire* – to convert) which looks like a guess based on superficial phonemic similarities.

Kowtow collocates with the metonymy *suit*, which also produced a range of translations, shown in Table 4. In class discussion of the students' translations, we reached the consensus that the best translation was simply *cravatta* ('tie'), which none of the students suggested in their written translation tasks: the eleven students who used *cravatta* (mainly grade bands B and C) did so in conjunction with *giacca* ('suit jacket'), and all but one added *uomo* (or synonym) to explicitate the metonymy as 'a man in a suit and tie'. A further ten students (examples from all grade bands, with a concentration at C and below) translated the item of clothing, using a range of possible synonyms, none of which adequately preserved the figurative meaning in the Italian text. Three students adapted the metonymy, demonstrating that they understood that *suit* referred to the person wearing a suit, e.g. *un uomo d'affari* ('a businessman') or a *manager*, or *qualche elegantone* ('some sharp-dresser', maintaining the tone of contempt in the ST). Four students (grades C and D) interpreted suit as *causa* ('law-suit'), despite the absence of a supportive context for this meaning.

Table 4: Translations of *suit* and their distribution over the five English proficiency grade bands.

Grade band	giacca e cravatta	literal translation	person	wrong meaning
A (30/ 30 *e lode*)	–	divisa (1)	elegantone (1)	–
B (27–29)	6	completo (1)	–	–
C (24–26)	4	completo (2) abito (1) tailleur (1) vestito (1)	un uomo d'affari	causa (2)
D (21–23)	1	completo (2)	un manager	causa (2)
E (18–20)	–	costume (1)	–	–
Total	11	10	3	4

As the data in Table 5 demonstrates, the fictitious placename *South Bacup* generated little in the way of variation, probably because language learners are encouraged early on not to translate proper names unless there is an existing translation in the TL. That said, from the tone of the earlier part of the sentence in which it occurs, a reader ought to understand that the place being referred to is insignificant, making South Bacup either a real place that is held as emblematic of

Table 5: Translations of *South Bacup* and their distribution over the five English proficiency grade bands.

Grade band	No translation	Literal translation	Creative translation
A (30/ 30 *e lode*)	2	–	–
B (27–29)	5	2	–
C (24–26)	8	2	Nulla (1)
			Ripiegoland (1)
D (21–23)	3	2	Merendine (1)
E (18–20)	–	–	Stocavolo (1)
Total	18	6	4

insignificance, or an invented place. Most students did not alter the place name, although one did put scare quotes around it. Six students Italianised the location by translating South as *sud* (5) or *meridionale* (1). This effectively reinforces the literal meaning, while the English term allows some ambiguity to remain.

Of the four creative translations, there are two 'real' words: *Nulla* ('nothing[ness]') and *Merendine* ('children's snacks') plus two creative forms: *Stocavolo*, derived from *'sto cavolo* (a euphemistic slang expression used to express sarcastic disaffection) and Ripiegoland, which draws on *ripiego* ('I fold/ bend over') attached to the suffix *–land*, used for the names of entertainment parks throughout Italy. All four variants work exceedingly well, conveying contempt, sarcasm and belittlement, and they were much appreciated by the students' colleagues – several of whom confessed that they had been unsure how much licence they could take in preparing their translations and had, as a consequence, chosen the safe option of non-translation. The higher-achieving students were, at least in this case, more conservative than their peers in preparing their work. It can be hoped that the class discussions of the examples give them more confidence in the future to attempt interpretative translations which depart from the source text wording.

This final extract adds a further nuance to the 'problem' of metaphor in translation: L2 competence. While it is impossible to make conclusive claims on the basis of one source language term, there seems to be enough evidence to support the idea that lower proficiency is linked to a tendency to interpret metaphorical language as literal, even when the context suggests otherwise. The higher the students' proficiency, the more likely they are to adapt and contextualise the translations proposed by bilingual dictionaries. Weaker students are less inclined to adopt translation solutions which deviate from the ST wording and may even fail to identify the correct meaning of figurative expressions. They appear to be more concerned with translating individual words than they are of translating texts, and as a result their efforts may feature inexplicable incongruities. That said, there are some aspects of learner behaviour which are not ascribable to proficiency level alone. Some students –including high-achievers– may be surprisingly conservative in their work, conscious as they are of having to fulfil the expectations of the academic environment in which they are operating. In the example discussed in this section, we have seen that students at the upper bands of level C1 almost always recognize metaphors and attempt to translate them as such, but they are inclined to explicitate, as in the translation of *suit* as *uomo in giacca e cravatta* ('*a man* in a suit'). Conversely, despite sometimes mistranslating metaphors (especially if they have interpreted them as literal), lower-achieving students also have their moments of glory, suggesting effective translations that their 'better' classmates can learn from. Clearly, a translation is evaluated as a whole and not for occasional flashes of brilliance, but the point here is that explicit training in how to deal with figurative language in translation does bear fruit.

7 Conclusions

In this chapter I have offered an overview of an ongoing research and teaching project dealing with metaphor in translation. It has emerged over the three years that I have been collecting and analysing data that metaphor is problematic in translation, mainly because learners have not acquired the necessary tools for identifying figurative language (idioms excepted), have not been encouraged to investigate polysemy, and at a certain point in their language learning they get stuck in the rut of literal meaning. By encouraging advanced learners to notice metaphors in non-fiction, to observe how they contribute to written texts and to appreciate how their meanings can be interpreted, we arm them with a set of essential skills. These help them to move forward both in their language learning and in their translator training by showing them how to deal with words and meanings that are not necessarily codified in dictionaries.

References

Dictionaries

Collins *COBUILD on CD ROM* v. 1.0. Glasgow: HarperCollins.
Oxford-Paravia Italian Dictionary, 2nd edn. 2006. Oxford: Oxford University Press.
Il Ragazzini Dizionario Inglese Italiano – Italiano Inglese 3rd edn. 1995. Bologna: Zanichelli.2

Other References

Anthony, Laurence. 2017. *AntConc* version 4.3.4. Waseda University: Tokyo http://www.lauren ceanthony.net/software/antconc/ (accessed 23 February 2018).

Bowker, Lynne & Peter Bennison. 2003. Student translation archive and student tracking system. Design, development and application. In Federico Zanettin, Silvia Bernardini & Dominic Stewart (eds.), *Corpora in translator education*, 103–117. Manchester: St Jerome.

Castagnoli, Sara, Dragos Ciubanu, Kerstin Kunz, Natalie Kübler & Alexandra Volanchi. 2011. Designing a learner translator corpus or training purposes. In Natalie Kübler (ed.), *Corpora, language, teaching, and resources: From theory to practice*, 221–247. Berlin: Peter Lang.

de Botton, Alain. 2012. *Religion for atheists*. London: Penguin.

van den Broeck, Raymond. 1981. The limits of translatability exemplified by metaphor translation. *Poetics Today* 2(4). 73–87.

Danesi, Marcel. 1994. Recent research on metaphor and the teaching of Italian. *Italica* 71. 453–464.

Dickins, James. 2005. Two models for metaphor translation. *Target* 17(2). 227–273.

Dobrzyńska, Teresa. 1995. Translating metaphor: Problems of meaning. *Journal of Pragmatics* 24(6). 595–604.

Gibbs, Raymond W. Jr. 1994. *The poetics of mind*. Cambridge: Cambridge University Press.

Goatly, Andrew. 2007. *The language of metaphors*. London: Routledge.

Graedler, Anne-Line. 2013. NEST – a corpus in the brooding box. *Corpus linguistics and variation in English: Focus on non-native Englishes*. http://www.helsinki.fi/varieng/se ries/volumes/13/graedler/ (accessed 6 April 2018)

Granger, Sylviane & Marie-Aude Lefer. 2017. *General report of the MUST kickoff meeting, 2–3 December 2016*. Centre for English Corpus Linguistics – Université catholique de Louvain. Louvain-la-Neuve.

Hanks, Patrick. 2006. Metaphoricity is gradable. In Anatol Stefanowitsch & Stephan Th. Gries (eds.), *Corpus-based approaches to metaphor and metonymy*, 17–35. Berlin: Mouton De Gruyter.

Kübler, Natalie. 2008. A comparable learner translator corpus: Creation and use." *LREC 2008 workshop on comparable corpora*, 73–78.

Lee, David. 2000. What contemporary art means to me. In Ivo Mosley (ed.), *Dumbing down: Culture, politics and the mass media*, 197–199. Bowling Green (OH): Imprint Academic.

Littlemore, Jeannette. 2009. Applying cognitive linguistics to second language learning and teaching. Basingstoke: Palgrave MacMillan.

Littlemore, Jeannette & Graham Low. 2006. *Figurative thinking and foreign language teaching*. Basingstoke: Palgrave MacMillan.

Moon, Rosamund. 1998. *Fixed expressions and idioms in English*. Oxford: Clarendon.

Nacey, Susan. 2013. *Metaphors in learner English*. Amsterdam & Philadelphia: John Benjamins.

Nacey, Susan. 2017. Metaphor in multiple learner corpus translations. In Pieter de Haan, Sanne van Vuuren & Rina de Vries (eds.), *Language, learners and levels: Progression and variation*. Corpus and language use – proceedings 3, 227–252. Louvain-la-Neuve: Presses Universitaires de Louvain.

Newmark, Peter. 1981. *Approaches to translation*. Oxford: Pergamon.

Packard, Vance. 1957. *The hidden persuaders*. London: Penguin.

Papadoudi, Dafni. 2010. *Conceptual metaphor in English popular technology and Greek translation*. Manchester: University of Manchester. PhD thesis. https://core.ac.uk/download/pdf/40036079.pdf (accessed 12/ 09/2018)

Philip, Gill. 2006. Metaphor, the dictionary, and the advanced learner. In Elisa Corino, Carla Marello & Cristina Onesti (eds.), *Proceedings XII EURALEX international congress*, 895–905. Alessandria: Edizioni dell'Orso.

Philip, Gill. 2010. "Drugs, traffic, and many other dirty interests": Metaphor and the language learner. In Graham Low, Lynne Cameron, Alice Deignan & Zazie Todd (eds.), *Researching and applying metaphor in the real world*, 63–79. Amsterdam & Philadelphia: John Benjamins.

Philip, Gill. 2011a. " . . . and I dropped my jaw with fear": The role of corpora in teaching phraseology." In Natalie Kübler (ed.), *Corpora, language, teaching and resources*, 49–68. Frankfurt: Peter Lang.

Philip, Gill. 2011b. Colouring Meaning. Collocation and connotation in figurative language. Amsterdam: John Benjamins.

Philip, Gill. 2016. Review of Miller, D. & Monti, E. (eds.). (2014). Tradurre figure/ Translating figurative language. *Metaphor and the Social World* 6(1). 156–168.

Pragglejaz group. 2007. MIP: A method for identifying metaphorically used words in discourse. *Metaphor and Symbol* 22(1). 1–39.

Prandi, Michele. 2010. Typology of metaphors: Implications for translation. *Mutatis Mutandis* 3(2). 304–332.

Schäffner, Christina. 2017. Metaphor in Translation. In Elena Semino & Szofia Demjén (eds.), *Routledge handbook of metaphor and language*, 247–257. London: Routledge.

Schäffner, Christina & Mark Shuttleworth. 2013. Metaphor in translation: Possibilities for process research. *Target* 25(1). 93–106.

Shuttleworth, Mark. 2014. Translation studies and metaphor studies: possible paths of interaction between two well-established disciplines. In Donna Miller & Enrico Monti (eds.), *Tradurre figure / Translating figurative language*, 53–65. Bologna: Bononia University Press.

Shuttleworth, Mark. 2017. *Studying scientific metaphor in translation*. London: Routledge.

Steen, Gerard. 2014. Translating metaphor: What's the problem? In Donna Miller & Enrico Monti (eds.), *Tradurre figure / Translating figurative language*, 11–24. Bologna: Bononia University Press.

Steen, Gerard, Aletta Dorst, Berenicke Herrmann, Anna Kaal, Tina Krennmayr & Trintje Pasma. 2010. *A method for linguistic metaphor identification: from MIP to MIPVU*. Amsterdam & Philadelphia: John Benjamins.

Uzar, Rafał & Jacek Waliński 2001. Analysing the fluency of translators. *International Journal of Corpus Linguistics* 6. 155–166.

Venuti, Lawrence. 1995. The translator's invisibility: A history of translation. London: Routledge.

Tina Krennmayr
Metaphorical Alignment in Cross-Cultural Office Hours' Consultations

1 Introduction

When people engage in conversations, about 7.7 per cent of their speech is metaphorical (Kaal, 2012). Metaphors in talk are largely conventional (Cameron, 2003; Kaal, 2012). They display dynamic patterns that develop as speakers take turns speaking. They may be repeated, relexicalized, contrasted, expanded or elaborated on (Cameron and Maslen 2010), thereby creating systematicity in metaphor use. People may be "bouncing them back and forth, co-creatively recycling, extending, fine tuning and retuning each other's metaphors" (Carter 2004: 121). When a topic is particularly difficult, metaphors tend to occur in clusters (Cameron and Stelma 2004). "People use metaphor to think with, to explain themselves to others, to organise their talk, and their choice of metaphor often reveals – not only their conceptualisations – but also (...) their attitudes and values" (Cameron 2008: 197). Metaphors in conversation thus fulfill a number of important roles.

In educational contexts, metaphor can be a powerful tool for lecturers to help their students understand new and abstract concepts (Beger 2011). Lecturers furthermore use metaphors to organize their lecture, to frame problems or to change topic (Corts and Pollio 1999, Low 2010, Low, Littlemore and Köster 2008). For international students who follow their education in a non-native language, this has important consequences. They need to be able to produce and understand metaphorical language. This is not easy. Knowing how to navigate metaphor in talk may contribute to a learner's ability to understand as well as to successfully convey meanings.

Conceptual and linguistic differences in metaphor may lead to miscommunications and misunderstandings in intercultural contexts. In their analysis of university lectures, Littlemore (2001) and Littlemore, Chen, Barnden, and Koester (2011) found that overseas students tended not to understand or to misinterpret metaphors. Misinterpreting metaphors means that the students failed to understand the meanings the lecturers intended and, at the same time, were not aware that they misunderstood. An example of such a misunderstanding is the metaphorical use of the conventional metaphor *point*, in 'some point over the next

Tina Krennmayr, Vrije Universiteit Amsterdam, Amsterdam, Netherlands,
e-mail: t.krennmayr@vu.nl

https://doi.org/10.1515/9783110630367-008

week' where a student interpreted the word to mean 'interesting topic', rather than a reference to a particular moment in time (Littlemore et al., 2011: 15). Learning to navigate metaphors in talk seems to be key to a learner's ability to understand as well as to successfully convey meanings.

In lectures, there is limited opportunity for engaging with the instructor, and failures to understand can be difficult to address. May face-to-face conversations between lecturers and students provide an opportunity to minimize non- and misunderstandings? Do they allow students and lecturers to communicative more effectively and may they thus provide better learning experiences for international students?

This study investigates metaphorical alignment of metaphor use in a teaching context where speakers use English as a lingua franca. It explores a new and relatively quick way of uncovering linguistic alignment (or the lack thereof) between speakers in the context of office hours' consultations at university: the software tool Wmatrix (Rayson 2008).

Students whose first language is not English tend to misinterpret English language metaphors used by lecturers (Littlemore 2001, 2003; Littlemore et al. 2011). This is because metaphors can differ across linguistic and cultural communities in several ways. Metaphors in one language can be rare or may not exist in another (e.g. Deignan 2003); they may be used in both but may differ in their frequency of use (e.g. Boers and Demecheleer 1997) or may differ in details. For example, anger metaphors in Chinese conceptualize heat as a hot gas – not as a liquid, as in English (e.g. Yu 1995).

The metaphors most likely to be culture-dependent are complex metaphors. For instance, the source domain of the THE MIND IS A COMPUTER metaphor (e.g. human *memory storage*) is probably unavailable in cultures not exposed to that technology. Primary metaphors (Grady 1997), on the other hand, are more closely rooted in physical experiences, and thus less likely to vary across cultures, since the physical experiences are shared (e.g. conceptual metaphors such as LESS IS DOWN; his results are *below* average).

Yet even metaphors rooted in physical experience have been shown to be instantiated in different ways across languages (see Ibarretxe-Antuñano 2013). While knowledge in the Western world is often talked about in terms of sight (e.g. I *see* what you mean; you can also *view* this from a different *perspective* (e.g. Danesi 1990; Sweetser 1991), this is not the case in many Australian languages where knowledge is talked about in terms of hearing (Evans and Wilkins 2000). Another example of a metaphor that is regarded as universal, namely anger as a pressurized container, has been shown to exhibit differences across languages. Differences pertain, for example, to the kind of container involved (the heart in Zulu, the belly in Japanese etc.), what kind of substance fills the container (a gas in Chinese, a liquid in English) and whether the substance is heated or not (Kövecses 2005).

While Zulu, Chinese and English are quite dissimilar, more closely related languages also display differences. For example, the metaphorical sense of *see* (understand) is used twice as often than the literal one in the British National Corpus. This difference is less pronounced with the Spanish (*veo*) and the Basque (*ikusten dut*) equivalents (Ibarretxe-Antuñano 2013). Clearly there are not just differences in metaphorical conceptualizations and linguistic form, but also differences in use.

Littlemore, MacArthur, Cienki and Holloway's (2012) data consisting of one-on-one sessions between lecturers and students reveal that native speakers share metaphors when talking to each other. They repeat them and toss them back and forth, thereby generating discourse coherence and shared understanding. This observation is along the lines of what Niederhoffer and Pennebaker (2002) found for other word categories than metaphor (e.g. prepositions or past tense verbs). They discovered that people communicating with each other seem to coordinate their interaction by "matching" their word use, both on a conversational and on a turn-by-turn level. In other words, even at the basic word level, conversational partners' choice of words unrelated to content is very similar. While non-native speakers participating in Littlemore et al.'s (2012) tutoring sessions are sometimes able to share and further develop metaphors, misunderstandings are common. The interlocutors are not always aware that one speaker used the words literally while the other one meant them metaphorically, and the other way around. As a consequence of the resulting misunderstandings, communicative goals may not be achieved.

MacArthur, Krennmayr and Littlemore (2015) have also gone beyond researching metaphors in the rather unidirectional discourse setting of the lecture, in their case by investigating office hours' consultations between lecturers and students using English as a lingua franca. Besides some overlap, they found divergent uses of the ways lecturers and students metaphorically talked about knowledge and understanding. They detected substantial differences in terms of frequency, forms and meanings of UNDERSTANDING IS SEEING metaphors. Successful metaphor use seems to be dependent on "the way the conversational partners enact their roles as collaborative participants" (MacArthur, 2016). Thus, what seems crucial in cross-linguistic and cross-cultural research on metaphor use in face-to-face conversations is to investigate in how far the conversational partners 'align' their use of metaphors. Do they take them up and repeat them? Do they reformulate them or expand and elaborate on them?

This is, to my knowledge, the first study combining computational tools for identifying metaphorical lexis and an investigation of metaphorical alignment between speakers in a lingua franca situation. An analysis of semantic domains, (which are treated as roughly corresponding to source domains) that are over- or underrepresented in the lecturer versus the student sub-corpus, can provide insight into the degree of alignment between speakers. It is important to note though, that lack of alignment does not automatically mean that listeners did not understand the metaphors introduced by their interlocutors. This research can serve as a basis for further research that examines whether conversational partners have actually understood the metaphors offered.

2 The Wmatrix Annotation Tool

Wmatrix (Rayson 2008), a web interface for corpus analysis, contains the USAS (UCREL semantic analysis system) (Rayson, Archer, Piao and McEnery 2004), a framework that automatically annotates each word of a running text semantically. It was not designed for the purposes of metaphor analysis. The system is built on a large semantic lexicon. Each item in this lexicon has a syntactic tag as well as one or multiple semantic tags assigned to it. The semantic tagset is categorized into 21 main semantic fields, which are further subdivided into 232 more fine-grained semantic labels. The original tagset was loosely based on the *Longman Lexicon of Contemporary English* (McArthur 1981) but has since been revised (Archer, Wilson and Rayson 2002). An example of the semantic field called *sensory* (X3) is presented below:

X3	Sensory
X3.1	Sensory: Taste
X3.1+	Tasty
X3.1–	Not tasty
X3.2	Sensory: Sound
X3.2+	Sound: Loud
X3.2–	Sound: Quiet
X3.3	Sensory: Touch
X3.4	Sensory: Sight
X3.4+	Seen
X3.4–	Unseen
X3.5	Sensory: Smell
X3.5–	No smell

The letters and the first digit designate a semantic field at its most general level. Added digits after a dot indicate subdivisions; the finer the subdivision, the more digits there are. The operators plus (+) and minus (–) indicate a positive or negative position on a semantic scale. The semantic groupings represent senses that "are related by virtue of their being connected at some level of generality with the same mental concept" (Archer et al. 2002: 1). When a text is uploaded and annotated by USAS, the output is a list in which each lexical unit is assigned one or more semantic tags, as shown in Table 1.

Table 1: Sample excerpt of the European Corpus of Academic Talk with semantic tags assigned.

POS-tag	Text	semantic tag
DD1	that	Z8 Z5
VBZ	's	A3+ Z5
APPGE	your	Z8
NN1	focus	X5.1+ X3.4 A4.2+ A11.1+

The first column in Table 1 lists the part-of-speech tags (POS-tags), the second column displays the words of the text and the final column indicates the semantic tags for each lexical unit. When there are multiple semantic tags for a word, the most likely tag is placed in initial position. The ranking is derived by a combination of factors such as, for example, the POS tag of the word (e.g. if *spring* has a noun tag, it filters out the *jump* sense), frequency (e.g. *green* as a color is more likely than *green* as in inexperienced), the context a word is likely to occur in (e.g. *account of* followed and preceded by a noun phrase most likely refers to narration), or the surrounding words (for more details on methods of disambiguation see Rayson (2003: 67–68) and Rayson et al. (2004). The codes can be checked against a document provided on the Wmatrix platform listing the labels for the semantic fields for each of the codes. In the example above, the first tag of *focus*, X5.1+ stands for "attentive", the second for "sensory: sight", the third for "detailed" and the last for "important".

3 Uncovering Alignment with Wmatrix

Uncovering in how far interlocutors align their use of metaphors requires identifying metaphors in the first place. Examples of metaphor identification procedures are MIP (Pragglejaz Group 2007), or MIPVU (Steen et al. 2010), a more detailed and refined variant of MIP. Both procedures analyze texts for metaphor manually on a word-by-word basis. The core of these procedures entails comparing and contrasting the contextual meaning with a more basic meaning of a word. For example, the contextual meaning of the adjective *high* in "high status" is "important compared to other people or things, especially in a particular system or organization." The lexical unit also has a more concrete, basic meaning, namely "large in size from the top to the ground" (Macmillan). The two meanings contrast, but the contextual meaning can be understood in comparison with the more basic meaning. Therefore, in this context, *high* is metaphorically used.

Going through extensive stretches of discourse in this way is a time-consuming task, primarily because it must be done manually. Current programs for automatic metaphor identification do not yet match human coding abilities, though there are some promising developments (e.g. Berber Sardinha, 2009; Dodge, Hong and Stickles, 2015; Mason, 2004; Neuman et al., 2013; Patwardhan and Pedersen, 2006; Shutova, Douwe and Jean, 2016).

In order to speed up identification and to process larger amounts of data, several studies combine manual and computer assisted approaches. This can be done by concordancing a predefined set of lexical items (e.g. Deignan, 2005; Koller, 2004; Musolff, 2004) or by hand-coding a small corpus sample and then performing a search in a bigger corpus based on what was found in the small sample (e.g. Cameron and Deignan, 2003; Charteris-Black, 2004).

Rather than searching for pre-selected lexical items Koller, Hardie, Rayson and Semino (2008) used a semantic approach to detect metaphorically used words. They reasoned that the semantic fields that the annotation tool Wmatrix automatically assigns to words of a text roughly correspond to metaphorical domains, as suggested by conceptual metaphor theory. They can thus be exploited for targeted metaphor analysis (Hardie, Koller, Rayson and Semino, 2007). While the tool yields semantic fields that may correspond to source domains, it does not identify metaphors. Concordances for all the lexical items in a semantic category can be generated. Decisions as to which of the target words are actually metaphorically used need to be made by the analyst, e.g. by employing metaphor identification procedures such as MIP or MIPVU. Wmatrix thus combines automatic and manual analysis: automatic retrieval of potentially relevant lexis and manual identification of metaphor.

A feature within Wmatrix that is particularly useful for uncovering alignment between (groups of) speakers is the 'keyness analysis'. The keyness analysis compares a corpus to a reference corpus (a normative corpus such as samples from the BNC or any other uploaded text). Semino, Hardie, Koller and Rayson (2009) have successfully used the keyness analysis to compare metaphor across genres. The comparison procedure produces those semantic categories that are significantly more or less frequently used in the analyzed text than in a reference corpus.

For the analysis of conversations, the results of such a comparison can serve as a first indication as to whether two (groups of) speakers are on the "same page."

The following section will apply Wmatrix to a corpus of office hours' consultations (European Corpus of Academic Talk) (MacArthur et al. 2014) between students and lecturers using English as a lingua franca to uncover alignment (or the lack thereof) between students and teachers when using metaphors from the semantic domain of SIGHT. Sight metaphors are expected to be prominent in academic discourse because of the close connection between vision and knowledge (Sweetser 1991) as noted above. For an overview of research on the domain of sight to refer to knowledge and mental processes, including cross-cultural variation, see MacArthur et al. (2015).

4 Method

4.1 The Corpus

The European Corpus of Academic Talk (EuroCoAT) consists of 27 conversations during office hours' consultations between Spanish Erasmus students and their lecturers at five European universities in Sweden, Ireland, the UK and the Netherlands. The participants' first languages are Spanish, English, Greek, Dutch, German, Chinese, and Swedish. The recordings amount to a total of about 350 minutes. To investigate (lack of) metaphorical alignment when the interlocutors draw on the domain of SIGHT, two sub-corpora are created (a lecturer and a student corpus) and one of them is used as a reference corpus for the other. The lecturer corpus consists of 40,432 and the student corpus of 17,317 words, totaling just under 60,000 words.

4.2 Detecting Over- or Underuse and Retrieving SIGHT Metaphors

The Wmatrix dictionary contains three fields relating to sight: "sensory: sight" (X3.4), "seen" (X3.4+) and "unseen" (X3.4−). As described above, when Wmatrix assigns multiple semantic tags for a word, they are ordered according to likelihood, placing the most likely tag in initial position. For example, *focus* in "that's your focus" is assigned the tag "attentive" first. It is the most likely tag and represents the contextual meaning of "the thing that people are concentrating on or paying particular attention to" (Macmillan). The tag representing the basic meaning of *focus* (the source domain tag), namely "the part of a camera, telescope, microscope etc that you turn until you can see something clearly" (Macmillan), is listed only second, indicating the high conventionality of the use of *focus* in the present context. As a consequence, when examining the concordances of the semantic field of "sight" they will not contain the lexical item *focus*. This is because the concordance list only contains items that were assigned the "sight" semantic tag in the first position. This ordering is thus detrimental to metaphor analysis, because it means that relevant lexical items will be missed. In order to retrieve a more comprehensive list, it is crucial that the tag corresponding to the more basic meaning of a word is assigned as a first tag.

In order to force the program to assign the semantic tag that closely corresponds to the most basic sense in first position, the lecturer corpus and student corpus are uploaded using the 'Domain Tag Wizard', a feature that Koller et al. (2008) added in order to facilitate metaphor analysis. It allows for privileging a semantic field, placing it in the first position of a word's tag list. This way the concordance list includes words that have the sight tag in the first position of the taglist and these are the words the metaphor researcher will be interested in. Taking the example of *focus* above, the tag order using the Domain Tag Wizard is X3.4 X5.1+ A4.2+ A11.1+ ("sensory: sight", "attentive", detailed", "important"). Using the Domain Tag Wizard (i.e. privileging the semantic field of sight) makes *focus* part of the concordances listed under the "sensory: sight" semantic field.

To be maximally inclusive it is additionally possible to examine the so-called *broad list* of each of the semantic fields related to "sight". The broad list includes all words that contain a certain semantic tag –regardless of its position in the taglist. The researcher can examine this list manually and decide if any of the words listed but not included in the concordances should be added to the semantic field of interest.

Once the lecturer and student sub-corpora are tagged, they are compared with each other performing the 'keyness analysis'. In other words, one of the two sub-corpora is used as a reference corpus to the other in order to give a first indication of (mis)alignment: the analysis yields semantic fields that are used more or less frequently in one corpus in comparison to the other ('over-' or 'underuse'), as measured by LogLikelihood values. A value of 6.63 is used as a cut-off point for 99% confidence of significance (Rayson 2003).

4.3 Coding Metaphors

While Wmatrix retrieves lexical units that belong to the domain of vision, it does not automatically retrieve metaphors. Metaphors were identified using the

MIP procedure (Pragglejaz Group 2007). For each sight term in the concordance line, it was determined if its contextual meaning could be compared, contrasted, and understood via a more basic meaning of the word. If so, it was coded as metaphorically used. The data set was coded by three researchers, each annotating a third of the complete corpus, cross-checking another third, and making notes when disagreeing on coding decisions. Disagreements (23 cases) were discussed and resolved as a group.

Lexical units were put into one of three categories: non-metaphor, metaphor, and a hybrid category. There were three cases for which the contextual meaning could not be established due to lack of context. They were discarded from metaphor analysis. Examples (1) – (4) illustrate each category (transcript identifier in parenthesis).

(1) let's *see* if I (.) find one I marked recently (UE1, England; lecturer)
(2) I can *see* that it is a (.) difficult area (.) for almost everyone (UE6, England; lecturer)
(3) I have some NOT so good responses to some questions and you will *see* what people have done in the past (UE7, England; lecturer)
(4) We'll we'll we'll *look at* you tell me what question (UI8, Ireland; lecturer)

The first example is a straightforward case of literal use of *see*: the lecturer is searching on the computer screen. (2) is a straightforward case of metaphorical use. *See* is used to mean *understand*. (3) is an example of an item in the hybrid category. This category comprises items where both non-metaphorical and a metaphorical meanings are at work at the same time. In this case, *see* is metaphorical because the student will understand what kind of answers are possible when she is shown old exams but it is also literal because she will also look (with her eyes) at the exam copies. (4) illustrates a case which was excluded from metaphor analysis. The utterance is incomplete; the contextual meaning of *look at* cannot be established.

5 Results

5.1 Keyness Analysis

There were three Wmatrix domains that clearly referred to 'sight'. "Sensory: sight," "seen," and "unseen". Using a value of 6.63 as a cut-off point for 99% confidence of significance (Rayson 2003), the semantic domain "sensory: sight" was used significantly more frequently in the lecturer corpus than in the student corpus, with a LogLikelihood value of 24.71 and a %DIFF of 46.57. The fields "seen" and "unseen" were also used more frequently by the lecturers than by the students but not significantly so. The number of lexical items in these latter fields was small, however, (only four in "seen" and nine in "unseen" consisting of only one lemma (*notice*) and two lemmas (*miss* and *blind*) respectively.) The significant difference between lecturers and students with regard to the use of lexical units from the semantic field of "sensory: sight", may indicate a lack of alignment in the use of sight lexis and calls for closer investigation.

5.2 Sight Terms

The following lemmas were retrieved in the lecturer corpus: *look, see, watch, reflect, observe, spot, visible, focus, follow, view, viewpoint* (semantic field "sensory: sight"), *blind, miss* (semantic field "unseen"), and *notice* (semantic field "seen"). In the student corpus the following items were found: *look, see, watch, visual, reflect, focus, view, follow* (semantic field of "sensory: sight"), *miss* (semantic field of "unseen"), and *notice* (semantic field of "seen").

Two of the terms retrieved, namely *follow* and *miss*, are not part of the sight domain. A more basic meaning of *follow* is "to walk, drive etc. behind someone, when you are going in the same direction as them", and a more basic meaning of *miss* is "to fail to hit or reach something that you aim at." These meanings are movement-related, not sight-related, and were therefore excluded from the analysis. This demonstrates that the concordances produced by Wmatrix still need to be subjected to careful and critical inspection by the researcher to manually filter out terms that do not actually belong to the sight semantic field.

Applying the Domain Tag Wizard catches most of the relevant lexis. In order to check if any items that fit into one of the three lexical fields related to sight have nevertheless been missed, the broad lists were checked for each of them. As explained in section 4.2, a broad list contains all items that have a sight-related field anywhere in the taglist, regardless of its position. The broad list for the semantic field of "sensory: sight" yielded 31 hits that had a sight-tag in their tagset but not in first position (see Table 2).

It is worthwhile to manually examine this list for potential sight lexis candidates. A number of items are clearly not related to sight. These are *face-* (part of the compound *Facebook*), *honor, internship*, and *note*. The 23 cases of *look* and the one case of *see*, however, are clearly sight terms and should be added to the concordance list. *See* contained the tag "sensory: sight" in the taglist but, even though the Domain Tag Wizard was used, it did not get pushed into first

Table 2: Broad list for the semantic field "sensory: sight" for the complete EuroCoAT corpus.

lemma (frequency)	first USAS tag	semantic field
look like (2)	A6.1+	comparing: similar
face- (1)	B1	anatomy & physiology
honor (2)	G2.2+	ethical
internship (3)	M6	location and direction
look scholarly (2)	P1/A8	education in general/seem
note (1)	Q1.2	paper documents and writing
look to (1)	S7.1-	no power
look for (18)	X2.4	investigate, examine, test, search
see (1)	X2.5+	understanding

position, which is why one case of *see* ("we are relatively lenient for plagiarism as you *see* that you you just fail the essay and not the module") did not show up in the concordances. Wmatrix treated *look like, look scholarly, look to,* and *look for* as single lexical units. While the lexical units *look at* and *look up* were assigned a sight tag in first position when uploading the corpus, *look like, look scholarly, look to,* and *look for* were not and were thus only detected through the broad list. The broadlists of "seen" and "unseen" did not reveal any new items. Inspecting the broad list added 26 relevant lexical units. This yielded a total of 334 concordance lines: 76 for the student corpus and 258 for the lecturer corpus.

Figure 1 demonstrates that lecturers use a wider range of terms related to sight than the students. The 258 tokens include twelve terms in the lecturer corpus, whereas the 76 tokens in the student corpus include only eight terms. Students thus make more limited use of sight terms, although this distinction may be attributable to the smaller size of the student subcorpus.

The top three sight terms in the lecturer corpus are *see* (39.9% of all sight terms), *look* (35.7 %) and *focus* (9.3%). These are also the top three in the student corpus but they are ordered differently: *focus* (40.8%), *look* (23.7%) and *see* (22.4%). Normed rates of all sight-related terms in both subcorpora are presented in Table 3.

5.3 Metaphorical Sight Terms

The top three sight terms in the corpus are also the top three metaphorically used sight terms in both the lecturer and the student corpus: *focus* (54.4%), *look* (21.1%) and *see* (15.8%) in the student corpus and *see* (40.4%), *look*

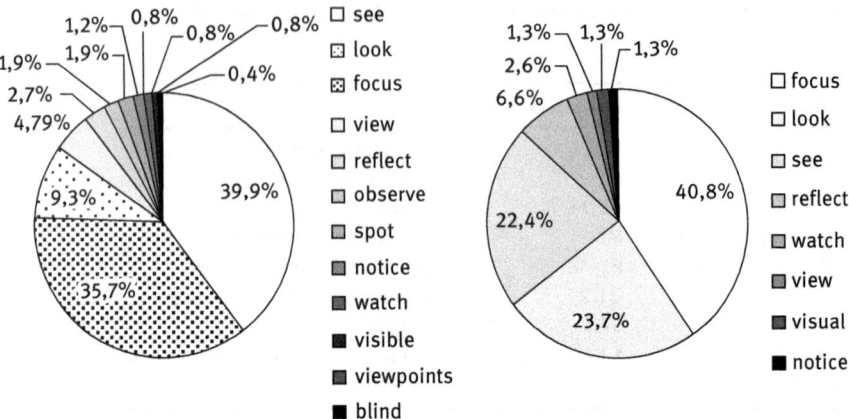

Figure 1: Sight terms in the lecturer (left) and the student sub-corpora (right) in per cent.

Table 3: Sight terms used by lecturers versus students
(normed per 10,000 words) (see also MacArthur et al. 2015).

sight term	lecturers	students
Focus	5.9	17.9
look	22.8	10.4
see	25.5	9.8
reflect	1.7	2.9
watch	0.5	1.2
view	3.0	0.6
visual	0.0	0.6
notice	0.7	0.6
observe	1.2	0.0
spot	1.2	0.0
visible	0.5	0.0
viewpoints	0.5	0.0
blind	0.2	0.0

(32.6%) and *focus* (12.4%) in the lecturer corpus (see Figure 2). As with sight terms overall, the lecturers use a wider range of metaphorical sight terms (*see, look, focus, view, spot, reflect, notice, observe* and *viewpoints*) than the students (*focus, look, see, reflect, view* and *notice*). *Spot, observe* and *viewpoints* were never metaphorically used by the students. *Visual, watch* and *visible* were never metaphorically by any of the speakers. Normed rates of all sight-related terms in both subcorpora are presented in Table 4.

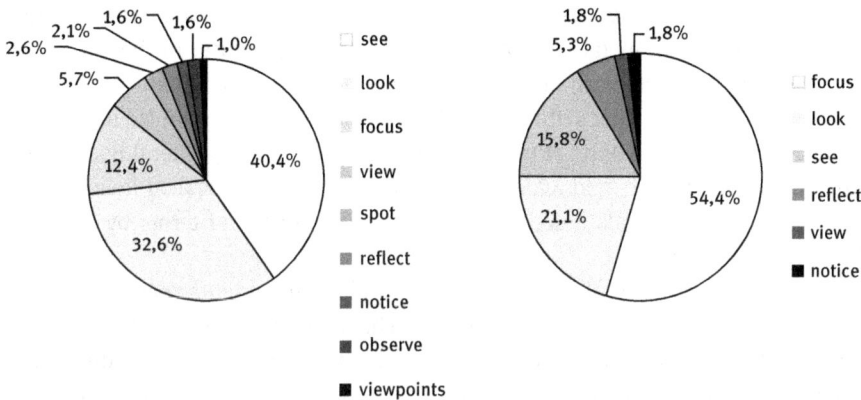

Figure 2: Metaphorical sight terms (clear cases and hybrid cases) in the lecturer (left) and the student sub-corpora (right) in per cent.

Table 4: Metaphorical sight terms used by lecturers versus students (normed per 10,000 words).

sight term	lecturers	students
focus	5.9	17.9
look	15.6	6.9
see	19.3	5.2
reflect	1.0	1.7
watch	0.0	0.0
view	2.7	0.6
visual	0.0	0.0
notice	0.7	0.6
observe	0.7	0.0
spot	1.2	0.0
visible	0.0	0.0
viewpoints	0.5	0.0
blind	0.2	0.0

6 Analysis and Discussion

The Wmatrix analysis reveals asymmetries in the use of sight metaphors used by lecturers and students, suggesting that the conversational partners may not always align their metaphor use. Lecturers use a wider range of metaphorical sight terms and largely make use of them more frequently than the students. While power relationships, proficiency, personal style or lack of engagement may play a role in this, the differences do not fully account for the lack of alignment. Note that the use of sight metaphors by a Spanish-speaking lecturer in the corpus resembled Spanish-speaking students' use more closely than use by English-speaking colleagues (MacArthur et al. 2015), which suggests that linguistic and cultural differences may be at play. Moreover, examination of literal uses of understanding (semantic field X2.5+ "understanding" with the lexical items *realize* and *understand*), reveals a significantly higher use of literal terms by students than by lecturers.

A closer inspection of the transcripts reveals that students seem to struggle with the lecturers' use of sight metaphors. This is corroborated by the students' short and restricted responses (e.g. *yeah, okay, uhu* and *mhm*.) Consider example (5) from UE2 (England) in which a lecturer (NT) tries to give advice to a student (MM) about how to best prepare for an exam:

(5) NT: but on the other hand you might *look* and *see* well actually when I *look*
      at those topics a couple of them actually go together so it's really only
      one topic
  MM: yeah yeah
  NT: that it's spread over two weeks
  MM: mhm
  NT: so you might *look at* that hh okay
  MM: yeah
  NT: so that that's what you need to do so you KNOW exactly what you have
      to do: so what i would say is the best thing to do is you you understand
      that you've got the theory of the lectures so you've got to *look through*
      your lecture
  MM: yes
  NT: notes

The lecturer frames the topic of exam preparation in terms of sight, drawing on metaphorically used sight lexis on several occasions within a very short timeframe: "you might *look* and *see*", "*look* at those topics", "*look at* that", and "*look through* your lecture". The student does not pick up any of the sight metaphors, however. She neither repeats nor elaborates on them. Her restricted responses may indicate that she is having difficulties understanding what the lecturer is trying to convey.

The student's apparent inability to respond using metaphors that continue or elaborate on those of the instructor, may seem surprising, given that this lecturer repeatedly frames knowledge and mental activity in terms of vision throughout the conversation. The lecturer used metaphors from the domain of sight 25 times in total. Unlike in conversations between native speakers where interlocutors share metaphors to create common ground and shared understanding (Cameron 2008; Littlemore et al. 2012), the student did not use a single sight term (neither metaphorical nor non-metaphorical) during the whole office hour consultation. There was complete lack of alignment. While the lecturer was heavily drawing on the sight domain to talk about exam preparation, it seems the student was some-what at a loss in her effort to understand the lecturer's advice. This becomes clearer as the conversation goes on, as illustrated in Example (6) – the student still does not know "what to talk about" (see also MacArthur et al. 2015).

(6) NT: exactly and the other thing is if you *look* HARD at (.) the (.) topic and
      you think (.) there is no debate here (.) it's just facts it probably isn't
      going to be on the exam paper
  MM: okay
  NT: okay
  MM: okay yeah
  NT: so that can help you *focus*
  MM: yeah
  NT: a little bit more
  MM: because (.) I'm I was really I really worried about that
  NT: yeah
  MM: because (.) sometimes you have a lot of theory but
  NT: mm
  MM: okay I can learn it but I don't know what to talk about

The lecturer frames intense mental activity and careful thinking in terms of di-recting one's eyes at a physical object. *Looking hard* at an object means that one can see it more clearly and detect its details and peculiarities. The metaphorical use of *looking hard* at a topic, thus thinking about something very deeply and carefully, can be understood via this more concrete meaning. The lecturer contin-ues that *looking hard* can help the student *focus*, that is, concentrate on a set of topics. Again, she uses a metaphor from the sight domain (*focus*), thereby con-tinuing the frame she had set up. However, the student still does not take up any of the metaphors from the visual domain. There is still no systematicity in the use of sight metaphors. In short, the interlocutors do not align.

What may be particularly difficult for the student is that many sight meta-phors tend to be simultaneously metaphorical and literal. For example, when the lecturer in (5) says "you might *look* and *see*", she refers to both the process of physical looking, which is followed by the 'product' of understanding.

Earlier in the conversation both meanings are again at play at the same time when the lecturer says "well actually when I *look* at those topics a couple of them actually go together". *Look at* here refers not only to mental activity (metaphorical) but also to reading (literal).

Students also seem to misinterpret metaphorical meanings as literal. Consider example (7) from UE1 (England), where the student wants to get feedback on his essay.

(7) AC: okay yeah that's fine you can also (.) ee as we saw in (.) as we saw in the: (.) in the film fresa y chocolate no (.) the character cause
MM: ah yes i saw the film it was

In her explanations, the lecturer refers to the film "fresa y chololate": *see* in "as we *saw* in the film" refers to more than watching – it also expresses the idea that the film was discussed. The student, however, seems to understand the meaning purely literally, reacting with "ah yes I *saw* the film". This mirrors Littlemore et al.'s (2012) data, which also revealed that non-native speakers may interpret metaphorically used words as literally used.

Examples (5) – (7) have illustrated a lack of alignment discovered by using the Wmatrix semantic annotation tool. While Wmatrix is certainly useful to uncover (lack of) alignment, there are some caveats the researcher needs to be aware of. Consider the following excerpt from US3 (Sweden) – a conversation between a lecturer (FL) and a student (RH) in which the student gets feedback on a written assignment.

(8) FL: you (.) need to correct me now because (.) when when I read your essay it was sort of a little (.) difficult to follow your
RH: mhm
FL: train of thought (.) but I think that what you want to do (.) is to say that he contradicts himself.
RH: yeah
FL: that is your main point
RH: mhm
FL: so this this ONE thing is something that you need to *pick out* from your essay, *lift out* and make *clearer* (.) this is your main idea (.) you're not talking about (.) Oscar Wilde or (.) or or the (.) article you are talking about how he contraDICTS himself in the article (.) this is your point (.) and you need to *lift it out*
RH: yeah (.) I have to be more *clear* (.) I know

The lecturer frames advice on how to improve an essay in terms of concrete, invisible things that need to be made visible (*pick out, lift out, clear*). The student continues the metaphor by repeating the metaphorical use of *clear*. In this excerpt is seems that the student actually understood the lecturer's advice – it is a rare example of alignment between the student and the lecturer. What is interesting to note is that the student chooses to repeat the most conventional of the lecturer's metaphorical expressions.

However, *pick out, lift out,* and *clear* were not retrieved by Wmatrix. This is due to the way the Wmatrix dictionary categorizes lexical items under specific semantic field labels. The sight terms turned up by examining the Wmatrix semantic fields that clearly reference "sight," belong to those describing the physical process of seeing (in their basic meanings) such as the ones in the metaphorically used examples below:

(9) *looking* at the way you answer exam questions (UE7, England, lecturer)
(10) Alejo Carpentier *sees* the problems ee in the black ee people (UI1, Ireland, lecturer)
(11) these people have this *view* (UE2, England, lecturer)

More peripherally related items were not found using Wmatrix. Danesi (1990: 223) established additional categories related to sight such as, for example metaphors that refer to "differences in the physical conditions (...) which affect the modalities of visual perception":

(12) That was a *brilliant* idea
(13) I take a *dim view* on that whole affair.
(14) What you are saying is not very *clear*
(15) That is a *transparent* argument.
(16) Can you *elucidate* your idea?

and vision metaphors "which enlist the modalities involved in visual perspective", such as:

(17) I have a different *outlook* than you do.
(18) Within *hindsight*, I would have done it in the same way.
(19) You have very little *foresight* on most issues.
(20) Please *look* your ideas *over*.
(21) Her speech *threw light* on the matter.
(22) Allow me to *point out* the weaknesses in your argument.

Also the lexical items from (23) – (25) that Sweetser (1991: 38) lists under the KNOWING IS SEEING metaphor would go undetected.

(23) a *clear* presentation
(24) an *opaque* statement
(25) a *transparent* ploy

Pick out, lift out, and *clear* in Example (8) were not revealed by Wmatrix, because none of them was categorized under any of the three sight-related semantic fields of "sensory: sight", "seen" and "unseen". For example, *clear* was not detected because it received the following semantic tags: "likely", "open; finding; showing", "colour and colour patterns", "general appearance and physical properties", "entire; maximum", and "weather". None of these semantic tags pertains to one of the three selected sight-related semantic fields. Instead, *clear* was assigned to the semantic category "likely" – its first tag – and was thus not retrieved. Instead, its 15 uses are buried in a set of 699 concordance lines mainly containing modals such as *would, can, may, might, could* and adverbs such as *certainly* and *probably*. As a consequence, it is difficult for the researcher who has no detailed knowledge of the complete corpus to detect this interesting section of discourse. In isolation, *pick out* and *lift out* are movement-related metaphors. Yet in this excerpt they surround to "make clearer" and together, they are "attracted" (Cameron and Low 2004) or drawn into the sight metaphor. This shows that conceptual domains are flexible structures which are not automatically pulled out by applying the Wmatrix tool. They require closer inspection of larger stretches of text surrounding metaphorical lexis.

A potential solution to these restrictions may be to run additional analyses that assign domains that are related to sight only indirectly as a first tag. For example, the three lexical units *clear, transparent* and *brilliant* share the tags "colour and colour patterns"; one can additionally decide to examine the concordances of that semantic field. While this is certainly possible, the following questions arises: Where do we draw the line between the core semantic fields describing the physical process of seeing and semantic fields that relate to sight more indirectly? "Colour and colour patterns" is indirectly related to sight because we see colors by distinguishing light of different wavelengths with our eyes. Following Danesi, the semantic fields of "light" and "darkness," which are semantic fields within Wmatrix, could arguably be included into the analysis as well. There are two instances of terms grouped under the semantic field of "light" in the corpus: the non-metaphorical "enjoy the *sunshine*" and the metaphorical "you need to think about these questions in that *light*."

However, there are other, more vague semantic field labels included in the Wmatrix tool such as "open/closed; hiding/hidden; finding; showing" (when something is open we can see it, if something is hidden we cannot see it), "general appearance and physical properties" or "judgement of appearance" (which both refer to the way something looks). Whether or not these should also be included seems a more difficult call.

Besides the challenge of determining where the border lies between fields within and outside of the domain of SIGHT, checking every semantic field that may be somehow related to sight, even if only remotely, and consequently sifting through each of the concordance lines (most of which will not contain the targeted word) defeats the purpose of searching a corpus relatively quickly with reliance on the built-in semantic dictionary. A possible approach is that of Demmen et al.'s (2015). They combine manual metaphor identification and semantic tagging of a corpus subset with computer-assisted analysis of the complete corpus to find lexical items in related semantic tags. This approach seems to be especially helpful with big datasets.

7 Conclusion

Conversational partners have been shown to coordinate their choice of words when talking to each other (e.g. Niederhoffer and Pennebaker 2002). Similarly, this has also been observed for metaphorical language use. When native speakers engage in conversations, they have been shown to repeat and expand on each other's metaphors in order to create knowledge and common understanding (Cameron 2008; Littlemore et al. 2012). In conversations between participants using English as a lingua franca in office hours' consultations, such alignment is less pronounced. The lecturers' metaphorical language use seems to be a stumbling block to creating common ground and shared knowledge.

Investigating metaphorical alignment between speakers in lingua franca contexts is crucial. Being able to understand and use metaphors in talk is key to successful conversations. Part of this skill involves being able to create discourse coherence and signaling understanding by repeating, expanding, changing, or elaborating on the interlocutor's metaphor use. Thus when participants in conversations align, they throw metaphors back and forth across turns. When metaphors are not systematically used (i.e. the conversational partner does not use metaphors from the same or related source domains) this can be an indication of lack of alignment.

This paper has shown that Wmatrix, through its semantic tagger and the keyness analysis, is a valuable tool for investigating metaphorical alignment between (sets of) speakers. Its value goes beyond the case-study presented here and promises to be useful for studies on different semantic domains that correspond to potential source domains (e.g. domains M1 to M8 for source domains related to movement or B1 "anatomy and physiology" for source domains related to the human body) or with different groups of speakers. The tool provides a quick way of detecting (lack of) alignment of metaphors from a pre-selected source domain (in this case, SIGHT) by comparing two corpora (in this case, lecturers and students). When comparing the two corpora, asymmetric use of words from semantic domains can be revealed. This case study has revealed an asymmetric use of the domain of sight between lecturers and students. Words from the semantic field of "sensory: sight" appeared far more often in the lecturer corpus than in the student corpus, which was a first indication of lack of alignment in student instructor interaction. Such a comparison can form the starting point of closer investigation of the discourse. In the present dataset lack of alignment was the norm. Students generally did not take up lecturers' sight metaphors. While not taking up metaphors does not automatically mean that they did not understand them, a close look at the discourse shows that they did not seem to understand the advice given and appeared to misinterpret metaphorical meanings as literal.

Wmatrix partly automates retrieval of relevant lexis as it automatically assigns semantic fields to each lexical unit in the corpus. Tagging accuracy is 96–97% for POS tags and 91–92% for semantic tags (Rayson et al., 2004). Wmatrix retrieves lexical items falling within a semantic field but it does not retrieve metaphors. It is still left to the analyst to determine which of the lexical items listed under a semantic field are indeed metaphorical. Nevertheless, the tool can tremendously speed up analysis.

While the program is a valuable tool for uncovering alignment, the researcher needs to be aware that the program may not detect all cases of (non)alignment in the corpus. The analysis of sight metaphors has shown that a small number of more peripherally related lexis will not be found. This is due to the way Wmatrix groups lexis under specific semantic field labels. Some of these potentially relevant sight-related terms may thus end up in semantic fields that do not explicitly refer to the targeted domain. There is also a small number of tokens that may not be listed under the pre-selected semantic fields (in this case "sensory: sight", "seen" and "unseen".) These can be added by making use of the Broad List function. The researcher also must critically evaluate whether all lexical items listed under the semantic fields of 'sight' indeed are a good fit, and those that are not need to be excluded. Unlike a keyword approach, however, Wmatrix allows searching for "open-ended sets" (see Demmen et al. 2015), meaning that the researcher is not restricted to pre-selected lexical items.

As long as its caveats are kept in mind, Wmatrix is a valuable tool for investigating (metaphorical) alignment in talk. It speeds up analysis dramatically and allows a quick way into the data. The analysis can provide a first step in understanding challenges that may arise through the use of metaphor for speakers communicating with each other using English as a lingua franca. Future research may additionally look into the time dimension and address the question of how alignment develops as the conversation unfolds.

References

Archer, Dawn Elisabeth, Andrew Wilson & Paul Rayson. 2002. Introduction to the USAS category system. *Benedict project report, October 2002*.

Beger, Anke. 2011. Deliberate metaphors? An exploration of the choice and functions of metaphors in US-American college lectures. *metaphorik.de* 20, 39–60.

Berber Sardinha, Tony. 2009. *A tool for finding metaphors in corpora using lexical patterns*. Paper presented at the Corpus Linguistics 2009, Liverpool.

Boers, Frank & Murielle Demecheleer. 1997. A few metaphorical models in (western) economic discourse. In Wolf A. Liebert, Gisela Redeker, & Linda R. Waugh (eds.), *Discourse and perspective in cognitive linguistics*, 115–129. Amsterdam: John Benjamins.

Cameron, Lynne. 2003. *Metaphor in educational discourse*. London & New York: Continuum.

Cameron, Lynne. 2008. Metaphor and talk. In Raymond W. Gibbs (Ed.), *The Cambridge handbook of metaphor and thought*, 197–211. Cambridge: Cambridge University Press.

Cameron, Lynne & Alice Deignan. 2003. Combining large and small corpora to investigate tuning devices around metaphor in spoken discourse. *Metaphor and Symbol* 18(3). 149–160.

Cameron, Lynne & Graham D. Low. 2004. Figurative variation in episodes of educational talk and text. *European Journal of English Studies* 8(3). 355–373.

Cameron, Lynne & Robert Maslen (Eds.). 2010. *Metaphor Analysis: Research practice in applied linguistics, social sciences and the humanities*. London & Oakville: Equinox.

Cameron, Lynne & Juurd H. Stelma. 2004. Metaphor clusters in discourse. *Journal of Applied Linguistics* 1(2). 107–136.

Carter, Ronald. 2004. *Language and creativity: The art of common talk*. London & New York: Routledge.

Charteris-Black, Jonathan. 2004. *Corpus approaches to critical metaphor analysis*. Houndmills, Basingstoke, Hampshire & New York: Palgrave Macmillan.

Corts, Daniel P. & Howard R. Pollio. 1999. Spontaneous production of figurative language and gesture in college lectures. *Metaphor and Symbol* 14(2). 81–100.

Danesi, Marcel. 1990. Thinking is seeing: Visual metaphors and the nature of abstract thought. *Semiotica* 80(3–4). 221–238.

Deignan, Alice. 2003. Metaphorical expressions and culture: An indirect link. *Metaphor and Symbol*, 18(4). 255–271.

Deignan, Alice. 2005. *Metaphor and corpus linguistics*. Amsterdam & Philadelphia: John Benjamins.

Demmen, Jane, Elena Semino, Zsófia Demjén, Veronika Koller, Andrew Hardie, Paul Rayson & Sheila Payne. 2015. A computer-assisted study of the use of Violence metaphors for cancer and end of life by patients, family carers and health professionals. *International Journal of Corpus Linguistics*, 20(2). 205–231.

Dodge, Ellen, Jisup Hong & Elise Stickles. 2015. MetaNet: Deep semantic automatic metaphor analysis. *Proceedings of the Third Workshop on Metaphor in NLP*, 40–49.

Evans, Nicholas & David Wilkins. 2000. In the mind's ear: The semantic extensions of perception verbs in Australian languages. *Language* 7(3). 546–592.

Grady, Joseph E. 1997. THEORIES ARE BUILDINGS revisited. *Cognitive Linguistics* 8, 267–290.

Hardie, Andrew, Veronika Koller, Paul Rayson & Elena Semino. 2007. Exploiting a semantic annotation tool for metaphor analysis. In Matthew Davies, Paul Rayson, Susan Hunston & Pernilla Danielsson (Eds.), *Proceedings of the Corpus Linguistics 2007 Conference*.

Ibarretxe-Antuñano, Iraide. 2013. The power of the senses and the role of culture in metaphor and language. In Rosario Caballero & Javier E. Dîaz-Vera (Eds.), *Sensuous cognition*, 109 –133. Berlin, Germany & New York: Mouton de Gruyter.

Kaal, Anna A. 2012. *Metaphor in conversation*. Oisterwijk: Boxpress.

Koller, Veronika. 2004. *Metaphor and gender in business media discourse: a critical cognitive study*. Basingstoke & New York: Palgrave Macmillan.

Koller, Veronika, Andrew Hardie, Paul Rayson & Elena Semino. 2008. Using a semantic annotation tool for the analysis of metaphor in discourse. *metaphorik.de* 15. 141–160.

Kövecses, Zoltan. 2005. *Metaphor in culture. Universality and variation*. Cambridge: Cambridge University Press.

Littlemore, Jeannette. 2001. The use of metaphor by university lecturers and the problems that it causes for overseas students. *Teaching in Higher Education* 6(3). 335–351.

Littlemore, Jeannette. 2003. The effect of cultural background on metaphor interpretation. *Metaphor and Symbol* 18(4). 273–288.

Littlemore, Jeannette, Phillys Chen, John Barnden & Almut Koester. 2011. Difficulties in metaphor comprehension faced by international students whose first language is not English. *Applied Linguistics* 32 (3). 408–29.

Littlemore, Jeannette, Fiona MacArthur, Alan Cienki & Joseph Holloway. 2012. How to make yourself understood by international students: The role of metaphor in academic tutorials. *ELT Resarch Papers* (12–06). 1–22.

Low, Graham. 2010. Wot no similes? The curious absence of simile in university lectures. In Graham Low, Zazie Todd, Alice Deignan & Lynne Cameron (eds.), *Researching and applying metaphor in the real world*, 291–308. Amsterdam, The Netherlands, Philadelphia, PA: John Benjamins.

Low, Graham D., Jeannette Littlemore & Almut Koester. 2008. Metaphor use in three UK university lectures. *Applied Linguistics* 29(3). 428–55.

MacArthur, Fiona. 2016. Overt and covert uses of metaphor in the academic mentoring in English of Spanish undergraduate students at five European universities. *Review of Cognitive Linguistics*, 14(1). 23–50.

MacArthur, Fiona, Rafael Alejo, Ana M. Piquer-Píriz, Carolina Amador-Moreno, Jeannette Littlemore, Annelie Ädel Krennmayr, Tina & Elaine Vaughn. (2014). *EuroCoAT. The European Corpus of Academic Talk* http://www.eurocoat.es.

MacArthur, Fiona, Tina Krennmayr & Jeannette Littlemore. 2015. How basic is "UNDERSTANDING IS SEEING" when reasoning about knowledge? Asymmetric uses of sight metaphors in office hours consultations in English as academic lingua franca. *Metaphor and Symbol* 30(3). 184–217.

Mason, Zachary J. 2004. CorMet: A computational, corpus-based conventional metaphor extraction system. *Computational Linguistics* 30(1). 23–44.

McArthur, Tom. 1981. *Longman lexicon of contemporary English*. London: Longman.

Musolff, Andreas. 2004. *Metaphor and political discourse: Analogical reasoning in debates about Europe*. Houndmills & Basingstoke: Palgrave Macmillan.

Neuman, Yair, Dan Assaf, Yohai Cohen, Mark Last, Shlomo Argamon, Newton Howard & Frieder Ophir. 2013. Metaphor identification in large texts corpora. *PLOS ONE* 8(4), e62343.

Niederhoffer, Kate G. & James W. Pennebaker. 2002. Linguistic style matching in social interaction. *Journal of Language and Social Psychology* 21(4). 337–360.

Patwardhan, Siddharth & Ted Pedersen. 2006. Using WordNet based on context vectors to estimate the semantic relatedness of concepts. *Proceedings of the Twentieth National Conference on Artificial Intelligence*. 1692–1693.

Pragglejaz Group. 2007. MIP: A method for identifying metaphorically used words in discourse. *Metaphor and Symbol* 22(1). 1–39.

Rayson, Paul. 2003. *Wmatrix. A statistical method and software tool for linguistic analysis through corpus comparison*. (Ph.D. thesis), Lancaster University, Lancaster.

Rayson, Paul. 2008. Wmatrix: a web-based corpus processing environment. Computing Department, Lancaster University http://ucrel.lancs.ac.uk/Wmatrix/.

Rayson, Paul, Dawn E. Archer, Scott Piao & Tony McEnery. 2004. The UCREL semantic analysis system. *Proceedings of the workshop on 'Beyond Named Entity Recognition Semantic labelling for NLP tasks' in association with 4th International Conference on Language Resources and Evaluation (LREC 2004), Lisbon, Portugal*, 7–12.

Semino, Elena, Andrew Hardie, Veronika Koller & Paul Rayson. 2009. A computer-assisted approach to the analysis of metaphor variation across genres. Paper presented at the *Corpus Linguistics Conference 2009*, July 2009, University of Birmingham.

Shutova, Ekaterina, Kiela Douwe & Maillard Jean. 2016. Black holes and white rabbits: Metaphor identification with visual features. *Proceedings of the 2016 Conference of the North American Chapter of the Association for Computational Linguistics: Human Language Technologies*, 160–170.

Steen, Gerard J., Aletta G. Dorst, Berenike Herrmann, Anna A. Kaal, Tina Krennmayr & Trijntje Pasma. 2010. *A Method for Linguistic Metaphor Identification: From MIP to MIPVU*. Amsterdam: John Benjamins.

Sweetser, Eve. 1991. *From etymology to pragmatics: Metaphorical and cultural aspects of semantic structure* (Vol. 54). Cambridge: Cambridge University Press.

Yu, Ning. 1995. Metaphorical expressions of anger and happiness in English and Chinese. *Metaphor and Symbol* 10(2). 59–92.

Susan Nacey
Development of L2 Metaphorical Production

1 Introduction

This chapter details a pseudo-longitudinal corpus-based exploratory study into the development of metaphorical production of foreign/second language (L2) learners of English as they progress through their school career. The particular focus here is on the written production of linguistic metaphors in the L2 English of pupils from the ages of 10–19 in Norway, where the subject of English is obligatory from the first grade (age six). The empirical data is retrieved from a longitudinal corpus currently under compilation called "Tracking Written Learner Language" (TraWL), consisting of authentic L2 texts written by Norwegian pupils from grades five through the final year in upper secondary school. All metaphors in 45 texts (5 per grade level) were identified using the Metaphor Identification Procedure Vrije Universteit (see Steen et al. 2010).

The overall objective is to shed light on how metaphorical production develops as proficiency increases. To do so, this study adapts the methods and many of the research questions from Littlemore et al.'s (2014) investigation into metaphor use at different levels of L2 writing. One main aim is thus to measure how overall metaphor density varies per grade level. A related aim is to uncover any patterns in the metaphor density for open-class versus closed-class metaphor, to identify any particular level at which the use of the former overtakes the latter, as has been observed in previous research. Moreover, this study investigates how the distribution of metaphor clusters varies across levels, since clusters have been found to serve important communicative functions and might therefore be expected to increase with improved proficiency (see Cameron and Low 2004). Finally, this study examines the discourse function of the observed metaphors (including metaphor clusters) in texts from the different grade levels, to explore potential differences with respect to the role metaphor plays as L2 proficiency increases.

2 Background

This section presents the background for the study. Section 2.1 first outlines the theoretical underpinnings for the view of metaphor adopted in this study, as

Susan Nacey, Faculty of Education, Inland Norway University of Applied Sciences, Hamar, Norway, e-mail: susan.nacey@inn.no

https://doi.org/10.1515/9783110630367-009

well as the links between metaphor and the L2 providing the motivation for the research presented here. Section 2.2 then briefly outlines previous research in the field, focusing on research that has contributed towards the development of the particular research questions addressed.

2.1 Why Metaphor Production in the L2?

My approach is framed by Conceptual Metaphor Theory (CMT), which holds that metaphor in language reflects metaphor structures in thought, i.e. "metaphors as linguistic expressions are possible precisely because there are metaphors in a person's conceptual system" (Lakoff and Johnson 1980: 6). These structures may or may not be consciously active in the mind of the producers or recipients of utterances. This means that people may not necessarily be aware of "doing metaphor" even when they are in fact doing so, partially because metaphor is so intrinsic to our understanding of the world around us that we do not always perceive of it as something extraordinary. Metaphor pervades our thought (i.e. *conceptual metaphor*) and is represented in language by conventional, and usually codified, ways of expressing something (i.e. *linguistic metaphor*).

The primary focus of this investigation is on the level of language, in that all linguistic metaphors produced in the pupil texts have been identified. Previous empirical studies have found that linguistic metaphors are ubiquitous in both the first language (L1) and in the L2. When it comes to the L1, Steen et al. (2010: 189, 195) identified all metaphors in roughly 200,000 words from the British National Corpus, and found that an average of one in every seven and a half words was related to metaphor. They explain, however, that the distribution of linguistic metaphors varies considerably according to register, with academic texts having the most metaphor (17.5%), followed by news (15.3%), fiction (10.8%), and finally conversation (6.8%). Nacey (2013: 139) provides further evidence of the ubiquity of metaphor in L1 English, reporting a metaphor frequency of 13.3% in almost 20,000 words of text written by British A-level pupils. Pasma (2011) reports similar findings for L1 Dutch, providing empirical evidence that the ubiquity of metaphor is not restricted to English alone.

When it comes to metaphor in the L2, Nacey (2013: 138) also investigates metaphor frequency in English argumentative texts written by Norwegian college students, and finds an overall metaphor frequency of 15.5%. Because metaphor is a frequent feature of both spoken and written discourse regardless of register or language, it clearly has important consequences for language learners. Production of metaphor is one facet of metaphorical competence, which in turn is an important component of learners' overall communicative competence (see e.g. Littlemore and Low 2006).

2.2 Previous Research into L2 Metaphorical Production

Previous research about metaphor and language learners has focused primarily on metaphor comprehension, interpretation and/or appreciation, with L2 studies frequently concentrating on metaphor in connection with vocabulary acquisition and retention. Much less work has been carried out on production of metaphor in the L2; those studies that have been conducted tend to offer "snapshot" views of L2 competence, through investigating metaphor production of a particular population at a particular point in time. In most studies, informants are college-age students, perhaps because they are the most readily accessible to researchers (see Nacey 2017 for a more comprehensive overview).

How metaphorical production develops as L2 proficiency increases is an under-researched area. One important exception is Littlemore et al. (2014), who investigated metaphorical use in 200 exam texts collected in the Cambridge Learner Corpus, half written by German learners of English and half written by Greek learners of English. Each set of 100 texts consisted of 20 texts graded at each of five of the Common European Framework of Reference for Languages (CEFR) levels, from A2 to C2 (elementary English to proficiency English). They find that the metaphor competence of L2 writers improves as proficiency increases, and use these findings to propose CEFR descriptors for metaphor use, something that had been missing from the framework.[1] The present study consolidates four of Littlemore et al.'s (2014: 120) research questions into three subordinate aims, asking them of the Norwegian learner texts. More specifically:

1. Does the amount of metaphor produced vary across grade levels, both overall and as a factor of word class (open versus closed)?
2. Does the distribution of metaphor clusters vary across the grade levels?
3. What function does metaphor play across grade levels?

Note that Littlemore et al. (2014) had access to texts that were already graded for CEFR proficiency levels. In the present study, by contrast, grade level and age serve as a proxy for proficiency level. An underlying assumption here is thus that L2 language proficiency generally rises with additional instruction, learning opportunity and exposure to a language.

---

1 Their findings were also reported in Littlemore et al. (2012).

The present chapter builds upon the work of Littlemore et al. (2014) by exploring metaphorical production in the context of English language learning in the Norwegian educational system, and by including young language learners as informants. This type of expansion follows in the footsteps of Hoang and Boers (2018), who also built upon Littlemore et al. (2014), albeit from a different perspective: their goal was to examine whether the patterns uncovered by Littlemore et al. (2014) hold equally true for texts written by a more homogenous group of L2 writers (Vietnamese university students).

3 Primary Material and Methods

This section discusses the material and methods employed in the present study. Section 3.1 provides details about the texts analyzed for metaphor use, together with information about the informants who produced those texts. Section 3.2 then explains the procedure employed for metaphor identification, including how learner errors were dealt with in the analysis.[2] Finally, section 3.3 discusses the procedure employed for identifying metaphor clusters.

3.1 TraWL corpus

The data for this study comes from "Tracking Written Learner Language" (TraWL), a longitudinal corpus whose compilation began in 2016. The corpus includes English texts written by Norwegian pupils from Grades 5 through the final year of upper secondary school – that is, pupils aged 10–19. These texts were collected from schools in five different Norwegian cities and towns, anonymized, computerized (necessary for the texts by youngest pupils, who write mainly by hand). Important to note is that in Norway, English is defined as a core subject already from the first grade, at the age of six. As a result, ten-year-old Norwegian pupils – the youngest included in the corpus – are already expected to be able to produce simple texts in English, about themselves and their surroundings.

The TraWL corpus contains all pupil-produced texts written in the participatory classes during the year(s) of collection, contingent upon consent from both the pupil and his/her parents or guardians. In addition, most collected texts are linked to some metadata about task type, instructions, writing aids, etc. No

---

2 Although the term "error" is employed here, this chapter is agnostic about whether the anomalies were errors (due to a lack of knowledge) or mistakes (due to oversight).

attempt was made by the corpus compilers to influence text production. The TraWL corpus therefore represents the type of authentic English texts that are "naturally" produced in the English language classroom in different grades in Norway.

Because text collection began in 2016, few texts had been through the entire preparation process by the start of the present exploratory study, so few were available for research. As a consequence, the material included here comprises only 5 texts per each of the 9 grade levels, the work of 45 different pupils; see Table 1 for an overview. Topics necessarily vary by grade, with the younger pupils writing about subjects that are familiar in their everyday lives, and frequently concrete in nature. Writing conditions also varied, with the texts from Grades 8–11 having been produced under examination conditions.

Table 1: Overview of data: Grade, ages, numbers of lexical units and topics.

Grade	Ages	Lexical units	Topic
5	10–11	331	My family
6	11–12	637	A fairy tale
7	12–13	1389	Drawing / dream
8	13–14	1083	My favorite artist
9	14–15	1147	The most interesting thing I know
10	15–16	1350	How to make newcomers feel welcome
11	16–17	2814	Why is it important to learn English?
12	17–18	4046	Problems immigrants face / prejudice
13	18–19	1749	A personal statement

A total of 14,546 lexical units[3] were analyzed for metaphorical use. The number of lexical units varies per grade level, with the fifth and sixth graders, perhaps unsurprisingly, writing the shortest texts. The boxplot in Figure 1 presents a more nuanced picture by showing the minimum and maximum text length per grade, along with the median and mean (indicated by the bold line in the boxes and the plus signs, respectively).[4] The shortest text analyzed is a 20-word-long text written by a fifth grader, while the longest text is 871 words long and written by a twelfth grader.

Variation in text length may be considered a challenge when investigating metaphor production. As an example, Hoang and Boers included text length as

---

3 The term "lexical unit" is defined in section 3.2.
4 The R software environment for statistical computing and graphics (2014) was employed to produce all plots in this chapter.

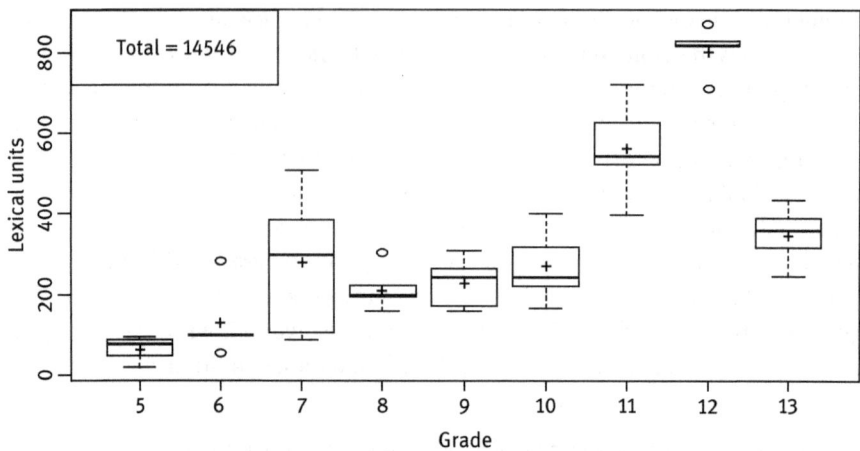

Figure 1: Numbers of lexical units per text and grade.

a factor for exclusion of texts from their investigation into metaphor production in L2 English essays written by Vietnamese university students. They chose to omit any text comprising fewer than 250 words, reasoning that "counts of metaphorical language in very brief essays with little content risk not being representative". As a consequence, Hoang and Boers felt compelled to exclude *all* essays written by first-year university students, because what remained after imposition of the minimum word count was considered too few to compare with the essays from the three higher year levels (Hoang and Boers 2018: 3).

The word length variation of the texts documented in Figure 1 is hardly unexpected, due to the difference in ages between the youngest and oldest learners. Text length was not considered as a factor for exclusion from the present analysis, unlike in Hoang and Boers (2018). Indeed, their assumption that metaphor production in the shortest texts would then be unrepresentative because of their short length begs the question of exactly what the texts are intended to represent. Imposing similar strict minimum word-length restrictions on the texts in this study would have entailed omitting all texts written by fifth and sixth graders (at a minimum), making it impossible to draw any conclusions about metaphor production at these levels. Such a decision would have been unfortunate.

3.2 Metaphor Identification

The Metaphor Identification Procedure Vrije Universiteit (MIPVU) was employed to identify all linguistic metaphors in the 45 texts. This procedure identifies both "indirect" and "direct" metaphor.[5] Indirect metaphors consist of those words where there is a contrast between the basic and contextual senses, where that contrast may be attributed to a relationship of comparison. As an example, consider the italicized word *step* in (1), found in a ninth-grade text about "the most interesting thing I know".

(1) I can **take** the next *step* and **push** myself even **further** . . .[6]

The basic meaning of *step* (that is, the most concrete, specific and human-oriented sense in the dictionary) is "a short movement made by putting one foot in front of the other", the first sense entry for the noun in the online version of the *Macmillan Dictionary* (MM).[7] By contrast, its contextual sense is MM's sixth sense entry for the noun: "one of the stages in a process, or one of the levels on a scale". These two senses are sufficiently distinct (i.e. represented by different sense entries), and are related through comparison whereby we understand an advance in an abstract process in terms of physical forward movement. In similar fashion, the words *take, push,* and *further*, in bold script in (1), are also indirect metaphors.

In direct metaphors, an underlying cross-domain metaphorical comparison is triggered through "direct" language use, i.e. by words where there is no contrast between the contextual meaning and a more basic meaning. An example is found in (2), from a twelfth-grade text.

(2) Do not *judge* a *book* by its *cover*.

In the cases of the verb *judge* and the nouns *book* and *cover*, there is no distinction between their more basic and contextual senses, even though there is an underlying conceptual metaphor because the topic under discussion is immigration, rather than books. Interpretation of this sentence, which directly evokes an "alien" physical source domain unrelated to the topic at hand, requires the addressee to set up a cross-domain comparison between the referents of the words in discourse.

---

5 MIPVU also identifies "implicit" metaphors, consisting of elements where the metaphorical relationship is due to an underlying cohesive grammatical link referring to metaphorical text, such as with anaphoric pronouns or determiners. Although implicit metaphors were identified during the analysis, they are arguably of lesser importance for the present research and are not discussed.

6 All quotations from pupil texts are reproduced here as written, including any mistakes/errors.

7 The Macmillan Dictionary is available at https://www.macmillandictionary.com/.

The basic unit of analysis for MIPVU is the lexical unit. In most cases, the lexical unit corresponds to the orthographic word, so the terms *lexical unit* and *word* are henceforth used synonymously in this chapter, for ease of reference. Note, however, that MIPVU also considers phrasal verbs, compounds, some proper nouns, and polywords (e.g. *of course, fait accompli*) as single lexical units even though they consist of more than one orthographic word; the identification procedure employed for this study followed the MIPVU guidelines when demarcating such multiword lexical units.

3.2.1 Learner Errors

Many of the texts contain errors, as is only to be expected in texts written by language learners at varying proficiency levels. For the purposes of the present investigation, errors that were of no consequence for either metaphor identification or word count were not adjusted. By way of example, consider the words *her self, now,* and *princesse* in the "Cinderella" text written by a sixth grader, shown in its entirety in Figure 2 below:

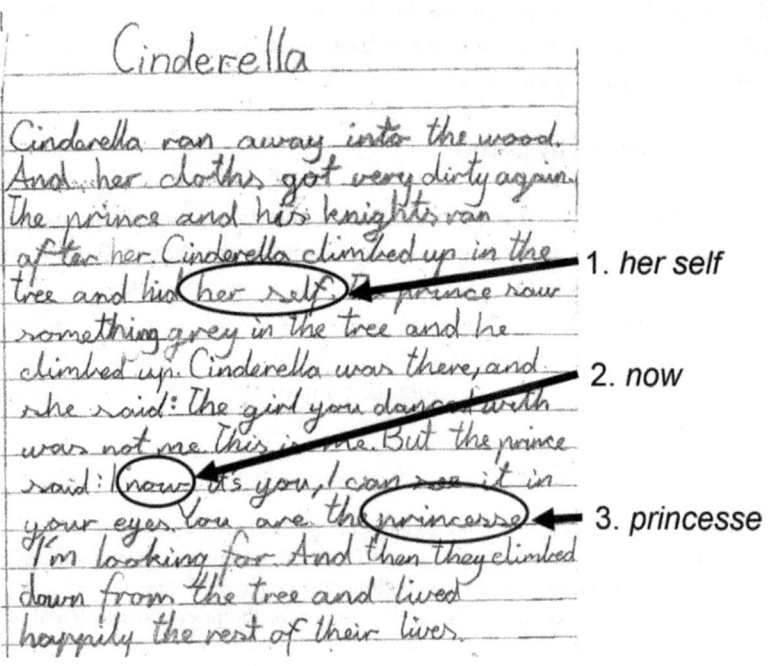

Figure 2: Sixth-grade "Cinderella" text.

When it comes to metaphor identification, the word *princesse* is unnecessary to alter. Its metaphorical status may be determined through consultation of MM's entry for the English noun *princess*, the only obvious intended target. By contrast, *her self* (written as two words) was corrected to *herself* (one word), because this type of error would have affected the calculation of both the overall number of lexical units analyzed and the overall metaphor density per text (that is, number of metaphorical words per number of total words). Finally, the adverb *now* was corrected to the verb *know*. Strict application of MIPVU would have required metaphor identification based on the word as written in the text, rather than on the basis of the analyst's interpretation of the intended word. This type of application was deemed overly strict for the present study, however, as it would have unduly skewed the numbers of potential metaphors. Whereas more comprehensive error tagging may be tricky (see e.g. Granger et al. 2009: 13), this type of minor adjustment of low-level errors proved unproblematic.

3.3 Metaphor Clusters

Identification of metaphor clusters was accomplished through a series of time analyses, one per text, following Littlemore et al. (2014: 123):

> A span size of 20 words was selected, and the metaphoric density across the words in this span was calculated. The result was placed at the mid-point (the 10th word). The span was then shifted one word down, and the metaphoric density calculated for the next 20-word span. The result was placed at the mid-point (the 11th word), and so on until the end of the text was reached.

Littlemore et al. adopted the span size of 20 words from Turner (2010: 65), who explains that while the choice was arbitrary, "choosing a different span length will retain the general shape of the moving metaphor density chart". The same 20-word span was adhered to in the present study, to more easily allow for the possibility of comparison between studies. By coincidence, the shortest text in the TraWL data under examination was exactly 20 words long, making the span meaningful for all texts.

This time analysis procedure allows for the production of charts illustrating the moving metaphor density of each text, such as that shown in Figure 3, which was created based on one of the longest texts in the material. The cut-off point for what is considered a metaphoric cluster is 30% metaphor density, indicated by the bold horizontal line in Figure 3. The choice of 30% also follows Littlemore et al. (2014: 124), a density they found to include "visible metaphor use

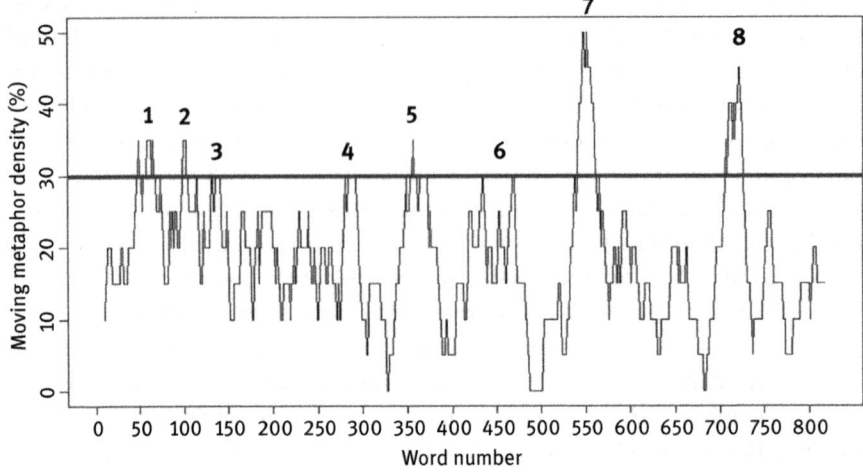

Figure 3: Moving metaphor density chart: 12th grade text, 828 words long.

above and beyond the sorts of highly conventionalized metaphorical uses of prepositions". A subsequent important procedural issue concerns identifying boundaries between clusters in those cases when there are many data points above the 30% threshold in close vicinity, an issue not explicitly dealt with in Littlemore et al. (2014). In the present study, consecutive peaks were considered part of a single cluster if the relevant 20-word spans overlapped.

In this way, eight metaphor clusters were identified in the text providing the data for Figure 3: these are numbered above each peak. In each case, we find a period of a relatively low level of metaphor use, followed by a burst of metaphor use indicated by a peak in the chart. As an example, the text in (3) forming Cluster 1 deals with problems facing second-generation immigrants, and runs as follows (with metaphor-related words in bold script):

(3)   Their parents are often eager to **get** them **into** a school, **give** them education to **get** a job, and to do well **in** life. **This** could **lead to** a huge amount of **stress** and cause **obstacles in** their children's life.

In essence, each moving metaphor density chart provides individual metaphor portraits for each text. This approach allows for relatively simple visual inspection and comparison of how metaphor usage varies in each of the 45 texts under investigation.[8] High localized metaphor density may prove informative for subsequent qualitative analysis, by providing indications of where analysts could focus attention.

4 Findings

The following subsections discuss findings for each of the study's three research questions. Section 4.1 concerns the overall metaphor density per grade level, as well as the variation in metaphor density in open-class versus closed-class words across grade levels. The variation in the distribution of metaphor clusters across grade level is addressed in section 4.2, while section 4.3 discusses the functions of metaphor across grade levels.

4.1 Metaphor Density per Grade Level and Word Class

The scatterplot in Figure 4, where each dot represents one text, indicates that there is a strong positive association between metaphor density and grade level. As the predictor variable of grade level increases, so too does the criterion variable of metaphoric density. The strength of this association is significant (r_s = 0.85, $p < 0.0001$).

Metaphor density starts off fairly low in the earliest grades, including one fifth-grade text and one sixth-grade text that contain no metaphor at all. In general, the metaphor density progressively increases by an average of 1.8% per year for each grade (indicated by the slope of the regression line), with only minor discrepancies. For instance, a ninth-grade text contains the highest overall metaphor density of 19.1%, but this is closely followed by a text from Grade 13 with a metaphor density of 19%.

The black horizontal line in Figure 4 represents the previously cited findings of Nacey (2013) for the 15.5% metaphor density in roughly 20,000 words of argumentative texts written in English by Norwegian college students. Some TraWL texts begin to approach the same metaphor density already in the ninth grade, but it is only in the upper secondary years (Grades 11–13) that most of the texts in this sample are on par with college students in this respect.

---

8 All 45 metaphor density charts, along with the data and R-code for this chapter, is available at https://susannacey.inn.no

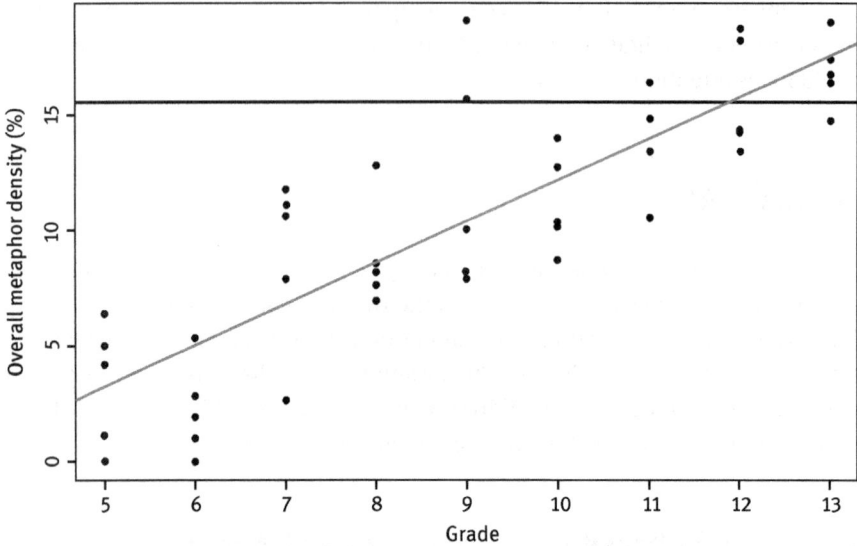

Figure 4: Metaphor density per grade level.

Figure 5 shows the identical scatterplot as in the previous figure, but where the regression lines indicate the trends for variation of the metaphor density per grade level of open-class words (dashed line) versus closed-class words (solid line). The strength of these associations is significant, r_s=0.76 and r_s=0.69 respectively (p < 0.0001 in both cases). Here we see that the metaphor density for open-class words grows more quickly than that of closed-class words. More specifically, this model shows us that we may expect an average growth of 2.2% metaphor density for the former, and 1.4% for the latter.

In their investigation, Littlemore et al. (2014: 128) found that the frequency of open-class metaphors overtook that of closed-class metaphors at the B2 (upper intermediate) level; they suggest that this development may indicate "a qualitative type of metaphor that learners need to use at this level". However, as we see by the crossing regression lines in Figure 5, this transition point appears much earlier in the TraWL texts. While the average metaphor density in the fifth-grade texts is higher for closed-class than for open-class words, this relationship begins

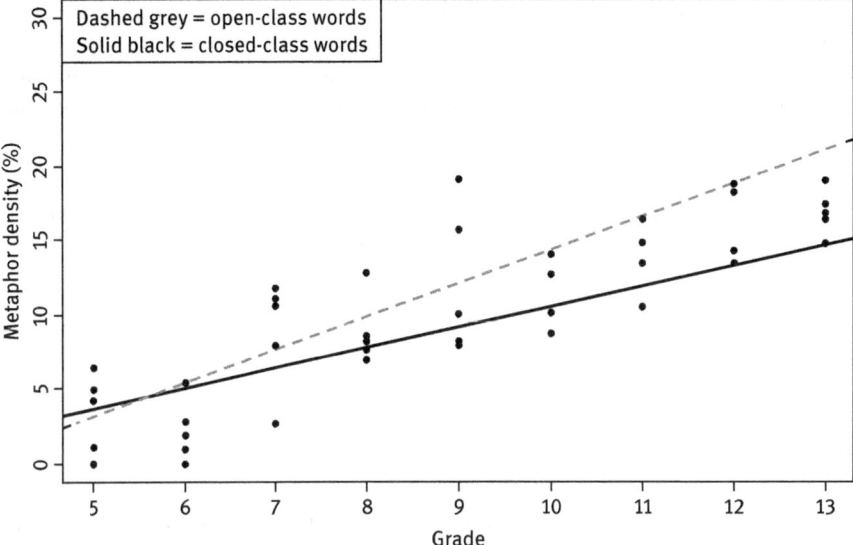

Figure 5: Metaphor density per grade level (regression lines for open-class and closed-class words).

to change already by the next grade – far below the B2 proficiency level – after which the difference steadily widens with each successive grade.[9]

The clear and strong correlation between the two factors of metaphor density and grade level, however, does not necessarily result from a causal relationship. Studies investigating metaphor use are subject to the confounding factor of topic. Indeed, Littlemore et al. (2014: 121) described their efforts to minimize the impact of topic type by extracting a selection of essays with some of the same words (e.g. *politician, politics, government*, etc.). Despite such mitigation attempts, however, there may still be minor variations in topic that inevitably effect the metaphorical language produced. By way of possible explanation for the increased use of open-class metaphor at B2 level and above, Littlemore et al. (2014: 128) acknowledge that "this is likely to be the result of tasks set".

In the present study, topic most probably has an even greater effect upon metaphorical production than in the Littlemore et al. (2014) study. This is partially due

---

9 The Norwegian Ministry and Research has determined successful completion of 11th grade English as the minimum threshold to satisfy university admission requirements, a level that is generally recognized as the equivalent of the CEFR B2 level (Hellekjær 2008: 13–14).

to the nature of the TraWL corpus, as it consists of assignments and examination texts that naturally occur in the pupils' classrooms. The corpus thus mirrors a general progression in language learning, where younger, less proficient learners first write about very concrete topics where metaphor often plays a subordinate role, appearing most often in function words such as prepositions and determiners. A typical such "concrete" topic was addressed in the fifth grade texts under study: "My family", exemplified in (4) below, presenting the shortest text in the data in its entirety. This text has only a single metaphorical word, the adjective *cool*.

(4)　　My family is crasy
　　　　My Family is **cool**
　　　　My broder cries alot
　　　　My grandmother is smart
　　　　My grandfather is friendly

More complex themes, such as the tenth-grade and twelfth-grade topic of immigration, involve more abstract issues. These naturally trigger the use of metaphorical language. Indeed, one of the main premises of CMT is that abstract concepts are structured and mentally represented in our thoughts in terms of concrete entities; these would then be expressed through linguistic metaphors in written texts. The increase in metaphor density across grades shown in Figures 4 and 5 is due to the increasingly abstract nature of the topics discussed, indicating a correlation between grade level and abstraction level. Ensuring uniformity of topic is thus a challenge in pseudo-longitudinal or longitudinal studies of metaphor development, in cases when the researcher is unable to influence topic choice and where the age of the informants greatly varies.

4.2 Does the Distribution of Metaphor Clusters Vary across Grade Levels?

The scatterplot in Figure 6 shows the observed occurrences of metaphor clusters per grade. Each dot represents one text, and a "jitter" function has been utilized to slightly separate otherwise overlapping dots that represent texts from the same grade containing the same number metaphor clusters.

　　We see here that no metaphor clusters were produced in texts from Grades 5–8, with the exception of a single outlier in a seventh-grade text. This testifies to the relatively low level of metaphor in texts written by the youngest children, perhaps due to task topic (as discussed above), and/or due to short text length. Other than that, the first clusters appear in the ninth grade, a trend that continues in the

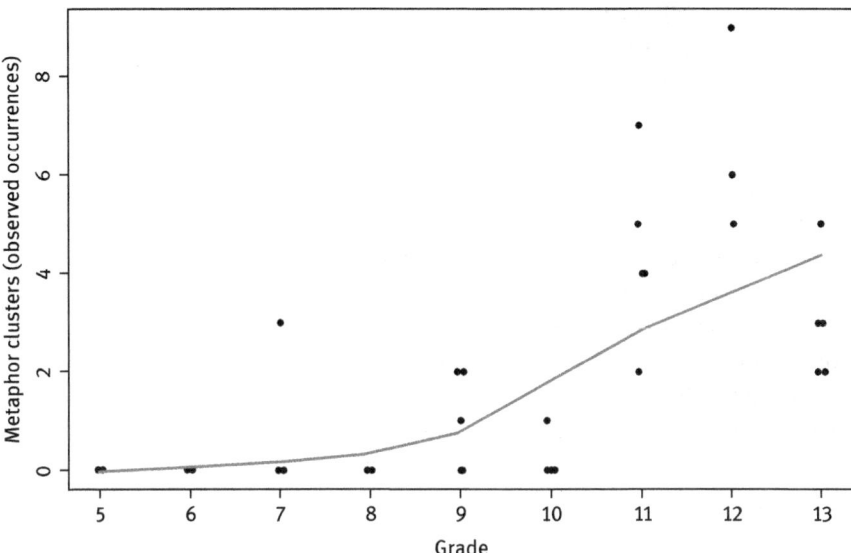

Figure 6: Observed occurrences of metaphor clusters per grade.

later grades. All texts in the upper secondary school grades 11–13 contain metaphor clusters, with one twelfth-grade text containing nine of them – the maximum number of metaphor clusters in a single text in my data. Pupils in the higher grades are thus using metaphor at a more sustained rate than earlier. The nonparametric regression curve in Figure 6 predicts that, after a certain point, the number of metaphor clusters will increase as grade increases. In brief, once pupils have begun to use metaphors in clusters, they will then continue to do so in increasing numbers (at least up to a certain, as yet undefined point).

4.3 What Function Does Metaphor Play across Grade Levels?

Addressing this question called for a manual search of all 45 texts to determine the main function of the identified metaphorically used words, both metaphors that appeared in clusters and those that did not. This analysis was informed by the functions of metaphors identified in the Littlemore et al. (2014) study:

- to serve an evaluative effect;
- to create a dramatic effect;
- to create dramatic contrasts;

- to organize discourse;
- to convey sarcasm;
- for humor; and
- to sum up/round off an argument.

The metaphorical language identified in the texts was also considered in light of the stated aims for writing English that are outlined in the Norwegian national curriculum, where being able to express oneself in writing is described as a basic skill in English (along with oral skills, being able to read, numeracy and digital skills). The curriculum provides competence aims for the conclusion of Grades 2, 4, 7, 10 (the final year of mandatory schooling), as well competence aims for the upper secondary years of Years 11–13.[10] While the competence aims for Grades 2 and 4 fall outside the scope of this study, the remaining descriptors are relevant for the present study.

4.3.1 Grades 5–7

The competence aims related to writing in English for the end of Grade 7 are to enable pupils to do the following:

- use reading and writing strategies
- understand and use a vocabulary related to familiar topics
- write coherent texts that narrate, retell and describe experiences and express own opinions
- use basic patterns for orthography, word inflection, sentence and text construction to produce texts

As touched on in section 4.1, metaphor appears to have little clear role at these levels, other than in incidental use with function words and with some highly frequent lexical verbs. Consider (5) and (6), where all metaphor-related words are written in bold text.

(5) I **have** a brother, a mother and a father.

(6) Once **upon** a time, there was three sister a dragon in a gingerbread house and a magic helper Mr Rock.

---

10 The Norwegian subject curriculum for English is available (in English) at https://www.udir.no/kl06/ENG1-03?lplang=http://data.udir.no/kl06/eng.

Example (5) is taken from a fifth-grade text where pupils were asked to write about their families, a topic which naturally triggers the metaphorical use of the verb *have* when discussing family members. Following MIPVU, the basic meaning of the verb *have* is that of showing possession (MM's third sense entry for the verb), while its contextual meaning is that of stating a relationship between someone and their family members (MM's fifth sense entry). These two senses are sufficiently distinct, and the contrast between them may be understood through comparison whereby we understand the relationship between people in terms of possession.

Example (6) is found in a sixth-grade text where pupils were asked to write a fairy tale. Here we find the metaphorical use of the preposition *upon*, whose basic sense corresponds to that of physically touching a surface or object. Metaphorical use of prepositions is hardly surprising, as previous empirical studies have found prepositions to be the most metaphorical word class of them all: "no other word class comes close to matching their metaphoricity" (Nacey 2013: 146). What is notable about this particular case, however, is that the preposition is contained in the fixed expression *once upon a time*, functioning as a discourse marker and thereby increasing cohesion. In this way, metaphor may begin to play a (minor) role in these earliest years towards achievement of the Grade 7 competence aim of writing coherent texts.

Despite a general tendency towards relatively little use of metaphor in the lower grades, individual differences can nevertheless be observed. Looking again at Figure 6 in section 4.2 showing the number of metaphor clusters per grade, we find a single seventh-grade text with three clusters. The moving metaphor density chart for this outlying text is presented in Figure 7. The text fragments forming the three identified metaphor clusters appear in sequential order immediately beneath the figure.

As shown in Table 1 in section 3.1, the topic of the seventh grade texts included in the present study was *Drawing / dream*. This broad topic resulted in rather varied written material, depending on the drawing or dream in question. The pupil responsible for the text from Figure 7 wrote about a crush he once had on a girl in school. Here he uses direct metaphor to explain the more abstract experience of love. Note that by the MIPVU protocol, all lexical words involved in a direct metaphor are coded as metaphor-related words (e.g. *heart*, *beating*, and *peices* [sic] in the first sentence of Cluster 2); in addition, direct metaphors may also contain function words that are also metaphorical in use (e.g. *in to* [sic], in the same sentence). This method for coding metaphor naturally results in a high concentration of words that are marked as metaphor. They thereby contribute to an increased metaphor density, and appear as metaphor clusters in metaphor density charts.

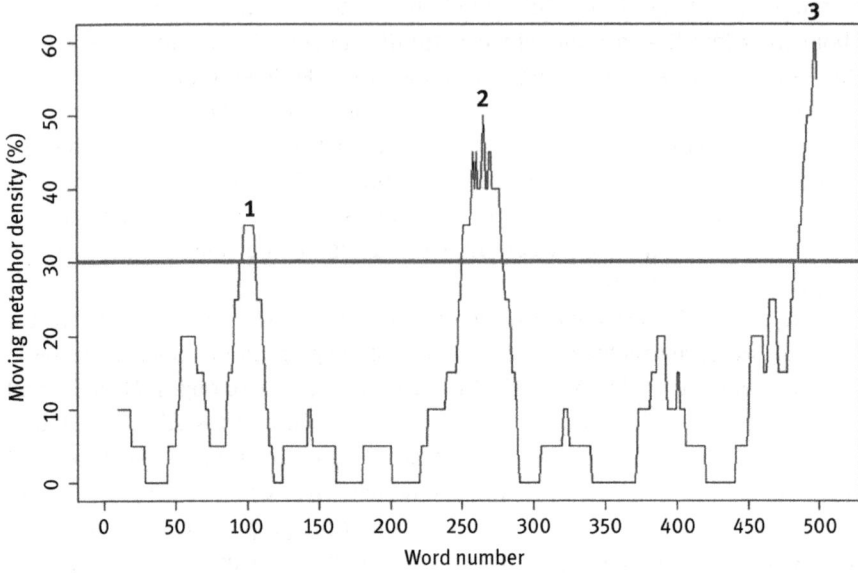

Figure 7: Moving metaphor density chart: 7th grade text, 508 words long.

Cluster 1= I remember that my **heart beating** and that I **had butterflies in** my **stomach**.
Cluster 2 = It *felt like* my **heart breaking in to** a thousand **peices**. It *felt like* I got **punched** in the **gut**. It hurt *like* **knives stabbing** me.
Cluster 3= It *felt like* someone **punched** my **balls** and **gut**. My **heart broke in to** a thousand **peices** and **started burning**. I'm **heart broken** and angry.

Bold black script = metaphor-related words; *Italics* = metaphorical flags;
Bold grey script = WIDLII

In Cluster 1, the pupil introduces an apparent shift in topic – from love to butterflies – that only makes sense when interpreted metaphorically. Added to this is the remembrance of his *heart beating*, which may be interpreted literally or metaphorically (categorized as the MIPVU "WIDLII" category [When in doubt, leave it in], and hence written here in bold grey rather than black script). Cluster 2 contains a series of metaphorical similes introduced by the italicized metaphor flags *felt like* and *like*, whereas a metaphorical simile in Cluster 3 is used to introduce an extended metaphor that continues to the end of the text. While all three clusters function as dramatic effect, this third cluster also functions as a conclusion.[11] In short, this student uses metaphor to "narrate, retell and describe experiences", Grade 7 competence aims that build upon those from earlier years.

4.3.2 Grades 8–10

The competence aims related to writing in English for the end of Grade 10 are to enable pupils to do the following:

- choose and use different reading and writing strategies that are suitable for the purpose
- understand and use a general vocabulary related to different topics
- demonstrate the ability to distinguish positively and negatively loaded expressions referring to individuals and groups
- write different types of texts with structure and coherence
- use central patterns for orthography, word inflection, sentence and text construction to produce texts

At these levels, we find more metaphors used with an evaluative function than in earlier texts. For instance, in eighth-grade texts, Selena Gomez is described as *sweet*, Gerard Way's music has a *dark aura*, Justin Bieber is a *big star*, and Austin Mahomed is characterized as *cool* – all (in these cases) positively loaded expressions about individuals that pupils are expected to learn to distinguish. Despite such examples, however, these pupils display a stronger tendency towards employing non-metaphorical language to describe individuals:

(7)   Selena Gomez have black/brown hair, brown eyes and are not that tall.

(8)   [Austin Mahomed] is also cut,[12] strong, **hot**, nice, fantastic, happy, and peaceful.

The pupil in (7) provides a physical, and hence non-metaphorical, description of the artist, reminiscent of texts from younger pupils who described their

---

11 Note that while metaphor clusters provide indications of where analysts could focus attention, not all clusters have a readily identifiable discourse function such as was observed in this seventh-grade text. For instance, the cluster documented as example (3) in section 3.3 does not appear to serve any particular unified role, despite containing a high concentration of metaphor.

12 Analyzed as the adjective *cute*.

family members almost exclusively in terms of their physical attributes. Even descriptions of other less concrete facets of artists, however, do not necessarily lead to great amounts of metaphorical production. For instance, only one of the seven adjectives used to characterize Austin Mahomed in (8) is a metaphor-related word.

Metaphor at these levels also plays additional roles beyond evaluation, apparent in the lower grades to a lesser extent. Examples are found in a text about ninth-grade handball, the assigned topic being "the most exciting thing I know". The author of this text writes about development of prowess in the game variously in terms of a battle, in terms of physical elevation, and in terms of a difficult journey; see examples (9), (10) and (11) respectively.[13]

(9)   personally I **struggled with having** confidence

(10) coaches **build up** players and **boost** their confidence

(11) I can **take** the next **step** and **push** myself even **further** and **show** everyone that I can manage anything I want to.

Example (11) is the closing sentence in the text, and serves to effectively round off the pupil's arguments in a strong and evaluative way, a function that Littlemore et al. (2014: 134) record observing at the CEFR C1 level. Other expressions involving metaphorical movement or journeys are evident in the tenth-grade texts. As an example, one pupil writes about adjusting to different cultures in terms of a path immigrants travel after they "**come into** my local community":

(12) To learn new and difficult languages and traditions **in** another community is difficult. Especially when you don't **get** help **along** the **way**.

Such movement metaphors arguably act as a cohesive element in texts, and hence contribute towards achievement of the Grade 10 competence aims of writing with structure and coherence.

---

13 Example (11) was previously cited as (1), but is reproduced here for the sake of convenience, with co-text added for clarity.

4.3.3 Grades 11–13

The competence aims related to writing in English for the end of Grade 13 are to enable pupils to do the following:

- evaluate and use suitable reading and writing strategies adapted for the purpose and type of text
- understand and use an extensive general vocabulary and an academic vocabulary related to one's education programme
- write different types of texts with structure and coherence suited to the purpose and situation
- use patterns for orthography, word inflection and varied sentence and text construction to produce texts

At these levels, pupils show some adeptness at using metaphor with appropriate phraseology and collocations, to a degree that is less evident in texts from Grades 10 or below. Examples include the following:

11th grade: **pursue** a scientific career, **consume** information, X allows you to **tap into far** more of the world's intellectual **resources,** X will **give** you the best **return** for your efforts

12th grade: **spend** time, a **cold** relationship [between children and parents], **confronted with** questions, it all **comes down to** X, **take** the initiative

13th grade: **make** a **mark on** this world, **make** X **see things in** a **different light**, a **dream come true**

Greater variation of discourse markers involving metaphorically used words are also evident in the Grades 11–13 texts: *on one side/on the other side, after all, to sum up, in this way, in* conclusion.

Note that not all collocations involving metaphorical expressions are completely successful, in the sense that they do not all adhere to conventionally established colligational or collocation patterns. Consider examples (13) and (14).

(13) [English is] an especially complex language to **get grips with** [11th grade]

(14) the kids are **keeping** secrets *for* their parents **about** their social lives and who they are **hanging out** with [12th grade]

In (13), we see an unconventional variation of the expression *to get to grips with,* where the pupil has omitted the preposition *to.* However, this omission does not interfere with successful communication; the text is still comprehensible and unlikely to be misunderstood. Such unconventional phrasing may be compared to that in (14), where the pupil substitutes the preposition *for* for the preposition *from* that normally appears in this collocation.[14] With the preposition as written, the sentence implies that the youth are protecting secrets that belong to the parents. The pupil arguably wanted to express the opposite – namely that the youth are protecting their own secrets, rather than those of their parents.

Personification first appears in the TraWL texts at these grade levels, as in (15) and (16), retrieved from two different eleventh-grade texts.

(15) ... your message **reaches out** to a **great deal** of more people ...

(16) Imagine if every country **spoke** only their own language ...

While the phrasal verb *reaches out*, whose basis sense denotes that of a person stretching out an arm, represents a clear case of personification, the sentence in (16) can be analyzed in more than one way. One could interpret *country* as a metonymy standing for the people within that country, in which case the verb *spoke* would not be metaphorical in use. Alternatively, this instance can be understood as personification where *country* is personified through the verb *spoke*, which normally has a human agent. Rather than viewing the distinction between metaphor and metonymy as an "either/or" dichotomy, however, it is more useful to view the two as a continuum between with two clear outer poles; between these poles, metaphor and metonymy interact in different ways (see e.g. Deignan 2005: 60–61). The co-occurrence of personification and metonymy was also observed in Littlemore et al. (2014: 132), and has been noted in other types of data and discussed in the relevant literature (e.g. Dorst 2011; Low 1999; Nacey 2013: 18)

Texts at these grade levels also evidence greater ability to use metaphor to create textual cohesion. As an example, one twelfth-grade text about challenges immigrants face in Norway begins with the metaphorical idiom "Do not judge a book by its cover" (previously cited as example (2)). The pupil employs this idiom to establish an overall cohesive framework for the text, whose main themes concern how immigrants may be unfairly judged due to their foreign-looking appearance. Further, some pupils at these levels display an ability to manipulate metaphor, as in (17) where the pupil alters the otherwise frozen metaphorical expression "needle in a haystack".

---

14 Following the MIPVU protocol, which does not consider the prepositions *for* or *of* for metaphoricity, the word *for* in this example is coded 'not metaphor'. By contrast, the preposition *from*, appearing in this same context, would be coded as in indirect metaphor. Its basic meaning is MM's 3a sense entry: 'starting at a particular place and moving away'.

(17) **From** the **big perspective** I'm no significance, not even the **slightest bit** of a **needle in** a **haystack**.

Such creative appropriation of an established English expression provides possible evidence of increasing metaphorical competence as the pupil's "feel" for the language grows, facilitating experimentation with wording (see MacArthur 2010: 164). It should be noted, however, that collocational deviation is a risky strategy for L2 learners, whose potential linguistic creativity may be taken for linguistic error, even when their production is understandable in context (see e.g. Nacey 2013: 163–168).

Finally, the use of metaphor to conclude arguments, while evident in earlier grades, may be observed more often in texts written in Grades 11–13. An example is provided in (18), serving as the conclusion of an eleventh-grade text about the importance of learning English.

(18) When a language **barrier** is **lifted**, there is more **space** for opportunities understanding and for common **ground**.

Here we find both *space* and *ground* from a source domain of some physical location, with *barrier* and *lifted* adding a sense of physical obstacle. Such close proximity of several metaphors from the same or related source domains contributes towards reawakening the perceived metaphorical nature of the words. This use represents an instance of potentially deliberate metaphor, intentionally produced as metaphor through the introduction of an alien element to change the reader's perspective (see Reijnierse et al. 2017). Littlemore et al. (2014: 137, 142) document parallel examples from their data, and argue that such production belongs in the CEFR descriptors for the C2 level.

5 Concluding Thoughts

The overall objective of the present explorative study has been to shed further light on the development and function of metaphorical production as proficiency increases. The investigative approach adopted here has featured the exploration of both quantitative and qualitative facets of English metaphorical production in L2 learner texts from the Norwegian Grades 5–13, where pupils range from ages 10–19.

When it comes to quantitative measures, we have first seen that the metaphor density of texts increases steadily as grade level increases (section 4.1). In addition, while the metaphor density of function words is greater than that of open-class words in texts written by the very youngest students (ages 10–11), this relationship quickly changes. Pupils begin to produce relatively more metaphors in the open-word classes than in the closed-word classes already by the next grade, when pupils are aged 11–12 – a trend that continues unabated as the grades and ages increase. Further, metaphor clusters, defined here as a 30% metaphor frequency over a minimum 20-word span, hardly appear in texts written in the lowest grades, arguably resulting from a short text length and relatively concrete topics. However, metaphor clusters do appear in texts from the higher grades, in increasing frequency as grade level rises.

When it comes to more qualitative analysis, this study indicates that the role of metaphor in discourse evolves as the grades increase. In the lowest grades (5–7), metaphor has no clear function, although there are individual exceptions. Texts in later grades (8–10) evidence functions such as evaluation and conclusion. In the uppermost grades (11–13), metaphor contributes to a wider variety of textual features: (mostly) appropriate phraseology and collocations, more varied discourse markers, greater textual cohesion, personification, along with summing up and concluding.

All texts at these highest levels in Grades 11–13 contain metaphor clusters. The occurrence of such concentrated pockets of metaphor may thus be indicative of a qualitative change in the type of metaphorical language required of more proficient language users, in discussions that address more abstract topics than those dealt with in lower grades. As discussed in section 4.1, Littlemore et al. (2014) suggest that such a qualitative change may be indicated by the point at which the metaphor density of open-class words becomes greater than that of closed-class words, found at the B2 level in their material. That this transition point appears so much earlier in the TraWL texts investigated here raises questions concerning the significance of this point, as well as the proficiency level at which it generally occurs.

The present chapter details an initial study of metaphor production across grade level, based on data from a longitudinal corpus that is currently under compilation. As a consequence, the findings presented here should be interpreted with caution, particularly as they are based upon only five texts per grade level. Moreover, future investigation into such issues should ideally control for the factors of topic uniformity and text length, considerable challenges for investigations into the development of metaphorical production in either longitudinal or pseudo-longitudinal investigations dealing with a wide range of ages and/or including young learners. This study nevertheless represents a first exploration of such data, paving the way for future research.

References

Cameron, Lynne & Graham Low. 2004. Figurative variation in episodes of education talk and text. *European Journal of English Studies* 8. 355–373.

Deignan, Alice. 2005. *Metaphor and corpus linguistics*. Amsterdam: John Benjamins.

Dorst, Aletta G. 2011. *Metaphor in fiction: Language, thought and communication*. Amsterdam: VU University Amsterdam dissertation. http://dare. ubvu.vu.nl/bitstream/handle/1871/19629/dissertation.pdf?sequence=1 (accessed 23 August 2018).

Granger, Sylviane, Estelle Dagneaux, Fanny Meunier & Magali Paquot (eds.). 2009. *International corpus of learner English: Version 2*. Louvain-la-Neuve: Presses universitaires de Louvain.

Hellekjær, Glenn Ole. 2008. Lesing som grunnleggende ferdighet: En utfordring for engelskfaget. [Reading as a basic skill: A challenge for the subject of English]. *Språk og Språkundervisning* (4). 10–15.

Hoang, Ha & Frank Boers. 2018. Gauging the association of EFL learners' writing proficiency and their use of metaphorical language. *System* 74. 1–8. doi:https://doi.org/10.1016/j.system.2018.02.004 (accessed 23 August 2018).

Lakoff, George & Mark Johnson. 1980. *Metaphors we live by*. Chicago, IL: University of Chicago Press.

Littlemore, Jeannette, Tina Krennmayr, James Turner & Sarah Turner. 2012. Investigating figurative proficiency at different levels of second language writing. *Cambridge ESOL* (47). 14–26.

Littlemore, Jeannette, Tina Krennmayr, James Turner & Sarah Turner. 2014. An investigation in metaphor use at different levels of second language writing. *Applied Linguistics* 35(2). 117–144.

Littlemore, Jeannette & Graham Low. 2006. *Figurative thinking and foreign language learning*. Basingstoke: Palgrave Macmillan.

Low, Graham. 1999. "This paper thinks… ": Investigating the acceptability of the metaphor AN ESSAY IS A PERSON. In Lynne Cameron & Graham Low (eds.), *Researching and Applying Metaphor*, 221–248. Cambridge: Cambridge University Press.

MacArthur, Fiona. 2010. Metaphorical competence in EFL: Where we are and where we should be going? A view from the classroom. *AILA Review* 23. 155–173.

Nacey, Susan. 2013. *Metaphors in learner English*. Amsterdam: John Benjamins.

Nacey, Susan. 2017. Metaphor comprehension and production in a second language. In Elena Semino & Zsófia Demjén (eds.), *The Routledge handbook of metaphor and language*, 503–516. London: Routledge.

Pasma, Tryntje. 2011. *Metaphor and register variation: The personalization of Dutch news discourse*. Amsterdam: VU University Amsterdam dissertation. http://dare.ubvu.vu.nl/handle/1871/19630 (accessed 23 August 2018).

R Core Team. 2014. R: A language and environment for statistical computing. Vienna, Austria: R Foundation for Statistical Computing. http://www.R-project.org/ (accessed 23 August 2018).

Reijnierse, W. Gudrun, Christian Burgers, Tina Krennmayr & Gerard J. Steen. 2018. DMIP: A method for identifying potentially deliberate metaphor in language use. *Corpus Pragmatics* 2(2). 129–147.

Steen, Gerard J., Aletta G. Dorst, J. Berenike Herrmann, Anna A. Kaal, Tina Krennmayr & Tryntje Pasma. 2010. *A method for linguistic metaphor identification: From MIP to MIPVU*. Amsterdam: John Benjamins.

Turner, James 2010. *Investigating figurative language in EFL learners' writing across levels of proficiency*. Birmingham: University of Birmingham MA thesis.

Irene Castellano-Risco and Ana M. Piquer-Píriz
Measuring Secondary-School L2 Learners Vocabulary Knowledge: Metaphorical Competence as Part of General Lexical Competence

1 Introduction

Figurative language pervades our daily communicative exchanges although it very often goes unnoticed by speakers, even in their native language (L1). In the process of learning a foreign language (L2), the importance of dealing with non-literal meanings has been widely recognised (Cameron and Low 1999; Littlemore and Low 2006b; Low 1988). Two main reasons seem to justify paying attention to figurative meanings in the L2 classroom: On the one hand, metaphor has been shown to be ubiquitous in language (Lakoff and Johnson 1980; 1999) and figurative uses are extensively employed in any communicative situation, including the very basic ones, from early infancy (see Özçalışkan 2011 for a review) and, therefore, L2 learners need to deal with them from the first stages of the L2 learning process and seem to be ready to do so (see Piquer-Píriz, this volume). On the other hand, the misuse and misunderstanding of this type of language has been reported as one of the reasons why non-native speakers are perceived as outsiders in social interactions. Some scholars (Danesi 1992, 2008, 2016; Littlemore 2001; Littlemore and Low 2006a) have even pointed at the importance for L2 learners of developing what has been labelled as "metaphorical competence". In practice, however, neither defining what this competence consists in nor finding ways to empirically measure it have proved to be easy tasks. Recently, some research studies have examined learners' production of metaphor (Hoang and Boers 2018; Littlemore, et al. 2014; Nacey 2013; Turner 2014). In this chapter, we focus on learners' understanding of metaphor and propose a way of measuring what could be a specific dimension of L2 learners' metaphorical competence, namely, their understanding of metaphorically-used words.

The chapter is structured as follows: first, the notion of metaphorical competence is analysed by considering the different theoretical approaches to this

Irene Castellano-Risco, English Philology Department, University of Extremadura, Badajoz, Spain, e-mail: ircastellano@unex.es
Ana M. Piquer-Píriz, English Philology (Faculty of Education), University of Extremadura, Badajoz, Spain, e-mail: anapiriz@unex.es

https://doi.org/10.1515/9783110630367-010

concept found in the literature as well as the main proposals that have been made to explore it in L2 learners' language. Here we outline our own proposal to measure what could be considered one dimension of learners' metaphorical competence, specifically, their ability to understand figurative meanings. After that, we present a study in which, following this proposal, we gauged the understanding and recognition of figurative meanings by a group of seventy-seven third grade secondary school learners of English (aged 14-15), combining tools that have been widely used and validated in vocabulary studies, i.e., the 2K and the Academic Level versions of the Vocabulary Levels Tests (Schmitt, Schmitt and Claphman 2001) and the Productive Vocabulary Levels Tests (Laufer and Nation 1999), in conjunction with methods developed by metaphor scholars (MIPVU, Steen et al. 2010) with the aim of highlighting how these two research areas can be mutually enriching.

2 Metaphorical Competence

The notion of metaphorical competence can be traced back to the 1970s in the work carried out in experimental psychology. In a seminal paper published in 1978, Gardner and Winner already attempted to establish the importance of this notion for the humanities (philosophers, literary critics and linguists) and how complementary research among psychologists and "humanistically oriented scholars" would mean that "future treatments of figurative language should be significantly enriched" (Garder and Winner 1978: 141). Over three decades later, it can be said that the treatment of figurative language, particularly that brought about by Cognitive Linguistics, has certainly been enriched by the complementary work of applied linguists (e.g. Cameron 2003 or Low 1988), psychologists (Gibbs 1994, 2008; Robinson and Ellis 2008), and cognitive linguists themselves (Lakoff and Johnson 1980, 1999; or Kövecses 2002, 2005, among others).

When considering specifically the notion of metaphorical competence, some key contributions have been made, mostly by applied linguists (for a recent review, see Nacey 2017: 504–505). In our view, two important insights have emerged from this literature: On the one hand, the recognition of the importance for L2 learners to develop this ability at the different stages of their process of acquiring the target language and, on the other, the idea that metaphorical competence is not restricted to a particular dimension but, rather, aspects of metaphor in lexis or discourse need to be addressed by learners in all four dimensions of communicative competence, i.e., linguistic, sociolinguistic, discourse and strategic (c.f. Littlemore and Low 2006a, 2006b).

A pioneering scholar in this field is Danesi, who has been working on metaphorical competence for the past two decades (1986, 1992, 2008, 2016). For this author, L2 learners' control of figurative language, which is what he defines as metaphorical competence, is essential for them to achieve real L2 proficiency (Danesi 1986). In his view, the idea of metaphorical competence in Second Language Acquisition (SLA) somehow overlaps with that of communicative competence and he formulated the notion of 'Conceptual Fluency' (Danesi 1992) which he defined as the learners' mental capacity to use figurative discourse systematically. Behind this conception is the implication that the systematic nature of figurative language makes it teachable in the same way as other aspects of the L2. Low's (1988: 129) definition of the construct, "a number of skills related to metaphor which native speakers are frequently expected to be good at, and which learners need to develop to some degree if they hope to be seen as competent users of the language", also highlights the importance for L2 learners of developing this ability to be perceived as competent users of the target language. Littlemore (2001: 461) went a step further in identifying these 'skills' and established four main components that make up learners' metaphorical competence: "(a) originality of metaphor production, (b) fluency of metaphor interpretation, (c) ability to find meaning in metaphor, and (d) speed in finding meaning in metaphor." These two authors together published a comprehensive monograph (Littlemore and Low 2006b) devoted to figurative thinking and foreign language instruction in which they highlight the importance of figurative language in the L2 learning process and show that learners have to deal with aspects of metaphor at all stages of proficiency and in all the different dimensions of communicative competence in the L2 (grammatical, textual, illocutionary and sociolinguistic). All these accounts of metaphorical competence illustrate the intrinsic complexity of the construct as well as applied linguists' concerns for its applicability in the process of learning a foreign language. These theoretical notions have recently given rise to some proposals to measure empirically L2 learners' metaphorical competence. Although there has been an attempt to relate learners' metaphorical competence and their overall language proficiency (Teymouri and Dowlatabadi 2014), the bulk of research studies in this area consists of corpus work that has focused on measuring learners' production of metaphor (Littlemore's [2001] first component, i.e., 'originality of metaphor production') in their written outputs. For example, Nacey (2013) reports a comparison between Norwegian, advanced learners' texts extracted from the *Norwegian subset of the International Corpus of Learner English* (NICLE) and those produced by British L1 novice writers from the Louvain Corpus of Native English Essays (LOCNESS), and Turner (2014) analyses the presence of metaphor in exam-based written production of French and Japanese learners of English. To the best of our knowledge, one of the most comprehensive and ambitious study into learners' production of metaphor so far is Littlemore et al (2014). Using the Cambridge Learner Corpus of exam scripts, they analysed two hundred essays produced by successful Greek and German learners of English across five of the levels (A2 to C2) established by the Common European Framework of Reference for Languages (CEFRL) in order to determine the amount of metaphor employed at the different stages and the different functions for which learners used those metaphors. The authors found that metaphor usage increased as students progressed through the levels, and so did the sophistication of the function for which learners used metaphors. However, error rates involving metaphor remained significantly higher than general error rates, even at the higher levels, and L1 transfer was seen to have an effect on metaphor-related errors. Along this line of research, Hoang and Boers (2018) have also explored the association of advanced, EFL learners' writing proficiency and their use of metaphorical language in a more homogenous corpus consisting of two hundred and fifty-two essays produced by language majors from three year levels in an undergraduate programme at a university in Viet Nam. Correct metaphor use was also found to be strongly correlated with the students' year levels and the grades awarded to the essays.

In this chapter, we propose the analysis of a different dimension of metaphorical competence, specifically, the understanding/recognition of metaphor (which corresponds to Littlemore's [2001] third dimension: 'ability to find meaning in metaphor'), as we consider that L2 learners' understanding of metaphorical meanings is part of their general lexical competence which is defined as the ability to recognize and use the words of an L2 in a native-like way (cf. López-Mezquita 2005). Studies on lexical competence date back to the beginning of the twentieth century, and, since early stages, researchers have attempted to identify the different types of knowledge involved in vocabulary development. In most of the proposals, metaphorical competence *per se* has not been explicitly mentioned, but it has been implicitly included in the aspects analysed since the very first attempts. For example, Cronbach (1942) distinguished between five main vocabulary knowledge dimensions, one of them being '*breadth of meaning*' (here 'breadth' is not related to vocabulary size but it refers the understanding and managing of those words with more than one meaning*)*, which made reference to the understanding and managing of polysemous words. Years later, Anderson and Freebody (1976) encapsulated this idea of polysemy and full understanding of a word by giving it a new label -'depth'- and defining it as follows: " ... [There] is a second dimension of vocabulary knowledge, namely the quality or "depth" of understanding. We shall assume that, for most purposes, a person has a sufficiently deep understanding of a word if it conveys to him or her all of the distinctions that would be understood by an ordinary adult under normal circumstances" (1981: 92-93). Meara (1996) went a step further and reflected on the importance of the interaction between both dimensions (*'breadth'* and *'depth'*), in his case labelled as 'size' and 'organization', proposing that, as a learner's lexicon grows, the importance of size decreases, while the importance of depth of knowledge or organisation of the lexicon increases. Recently, in a study about L2 learners' vocabulary knowledge of primary and peripheral meanings, Aizawa (2018: 31) acknowledged that: "We still do not know whether the knowledge of words with multiple meanings should be categorized as width or depth of vocabulary knowledge". But, he concludes, following Meara, that 'breadth of knowledge' is more important for lower-intermediate learners while 'depth of knowledge' is more important at advanced stages.

Finally, Nation (2001) developed the most comprehensive categorization of lexical competence up to that moment, by identifying three main categories of word knowledge, namely, *form, meaning* and *use*; each of which containing specific aspects. In the case of the category *meaning*, he distinguished also between three aspects of knowledge: *form and meaning, concepts and references* and the different *associations* that learners may have when meeting the word. It is in these two latter concepts that metaphorical competence could be considered. In addition, he included a second classification that had been developed in parallel to all these proposals: the distinction between receptive and productive knowledge. With this distinction, grounded in the experience of many teachers, and reflected, among others, in Palmer's (1921) and Henriksen's (1999) proposals, the understanding of a term and the production of the same term are seen as different processes, i.e., it is recognized that a learner may be able to understand or recognize a word, but at the same time, may not have total control of it and may experience difficulties in recalling or producing the word. This distinction is also relevant to the conceptualization of metaphorical competence, because, as Littlemore and Low (2006b: 46) pointed out "foreign language learners probably need to understand metaphor more often than they need to produce it" and this is particularly the case at basic levels of proficiency (A1-B1 CEFRL levels), which would correspond to the most common levels of learners of English in mainstream education in many countries around the world.

In our view, metaphorical competence is strongly linked to a more global capacity in the sense of Danesi's 'conceptual fluency' or Littlemore and Low's 'figurative thinking' that consists in the ability to use our knowledge of concrete things to understand abstract concepts. As is well known, this is the basis of the Cognitive Linguistic paradigm (Lakoff and Johnson 1980, 1999). This natural ability is conceptual and, therefore, not restricted to the way we reason in our native language but also applicable to other languages we may happen to speak and is part of the human reasoning abilities from early infancy (cf. Özçalışkan 2011). In the early 1990s, Levorato and Cacciari (1992: 416-417) already highlighted the importance, even for children, to develop a 'figurative competence'. It has been shown that even very young L2 learners are able to reason metaphorically and metonymically when confronted with non-literal L2 meanings (Piquer-Píriz 2005, 2008a, 2008b, 2010). These studies show that children as young as five years of age resort to analogical (metaphorical) or associative (metonymical) reasoning when asked to explain some of the semantic extensions of specific words in English whose core meanings they know.

At this point, it is also very important to distinguish between the mental process and its linguistic products (cf. Gibbs' [1999] for a seminal discussion on this issue). Although human beings seem to be endowed with this natural ability to perceive the underlying motivation of non-literal meanings from early infancy, a direct extrapolation of this strategy to lexical items in an L2 is not possible because different languages may encode figurative meanings in different ways. For instance, the long parts of a watch or clock that move around and show the time are called *'hands'* in English. This figurative meaning of the body part term seems to be motivated by a metonymy-based metaphor where the shared standard information about one specific function of the human hand, i.e., pointing or indicating, and the same function of the device of a watch or clock may have given rise to this semantic extension. In Spanish, the preferred realisation for the *'hands of a watch'* is *'agujas'* ('needles') although *'manecillas'* (literally, 'little hands') also exist. The Spanish realisation *'agujas'* focuses on shape rather than on function. Boers (2013) makes a fundamental point in relation to this aspect that may, perhaps, explain why the important findings of the research literature into the applications of some of the main tenets from CL to foreign language instruction (see Piquer-Píriz and Alejo-González 2016 for an overview, and Boers 2011 for an insightful discussion of the contributions to the field but also the main methodological limitations of these studies) have not reached L2 classrooms as much as it would be expected: The fact that figurative meanings are motivated does not mean that they are predictable. But this is, precisely, according to Boers, why enhancing and promoting figurative awareness can be of help for L2 learners:

> It cannot be overemphasised that 'motivated' in CL jargon is not synonymous with 'predictable' [...] If there were no room for arbitrariness, then all natural languages would look and sound identical. If the CL endeavour to describe linguistic phenomena as motivated holds a certain promise for language pedagogy, it is precisely because in many cases the motivation is not blatantly obvious to the learner. (Boers 2013: 211).

This author has suggested that rather than encouraging learners to generate L2 metaphors, it may be more successful to instil a 'metaphor awareness' in learners to "organize the steady stream of figurative language they are exposed to" (Boers 2000: 564). In this same line is MacArthur's (2010) seminal paper on metaphorical competence in EFL where she argues for the importance of adding 'metaphor awareness' generally to the experience of learning English in instructed L2 setting:

> In this approach, the specific pedagogical techniques employed [...] are seen to be less significant than the general foregrounding of metaphor and the effect(s) this may have on learners' growing awareness of how metaphor permeates language (their own and the L2 to be learnt) as reflected in the growing felicity of the metaphorical language used in their written work. (ibid.: 157)

In our view, any understanding of metaphorical competence as a strategy employed by L2 learners cannot be seen in isolation from the rest of strategies they may resort to when confronted with new lexical items in the target language. However, scant attention seems to have been paid to metaphorical competence in vocabulary studies. Since the 1990s, there has been a soaring interest in the identification of the strategies learners use to develop their lexical competence. In this regard, a large number of taxonomies have been proposed (Stöffer 1995; Gu and Johnson 1996; Schmitt 1997; Nation 2001; Tseng, Dörnyei and Schmitt 2006; or Siriwan 2007). Yet, these proposals show little consideration for the development of metaphorical competence. For example, the two best-known taxonomies (Schmitt 1997; Nation 2001) mention no strategies to develop learners' capacity to understand/produce metaphorical terms. Schmitt (1997) identified a total of fifty-eight strategies, none of which seems to be specifically focused on aiding the understanding of figurative meanings. Similarly, Nation (2001) mentioned sixteen general strategies, and these were all devoted to the expansion of other vocabulary dimensions, neglecting, once again, the metaphorical dimension.

To be fair, it must be acknowledged that, conversely, few metaphor scholars, with the exception of Boers (e.g. 2013), tend to take into consideration research findings from vocabulary studies in mainstream applied linguistics.

This chapter is an attempt to connect two fields that can enrich one another. In order to do so, it presents an exploratory study in which well-known vocabulary tests that have been validated and are widely used with different learners in many parts of the world (Schmitt 2010) were employed to measure secondary-school learners' general lexical competence as well as their understanding/recognition of figurative word meanings.

3 The Study: Measuring L2 Secondary School Learners' Vocabulary Knowledge: Metaphorical Competence within Lexical Competence

3.1 Objectives

Two main objectives were established for the study:

1. To measure L2 secondary school learners' understanding of figurative meanings in English using a validated test to measure lexical competence.
2. To compare their understanding of figurative meanings with their understanding of non-figurative senses.

3.2 Design of the Study

3.2.1 Participants

The study was conducted in a medium-size town of Extremadura (western Spain) as part of a bigger project (Castellano-Risco, in preparation). A convenience sample of seventy-seven students (thirty-eight boys and thirty-nine girls) was analysed. Participants were asked to complete the Vocabulary Levels Tests (VLT) and the Productive Vocabulary Levels Tests (PVLT) at two points within two different academic years, the first time when they were in 3rd year (Year 9) and a year after, when they were in 4th year of Compulsory Secondary Education (Year 10).

3.2.2 Instruments

Two instruments were used in the study. In order to measure their receptive vocabulary size, students were asked to complete the 2K and academic bands of the VLT (Schmitt, Schmitt and Claphman 2001). Developed by Nation (1983) and refined by Schmitt et al. (2001), this test has been validated and is one of the most widely used tests when measuring L2 vocabulary knowledge (Schmitt 2010). It consists of five levels and, in each level, thirty words, grouped in ten clusters, are presented to the test-takers. In each cluster, there are three definitions and six options, and test-takers are asked to match the definitions with their corresponding word. The test is designed in a way that minimizes the guessing aids and all the words, the tested ones and those presented in the definitions, belong to the level tested or to lower levels.

In order to measure productive vocabulary size, the 2K and academic bands of the PVLT (Laufer and Nation 1999) were used. This set of tests measures the productive knowledge of five main bands of vocabulary: four frequency levels and an academic band. In each, eighteen sentences are presented. These sentences include an incomplete word and test-takers are asked to complete the word, bearing in mind the context provided with the sentence. In spite of being called a "productive" test, Schmitt (2010) argues that it can be considered a form-recall test, as test-takers are asked to recall some words, but they are not actually producing any lexical item. Similarly, Read (2000) defines it as a "selective" test, because the target language is pre-selected. From their point of view, the PVLT cannot be considered a productive test properly, because it does not measure what is produced by the learners, but how test-takers are able to create connections with other words.

The VLT and the PVLT are similar in the sense that they measure the same bands that correspond to the number of word families considered sufficient to engage in a daily conversation (2,000); and the academic band that measures knowledge of the words included in the Academic Word List (Coxhead 2000) and its precedessor, the University World List (Xue and Nation 1984). Moreover, they also present the same distribution of word classes, following a 3 (noun): 2 (verb): 1 (adjective) ratio (Schmitt, Schmitt and Clapham 2001).

3.2.3 Procedure

Following the objectives that were established for the general project (Castellano-Risco in preparation), the tests were administered at two different times within two academic years: March, 2016 (T1) and February, 2017 (T2). At T1, the data collection took one day, but at T2, two days were needed: the first day, the test-takers answered the VLT and, on the second day, the PVLT was administered. Students, thus, had to complete six different tests in total, as shown in Table 1.

Table 1: Data collection periods.

Data collection period	Tests
Time 1 (March, 2016)	– Version 1 of the 2K and academic bands of the VLT (2 tests)
Time 2 (February, 2017)	– Version 2 of the 2K and academic bands of the VLT (2 tests) – Version 1 of the 2K and academic bands of the PVLT (2 tests)

After their administration, the tests were scored and the data were processed and coded manually. In the scoring process of the PVLT, bearing in mind that the aim was to explore the learners' lexical knowledge and not grammatical competence, certain decisions were made in relation to the 'correctness' of the answers provided by the students: Spelling mistakes invalidated the answer but the use of the wrong tense in the case of verbs or the incorrect choice of a singular or plural form for nouns was not penalised.

In order to explore the participants' understanding of figurative meanings, an identification of the metaphorical uses in the tests was carried out. To do so, the metaphor-identification procedure used was MIPVU (Steen et al. 2010) which has been extensively applied to identify metaphors in research studies. As is well-known, this procedure is a refined version of the Metaphor Identification Procedure (MIP) devised by the Pragglejaz group (2007). In order to apply MIPVU, the analyst has, first of all, to identify the different lexical items, then, establish their meaning in that specific context and, finally, decide whether it has a more basic contemporary meaning in other contexts. If it does, that lexical item is considered to be metaphorical. Three raters applied the method to the vocabulary items included in the tests listed in Table 1. A total of one hundred fifty-six items were examined (thirty words per level and version in the VLT and eighteen words per level in the PVLT), and, only five metaphorical uses were found: *charm* (2K band of the VLT, version 1), *admire* (2K band of the VLT, version 2), *highlight* (academic band of the VLT, version 1), *limit* (2K band of the PVLT) and *attain* (academic band of the PVLT). Then, these results were correlated with participants' overall lexical competence. Finally, the results obtained for these specific terms were compared with the results obtained for other terms belonging to the same grammatical category. Specific details of these analyses are provided in the following section.

4 Results

Starting first with an overall analysis of the global score differences between the metaphorical and the non-metaphorical terms, we performed a Wilcoxon test, which is the appropriate statistical measure when the data are not normally distributed. The test was statistically significant ($z = -7.272$, $p = .000$) and showed that non-figurative terms obtained a higher mean score (52.77%) than metaphorical ones (34.81%). In other words, participants were able to recognise and produce literal meanings more frequently than metaphorical ones.

This result was confirmed when we separately analysed the terms in both the VLT ($z = -5.975$, $p = .000$) and PVLT ($z = -5.423$, $p = .000$). With respect to the results of the VLT, participants understood non-figurative terms (66.87%, SD = 19.38) better than figurative terms (51.08%, SD = 25.79). As explained above, in the VLT three items were identified as metaphorical. Two of them, *charm* and *admire*, are found in the 2K band, whereas *highlight* belongs to the academic band. To check whether each of these metaphorical terms individually correlated with the non-figurative total score obtained in the corresponding vocabulary band, a calculation of Spearman's rho was carried out. The results show that a correct recognition of the two metaphorical terms identified (*charm* and *admire*) correlates (N= 77; p < .01) with a larger receptive knowledge of the 2K band (*charm*: $r = .346$, $p = .002$; and *admire*: $r = .304$, $p = .007$) and that the understanding of *highlight* correlates with a greater recognition of the academic band (*highlight*: $r = .395$, $p = .001$). In other words, it seems that the recognition of the metaphorical terms is related to a better performance in the whole test.

Moving on to the metaphorical terms identified in the PVLT, there were only two items identified as metaphorical: *attain* belonging to the academic band and *limit* to the 2K band. In the analysis of the difference between the global scores of the metaphorical and non-metaphorical terms, which again was statistically significant ($z = -5.423$, $p = .000$), it was also found that the figurative terms (10.39%, SD = 20.41) were significantly less recalled than the non-metaphorical ones (31.60%, SD = 18.32).

However, in the detailed analysis of the relationship between each item and the band to which it belonged, unlike in the previous items, a calculation of Spearman's rho only found a positive significant correlation (N= 77; p < .05) between a correct production of the metaphorical term *attain* and the global score of the 2K PVLT ($r = .300$, $p = .008$), whereas in the case of *limit*, no correlation was found ($r = .078$, $p = .499$).

In sum, four out of the five metaphorical items correlated positively with the overall results of the tests, which seems to indicate that recognition or understanding of figuratively-used words is related to students' larger vocabulary size. These results will be taken up in the discussion.

We also analysed the differences between the success rate of metaphorical items and the rest of terms belonging to the same grammatical category. The success rate for each of them was calculated by dividing the number of participants that provided the correct answer by the total number of participants. In order to do so, each of the participants' responses was given 0 or 1, where 0 meant that this item was not recognised or produced and 1 meant that the participant got the correct answer. Then, the mean score for each item was calculated (see Table 2).

Table 2: Descriptive analysis of learners' success rate with figurative terms.

	N	Mean	Std. Deviation
Charm	77	.30	.461
Admire	77	.83	.377
Highlight	77	.40	.494
Limit	77	.17	.377
Attain	77	.04	.195

Finally, a Wilcoxon test was carried out to analyse the significance of the differences. These results will be shown individually for each of the items. To start with, the success rate of each metaphorical term found in the VLT (*charm, admire and highlight*) in comparison to the rest of the words belonging to the same category in the same test was examined. First, it was found that the success rate for *charm* ($\bar{x}$ = .30) was lower than that of the rest of nouns (see Table 3 below). The analysis of the significance of this difference showed that all the differences between the success rates of *charm* and the rest of nouns were significant ($p < .001$) with the exception of flesh (z= .000, p = 1.000).

Table 3: Descriptive analysis of the nouns found in the 2K band of the VLT.

	Victory	Birth	Temperature	Flesh	Journey	Education	Scale
N	77	77	77	77	77	77	77
$\bar{x}$	.96	.83	.77	.30	.92	.95	.82
SD	.195	.377	.426	.461	.270	.223	.388

	Salary	Treasure	Charm	Lack	Cream	Wealth	Pupil
N	77	77	77	77	77	77	77
$\bar{x}$	.56	.66	.30	.45	.87	.38	.58
SD	.50	.476	.461	.501	.338	.489	.496

This was not the case for *admire*. As can be seen in Table 4 below, it presented in general a higher, and, in some cases, significantly higher, success rate ($\bar{x}$ = .83) in comparison to the rest of verbs of the test. In this case, it was found that the success rate of admire was significantly higher than that of *strengthen* (z= −4.116, p = .000), *develop* (z= −4.333, p = .000), *arrange* (z= −5.145, p = .000), *manufacture* (z= −2.20, p = −.028) and *elect* (z=−2.111, p = .035).

Table 4: Descriptive analysis of the verbs found in the VLT v.2.

	Strengthen	Introduce	Admire	Develop	Arrange	Prefer	Manufacture	Elect	Melt
N	77	77	77	77	77	77	77	77	77
$\bar{x}$	.52	.78	.83	.51	.44	.71	.69	.92	.82
SD	.50	.42	.38	.50	.50	.46	.47	.28	.39

However, in the analysis of *highlight*, an academic metaphorical term also found in the first version of the test, as in the case of *charm*, it was found again that the success rate ($\bar{x}$= .40) was lower than with the rest of the verbs. In fact, the statistical analysis indicated that all the differences between *highlight* and the rest of verb terms were statistically significant (p <.001) (see Table 5).

Table 5: Descriptive analysis of the verbs found in the academic band of the VLT v1.

	Alter	Deny	Specify	Retain	Correspond	Highlight	Minimize	Estimate	Identify
N	77	77	77	77	77	77	77	77	77
$\bar{x}$	.73	.66	.71	.60	.57	.40	.86	.61	.77
SD	.45	.48	.46	.49	.50	.49	0.35	.49	.43

Moving on to the analysis of the success rate of the metaphorical terms identified in the productive tests, in the case of *limit*, the metaphorical term found in 2K band of the PVLT, a lower rate in comparison to the rest of the items ($\bar{x}$= .17) was observed (Table 6). The significance of this difference between terms was examined and the Wilcoxon test results showed a significantly lower production of the term *limit* in comparison to *climb* (Z= −4.743, p = .000), *examine* (Z= −3.053, p = .002), and *connect* (Z= −3.402, p = .001).

Table 6: Descriptive analysis of the verbs found in the 2K band of the PVLT.

	Climb	Examine	Surround	Connect	Wander	Limit
N	77	77	77	77	77	77
$\bar{x}$	0.56	0.39	0.27	0.4	0.18	0.17
SD	0.5	0.491	0.448	0.494	0.388	0.377

Finally, the analysis of the metaphorical term *attain*, an academic term included in the PVLT, was carried out. Similar to previous results, the success rate of *attain* ($\bar{x}$ = .04) was found to be lower in comparison to the success rate of the rest of verb terms in the academic band of the PVLT. The statistical analysis showed that the differences between the success rates of *attain* and the rest of terms were statistically significant at the .01 level ($p < .01$) with the exception of the difference between *attain* and *rely*, whose difference was significant at a .05 level ($z= -2.138$, $p = .033$).

Table 7: Descriptive analysis of the verbs found in the academic band of the PVLT.

	Inspect	Accumulate	Saturate	Rely	Evaluate	Attain
N	77	77	77	77	77	77
$\bar{x}$	.21	.43	.36	.14	.38	.04
SD	.41	.50	0.48	0.35	.49	.19

In general, a pattern seems to be found in the differences between the success rate for the metaphorical terms and the other terms belonging to the same word class: in two out of the three terms identified in the receptive VLT, and in the two metaphorical terms found in the PVLT, the metaphorical terms presented a lower success rate in comparison to other items occurring in the same frequency band and within the same grammatical category of the tests employed. The only exception was found in the term *limit* and different reasons could explain this difference, as will be explained in the next section.

In order to facilitate the interpretation of the results, it is important to consider the participants' performance overall in the tests. Starting with the 2K band of the VLT, in the first version, participants obtained a mean score of 58.90% of the words, whereas in the second version, administered one year later, they got a mean score of 75.47% of the 2K band. In relation to the academic band, in the first version, participants recognised a total of 48.38% of the academic terms, whereas in the second version, administered one year after, they recognised 60.9% of the items. First of all, the mean scores of the tests were explored. In the case of the 2K band of the PVLT test, learners successfully produced 37.55% of the words, a percentage well below that found in the receptive version of the 2K band, whereas in the academic band, participants were able to produce a mean of 23.12% of the academic words. This low performance was also observed in the success rate of the different items. As will be seen later, this may also explain some of the findings.

5 Discussion

This study has attempted to present a preliminary analysis of the use of standardised tools in second language acquisition for estimating L2 vocabulary size with the objective of measuring L2 learners' understanding of figurative meanings.

The results show that, first of all, a general positive correlation between the recognition or understanding of each metaphorical term and the global score of the corresponding test was found. This seems to indicate that the mastery of the metaphorical terms is clearly related to that of general vocabulary items. The only exception is found in the term *limit*, and the lack of connection between the metaphorical term and the global score of, in this case, the 2K band of the PVLT could be related to two factors: on the one hand, participants were able to produce 30.07% of the words, which is well below the performance in the receptive tests. This low performance is in line with other studies (Fan 2000; Laufer 1998; Laufer and Paribakht 1998; Melka 1997; Takala 1984) that conclude that leaners' productive mastery of vocabulary items lags behind their receptive knowledge of them. On the other hand, if the metaphorical term *limit* presents an unusual higher success rate in comparison to the other terms in the test, this is probably due to its resemblance to its Spanish equivalent (lit. *limitar*) and thus reflects a likely cognate effect. When dealing with this term, it is possible that the learners resorted to their mother tongue aiming to look for some kind of help. This fact may have produced a higher capacity of production of the word, which, together with a low performance in general in the test, could have led to this lack of difference with other terms.

Considering the results obtained from the analysis of a difference between the success rate of each metaphorical item and other terms belonging to the same grammatical category and test, it has been found that, in four out of the five items examined, the success rate for the metaphorical term is significantly lower in comparison to other terms in the same test. This finding is in line with the outcomes obtained by Littlemore et al. (2014), who, as has been noted above, also identified a greater proportion of errors in metaphorical items when compared to non-metaphorical terms. This outcome seems to corroborate that participants find it more challenging to understand the metaphorical items and this leads to a lower rate of recognition or production. However, in this analysis, an exception is found: *admire*, which, in fact, presented a greater success rate than other words with the same category and test. This finding may be related, again, to the particularities of the term: *admire*, like *limit*, is also a cognate in Spanish (literally, *admirar*) and it could be expected that learners find this term easier to recognise. It seems that cognation seems to work as a facilitator, not only in general acquisition of vocabulary, but also in the case of metaphorical items.

6 Conclusion

After over three decades of research into the notion of metaphorical competence, it can be said that, despite the complexity of the construct, important progress has been made into our understanding of this concept, particularly, from a theoretical perspective and in terms of identifying its importance in foreign language instruction. As has been noted above, recent research studies in the field (Hoang and Boers 2018; Littlemore et al. 2014; Nacey 2013; Turner 2014) have focused on measuring learners' production of metaphor providing insightful accounts of this dimension of learners' metaphorical competence. However, the receptive domain has not received so much attention despite the fact that it would seem that L2 learners need to understand figurative meanings more often than they need to produce them and this is particularly so at the basic levels of L2 proficiency (A1-B1) which would correspond to the most common levels for most learners of English in mainstream education worldwide.

In this chapter, we have focused on this somehow neglected dimension by trying to bridge a gap between general vocabulary studies and metaphor research. Especially relevant would be the design of instruments that would measure L2 learners' capacity to understand and produce figurative meanings, either with the inclusion of metaphorical items within the general vocabulary tests, or with the development of tests specifically designed for this aim. Our exploratory study is a first attempt in this regard but this area is in need of further research that uses insights and tools from both fields that would enrich our understanding of metaphorical competence as part of L2 learners' general lexical competence.

References

Aizawa, Kazumi. 2018. Exploring L2 learners' vocabulary knowledge of primary and peripheral meanings. *Research Bulletin* 77. 31–40

Anderson, Richard C. & Peter Freebody. 1981. Vocabulary knowledge. In John T. Guthrie (Ed.), *Comprehension and teaching: Research reviews*, 77–117. Newark, D.E.: International Reading Association.

Boers, Frank. 2000. Metaphor awareness and vocabulary retention. *Applied Linguistics* 21. 553–571.

Boers, Frank. 2008. How cognitive linguistics can foster effective vocabulary teaching. In Frank Boers & Seth Lindstromberg (eds.), *Cognitive linguistic approaches to teaching vocabulary and phraseology*, 1–61. Berlin: Mouton de Gruyter.

Boers, Frank. 2011. Cognitive semantic ways of teaching figurative phrases: An assessment. *Review of Cognitive Linguistics* 9. 227–261.

Boers, Frank. 2013. Cognitive linguistic approaches to teaching vocabulary: Assessment and integration. *Language Teaching* 46. 208-224.

Boers, Frank & Murielle Demecheleer. 2001. Measuring the impact of cross-cultural differences on learners' comprehension of imageable idioms. *ELT Journal* 55. 255–262.

Cameron, Lynne. 2003. *Metaphor in educational discourse*. New York: Bloomsbury Continuum.

Cameron, Lynne & Graham D. Low. 1999. *Researching and applying metaphor*. Cambridge: Cambridge University Press.

Castellano-Risco, Irene. forthcoming. The impact of vocabulary learning strategies on vocabulary size: a study of secondary learners in Content and Language Integrated Learning programmes. Badajoz: University of Extremadura PhD dissertation.

Cronbach, Lee J. 1942. Measuring knowledge of precise word meaning. *The Journal of Educational Research* 36(7), 528–534.

Coxhead, A. 2000. A new Academic Word List. *TESOL Quarterly* 34(2). 213–239.

Danesi, Marcel. 1986. The role of metaphor in second language pedagogy. *Rassegna Italiana di Linguistica Applicata* 18. 1–10.

Danesi, Marcel. 1992. Metaphorical competence in second language acquisition and second language teaching: The neglected dimension. In James E. Alatis (ed.), *Language communication and social meaning (Georgetown University Round Table on Languages and Linguistics)*, 489–500. Washington: Georgetown University Press.

Danesi, Marcel. 2008. Conceptual errors in second-language learning. In Sabine De Knop & Antoon De Rycker (eds.), *Cognitive approaches to pedagogical grammar*, 231–256. Berlin: Mouton de Gruyter.

Danesi, Marcel. 2016. Conceptual fluency in second language teaching: An overview of problems, issues, research findings and pedagogy. *International Journal of Applied Linguistics & English Literature* 5(1). 145–153.

Fan, May. 2000. How big is the gap and how to narrow it? An investigation into the active and passive vocabulary knowledge of L2 learners. *RELC Journal* 31. 105–119.

Gardner, Horward & Ellen Winner. 1978. The development of metaphoric competence: Implications for Humanistic disciplines. *Critical Inquiry* 5(1). 123–141.

Gibbs, Raymond W. 1994. *The poetics of mind: Figurative thought, language, and understanding*. Cambridge: Cambridge University Press.

Gibbs, Raymond W. 1999. Researching metaphor. In Lynne Cameron & Graham D. Low (eds.), *Researching and Applying Metaphor*, 29–47. Cambridge: Cambridge University Press.

Gibbs, Raymond W. 2008. *The Cambridge handbook of metaphor and thought*. Cambridge: Cambridge University Press.

Gu, Yongqi & Robert K. Johnson.1996. Vocabulary Learning Strategies and Language Learning Outcome. *Language Learning* 46(4). 643–679.

Henriksen, Birgit. 1999. Three dimensions of vocabulary development. *Studies in Second Language Acquisition* 21(2). 303–317.

Hoang, Ha & Frank Boers. 2018. Gauging the association of EFL learners' writing proficiency and their use of metaphorical language. *System* 74. 1–8.

Kövecses, Zoltán. 2002. Cognitive-linguistic comments on metaphor identification. *Language and Literature* 11(1). 74–78.

Kövecses, Zoltán. 2005. *Metaphor in culture*. Cambridge: Cambridge University Press.

Lakoff, George & Mark Johnson. 1980. *Metaphors we live by*. Chicago: University of Chicago Press.

Lakoff, George & Mark Johnson. 1999. *Philosophy in the flesh: The embodied mind and its challenge to western thought*. New York: Basic Books.

Laufer, Batia. 1998. The development of passive and active vocabulary in a second language: Same or different? *Applied Linguistics* 19(2). 255–271.

Laufer, Batia & Paul Nation. 1999. A vocabulary-size test of controlled productive ability. *Language Testing* 16(1). 33–51.

Laufer, Batia & Taherek S. Paribakht. 1998. The relationship between passive and active vocabularies: effects of Language Learning context. *Language Learning* 48(3). 365–391.

Levorato, Chiara & Cristina Cacciari. 1992. Children's comprehension and production of idioms: the role of context and familiarity. *Journal of Child Language* 19(2). 415–433.

Littlemore, Jeannette. 2001. Metaphoric competence: A possible language learning strength of students with a holistic cognitive style? *TESOL Quarterly* 35(3). 459–491.

Littlemore, Jeannette, Tina Krennmayr, James Turner & Sara Turner. 2014. An investigation into metaphor use at different levels of second language writing. *Applied Linguistics* 35(2). 117–144.

Littlemore, Jeannette & Graham D. Low. 2006a. Metaphoric competence and communicative language abilities. *Applied Linguistics* 27 (2). 268–294.

Littlemore, Jeannette & Graham D. Low. 2006b. *Figurative thinking and foreign language learning*. Basingstoke: Palgrave Macmillan.

López-Mezquita, María T. 2005. *La evaluación de la competencia léxica: test de vocabulario, su fiabilidad y validez*. Universidad de Granada: Universidad de Granada PhD dissertation.

Low, Graham D. 1988. On teaching metaphor. *Applied Linguistics* 9(2). 125–147.

MacArthur, Fiona. 2010. Metaphorical competence in EFL: Where are we and where should we be going? A view from the language classroom, Applied Cognitive Linguistics in Second Language Learning and Teaching. *AILA Review* 23. 155–173.

MacArthur, Fiona & Ana M. Piquer-Píriz. 2007. Staging the introduction of figurative extensions of familiar vocabulary items in EFL: Some preliminary considerations. *Ilha de Desterro: A Journal of English Language, Literatures in English and Cultural Studies* 53. 123–134.

Meara, Paul. 1996. The dimensions of lexical competence. In Gillian Brown, Kristen Malmkjaer & John Williams (eds.), *Performance and competence in second language acquisition*, 35–53. Cambridge: Cambridge University Press.

Melka, Francine. 1997. Receptive vs. productive aspects of vocabulary. In Norbert Schmitt & Michael McCarthy (eds.), *Vocabulary: Description, acquisition, and pedagogy*, 84–102. Cambridge: Cambridge University Press.

Nacey, Susan. 2013. *Metaphors in learner English*. Amsterdam: John Benjamins.

Nacey, Susan. 2017. Metaphor comprehension and production in a second language. In Elena Semino & Zsófia Demjén (eds.), *The Routledge handbook of metaphor and language*, 503–515. Abingdon and New York: Taylor & Francis.

Nation, Paul. 1983. Testing and teaching vocabulary. *Guidelines* 5(1). 12–25.

Nation, Paul. 2001. *Learning vocabulary in another language.* Cambridge: Cambridge University Press.

Özçalışkan, Şeyda. 2011. Acquisition of metaphor. In Patrick Hogan (ed.), *Cambridge encyclopedia of language sciences*, 486–488. Cambridge: Cambridge University Press.

Palmer, Harold E. 1921. *The principles of language-study.* London: Harrap.

Pragglejaz Group. 2007. MIP: A method for identifying metaphorically-used words in discourse. *Metaphor and Symbol* 22, 1-40.

Piquer Píriz, Ana M. 2005. *La comprensión de algunas extensiones semánticas de los lexemas "hand", "mouth" y "head" en las primeras etapas del aprendizaje del inglés.* Cáceres: Servicio de Publicaciones de la Universidad de Extremadura.

Piquer-Píriz, Ana M. 2008a. Reasoning figuratively in early EFL: some implications for the development of vocabulary. In Frank Boers & Seth Lindstromberg (eds.), *Cognitive linguistic approaches to teaching vocabulary and phraseology*, 233–257. Berlin: Mouton de Gruyter.

Piquer-Píriz, Ana M. 2008b. Young learners' understanding of figurative language. In Mara S. Zanotto, Lynne Cameron & Marilda C. Calvacanti (eds.), *Confronting metaphor in use: An applied linguistic approach*, 183-198. Amsterdam: John Benjamins.

Piquer-Píriz, Ana M. 2010. Can people be cold and warm? Developing understanding of figurative meanings of temperature terms in early EFL. In Graham D. Low, Zazie Todd, Alice Deignan & Lynne Cameron (eds.), *Researching and applying metaphor in the real world*, 21–33. Amsterdam: John Benjamins.

Piquer-Píriz, Ana M. 2011. Motivated word meanings and vocabulary learning: The polysemy of *hand* in the English for Young Learners classroom. *Metaphor and the Social World* 1(2). 154-173).

Piquer-Píriz, Ana M. & Rafael Alejo-González. 2016. Applying cognitive linguistics: Identifying some current research foci (figurative language in use, constructions and typology). *Review of Cognitive Linguistics* 14 (1).1-20.

Read, John. 2000. *Assessing vocabulary.* Cambridge: Cambridge University Press.

Robinson, Peter & Nick C. Ellis. 2008. *Handbook of cognitive linguistics and second language acquisition.* New York: Routledge.

Schmitt, Norbert. 1997. Vocabulary learning strategies. In Norbert Schmitt & Michael McCarthy (eds) *Vocabulary: Description, acquisition and pedagogy*, 199–227. Cambridge: Cambridge University Press.

Schmitt, Norbert. 2010. *Researching vocabulary: A vocabulary research manual.* Basingstoke: Palgrave Press.

Schmitt, Norbert, Diane Schmitt & Caroline Claphman. 2001. Developing and exploring the behaviour of two new versions of the Vocabulary Levels Tests. *Language Testing* 18(1). 55–88.

Steen, Gerard J., Aletta G. Dorst, Berenike Herrmann, Anna A. Kaal, Tina Krennmayr & Trijntje Pasma. 2010. *A Method for linguistic metaphor identification: From MIP to MIPVU.* Amsterdam: John Benjamins.

Siriwan, Mayuranee. 2007. English Vocabulary learning strategies employed by Rajabhat University Students. Nakhon Ratchasima: Suranaree University of Technology PhD dissertation.

Stöffer, Ilka. 1995. *University foreign language students' choice of vocabulary learning strategies as related to individual difference variable*. Alabama: University of Alabama PhD dissertation.

Takala, Sauli. 1984. Evaluation of students' knowledge of English vocabulary in the Finnish comprehensive school. Jyväskylä, Finland: Institute of Educational Research.

Tseng, Wenta T., Zoltán Dörnyei, & Norbert Schmitt. 2006. A New approach to assessing strategic learning: The case of self-regulation in vocabulary acquisition. *Applied Linguistics* 27(1). 78–102.

Teymouri Aleshtar, Maryam & Hamidreza Dowlatabadi. 2014. Metaphoric competence and language proficiency in the sameboat. *Procedia - Social and Behavioral Sciences (Proceedings of the International Conference on Current Trends in ELT)* 98. 1895–1904.

Turner, Sarah. 2014. *The development of metaphoric competence in French and Japanese learners of English*. Birmingham: University of Birmingham PhD dissertation.

Xue, Guo-yi & Paul Nation. 1984. A university word list. *Language Learning and Communication* 3(2). 215–229.

Part II. 2. **Fostering Knowledge of L2 Figurative Language**

Xinqing Wang, Frank Boers and Paul Warren
Using Literal Underpinnings to Help Learners Remember Figurative Idioms: Does the Connection Need to Be Crystal Clear?

1 Introduction

Several idiom dictionaries for language learners include information on the origins or literal underpinnings of idioms (e.g., *American Heritage Dictionary of Idioms 2003; Collins Cobuild Idioms Dictionary 2012; Oxford Idioms Dictionary for Learners of English 2009* and https://idioms.thefreedictionary.com/). This suggests that many dictionary makers assume that this kind of information must be helpful or at least appealing to learners. Its actual benefits for language learners have not yet been thoroughly evaluated, however. One proclaimed benefit (e.g., Liontas 2017) is that information about the origins of idioms helps learners to appreciate the connection between metaphorical language and culture. Another proclaimed benefit – and the focus of the present chapter – is that awareness of their literal underpinning can aid learners' retention of the idioms (e.g., Boers, Demecheleer, and Eyckmans 2004). This expectation rests on at least three theories.

One of these theories is that knowledge of the literal underpinning of idioms renders their meaning more transparent. For example, taking a back seat in a vehicle implies that someone else will be at the steering wheel and will thus likely be in control. By analogy, then, the meaning of the idiom *take a back seat* to refer to one's non-determining role in a project or activity makes sense against the backdrop of a more generic conceptual metaphor (Lakoff and Johnson 1980), according to which projects or activities are likened to journeys. In other words, the idiomatic meaning is *motivated*, to use a term from cognitive linguistics. If this indeed results in a clearer link between the form and the idiomatic meaning of the expression, it may be expected to facilitate acquisition (e.g., Steinel, Hulstijn, and Steinel 2007).

Xinqing Wang, School of Linguistics and Applied Language Studies, Victoria University of Wellington, Wellington, New Zealand, e-mail: aileen.wang@vuw.ac.nz
Frank Boers, Faculty of Education, The University of Western Ontario, London, Canada, e-mail: fboers@uwo.ca
Paul Warren, School of Linguistics and Applied Language Studies, Victoria University of Wellington, Wellington, New Zealand, e-mail: paul.warren@vuw.ac.nz

https://doi.org/10.1515/9783110630367-011

The second theory is Paivio's (1986) *Dual Coding Theory*, according to which concrete concepts (or lexical items with concrete meaning) are easier to remember than abstract ones owing to their imageability, i.e., their association with a mental image of the referent. Although idioms have abstract meanings, resuscitating the context in which they were originally used in a literal sense is likely to evoke images of concrete scenes, and this may thus render them memorable.

The third relevant theory is *Levels of Processing* theory (e.g., Cermak and Craik 1979), according to which "deep" processing creates stronger memories than "shallow" processing. Mental operations – called *elaborations* – that build rich semantic associations around lexical items are considered deep in this model. Connecting the meaning of an idiom to its literal underpinning qualifies as an example of this, and the label coined by Boers et al. (2004) for this particular type of elaboration is *etymological elaboration*. The term etymological should be interpreted here broadly as the original context in which the expression was (and sometimes still is) used literally. We shall call this the literal underpinning of an idiom.

One may justifiably wonder whether language learners truly experience information about the literal underpinning of an idiom as helpful. There is evidence, however, that many learners presented with L2 idioms spontaneously activate images related to the literal meaning of constituent words (e.g., Cieślicka 2006). This inclination seems different from most native speakers, where the experimental evidence suggests that idiomatic meaning is by default accessed directly (e.g., Siyanova-Chanturia, Conklin, and Schmitt 2011), although imagery can be triggered also in L1 speakers of a language (e.g., Gibbs, Nayak, and Cutting 1989). If it is true that many learners are inclined to activate imagery when they process L2 idioms, then pointing them to the "right" literal underpinning of an idiom (or, at least, a literal reading that is congruent with the figurative meaning of the idiom) may harness an inclination that is already present. That pointing learners to that underpinning will often be necessary is illustrated in the following section.

2 Obstacles to Learners' Autonomous Recognition of the Literal-Figurative Link

Learners face diverse challenges should they try to establish a connection between the literal and figurative meanings of idioms. For starters, the idiom may contain a key content word that is simply not yet known by the learner, as would likely be the case for low-frequency words (e.g., *in the doldrums; get short shrift; at the end of one's tether; bury the hatchet; pass on the baton*). In addition, content words may look deceptively transparent owing to homonymy. For example, learners may assume *suit* in *follow suit* refers to clothing (while it refers to playing cards) and they may assume *wake in the wake of* relates to being awake. In a similar vein, polysemy may cause misinterpretations. For instance, *gun* in *jump the gun* could easily be misinterpreted as a weapon (rather than a starting pistol) and *wings* in *waiting in the wings* could be mistaken for a bird's wings (rather than a theatre's wings). It is also possible for learners to mistake new words for already known ones because of formal resemblance (e.g., *reign* for *rein* in *on a tight rein*, *limp* for *limb* in *out on a limb*, and *tower* for *towel* in *throw in the towel*). Because the wording of idioms is often elliptic, learners may have insufficient clues to work out a plausible literal reading. For example, it is unclear what *thin* and *thick* refer to in *through thick and thin* (allegedly referring originally to making one's way through thick and thin bushes).

Even if a learner does recognize the literal meaning of an expression, this does not guarantee an accurate connection between that literal reading and the actual idiomatic meaning. For example, literally *having a lot on one's plate* may well be experienced as a good thing (especially if one is feeling hungry), and so the more negative meaning of the idiom ('being very busy; having a lot of work') seems not to follow logically from this. Besides, understanding the literal underpinning of idioms may require cultural knowledge that the learner may not yet have. This regards culture-specific experiential domains. For instance, a learner may be unfamiliar with sports such as cricket and golf, and so fail to recognize the underpinning of *hit someone for six* and *be par for the course*. It also concerns knowledge of historical events, myths, legends and fables behind expressions such as *cross the Rubicon, hang on a thread, a Trojan horse* and *a white elephant*. Moreover, even familiar-looking content words may prompt associations that are not shared cross-culturally. For example, the heart is conventionally referred to in western culture as the seat of emotions such as romantic love, while reason supposedly resides in the mind. This duality seems absent from Chinese, however, where the heart can symbolize both reason and emotion. It is not surprising, then, that Chinese learners of English find idioms containing the words *heart* or *mind* comparatively hard to interpret (Hu and Fong 2010).

It also needs to be acknowledged that the literal-figurative link can simply be too obscure for the literal meaning to serve as a clue for interpretation. Examples here include idioms such as *a red herring, kick the bucket* and *break a leg*. The origins proposed in dictionaries (e.g., that the distracting scent of smoked herring was used to train hunting dogs) may consequently be felt by learners to be rather far-fetched.

The general question raised by these observations is whether all literal-figurative links can be expected to be helpful. More specifically, the question we attempt to answer in the study reported in the present chapter is whether the degree of transparency of the literal-figurative connection matters for the mnemonic effect of etymological elaboration. First, however, we need to review a small number of earlier experiments that have evaluated this instructional approach to idiom learning.

3 Some Earlier Experiments

A number of studies have already shown that raising learners' awareness of the literal senses of polysemous words (e.g., *hurdles* referring to obstacles for athletes to jump over in track sports; *soar* in the sense of physical upward motion) benefits their comprehension and retention of the abstract or figurative uses of said words (e.g., *hurdles* referring to problems to be overcome; *soar* to denote upward trends in economics) (see Boers 2013, for a review). Focusing more specifically on the use of literal underpinnings in teaching figurative idioms, Boers et al. (2004) reported two experiments conducted with computer-aided exercises, where each idiom was tackled in three exercise components. In one component, learners were presented with the idiom in isolation and asked to choose the most likely domain of origin. For example, when presented with *jump the gun,* they could choose between source domains such as sports, war, jurisdiction, etc. Following this, the literal underpinning was displayed for learners (e.g., an athlete who *jumps the gun* in a racing contest sets off before the starting pistol has been fired). The second component asked learners to choose the correct figurative meaning of the expressions. For *jump the gun*, for example, they were given the choice between (a) defend someone at your own risk, (b) do something before the appropriate time, and (c) be startled by an unexpected event. The correct choice was subsequently pointed out to them. The third component presented learners with a completion task, where the idiom was incorporated in a meaningful context and a missing content word needed to be supplied. For example, "Although we had agreed not to tell anyone about my pregnancy yet until we were absolutely sure, my husband jumped the _____ and told his parents straightaway." This exercise was used as a post-test to evaluate the effectiveness of the preceding steps.

The first experiment reported in Boers et al. (2004) aimed to assess the mnemonic effect of presenting the literal underpinning of the idioms. In one condition learners tackled the multiple-choice exercise on origins followed by feedback, and they were then asked to do the completion exercise, i.e., they skipped the exercise on the actual figurative meaning of the idioms. In the other condition, the learners did the multiple-choice exercise on the figurative meaning of the idioms and they were then asked to do the completion exercise. The former condition was found to yield the better scores in the completion exercise, which the authors took as evidence of the mnemonic effectiveness of etymological elaboration. Of particular relevance for the present chapter is the distinction which Boers et al. then made between idioms whose source domains were identified readily in the multiple-choice exercise and those which were not. In the case of idioms whose source domains were hard to guess, recall turned out *not* to be better after etymological elaboration than in the comparison condition.

In the second experiment reported in Boers et al. (2004), all participants tackled the three exercise components of the program, in the order of (1) the multiple-choice exercise on the figurative meaning of the idioms (followed by feedback), (2) the multiple-choice exercise on the idioms' origins, and (3) the completion exercise, which served as a post-test again. This time, the average post-test scores for idioms whose source domains were hard to guess were very similar to those for idioms with better guessable source domains.

Leaving aside the inconsistent nature of the findings reported in Boers et al.'s (2004) two experiments, what the findings do *not* tell us is whether it matters if learners find the proposed motivation of an idiom's meaning transparent *after* it is presented to them. For example, learners may understandably fail to guess that *jump the gun* originates from track sports, but they might nonetheless find that the latter explanation makes good sense when it is subsequently given to them. By contrast, in a case such as *follow suit* they may not only fail to guess that the expression originates from a card game, but perhaps also find the information about this origin non-illuminating if they happen to be unfamiliar with that card game. In the experiment reported below, we therefore asked learners to evaluate the connection between the proposed literal underpinning of idioms and their figurative meaning after these were both explained to them. A week later, the participants were asked to recall the meaning of the idioms, and so we could examine if there was an association between each learner's ability to recall an idiom and their appreciation of its proposed underpinning.

First, however, we need to point out that not all experimental evidence to date has been favourable of etymological elaboration. Szczepaniak and Lew (2011) asked upper-intermediate EFL learners to study booklets with information about 18 idioms for ten minutes under one of four presentation conditions, with differing amounts of information. The minimal condition consisted of a definition of the idiomatic meaning and an example sentence. The richest condition included, in addition, a picture of a literal interpretation of the expression and an etymological note. The learners were subsequently tested on their recall of the form of the idioms (by means of a completion task where they were required to supply a missing content word) and on their recognition of the meaning of the idioms (by means of a multiple-choice task). The test was administered again three weeks later. While both the immediate and the delayed post-tests furnished evidence in favour of adding pictures to the definitions of idiomatic meaning, neither produced evidence of the effectiveness of etymological notes. It could be argued that the ten minutes of study time allowed in Szczepaniak and Lew (2011) was perhaps insufficient for the participants who were presented with the (longish) etymological notes. It takes much less time and effort to take in a picture than a text passage, after all (Boers, Warren, Grimshaw, and Siyanova-Chanturia 2017). Because this was exclusively a pen-and-paper experiment, it is not known to what extent the participants engaged with the etymological notes that were included in the booklets. If they did not actually take in the information provided there, then it would not be surprising that it left no impact. In our experiment, we therefore used a one-on-one interview procedure to make sure the participants did consider the information given about the idioms' literal underpinnings. A second possible account for the lack of evidence in favour of the etymological elaboration in Szczepaniak and Lew's experiment could be that a fair number of the target idioms used (e.g. *a white elephant, a loose cannon, a red herring* and *have an axe to grind*) were arguably ones where the learners found it hard to follow the explanations for the connection between the origin and the actual idiomatic meaning. Szczepaniak and Lew did not examine (through an analysis at the level of individual items) whether etymological notes perceived to be relatively transparent by the participants were the more helpful ones. In the study we report next, we did examine this.

Something else that is largely missing from the available body of research on L2 idiom learning is the potential role of individual learner traits. Exceptions are explorations of the role of (young) age on L2 metaphor comprehension (Piquer-Piriz, 2008) and explorations of so-called cognitive style differences among learners when they are taught idioms with the etymological elaboration technique (Boers, Eyckmans, and Stengers 2006). It is conceivable that some learners experience etymological elaborations as more useful than other learners do and are thus more inclined to appreciate the potential mnemonic potential of such elaborations even in cases where they seem far-fetched. By contrast, for learners who find it harder to appreciate the connection between an idiom's meaning and its proposed literal underpinning, the mnemonic benefits of etymological elaboration may be confined mostly to relatively transparent connections. What seems worth exploring, then, is whether such predispositions might be related to L2 student profiles more generally. For example, one may wonder if high achievers within a given student population reap the mnemonic benefits of etymological elaboration more readily than their comparatively low-achieving peers. This possibility appears compatible with findings from research on language-learning aptitude (Robinson 2013; Skehan 2015), where one of the known predictors of learning success is associative memory ability. High achievers are likely to have an advantage in this regard, and, in theory, this could also apply to their remembering the meaning of an idiom in association with additional information, such as its literal underpinning. The possibility that high achievers might benefit the most from etymological elaborations is also compatible with research on vocabulary learning strategies (Gu 2003, 2013) which suggests that it is individuals who welcome a wide range of strategies who tend to be relatively successful learners. In addition, the high achievers within a student population are also likely to have built a larger L2 vocabulary and to have developed greater familiarity with the L2 in general. If so, they will be more likely to be familiar with the lexical constituents of new idioms, and this could reduce the learning burden. It is now relatively well established that the ability to learn new L2 lexical items tends to increase as one becomes more proficient in the language (e.g., Elgort and Warren 2014), which is sometimes referred to as the *Matthew effect* (i.e., the rich get richer faster). In sum, there are indeed grounds for hypothesizing that, within an otherwise homogeneous population of L2 students, those who have been comparatively successful may be more inclined to engage with and remember the etymological elaborations proposed by a teacher, regardless of whether some of these elaborations seem far-fetched. An evaluation of this hypothesis will therefore be part of the present study as well.

4 The Present Study

4.1 Method

4.1.1 Participants

The participants (N = 25), 22 females and 3 males aged between 19 and 22 (medium age = 20), were Chinese EFL learners majoring in English at a university in mainland China. They were all in their third year of study at the university. They shared very similar histories of EFL learning and were all considered to have intermediate-to-high proficiency in English. They thus made up a rather homogeneous population. They had all passed the Test for English Majors 4 (TEM-4) before the end of their second year at the university. This criterion-referenced test is widely used in China to gauge the English proficiency of university undergraduate English majors in accordance with the National College English Teaching Syllabus for English

Majors. The mean grade of the participants on this test was 75.72 (SD 6.52), and the grades ranged from 61 to 89 (and showed a normal distribution). According to the TEM descriptors, a grade of 60–69 qualifies as a pass grade, one of 70–79 is considered a good grade, and one of 80 or above is an excellent grade. So, although the sample of participants was homogeneous in terms of L1 background and EFL learning history, the TEM-4 grades demonstrate different levels of EFL achievement. Whether this made a difference to their performance in the actual study will be explored further below.

The participants were informed the study was about strategies for learning English idioms, but the precise purpose was only explained to them after data collection was completed. They all gave written consent for their data to be used for this research project.

4.1.2 Instruments and procedure

The idioms presented to these participants were semi-randomly selected from dictionaries such as *Collins Cobuild Idioms Dictionary* (2012), *Oxford Idioms Dictionary for Learners of English* (2013), and *American Heritage Dictionary of idioms* (2003). These were all expressions whose dictionary entries included notes about their origins (not all entries do) and/or for which origins are proposed in online resources (e.g., *the Phrase Finder* on https://www.phrases.org.uk/ and *the Free Dictionary* on https://idioms.thefreedictionary.com/) (retrieved in September 2016). As we were interested in the role of item properties, we needed a substantial number of idioms. Altogether, 80 idioms without close equivalents in the learners' L1 (Mandarin) were selected. Because interviewing each participant about so many idioms was deemed unrealistic, the collection of idioms was divided into four equal sets of 20 idioms each. Each set was then used in interviews with separate groups of six (and in one case, seven) participants. For motivational reasons, we also added a small number of idioms that do have close equivalents in Mandarin and that were thus easier to guess the meaning of, but these were excluded from the analysis.

The two interviews were conducted a week apart. During the first interview (which took about an hour on average), the learner was informed about the meaning and the literal underpinning of the idioms and was asked to evaluate the clarity of the link between the two. The second, shorter, interview served to determine how well the participants remembered the meaning of the idioms, and if they remembered this in conjunction with the literal underpinnings they had been told about. The interaction in both interviews was in the participants' L1 whenever they preferred so. All the interviews were audio-recorded and transcribed. The

Mandarin excerpts were translated into English by the first author (who is a native speaker of Mandarin) to facilitate inter-rater reliability procedures (see below).

The first interview proceeded along the following steps per idiom:

1. The idiom was presented in isolation (e.g., *pull one's weight*) and the participant was asked if he or she was familiar with it, and, if so, to give its meaning. The purpose of this step was merely to ascertain that the participant was not yet familiar with the idiom. If a participant did give evidence he or she already knew the idiom, the interview moved on to the next idiom on the list.

2. The idiom was presented in a short sentential context without revelatory semantic clues (e.g., *He needs to pull his weight*), and the interviewee was asked to hazard a guess at the meaning of the expression. Embedding the idiom in a sentence served to illustrate at least the word class of its constituents and thus made the interpretation task more realistic than guessing the meaning of a completely decontextualized expression. At the same time, keeping the sentential context minimal was a way of avoiding variability in the interpretability of the idioms owing to a factor (i.e., the availability of contextual clues) extraneous to the semantic transparency of the idioms as such.

3. The origin of the expression was explained and then the interviewee was asked to make another guess at the figurative meaning of the idiom (or if the new information confirmed their earlier interpretation). The information about the origin of the idioms was taken from dictionaries or online resources. For example, according to *American Heritage Dictionary of Idioms*, *pull one's weight* comes from rowing, where all crew members are expected to pull on their oar(s) to give momentum to the boat. In case more than one origin was proposed by different sources, the one that seemed the most plausible was chosen.

4. The researcher then explained the meaning of the idiom given in the dictionary (or confirmed the interpretation proposed by the participant in the previous step, if that happened to be correct). The idiom was then also presented in a slightly more elaborate context to illustrate its meaning and use (e.g., *If he doesn't start pulling his weight, he'll lose his job*). These example contexts were borrowed mostly from the dictionaries. After both the literal underpinning and the actual idiomatic meaning of the expression were clarified, the interview moved on to the next idiom in the set.

After their set of 20 idioms had been tackled following the above steps, the participants were given a list of them, preceded by the following instruction:

You may feel that the figurative (idiomatic) meaning of some idioms follows in a straightforward manner from the literal (source) meaning of the expressions. For other idioms, you may find it much less obvious how the figurative (idiomatic) meaning is derived from the literal (source) meaning. You may even feel that there is no clear link at all.

Now that you know the literal meaning as well as the figurative meaning of the idioms, please circle the number on the scale below that best represents how you feel about the relationship between the literal meaning and the figurative meaning of the idiom.

5= The link between the literal and the figurative meaning of the expression is very clear to me. Given the literal use of the expression, it is easy for me to see how the figurative use is derived from it.

0 = The link between the literal and the figurative meaning of the expression is not at all clear to me. Although I (now) know both the literal (source) meaning of the expression and its idiomatic meaning, I cannot see how the literal use could have given rise to the figurative use of the expression.

non-transparent   transparent

←——→

0	1	2	3	4	5
The link between the literal and figurative meanings is not transparent at all.	*The link between the literal and figurative meanings is very vague.*	*The link between the literal and figurative meanings is vague.*	*The link between the literal and figurative meanings is somewhat clear.*	*The link between the literal and figurative meanings is clear.*	*The link between the literal and figurative meanings is very clear.*

The participants were encouraged to express their thoughts (in L1 if they wished) and explain their reasoning as they carried out this rating task per idiom. At the end of the interview, the participants were asked not to discuss individual items encountered in the interview with other students. They were not told they would be asked to recall the meaning of the idioms the following week.

One week later, in the second interview, the participants were presented with the same set of idioms and asked to try and recall their figurative meaning. They were also asked if they could recall anything else they had learned about the idioms in the first interview. The latter question was intended to gauge if successful recall of the idiomatic meaning often coincided with recall of the literal underpinnings.

4.1.3 Analysis

The participants' meaning guesses in the first interview and their meaning recall responses in the second interview were assessed by the first author and two L1 speakers of English (PhD students in Applied Linguistics). A three-point scoring protocol was adopted, distinguishing between no or incorrect responses, partially correct responses, and fully correct responses. It was agreed that responses were counted as correct if they contained all the meaning aspects contained in the definition from the dictionary that was used in the interview. For example, *pull one's weight* was defined as doing one's share in a common task – or, in other words, to work as hard as other people in a group. If the response was "to do one's share in teamwork", it was rated as 1. If it was just "to make an effort" or "to do one's best", it was rated as 0.5. Inter-rater reliability was high (Krippendorff α=.78). In case of disagreement, a verdict was made by majority vote.

As explained, step 1 in the interview sequence helped us to identify which idioms were already known by any given participant. For example, some participants remembered learning idioms such as *let the cat out of the bag, a rule of thumb* and *make ends meet* from their EFL textbooks. Step 2 revealed which (if any) idioms a participant correctly guessed the meaning of even before any hint about its origin was given. New idioms that at least some participants managed to guess the meaning of in step 2 included *a drop in a bucket, have a lot on one's plate* and *in the driver's seat*. If a learner already knew or understood a given idiom, such an item would likely still be known and understood one week later also in the absence of any intervention, and so these instances were discarded from further analysis. Some initial meaning responses generated in step 2 were not fully correct and thus given a score of 0.5. These instances were retained for analysis because they did entail room for further learning. This pruning procedure left us with 360 initial responses indicating no knowledge or comprehension of the given idioms and an additional 54 initial responses demonstrating partial comprehension of the given idioms, that is, 414 out of the total 500 initial responses (25 participants x 20 idioms). The idioms, with exclusion of those which all members of the group already knew or interpreted correctly at the start, are listed in the appendix.

4.2 Results and Discussion

Informing the participants about the origin of the expressions was found to considerably increase the likelihood of correct inferences in the first interview. In 49.7% of the 360 instances where participants had initially failed entirely to propose a correct interpretation, they now produced correct interpretations, and in an additional 19.5% they produced partially correct ones. For the 54 instances where guessing had initially already been partially successful, the information about the origin of the idiom also occasionally (11.1%) helped learners to arrive at a fuller understanding.

One week later, no fewer than 65% of the items which participants had demonstrated no comprehension of at the start of the first interview were re-called correctly, and an additional 10.5% of the recalls were partially correct. In addition, 44.5% of the items that had already elicited partially correct guesses at the very beginning were now accurately recalled. In sum, learning gains were thus attested for close to 71.5% of the instances where learners' prior com-prehension was either nil or incomplete. When the participants recalled the precise meaning of an idiom in the second interview, this typically (91.25%) co-incided with their recollection of the idiom's suggested origin, as displayed in Table 1. If they failed to recall an idiom's meaning altogether, they would often (65.59%) also fail to recall its origin.

Table 1: Meaning recall and recall of literal underpinnings (total N = 414).

Meaning recall	Recall of origin			No recall of origin	
	n	%		n	%
Correct	240	91.25		23	8.75
Partially correct	45	77.59	Versus	13	22.41
Failed	32	34.41		61	65.59

The next question is whether the proposed literal underpinnings of the idioms were perceived by the learners as relatively transparent motivations of the idi-oms' meanings. The participants' ratings of the degree of transparency (at the end of the first interview) were very unevenly spread across the six-point scale, with the lowest points, 0 to 2, ticked very seldom (together only about 8%). Idioms and their motivations that attracted such occasional low ratings in-cluded *on the back burner, let the cat out of the bag, take a back seat, hit the roof, a loose cannon, a wet blanket, hit the roof, jump the gun, have cold feet, be on the same page, in the wake of, not be up to scratch, hold your horses, bark up the wrong tree* and *hand over fist*. The two highest points on the scale, 4 and 5, were selected the most often (together about 73.5%), which suggests that, by and large, the participants thought the origin of the idioms that they had been presented with offered a relatively clear motivation for the idioms' meanings. It is worth mentioning, however, that there was considerable disparity among participants' judgements. It was not uncommon for idioms to receive a rating of 1 or 2 from one learner but ratings of 4 or 5 from others. Making predictions about which etymological notes will strike individual learners as clear vs. far-fetched thus appears problematic, even within a relatively homogeneous group of learners. This is also one of the reasons why we felt it was important to analyse the data by individual responses instead of using averaged ratings (see below).

It is somewhat ironic that the ratings for some of the idioms which we mentioned earlier as examples of likely transparent versus non-transparent cases did not confirm our expectations. For instance, *take a back seat* elicited an average rating of only 3.50, whereas *red herring* elicited an average rating of 4.33. We need to be cautious about these comparisons, though, because they cross over from one idiom set to another and do thus not reflect the same learners' judgements. Still, the data do suggest that it may be very hard for teachers, lexicographers and researchers to make reliable predictions about which motivations for idioms' meanings will be experienced as "making good sense" by an individual learner or group of learners.

The literal underpinning that elicited the lowest average rating (the only average below 3.00) concerned *a wet blanket*. One participant explained his low rating (0) as follows: "If it [the idiom] comes from putting out fire, I see it as something useful in a difficult or dangerous situation. This is in contrast with the negative meaning of the expression as stopping other people's enthusiasm" (translated from Mandarin by the first author). It seems this learner found the proposed source-target domain mapping improbable, because of his association of fire with danger. His low transparency rating did not, however, prevent him from accurately recalling both the idiom's meaning and its proposed origin one week later.

This brings us to the key question we set out to address here, notably whether the degree of perceived transparency of the literal-figurative link influences the mnemonic effect of etymological elaboration. Table 2 gives a first impression of a trend that appears to be in favour of idioms receiving relatively high transparency ratings. Because the participants' ratings were so unevenly distributed, we divide them here into just two categories for preliminary, descriptive purposes: ratings 0 to 3 ("low") versus ratings 4 and 5 ("high").

What Table 2 fails to capture, of course, is variation in recall successes due to many other potentially influential characteristics of individual idioms as well as characteristics of the individual participants. Regarding the latter (and as discussed previously), the students' comparative success as EFL learners may be particularly relevant.

Table 2: Meaning recall of idioms: Transparent vs. non-transparent underpinnings (N = 414).

| | Meaning recall | | | | | |
| | Correct | | partially correct | | failed | |
Transparency	n	%	n	%	n	%
0–3	66	60.55	14	12.84	29	26.60
4–5	192	62.95	49	16.07	64	20.98

We therefore turned to mixed-effects regression models for ordinal data, using *clmm* (cumulative link mixed modelling) in the *ordinal* package in R (Christensen, 2018). The dependent variable was the Recall score, with the scores of 0, 0.5 and 1, representing ordered categories of wrong/null, partially correct and fully correct. The fixed effect predictors were Transparency (i.e., the learner's rating of the transparency of the proposed connection between the literal underpinning and the meaning of the idiom) and the student's TEM-4 grade (i.e., the measure of the learner's EFL achievement or English proficiency). Since we hypothesized (see above) that the effect of perceived transparency may vary with the level of EFL achievement or proficiency, we included the interaction between Transparency and TEM-4 grade as another predictor. The random effects were participants and items (i.e., the different idioms). Including these random effects allowed the models to take into account variation both between participants and between idioms. Comparison of models with and without the interaction of Transparency and EFL achievement showed that the interaction made a significant contribution to explaining the variance in recall scores (χ^2 (1) = 4.72, p < .05). The full model, with the two simple fixed effects and their interaction, was therefore retained. A Type-III ANOVA test showed that in addition to the interaction, the simple fixed effects of Transparency (χ^2 (1) = 4.01, p < .05) and TEM-4 grade (χ^2 (1) = 7.13, p < .01) also made significant contributions to the full model. The interaction effect is illustrated in Figure 1.[1]

These effects reflect the following patterns. Overall, fully correct recall was more likely for idioms perceived to have transparent literal-figurative connections, while unsuccessful recall was more likely for those whose proposed underpinnings were perceived to be rather obscure. This supports an affirmative answer to

---

[1] Because the *predict* function has not been developed for *clmm*, this plot shows values derived using the *predict* function in *clmm2*. However, because *clmm2* only allows one random effect, we chose to keep items as the random effect since items explain more variance than participants.

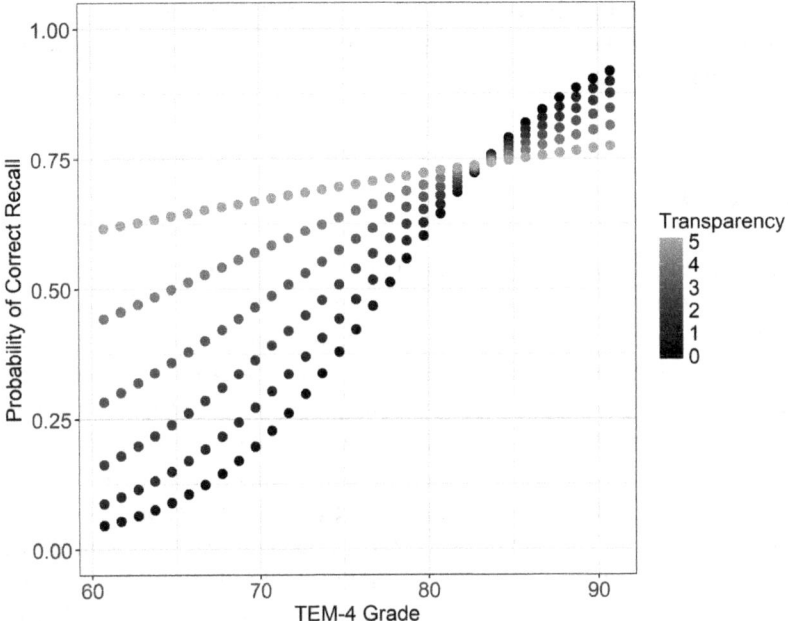

Figure 1: Probability of correct recall based on TEM-4 grade and transparency.

our principal research question: Transparency matters. Fully correct recall was also more likely for the learners with comparatively high TEM-4 scores. This is in line with our prediction that the high-achieving students in the EFL programme would also be the high achievers in our experiment.

The interaction effect revealed by the regression model is as follows. While the students with low TEM-4 grades performed generally more poorly than their high-achieving peers on the recall test, this was especially acute for idioms whose transparency they had rated as low. Idioms whose literal-figurative connection they deemed highly transparent were recalled the best at this lower end of the TEM-4 grades. However, as TEM-4 grades increased, the impact of transparency gradually diminished and disappeared by grade 80 (see Figure 1). So, if the transparency factor was found to be a predictor of recall, this is attributable to the low achievers' data. Returning to the example of the student who had given *a wet blanket* the lowest transparency rating but nonetheless successfully recalled it, it is perhaps no coincidence that this was a student with a relatively high TEM-4 grade (78). According to the interview data, this student was clearly willing to reflect on the literal underpinning of the idiom proposed by the researcher, perhaps precisely because its motivation for the idiomatic meaning was puzzling to him. It is possibly this willingness to put a certain effort into evaluating a proposed literal-figurative connection that helped him to entrench this association in memory (recall that the student remembered both the idiom's meaning and its proposed underpinning).

5 Conclusion

The findings presented here suggest that, if etymological elaboration aids learners' retention of the meaning of idioms, its effect is not confined to idioms whose meaning learners find to be straightforwardly derived from the proposed origins. Rather, it appears that explanations about origins that are experienced as somewhat far-fetched can also serve this mnemonic purpose. However, the findings also indicate that this mnemonic purpose is generally served more easily in the case of idioms where the learner finds the proposed literal underpinning comparatively straightforward or plausible. Interestingly, the interaction effect that emerged from our mixed effects regression model suggests that this influence of the perceived transparency of the literal-figurative connection was the greatest for students who obtained comparatively low TEM-4 exam grades, and who could by that proxy be considered the less successful or less advanced EFL students in the sample. For the participants with the higher TEM-4 grades, who could be considered the high achievers in this student population, there was no noticeable impact of the transparency variable on idiom recall.

Despite the role of said variables, the fact remains that most of the students in this study gained knowledge of a considerable number of new idioms through an instructional procedure which engaged them with the literal underpinnings of the expressions. We need to be cautious not to oversell the proclaimed benefits of this etymological elaboration approach, however. As mentioned, not all evidence to date has been favourable of its implementation (Szczepaniak and Lew 2011). We also need to bear in mind that the present study did not include a comparison treatment. As such, it provides no evidence that learning idioms through etymological elaboration should be given precedence over other learning procedures. The jury is still out, so to speak. What we can say with a degree of confidence is that the learning gains attested here were quite substantial, at least according to a one-week delayed post-test. Of course, a further delayed post-test would be required to check if the observed learning gains are truly durable.

At the same time, it is possible that idiom knowledge was underestimated in our experiment. That is because we only gave full credit to learners' paraphrases of the idioms if these paraphrases included all the meaning components mentioned in the dictionary entry that was used as a benchmark. It cannot be ruled out that one or the other meaning component was implied rather than explicitly verbalized in a respondent's paraphrase. Even in an interview procedure that takes recourse to the respondent's L1, an interviewer's efforts to solicit nuanced knowledge may fail. In future (conceptual) replications, it might be worth adding a different type of test, such as a multiple-choice meaning-recognition test where the respondent is required to select the meaning paraphrase that best captures the idiom's meaning.

If degree of transparency of the literal-figurative connection was found to play a role in learners' recall of the idioms' meanings in this study, this raises the question what other variables might play a part in this regard. Further analyses of the interview and test data and inclusion of alternative idiom-related variables in new mixed effects models will be required to identify these. In a similar vein, the potential influence of other learner traits than proficiency merits further investigation in future research on L2 idiom learning and teaching.

Finally, we need to be aware that the learning aim in the present experiment may in one respect be considered modest – that is, remembering the meaning of the idioms. For one thing, the post-test presented the learners with the English idioms again, and thus did not require them to recall the lexical makeup of the expressions. For another, it is well documented that idioms serve subtle pragmatic and evaluative functions in discourse (e.g., O'Keeffe, McCarthy and Carter 2007: 80–99) which are often not captured by dictionary definitions. Developing expert productive knowledge of idioms would take extensive exposure to L2 natural discourse (MacArthur 2010). It would nonetheless be interesting to explore, by means of a longitudinal investigation, if the intervention we have described here stimulates learners' long-term engagement with the idiomatic dimension of their target language.

Acknowledgements: We are grateful to the 25 students who volunteered to participate in this study, to Lisa Woods and Rolando Coto Solano for their advice on inferential statistics, and to Mark Toomer and Brian Strong for the many hours they invested in assessing and discussing the participants' meaning guesses and post-test responses.

References

Boers, Frank. 2013. Cognitive semantic ways of teaching figurative phrases: An assessment. In Francisco Gonzálvez-García, María S. Peña Cervel & Lorena Pérez Hernández (eds.),

Metaphor and metonymy revisited beyond the contemporary theory of metaphor,
229–263. Amsterdam: John Benjamins.

Boers, Frank, Murielle Demecheleer & June Eyckmans. 2004. Etymological elaboration as a
strategy for learning figurative idioms. In Paul Bogaards & Batia Laufer (eds.), *Vocabulary
in a second language: Selection, acquisition and testing,* 53–78. Amsterdam: John
Benjamins.

Boers, Frank, June Eyckmans & Hélène Stengers. 2006. Motivating multiword units: Rationale,
mnemonic benefits, and cognitive style variables. In Susan H. Foster-Cohen,
Marta M. Krajnovic & Jelena M. Djigunovic (eds.), *EUROSLA Yearbook Vol. 6,* 169–190.
Amsterdam: John Benjamins.

Boers, Frank, Paul Warren, Gina Grimshaw & Anna Siyanova-Chanturia. 2017. On the benefits
of multimodal annotations for vocabulary uptake from reading. *Computer Assisted
Language Learning* 30. 709–725.

Cermak, Laird S. & Fergus I. M. Craik. 1979. *Levels of processing in human memory.* Hillsdale,
NJ: Lawrence Erlbaum.

Cieślicka, Anna B. 2006. Literal salience in on-line processing of idiomatic expressions
by second language learners. *Second Language Research* 22. 115–144.

Christensen, Rune H. B. 2018. Ordinal - regression models for ordinal data. R package version
2018.4–19. http://www.cran.r-project.org/package=ordinal/.

Elgort, Irina & Paul Warren. 2014. L2 vocabulary learning from reading: Explicit and tacit
lexical knowledge and the role of learner and item variables. *Language Learning* 64.
365–414.

Gibbs, Raymond W., Nandini P. Nayak & Cooper Cutting. 1989. How to kick the bucket and not
decompose: Analyzability and idiom processing. *Journal of Memory and Language* 28.
576–593.

Gu, Yongqi. 2003. Fine brush and freehand: The vocabulary learning art of two successful
Chinese EFL learners. *TESOL Quarterly* 37. 73–104.

Gu, Yongqi. 2013. Vocabulary learning strategies. In Carole A. Chapelle (ed.), *The encyclopedia
of applied linguistics.* Oxford: Wiley-Blackwell.

Hu, Ying-hsueh & Yu-Ying Fong. 2010. Obstacles to conceptual-metaphor guided L2 idiom
interpretation. In Sabine De Knop, Frank Boers & Antoon De Rycker (eds.), *Fostering
language teaching efficiency through cognitive linguistics,* 293–317. Berlin: Mouton de
Gruyter.

Lakoff, George & Mark Johnson. 1980. *Metaphors we live by.* Chicago, IL: University of Chicago
Press.

Liontas, John I. 2017. Why teach idioms? A challenge to the profession. *Iranian Journal of
Language Teaching Research* 5: 5–25.

MacArthur, Fiona. 2010. Metaphorical competence in EFL: Where are we and where should we
be going? A view from the language classroom. *AILA Review* 23. 155–173.

O'Keeffe, Anne, Michael McCarthy & Ron Carter. 2007. *From corpus to classroom: Language
use and language teaching.* Cambridge, UK: Cambridge University Press.

Paivio, Allan. 1986. *Mental representations: A dual coding approach.* New York, NY: Oxford
University Press.

Piquer-Píriz, Ana M. 2008. Reasoning figuratively in early EFL: some implications for the
development of vocabulary. In Frank Boers & Seth Lindstromberg (eds.), *Cognitive
Linguistic Approaches to Teaching Vocabulary and Phraseology,* 233–257. Berlin: Mouton
de Gruyter.

Robinson, Peter. 2013. Aptitude in second language acquisition. In Carole A. Chapelle (ed.), *The encyclopedia of applied linguistics*. Oxford: Wiley-Blackwell.

Siyanova-Chanturia, Anna, Kathy Conklin & Norbert Schmitt. 2011. Adding more fuel to the fire: An eye-tracking study of idiom processing by native and non-native speakers. *Second Language Research*, 27. 251–272.

Skehan, Peter. 2015. Foreign language aptitude and its relationship with grammar: A critical overview. *Applied Linguistics* 36. 367–384.

Steinel, Margarita. P., Jan H. Hulstijn & Wolfgang Steinel. 2007. Second language idiom learning in a paired associate paradigm: Effects of direction of learning, direction of testing, idiom imageability, and idiom transparency. *Studies in Second Language Acquisition* 29. 449–484.

Szczepaniak, Renata & Robert Lew. 2011. The role of imagery in dictionaries of idioms. *Applied Linguistics* 32. 323–347.

Appendix

Target idioms (excluding ones known/understood by all respondents in the group already before the instructional procedure)

<u>Set A</u>: go belly-up; a drop in the bucket; on the same wavelength; get into gear; red tape; follow suit; pull one's weight; bread and butter; throw in the towel; a sitting duck; give the green light; spill the beans; have/get cold feet; jump ship; play into someone's hand; par for the course; on the back burner; take the bull by the horns; take it on the chin.

<u>Set B</u>: the ball is in your court; win hands down; on the ropes; weigh someone down; pass the baton; give someone the cold shoulder; leave someone high and dry; in the doldrums; beat around the bush; waiting in the wings; a shot in the arm; throw your hand in; a loose cannon; on the same page; let the cat out of the bag; (not) up to scratch; take a back seat; hit the roof/ceiling; a feeding frenzy.

<u>Set C</u>: in the driving/driver's seat; play your cards close to your chest; down and out; rub someone the wrong way; turn over a new leaf; (hit) below the belt; make ends meet; ring a bell; a red herring; bury the hatchet; have a lot on your plate; sit on the fence; pass the buck; jump the gun; stick your neck out; take the plunge; teething problems; hold your horses; in the wake of something; a rule of thumb; show someone the ropes.

<u>Set D</u>: a hot potato; have a green thumb; go with the flow; (start) from scratch; a can of worms; flex your muscles; give someone a leg up; pull a rabbit out of the hat; bite the bullet; get your second wind; cut corners; on automatic pilot come out of your shell; get something off your chest; hand over fist; throw your hat/cap into the ring; play it by ear; a wet blanket.

Rafael Alejo-González and Verónica García-Bermejo

"The Manage of Two Kingdoms Must": An Analysis of Metaphor in Two CLIL Textbooks

1 Introduction

In the last two decades, Content and Language Integrated Learning (CLIL) has become a common educational approach widely implemented in European Primary and Secondary schools. Following on the footsteps of Canadian bilingual experiences and promoted by the European Union, CLIL refers to those bilingual school experiences in which a foreign language, typically English, is used to teach, in part or in whole, Science, History, Mathematics, Physical Education, Music or other subjects of the school curriculum (Coyle, Hood and Marsh 2010; Marsh 2008).

As a result of its considerable expansion, CLIL has attracted the attention of applied linguists, who have turned their attention to the analysis of its impact in terms of language acquisition, cognitive development or content education, the general consensus being that CLIL programmes are helpful in developing both students' foreign language abilities and content learning (cf. Pérez-Cañado 2012 for an overview, although see Fernández-Sanjurjo, Fernández-Costales and Arias Blanco 2017 for a less optimistic view). There has also been much attention to the role of language and pragmatics in CLIL and to the different discourse functions and speech acts (e.g., questions, requests, directives) that are typically used in CLIL contexts (see for example Dalton-Puffer 2007; Llinares, Morton and Whittaker 2012), an analysis which has mostly been carried out within the framework of Systemic Functional Linguistics. The type of interaction in CLIL classrooms, following an interactionist approach, has also been the focus of some other research showing in what way the interaction happening in content subjects is supportive of L2 learning (see García Mayo and Basterrechea 2017). However, to the best of our knowledge, the research on CLIL has not incorporated a cognitive-linguistic perspective to the examination of the language being used in these experiences and, although another kind of metaphor, i.e."grammatical metaphor", has been

---

Note: King John 1.1, 35.

Rafael Alejo-González, English Philology (Faculty of Education), Universtiy of Extremadura, Badajoz, Spain, e-mail: ralejo@unex.es
Verónica García-Bermejo, Badajoz, Spain, e-mail: veronicagb@unex.es

https://doi.org/10.1515/9783110630367-012

studied with some detail (cf. Llinares et al. 2012; Järvinen 2010), metaphor, as understood in Cognitive Linguistics, has not been considered when providing a characterisation of this educational approach.

Given our focus on CLIL as a communicative context and a methodology based on the analysis of real CLIL textbooks, the present paper adheres to what some scholars call 'real world metaphor research' (cf. Deignan, Littlemore and Semino 2013), a research strand which has revealed the role of this figure of speech in a diversity of communicative contexts (e.g., Koller 2006 in business, Charteris-Black 2004 in political communication, Pérez-Sobrino 2016 in advertising and Caballero 2012 in tennis commentaries), among which university contexts feature prominently (Littlemore 2001; Littlemore, Chen, Barnden and Koester 2011; MacArthur 2016). This same research perspective was the one adopted to analyse metaphor use in the two educational contexts that more closely relate to CLIL, i.e. L1 school contexts (cf. Cameron 2003) and foreign language teaching (see MacArthur 2017 for an overview), in which metaphor, although not particularly frequent, is mainly used to mitigate potentially face threatening situations to children in the classroom or to provide support for vocabulary learning to L2 learners respectively.

The peculiarities of CLIL, described above, impose a research programme that analyses to what extent the basic metaphor patterns and goals revealed for L1 school settings (cf. Cameron 2003) will be affected by the use of a language in which the main participants (teachers and learners) are not fully proficient. In other words, we need to investigate whether the use of an L2 will make metaphors less frequent, whether this will change some of its functions, or whether there will be variation according to the topic or the specific moment of the pedagogic process. For example, it would be important to know if metaphor still plays a role in explanations in facilitating access to the abstract content of the academic curriculum. It must be borne in mind that in order to do this one has to assume the previous knowledge of the more concrete vocabulary used as metaphor vehicles, a knowledge that many L2 learners may not have.

It is the purpose of the present study to provide a first approach to the importance of metaphor in CLIL by analysing textbooks as one of the main sources of input. As an exploratory study, this paper describes some of the metaphors used by two textbooks used by a group of CLIL students in year 5 of Primary Education in a bilingual school in Extremadura, Spain. More precisely, we report the results of the identification of open-class metaphors (i.e. adverbs, adjectives, verbs and nouns) in selected lessons from the Social and Natural Science books. The importance of this exploration is highlighted by two factors. First, together with teachers' explanations, written language input has a fundamental role in students' educational success and development, and it is to be expected that in CLIL contexts, where teachers will feel less confident in their ability to provide explanations in an L2, this role becomes reinforced. Second, the ability to use the textbooks will depend, on the one hand, on the students' reading abilities, which as shown by the literature, are fundamentally determined by their vocabulary knowledge, and, on the other hand, the characteristics of the vocabulary used in the textbooks (see de Zeeuw, Grootjen, Jan Kootstra and Tellings 2019). These vocabulary features are related to word properties such as word frequency, morphological family size or polysemy and, although metaphor is not included among them, it seems only natural to hypothesize that this figure of speech will also have an impact on students' understanding of texts.

The chapter is organised as follows. After introducing the relevant literature on the subject and reporting the methodology used, we present the results of our metaphor identification for tokens and lemmas together with the distribution of this figure of speech by Part of Speech (PoS). We also analyse the internal distribution of metaphors in the text taking into account the different stages or moves that can be defined within the lessons. We finish by discussing the results obtained and by giving a preliminary characterisation of the use of metaphor in CLIL textbooks.

2 Metaphor Variation

2.1 Register

The importance of the relationship between metaphor and register has been highlighted by Berber Sardinha (2015), who has explored how metaphor – together with tense, aspect, modality, etc.- is another of the linguistic features that can help us identify the different functional dimensions of register, understood here as "a language variety associated with both a particular situation of use and with pervasive linguistic features" (Biber and Conrad 2009: 31). Replicating the methodology used by Biber and associates (Biber 1988, 2006; Biber and Conrad 2009) Berber Sardinha's research shows how metaphor contributes to the different dimensions of language and as a result metaphor can explain up to 41% of the variation between registers (cf. Berber Sardinha 2015).

By using a multi-dimensional (MD) statistical analysis, Berber Sardinha's work elaborates on the analysis started by the VUAMC (Vrije Universiteit Amsterdam Metaphor Corpus) team, who had already undertaken the study of metaphor in four major registers in the English language (Steen et al. 2010). Using a sample of the BNC Baby corpus, this group of researchers analysed the presence of metaphor in academic discourse (Herrmann 2013), news (Krennmayr 2011), fiction (Dorst 2011) and conversation (Kaal 2012). Contrary to expectations, academic discourse, whose subject matter would seem to require the use of literal meanings and avoidance of meaning displacements, was found to be the most metaphorically dense register (18.5%). Another informational register, the news, was the second most metaphorically dense register (16.4%), ahead of fiction (11.9%), which in principle could be assumed to be prone to making more use of expressive resources like metaphor. Finally, at a great distance from the rest, conversation showed the least metaphorically dense language (7.7%).

From a functional perspective, these results are less of a surprise. Using Biber's functional dimensions, we learn that texts with a high informational value, rich on explicit reference and a non-narrative dimension would provide 'a natural environment' for metaphor to thrive. The information packaging and abstraction that is typical of academic discourse and news could explain their higher densities, while the involved and situational dependence of conversation could account for its low density.

2.2 Part of Speech

However, metaphor density is not the only element of variation among the different registers. The VUAMC team also analysed the distribution of metaphors according to PoS. It was found (see Krennmayr 2017 for a summary of the finding by the VUAMC team) that register and PoS together interacted significantly with metaphor in such a way that certain registers had a higher proportion of metaphorical word classes. Thus, in the academic register, prepositions, verbs and adjectives have a greater metaphorical weight than other PoS, including nouns, which, although particularly frequent in that register, are not used as much with metaphorical senses. This distribution of metaphorically-used PoS is almost reproduced in the case of the news, the only difference being that, in this case, metaphorical nouns are also common. For their part, fiction and especially conversation show a different profile, the former having adjectives and prepositions at the top of their list and verbs in third position, and the latter incorporating prepositions, determiners and adjectives as the PoS with greatest metaphorical weight.

The analysis of PoS is interesting because it forms the basis of many of Biber's analyses and because, as Krennmayr (2017) acknowledges, "associations between metaphor and register cannot be interpreted directly but need to be interpreted by looking at the distribution of metaphor across word classes per register" (2017: 173). In other words, the number of metaphors per word class needs to be put into perspective as, for example, a high number of noun metaphors might be expected in academic discourse given that nominal groups are typical of this register (Biber 2006; Conrad 2001).

2.3 Disciplinary Variation and Genre

An additional dimension of variation is disciplinary variation, a topic dealt with by Herrmann (2015). In her study, this author analyses the different distributional patterns of metaphor use in the four general 'subregisters' or broad disciplines that she defines within academic discourse: 1) Natural Science; 2) Humanities and Arts; 3) Politics, Law and Education; and 4) Social Science. The general conclusion is that there seem to be no significant differences in metaphor density between the 'subregisters' with the one exception of Natural Science, which shows a lower percentage of Metaphor Related Words (MRW). However, the differences are not marked (17% in Natural Science vs 18.8% in the Humanities, 18.1% in Politics and 19% in Social Science).

Finally, genre, whose defining feature is not a broad situation, as in the case of register, but the specific purpose and the discourse community with which a text type is created (cf. Deignan et al. 2013: 40), provides a more precise source of variation (see Caballero 2017 for a review), although it has not been explored as much as register when dealing with metaphor in general and with metaphor density in particular. The reason could be that for a linguistic feature to be typical of a specific genre it need not be very frequent. For example, the expressions and linguistic elements used in the opening salutation of a letter (cf. Biber and Conrad 2009) are bound to be infrequent, although are actually part the conventions characterising that genre. Thus, if a linguistic element, in our case metaphor, is described as frequent it certainly is a feature to consider when describing that genre.

However, the number of studies giving an account of metaphor frequency in specific genres is relatively low. Exceptions include Low, Littlemore, and Koester's (2008) article on lectures, where we learn that the sample studied ranges from 11 to 13%, and MacArthur's (2016) study on office hours consultations, another oral academic genre, which is reported to have a metaphor density of 12.2%. Other authors approach the phenomenon from a different angle and, instead of concentrating on metaphor density overall, they focus on the presence of metaphor bursts, i.e. on the specific stretches of text where metaphor is highly frequent (cf. Corts and Pollio 1999). In this way, specific rhetorical or communicative goals of the participants of the discourse can be identified. Metaphor is thus examined as one of the features of genres, i.e. their staged nature (Caballero, 2017). The extent to which metaphor frequency fits a previously defined move structure of a specific genre has yet to be explored.

3 Metaphor in School Contexts

As already stated, the focus of the present article is not only linguistically defined by register or genre, it is also established by the situational context in which the textbooks under analysis are used, i.e. the Primary School context. Unfortunately, in spite of the amount of attention that metaphor has attracted in educational contexts, the school context has been neglected. According to Littlemore, with the exception of Cameron's (2003) seminal work, "there have been no other detailed studies of metaphor use in either primary or secondary education" (2017: 285). But even Cameron's work cannot strictly provide a model for the present research as it was carried out in a primary school in the UK, where the L1 of the students was English and the educational context was British education, and the main source for her corpus was the oral interaction in the classroom. We cannot take for granted that the use of metaphor by teachers with the function of agenda management, summarizing, providing feedback to the students or helping in giving explanations is an adequate model for the role of metaphor in a context or for a genre like the ones studied here.

Another strand of research related to teaching or educational contexts is the one dealing with second/foreign language learners. According to Hoang and Boers (2018), this exploration has mostly focussed on four main areas: metaphors conforming teachers' and learners' mind-set (Wan and Low 2015), awareness raising or use of linguistic motivation (MacArthur 2017), metaphor related comprehension problems (Littlemore 2001) and learners' production (Nacey 2013; Littlemore, Krennmayr, Turner, and Turner 2014). However, as in L1 contexts, young learners have not explicitly been the focus of attention in the literature on metaphor use in L2 learning (for an exception see Piquer-Píriz 2008). In all these cases, the studies are performed in the context of EFL classes, materials or activities addressed at improving the learners' competence in a foreign or second language. As we stated in the introduction, there is, to the best of our knowledge, no similar research on CLIL contexts, where the attention is not uniquely placed on how to learn a language but also on how to acquire the subject content, which makes it particularly interesting to investigate metaphor in this context.

It seems, therefore, appropriate to explore more in depth the CLIL context and to analyse the textbook as a particularly prominent genre by addressing the following research questions:
- What are the patterns of metaphor use in CLIL textbooks and how do these patterns expose, or not, connections to the registers described by the research? That is:
    - Is metaphor a frequent phenomenon in CLIL textbooks? Are these texts metaphorically dense?
    - Are certain parts of speech overused or underused as metaphors?
- What are the main sources of internal variation in metaphor use?
    - Is there disciplinary variation in metaphor use?
    - Is there variation in the different moves or stages of a CLIL lesson?

4 Methodology

To carry out the proposed analysis, we selected, from a corpus of textbooks previously compiled (García-Bermejo 2015), six lessons belonging to two different textbooks, which gave a total of 18,023 tokens, a figure that was considered more manageable given that the time-consuming process of metaphor tagging was carried out manually.

The two textbooks selected were *Natural Science ByMe: Primary 5* (2014) and *Social Science ByMe: Primary 5* (2014), which were used to teach two compulsory subjects, Natural Science and Social Science respectively, to students in 5th grade of Primary Education in Spain (10–11 years old). These textbooks are widely used in bilingual programmes in Spain and, as a consequence, they provided a good example of some of the language students are exposed to in these programmes.

The units to be analysed were chosen so that the first lesson of each academic term (i.e., units 1, 4 and 7 of each textbook) was included. In this way, we made sure that different thematic subjects were covered and a that the progression from beginning to end was also taken into account.

Once the corpus had been compiled, the text was scanned to tag open class parts of speech, i.e., nouns, verbs, adverbs and adjectives, a process that was carried out using the PoS tagger provided by the Wmatrix online software (Rayson 2008). The identification of metaphor related words (MRWs) was carried out manually by the two authors. Each researcher read the selected chapters from the books cited above and tagged potential MRWs individually. The researchers then met to reach a final agreement on the words we considered metaphor-related. In this process of MRW identification we followed MIPVU (Steen et al. 2010).

248 ━━━ Rafael Alejo-González and Verónica García-Bermejo

The only case in which we did not follow MIPVU was phrasal verbs, considered within MIPVU's methodology as polywords. As explained by Nacey (2013:86), MIPVU analyses phrasal verbs as a single unit because there is evidence that speakers 'lump' them as a whole. However, if we take into account the rich cognitive-linguistic literature on prepositions and particles (Lakoff 1989; Tyler and Evans 2003), it would be difficult to argue that these constituents of phrasal verbs, i.e. verbs and particles, do not contribute a meaning of their own, a stance also taken by other metaphor researchers (MacArthur 2016; MacArthur, Krennmayr, and Littlemore 2015).

The dictionary used to establish the basic meaning of the words was the *MacMillan Dictionary for Advanced Learners*, which is the usual reference work used in metaphor identification procedures (cf. MacArthur 2015; Steen et al. 2010). However, when there were instances where the dictionary was not helpful (see MacArthur 2015 for a complete explanation), we consulted the VUAMC corpus (available online at http://www.vismet.org/) to see whether instances similar to ours had been identified. If after all these steps, we still felt that the information provided in the dictionary was not helpful, we consulted other dictionaries, especially the *Longman Dictionary of Contemporary English*, to check for the basic meaning of lexical units.

It was also important to establish how to proceed with the specific terminology related to Biology or to History. As pointed out by Herrmann (2013), it is sometimes difficult to establish how incongruent the meaning of some terms can be in relation to the context in which they are used. This is the case, for example, of certain verbs like *breathe,* whose meaning is usually applied to mammals but it is not exactly clear to what extent it is used metaphorically when applied to plants. Do plants literally breathe? Here we follow Cameron (2003: 67), who suggests that in educational contexts technical language may be more prone to be interpreted metaphorically. As a result, we consider these terms as metaphorical.

Given the pedagogic goal of the texts, direct metaphors were also tagged. It is undertandable that some of the comparisons should be made directly to facilitate students' comprehension. We read the text and looked for the typical markers, or flags, of direct metaphors, which include 'like', 'as', 'seem', 'appear', 'sort of', 'kind of', etc. We also discovered that there was a section –'In other words'-, which typically featured a simile to help students to understand specific concepts explained in the text.

Once the text had been tagged for metaphor, a database using Excel was created and processed (i.e. tags converted to numbers) to be able to carry out the different statistical analyses by using the SPSS statistical package (v.17.0).

5 Results

5.1 Metaphor Density

The first research question concerns the frequency of metaphor in CLIL textbooks. We were surprised by the constant presence of this figure of speech in the discourse. See for example the opening paragraph of the Science book:

> Science helps us understand the world we live in. It shows us the importance of asking questions about natural phenomena that occur around us. Science helps us answer these questions by observing, predicting, researching, doing experiments and drawing conclusions. It also shows us the importance of technological and scientific advances in our lives.

The use of 7 metaphors in a paragraph with 53 words at the beginning of lesson 1 clearly shows that this figure of speech is going to play an important role in this textbook. A good initial explanation could be that personifying Science brings it closer to the students, who can thus see it not so much as an abstraction but as a person, a 'helping teacher', who is going to 'accompany' them in the learning process.

The importance of metaphor in the complete corpus is not just a mere first impression but is supported by a global quantitative analysis (see Table 1). Thus, the total number of open-class metaphors identified in the 6 lessons used in this study is 1,204, which given the number of tokens amounts to a density of 10.5%. This means that 1 in every 10 open class words is used metaphorically in the texts.

Table 1: Number of metaphor related words (tokens and lemmas).

Open class words	Tokens	%	Lemmas	%	Lemma/ token ratio
MRW	1204	10.5%	289	13.1%	31.90
Non- MRW	10211	89.5%	1925	86.9%	45.76
Total	11415	100.0%	2214	100.0%	38.83

It must be pointed out that the metaphor density of CLIL textbooks is not the result of the repetition of the same metaphors again and again. Thus, if we consider the number of lemmas used metaphorically, we can see that the figure of metaphor density is even higher (13.1%) than that of tokens or that the standardized type/token ratio is also quite high: 31.9. In other words, 1 in every 3 lemmas used metaphorically is not repeated. This means that, when reading these textbooks, students will be frequently faced with the task of understanding words used with a meaning that is different from their basic one.

5.2 Metaphor Density and Part of Speech

Nouns and verbs are the most important word classes found in the textbooks analysed. Together, nouns (with 41.03%) and verbs (with 40.37%) comprise more than three quarters of the open-class metaphors used in these texts, while metaphorically used adverbs and adjectives make up a smaller fraction of the total number of metaphorically used words. However, nouns and verbs are the most frequent PoS in the textbooks and so it is to be expected that many instances of metaphor will involve these word classes.

We therefore performed a Chi square analysis of the percentages of MRWs per word class (see Table 2) as a way to avoid the uneven representation of certain PoS in the corpus. The results are statistically significant (χ^2 = 173.664; df=3; p<.0001; Cramer's V 0.123) and clearly show that adjectives and nouns are less likely to be used metaphorically, while verbs and adverbs occur comparatively often with a metaphorical meaning. Unlike verbs, the predominance of metaphor-related nouns in absolute terms does not reflect a particular tendency to use them metaphorically but is a side-effect of the higher frequency of this PoS in the textbooks analysed.

Table 2: Metaphor tokens and parts of speech.

	MRW	%	Non-MRW	%	total tokens
Adverbs	117	17.4%	556	82.6%	673
Verbs	486	15.6%	2639	84.4%	3125
Nouns	494	8.0%	5687	92.0%	6181
Adjectives	107	7.5%	1329	92.5%	1436
Total	1204	10.5%	10211	89.5%	11415

As far as lemmas are concerned (see Table 3), the results are also statistically significant (χ^2 = 164.46; df=3; p<.0001; Cramer's V 0.26) and the analysis of residuals shows that, as with tokens, the proportion of metaphorically used adjectives and nouns is comparatively small, particularly so in the case of nouns (Std. Res.=−5.92), whereas the proportion of metaphorically used verbs and adverbs is more substantial, most notably so in the case of verbs (Std. Res.=+10.44).

Table 3: Metaphor lemmas and parts of speech.

	MRW	% MRW	Non-MRW	% NON.MRW	total lemmas
Adjectives	44	11.3%	345	88.7%	389
Nouns	113	7.9%	1311	92.1%	1424
Verbs	126	29.5%	301	70.5%	427
Adverbs	25	19.7%	102	80.3%	127

5.3 Disciplinary Variation

Our analysis on whether metaphor density was affected by the topic focussed on two of the most important subjects in the Spanish curriculum: Natural Science and Social Science.

By comparing the metaphors used in Natural Science with those used in Social Science (see Table 4), we find that there is a statistically significant difference in metaphor use ($\chi2$ = 60.640; df=1; p<.0001; Cramer's V 0.073) and that the number of metaphors used in the Natural Science textbook is greater than in Social Science. Thus, while Natural Science lessons have a density of nearly 13.0%, Social Science texts only reach 8.4%, which means a difference of 4.5 percentage points, enough to indicate that there is a substantial difference between the two textbooks analysed in terms of metaphor use.

Table 4: Percentage of MRWs by subject.

	MRW	%	Non-MRW	%	Total tokens
Natural Sc.	692	12.9%	4655	87.1%	5347
Social Sc.	512	8.4%	5556	91.6%	6068
Total	1204	10.5%	10211	89.5%	11415

5.4 Move Variation

The second source of internal variation that we set out to examine is the structure of the textbooks and the lessons in our corpus. The structure is described in Table 5, where we include labels for each part together with a short explanation, the corresponding move according to Parodi's (2010) taxonomy of textbooks moves and the kind of pedagogic function they perform. This structure is easily identifiable as its limits are marked by page breaks, except in the case of

Table 5: Structure of the textbooks' lessons.

Textbook label	Description	Move (cf. Parodi 2010)	Pedagogic function
Getting started	Opening introduction to the textbooks. Only before unit 1 of each textbook	Preamble (Macro-move)	Introductory
Read and discover	Short overview of unit's topic followed by questions	Practice	Warm up
Analyse and organize	Exercises to activate previous knowledge		
Content	Explanations about the topic of the unit It is the only section consisting of more than one page	Concept definitions	Explanation
Project	Practical work on the topic of the subject	Practice	Follow up
Fragile World	Focus on a specific issue related to the topic of the unit	Concept definitions	
Revise	Exercises to monitor comprehension and learning	Recapitulation	

the *Content* section (see Table 5), which consists of more than one page and uses titles identifying the topic. The structure is fixed to such an extent that, except for the opening macro-move in each textbook (*Getting started*), it is repeated in both the Natural Science and the Social Science lessons in the order appearing in the table.

To check whether metaphor densities varied across these moves, we carried out a Chi square analysis, whose results, shown in Table 6, are statistically significant (χ^2 = 20.837; df=6; $p<.002$; Cramer's V 0.043). The association is not very strong, as shown by the low Cramer's V value, but certain sections do tend to show greater metaphor use than others. These are *Getting started, Read & Discover* and *Fragile World*. This would indicate that there is greater reliance on metaphors in these sections, which in principle do not seem to share a common pedagogic function. At the same time, there is much less use of metaphor in the case of sections more related to practical work like *Analyse & Organise, Project* or *Revise*. The central section of *Content*, considered by Parodi (2010) the nucleus of a chapter and usually making up the bulk of the unit, does not stand out as having either particularly high or low metaphor density.

Table 6: MRW frequency by move.

	MRW	%	Non-MRW	%	total
Getting started	43	**12.4%**	303	87.6%	346
Read & discover	98	**14.1%**	597	85.9%	695
Analyse & organise	121	*9.5%*	1152	90.5%	1273
Content	512	10.2%	4489	89.8%	5001
Project	75	*9.4%*	726	90.6%	801
Fragile World	127	**12.9%**	856	87.1%	983
Revise	228	*9.8%*	2088	90.2%	2316
Total	1204	10.5%	10211	89.5%	11415

6 Discussion

After having presented the results, we are now in a position to discuss the research questions posed in our introduction. The first question sought to establish whether CLIL textbooks had a high, or low, degree of metaphor density, a question that can only be answered by referring to benchmarks against which our results can be measured. Two main points of reference are available.

First, we can compare our results to the percentages provided by the VUAMC team (Steen et al. 2010; Krennmayr 2011; Dorst 2011; Kaal 2012; Herrmann 2013). This comparison should be taken with a certain degree of caution as there is a methodological difference – relating to phrasal verbs – between our identification procedure and MIPVU's (see methodology). However, it is not very likely that this should essentially alter the percentages, as only a small number of words are affected by this methodological decision.

Given the nature of CLIL textbooks, one would expect to find a metaphor density typical of non-involved informational texts. In other words, the number of metaphors to be found in the textbooks should be closer to that of academic register (Herrmann 2013). In fact, this is not what we find if we look at Figure 1, where we can see that the density in our corpus is nearer the Conversation register (Kaal 2012). This would mean that the density could be considered as low and that school textbooks do not follow the patterns of metaphor use that are common in academic texts in general.

Secondly, we can consider the most important study to date on metaphor use in educational contexts (Cameron 2003). In this case, we can see that the figure obtained in our study for just the open class words (10.5%) is clearly higher than the 2.7% which Cameron identified in her corpus. We must acknowledge that Cameron's results are less comparable to ours than the VUAMC

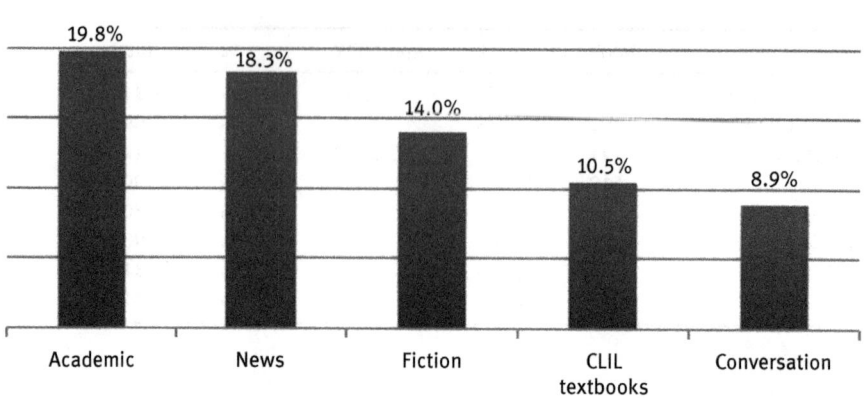

Figure 1: Comparison of metaphor density in CLIL textbooks with other registers.

team's cited above (Steen et al 2010), as she used a different method of metaphor identification and her corpus is made up of mostly spoken language. However, the number of metaphors that would be added by transforming Cameron's unit of analysis into words, a calculation that can be easily made as she provides the number of single metaphors (i.e. words) and the number of metaphorical phrases (noun, verb, etc., cf. Cameron 2003:88), would not significantly alter the tentative conclusion that oral school language in L1 educational contexts would have a lower metaphor density than the textbooks we are analysing. Other studies on metaphor density in texts directed at children, also cited by Cameron, would provide a similar conclusion as "around 10 metaphors per 1000 words might be expected in classroom texts" (Cameron 2003: 57).

In short, although the number of metaphors found in our corpus could be considered small if compared with academic texts in general, it seems that high metaphor densities are not to be expected in school texts directed at children, much less in those addressed to L2 learners. As a consequence, a figure of 10.5% may very well describe a not unimportant role for metaphor in the texts analysed, especially if we take into account that the type/token ratio indicates a high degree of variation in the metaphors used.

This conclusion is reinforced by our results on the breakdown of metaphors by PoS, which relates to our second research question. The relatively high proportion of metaphorically used verbs and a comparatively smaller proportion of metaphorically used nouns was also characteristic of the academic register (Herrmann 2013), which in this case matches what happens in school language (Cameron 2003). These PoS results therefore corroborate that patterns of metaphor use also conform to the academic register, although an explanation for each word class is needed.

The explanation for the high number of verbs is provided by Krennmayr (2017). According to her, the use of verbs is related to personification, which renders the text more comprehensible and accessible for students by providing them with a 'human-like' approach to abstract concepts. This personification function of metaphor related verbs is at its peak in textbooks when definitions are provided. General abstractions are thus rendered more manageable:

> Volume describes how much space matter occupies." (Nat. Science, less.7)
> Density explains why some objects float in water while others sink (Nat. Science, less.7)
> A force is a push or pull that acts on an object. (Nat. Science, less.7)
> Friction acts in the opposite direction to the direction of movement (Nat. Science, less.7)

Unlike verbs, the results for adverbs were unexpected, as adverbs have not been shown to be particularly prone to being used metaphorically in the academic register (Herrmann 2013). Here the explanation is simple. On the one hand, it is related to our methodological decision to consider the particle of phrasal verbs not as parts of a single multi-word verb but as an adverb. On the other, as typical of academic discourse, adverbs are used as metadiscursive devices which indicate that texts are conceived as locations (Herrmann 2013: 199). Here are some examples of this use in CLIL textbooks:

> What are the functions of the elements in a city listed above? (Nat. Science, lesson 1)
> What does the image above illustrate? (Soc. Science lesson 4)
> Explain the importance of the advances listed below. (Soc. Science lesson 7)
> Use the words from the words in the box below. (Nat. Science, lesson 1)
> In your notebook, complete the graphic organiser below by choosing the words from the box. (Nat. Science, lesson 1)

As for metaphorically-used nouns, contrary to what has been shown in academic discourse, where their frequency is the same as in the overall discourse (Herrmann 2013: 197), the relatively small proportion of metaphor-related nouns in our corpus was not expected and seems to be a characteristic of the textbooks we have analysed. If we have a look at the list of 15 most frequent nouns in our corpus, we find that there are only 3 nouns that are frequently used metaphorically: *kingdom, cell and thing*. The rest, as can be seen from Table 7 are concrete nouns referring to the basic entities or components of the disciplines being studied (*plant, water, matter, city*), to specific singular items (*Earth, Moon, Spain*) or to the materials used in class (*notebook*). Reference rather than explanation makes it appropriate to avoid metaphor.

Table 7: Most frequent nouns in the corpus studied.

	Lemma	Freq	% of Nouns		Lemma	Freq	% of nouns
1	plant	116	1.88%	9	Moon	42	0.68%
2	water	94	1.52%	10	City	40	0.65%
3	Earth	75	1.21%	11	matter	39	0.63%
4	kingdom	59	0.95%	12	Force	39	0.63%
5	cell	56	0.91%	13	Space	37	0.60%
6	Spain	52	0.84%	14	Word	35	0.57%
7	notebook	47	0.76%	15	animal	34	0.55%
8	planet	45	0.73%				

We now move on to our third research question, which asked whether there was disciplinary variation (Social vs. Natural Science) in our corpus. The results indicate a positive answer, although they contradict the ones obtained by Herrmann (2015), where the Natural Science 'subregister' shows a lower metaphor density. It would be fair to say that the jury is still out since neither Herrmann's nor the present study offer conclusive statistical results.

From a qualitative perspective, though, this different behaviour of the two 'subregisters', or thematic areas, can be best exemplified by looking at a specific noun like *kingdom* (see Table 8), which is used 33 times in the Natural Science textbook and 26 in the Social Science textbook.

As the Shakespearean quote in our title indicates, it seems that Primary school children have to learn how to interpret the word kingdom in two clearly differentiated contexts. In the context of the Natural Science textbook, the word is exclusively used metaphorically and appears in the beginning chapters of the book. In contrast, in the Social Science textbook the meaning is literal and the word is used in the middle and final chapters. In terms of language processing, this separation of contexts is probably helpful for students. What remains to be explored is whether the use of the metaphorical meaning before the literal sense, as the former is used in the beginning chapters, may pose a problem to them.

Finally, as regards the distribution of metaphors in the different sections of the lessons, i.e. the fourth research question, the results obtained are also statistically significant but in this case there are no similar studies with which they can be compared. The explanation does not pose a problem in the case of sections where metaphor density is relatively low. In these sections, the main concern is with practical work, which means that in terms of language there is greater use of a regulative register (Christie 2000). Students are given

Table 8: Concordance of 'kingdom' in the two subcorpora.

Natural	1	tula belongs to the Animal Kingdom. 2 It 's usual
Science	2	d into five groups called kingdoms. Organisms of
	3	Organisms of the same kingdom share similarities
	4	t from organisms in other kingdoms. Plant Kingdom
	5	kingdoms. Plant Kingdom. Plants are multicellu
	6	MRW oxygen. Protist Kingdom. Protists are usually
	7	tosynthesis. Monera Kingdom. All organisms in this
	8	_All organisms in this kingdom are unicellular.
Social	9	r false . Visigothic Kingdom. The Middle Ages began in
Science	10	ished the capital of their kingdom in Toledo and adopted
	11	redo I, converted his kingdom to Catholicism during the
	12	iscuss any problems in the kingdom. The rest of the p
	13	tal city of the Visigothic Kingdom. c . The Vis
	14	ans invaded the Visigothic Kingdom in AD 711. San Isi
	15	ical system Christian Kingdoms The Reconquista began

instructions that need to be precise and factual. As a consequence, there is less room for meaning displacements and for metaphor.

The reason behind the greater metaphor density of the introduction to the books (*Getting started*), the warm-up section giving an overview of the unit's topic (*Read & Discover*) and the follow-up focus section on a specific issue related to the subject matter (*Fragile World*) is less obvious. We would argue that it has to do with the wider scope and the more abstract nature of these sections. It seems as if their preparatory and exploratory nature calls for summarizing and generalizing statements for which metaphor is particularly apt. See for example this *Read & Discover* extract from unit 7, which is not particularly dense in terms of metaphor:

> During the Middle Ages, different civilisations lived on the Iberian Peninsula. Visigoths settled after the Roman Empire fell. Then Muslims invaded, calling their new territories Al-Andalus. Here, three religious groups lived together: Muslims, Jews and Christians. Over the next centuries, the Christians in the north fought against the Muslims. By the end of 1492, the whole Iberian Peninsula was under Christian rule again. What was the period before the Middle Ages called?

In this extract, the whole series of defeats and the collapse of the Roman army and institutions, which developed over a long period of time, and the emergence of a new social and political system after the *Reconquista*, which took several centuries to enforce, are condensed by using a verb of motion (*fell*) and a specific noun (*rule*). For their part, religious groups are personified (*live*) to indicate that they can have a particular kind of life whose limits go beyond individual human beings.

Finally, the content section is focussed on providing the basic definitions and explanations of the topic and, as a consequence, tends to make use of specific vocabulary and terminology, which is sometimes metaphorical, together with more general language used to perform the basic functions of scientific and academic language (e.g., defining, classifying, describing, giving examples, comparing and contrasting).

It is interesting to note that, in spite of metaphor not being manifested especially frequently in this central section, it is here where we can find most of the examples of direct metaphor. In fact, incorporated to all the content sections of the Natural Science book we can find a subsection called *In other words*. This subsection is nothing but an analogy expressed as a simile and intended to help students understandthe concepts explained in the lesson. Here we include the subsection in unit 4:

> Chloroplasts are like solar panels. They capture solar energy and transform it. Instead of electricity, chloroplasts produce glucose.

Typographically separated from the rest of the section and accompanied by a photograph of solar panels, this subsection is clearly designed to explain some of the concepts being used. Sometimes, it is the learners who have to provide the explanation, as in this example from unit 1 from the Natural Science book:

A cell is like a city:
nucleus=town hall
vacuole=water tower
cytoplasm=atmosphere
cell membrane=guards
chloroplasts=parks
cell wall= city wall
What are the functions of the elements in a city listed above?

These are clearly examples of direct metaphors being used with a pedagogic or illustrating function, but they are not used frequently (once in a whole unit) and are not given particular prominence as they are placed in a corner of the content pages. We can only find two other examples of metaphor being signposted. In a less obvious and more condensed simile, a part of the cell, the cytoplasm, is described as *jelly-like* and the leaves of a tree are referred to as *needle-like*. MacArthur (2016) already pointed out the relatively low frequency of similes and direct metaphors in a corpus of office hour consultations (EuroCoAT). Skorczynska and

Deignan (2006) obtained similar findings in other genres like research and periodical articles related to economics. They predicted, however, a higher proportion in textbooks given their pedagogical goals. However, it seems that this is not the case of CLIL textbooks.

All in all, indirect metaphor seems to be the order of the day, especially in those sections less directly focussed on either the specific content (definitions and explanations) or on the practical work students have to carry out. The more prominent and more marked use of direct metaphor, however, should not conceal its low frequency.

7 Conclusion

The present chapter has attempted to make a preliminary analysis of metaphor in CLIL. This educational approach to bilingualism, mostly adopted in Europe, has attracted a lot of attention from applied linguists, but up to now has been neglected in the extensive literature on metaphor, which is increasingly covering a wider range of communication contexts but has left this one unattended. The study of metaphor in two CLIL textbooks has provided us with a preliminary picture of the workings of metaphor in this context and has shown that, although it is not as frequently used as in academic prose (Herrmann 2013), the density is quite high, especially if we compare it with the levels found by Cameron (2003) for L1 educational contexts, which in a way points to the difficult task students reading these textbooks are faced with. However, the textbooks show similarities with some of the patterns found by Cameron (2003), as we found that they make use of a great number metaphorical verbs, in contrast to the relatively low now number of nouns, for example, which indicates a need to make the actions they express more accessible to the students by personifying the abstract nominal phrases used as their subjects. The picture of the use of metaphor in CLIL textbooks is completed by the study of the two main sources of variation we identified. On the one hand, the use of metaphor in the Natural Science textbook is clearly higher than in the Social Science one, which indicates that even at these initial stages of education the discourse strategies used are not homogenous and that the different subjects are already beginning to impose their stamp on the language used. On the other hand, we found that there are certain parts of the units when metaphor is more frequent and the internal variation between the different structural elements of the lesson evidences the need to pay more attention to those areas where the use of metaphor may go unnoticed, like for example the introduction of lessons. These conclusions should, however, be taken with caution as the study is only preliminary and another study with a corpus including a greater number of books and lessons would be needed.

References

Berber Sardinha, Tony. 2015. Register variation and metaphor use: A multi-dimensional perspective. In Berenike Herrmann & Tony Berber Sardinha (eds.), *Metaphor in specialist discourse*, 17–52. Amsterdam: John Benjamins.

Biber, Douglas. 1988. *Variation across speech and writing*. Cambridge: Cambridge University Press.

Biber, Douglas. 2006. *University language: A corpus-based study of spoken and written registers*. Amsterdam: John Benjamins.

Biber, Douglas & Susan Conrad. 2009. *Register, genre and style*. Cambridge: Cambridge University Press.

Caballero, Rosario. 2003. Metaphor and genre: The presence and role of metaphor in the building review. *Applied Linguistics* 24(2). 145–67.

Caballero, Rosario. 2017. Genre and metaphor: Use and variation across usage events. In Elena Semino & Zoltán Demjén (eds.), The Routledge handbook of metaphor and language, 193–218. London: Routledge.

Caballero, Rosario. 2012. The role of metaphor in tennis reports and forums. *Text & Talk* 32 (6). 703–726.

Cameron, Lynne. 2003. *Metaphor in educational discourse*. London: Continuum

Cameron, Lynne & Juurd H. Stelma. 2004. Metaphor clusters in discourse. *Journal of Applied Linguistics* 1(2). 107–36.

Charteris-Black, Jonathan. 2004. Why "an angel rides in the whirlwind and directs the storm": A corpus-based comparative study of metaphor in British and American political discourse. *Language and Computers* 49. 133–50.

Christie, Frances. 2000. The pedagogic device and the teaching of English. In Frances Christie (ed.), *Pedagogy and the shaping of consciousness*, 156–184. London: Continuum.

Conrad, Susan. 2001. Variation among disciplinary texts. A comparison of textbooks and journal articles in Biology and History. In Susan Conrad & Douglas Biber (eds), *Variation in English: Multidimensional studies*, 94–107. London: Routledge.

Corts, Daniel P. & Howard R. Pollio. 1999. Spontaneous production of figurative language and gesture in college lectures. *Metaphor and Symbol* 14(2). 81–100.

Coyle, Do, Philip Hood & David Marsh. 2010. *CLIL: Content and language integrated learning*. Cambridge: Cambridge University Press.

Dalton-Puffer, Christiane. 2007. *Discourse in content and language integrated learning (CLIL) classrooms*. Amsterdam/Philadelpia: John Benjamins.

Deignan, Alice, Jeannette Littlemore & Elena Semino. 2013. *Figurative language, genre and register*. Cambridge: Cambridge University Press.

Dorst, Aletta G. 2011. *Metaphor in Fiction: Language, thought and communication*. Oisterwijk: Box Press Uitgeverij.

Dorst, Aletta G. 2017. Textual patterning of metaphor. In Elena Semino and Zoltán Demjén (eds.), *The Routledge handbook of metaphor and language*, 178–92. London: Routledge.

Fernández-Sanjurjo, Javier, Alberto Fernández-Costales & José Miguel Arias Blanco. 2017. Analysing students' content-learning in science in CLIL vs. non-CLIL programmes: Empirical evidence from Spain, *International Journal of Bilingual Education and Bilingualism*. 1–14.

García-Bermejo, Verónica. 2015. Análisis del vocabulario en libros de texto para la enseñanza AICLE en 5º de educación primaria. *Campo Abierto. Revista de Educación* 34 (1). 29–47.

García-Mayo, María del Pilar & María Basterrechea. 2017. CLIL and SLA. In Ana Llinares & Tom Morton (eds.), *Applied Linguistics Perspectives on CLIL*, 33–50. Amsterdam: John Benjamins.

Herrmann, Berenike. 2013. *Metaphor in academic discourse: Linguistic forms, conceptual structures, communicative functions and cognitive representations*. Utrecht: LOT dissertation series.

Herrmann, Berenike. 2015. High on metaphor, low on simile? An examination of metaphor type in sub-registers of academic prose. In Berenike Herrmann & Tony Berber Sardinha (eds.), *Metaphor in specialist discourse*, 163–190. Amsterdam: John Benjamins.

Hoang, Ha & Frank Boers. 2018. Gauging the association of EFL learners' writing proficiency and their use of metaphorical language. *System 74*. 1–8.

Järvinen, Heini-Marja. 2010. Language as a meaning making resource in learning and teaching content. in Christiane Dalton-Puffer, Tarja Nikula & Ute Smit (eds.), *Language use and language learning in CLIL classrooms*,145–168. Amsterdam: John Benjamins.

Kaal, Anna A. 2012. *Metaphor in conversation*. Oisterwijk: Uitgeverij BOX Press.

Koller, Veronika. 2006. Of critical importance: Using corpora to study metaphor in business media discourse. In Anatol Stefanowitsch & Stefan T. Gries (eds.), *Corpus-based approaches to metaphor and metonymy*, 229–257. Berlin: Mouton de Gruyter.

Krennmayr, Tina. 2011. *Metaphor in newspapers*. Utrecht: LOT dissertation series.

Krennmayr, Tina. 2017. *Metaphor and parts-of-speech*. In Elena Semino and Zoltán Demjén (eds.), The routledge handbook of metaphor and language, 165–177. London: Routledge.

Lakoff, George. 1989. *Women, fire and dangerous things: What categories reveal about the mind*. Chicago: University of Chicago Press.

Littlemore, Jeannette. 2001. The use of metaphor in university lectures and the problems that it causes for overseas students. *Teaching in Higher Education* 6(3). 333–49.

Littlemore, Jeannete, Phillys Chen, John Barnden & Almut Koester. 2011. Difficulties in metaphor comprehension faced by international students whose first language is not English. *Applied Linguistics* 32(3). 408–29.

Littlemore, Jeannette, Tina Krennmayr, James Turner & Sara Turner. 2014. An investigation into metaphor use at different levels of second language writing. *Applied Linguistics* 35(2). 117–144.

Llinares, Ana, Tom Morton & Rachel Whittaker. 2012. *The roles of languages in CLIL*. Cambridge: Cambridge University Press.

Low, Graham D., Jeannette Littlemore & Almut. Koester. 2008. Metaphor use in three UK university lectures. *Applied Linguistics* 29(3). 428–55.

MacArthur, Fiona. 2015. On using a dictionary to identify the basic sense of words. *Metaphor and the Social World*. 5(1). 124–136.

MacArthur, Fiona. 2016. Overt and covert uses of metaphor in the academic mentoring in English of Spanish undergraduate students at five European universities. *Review of Cognitive Linguistics* 14(1). 23–50.

MacArthur, Fiona. 2017. Using metaphor in the teaching of second/foreign language. In Elena Semino & Zoltán Demjén (eds.), *The Routledge handbook of metaphor and language*, 193–218. London: Routledge.

MacArthur, Fiona, Tina Krennmayr & Jeannette Littlemore. 2015. How basic Is UNDERSTANDING IS SEEING when reasoning about knowledge? Asymmetric uses of SIGHT metaphors in office hours' consultations in English as academic lingua franca. *Metaphor and Symbol* 30(3). 184–217.

Marsh, David. 2008. Language awareness and CLIL. In Jasone Cenoz & Nancy Hornberger (eds): *Encyclopedia of Language and Education*, vol 6. Knowledge about language. 233–46. Boston, MA: Springer.

Nacey, Susan. 2013. *Metaphors in learner English*. Amsterdam: John Benjamins.

Parodi, Giovanni. 2010. The rhetorical organization of the textbook genre across disciplines: A 'colony-in-loops'? *Discourse Studies* 12(2). 195–222.

Pérez-Cañado, María Luisa. 2012. CLIL research in Europe: Past, present and future. International *Journal of Bilingual Education and Multilingualism* 15(3). 315–41.

Pérez-Sobrino, Paula. 2016. Multimodal metaphor and metonymy in advertising: A corpus-based account. *Metaphor and Symbol* 31(2). 73–90.

Piquer-Píriz, Ana M. 2008. Young learners' understanding of figurative language. In Maria S. Zanotto, Lynne Cameron & Marilda C. Cavalcanti (eds.), *Confronting metaphor in use: An applied linguistic approach*, 183–198. Amsterdam: John Benjamins.

Rayson, Paul. 2008. *Wmatrix: A web-based corpus processing environment (version 2009)*. Lancaster University: Computing department.

Skorczynska, Hanna & Alice Deignan. 2006. Readership and purpose in the choice of economics metaphors. *Metaphor and Symbol* 21(2). 87–104.

Steen, Gerard J., Aletta G. Dorst, Berenike Herrmann, Anna A. Kaal, Tina Krennmayr & Trijntje Pasma. 2010. *A method for linguistic metaphor identification: From MIP to MIPVU*. Amsterdam: John Benjamins.

Tyler, Andrea & Vyvyan Evans. 2003. *The semantics of English prepositions explained*. Cambridge: Cambridge University Press.

Wan, Wan & Graham D. Low. 2015. *Elicited metaphor analysis in educational discourse*. Amsterdam: John Benjamins.

Zeeuw Marlies de, Franc Grootjen, Gerrit Jan Kootstra & Agnes Tellings. 2019. Lexical characteristics of written language input across primary grades: An analysis of a Dutch corpus based lexicon. *Linguistics and Education* 49, 11–21.

Rawan A. Saaty

An Enactment-Based Approach to the Teaching of Metaphoric Expressions: A Case of Saudi EFL Learners

1 Introduction

Metaphor awareness-raising activities which are based on enactment involve promoting awareness of the embodied motivations behind conceptual metaphors. This approach to the teaching of EFL metaphors draws on insights from embodied cognition research (Barsalou 2009; Gibbs 2006), which views embodied metaphors as grounded in sensorimotor experience. Gibbs (2014) described embodied metaphors as being more fundamental than conceptual metaphors because they unfold through human actions and interactions with the world. This study is based on the hypothesis that promoting awareness of embodied metaphor in the EFL/ESL classroom through actions can improve the learning of related metaphoric expressions. To investigate this, the study examines the impact of enactment-based metaphor awareness on learners' comprehension and retention of the meaning of 11 metaphoric expressions instantiating the conceptual metaphor LIFE IS A JOURNEY. It also explores whether the intervention leads to productive use of the target vocabulary in writing.

As outlined by Lindstromberg and Boers (2005), enactment-based metaphor awareness involves encouraging language learners to enact the literal meanings of metaphorically used lexical items. Lindstromberg and Boers found inspiration in Asher's ([1977] 2012) Total Physical Response (TPR) for the teaching of metaphoric expressions as it allows for the natural acquisition of vocabulary in a physically active environment. Through the use of repetitive commands, learners experience the physical meaning of vocabulary from hearing and performing it multiple times, thereby taking an active role in vocabulary understanding (Asher ([1977] 2012). Applied to enactment-based metaphor awareness, learners can act out 'sailing through life' by waving their hands forwards to help them internalise the image of sailing in terms of life. Ray and Sealy's ([1998] 2004) advanced version of TPR, Teaching Proficiency through Reading and Storytelling (TPR Storytelling), relies on students enacting short stories rather than single words and allows them to learn vocabulary items in context. Both variations of TPR are

Rawan A. Saaty, English Language Institute, King Abdulaziz University, Jeddah, Saudi Arabia, e-mail: rsaaty@kau.edu.sa

https://doi.org/10.1515/9783110630367-013

employed in this study, so metaphoric expressions are learned both individually and in context.

2 Awareness of Conceptual Metaphor and Semantic Clustering

Figurative language teaching research has raised awareness of conceptual metaphor in L2 and guided this awareness through guessing strategies (Skoufaki 2008), etymological elaboration (Boers, Demecheleer, and Eyckmans 2004; Boers, Eyckmans, and Stengers 2007) and pictorial elucidation (Boers et al. 2008; Boers et al. 2009) among others. In an experimental study with 30 EFL Greek learners, Skoufaki (2008) employed learners' problem-solving skills to promote awareness of conceptual metaphors. The study involved three metaphor groups. Group 2 (the metaphor-guessing group) obtained meaning clues that helped them guess the relationship between the target idioms and conceptual metaphors. Groups 1 and 3, on the other hand, received conceptual metaphor awareness training minus the guessing, and differed only in that group 1 focused on meaning while group 3 focused on form. The metaphor-guessing group received higher scores than the metaphor-only groups in a cloze test (4.30 versus 1.60 and 1.90) as well as a comprehension test (62.50% versus 50% and 42.50%). Skoufaki concluded that the cognitive effort used in mental reasoning benefited the learners' retention of the metaphoric expressions. In another study, Boers, Demecheleer and Eyckmans (2004) employed etymological elaboration to promote awareness of the literal, historical and cultural origins of idioms. Results from the 2002 experiment indicated that the etymology group outperformed the control group by 11% in post-tests which required students to recall the key content words of the idioms in a blank-fill test format.

While figurative language teaching research calls for promoting awareness of metaphor in language teaching, most current EFL/ESL textbooks present metaphoric vocabulary in general semantic clusters with no reference to the metaphorical motivations behind them. Wilcox and Medina (2013: 1057) define semantic clustering as the presentation of vocabulary items as "groups of words whose meaning would fall under one superordinate concept" without further indication of the items' contextual use or cognitive motivation. Tinkham (1993) argued that textbooks often present new vocabulary items under semantic clusters, such as *words for animals*. He clarified that although learners would be able to memorize such lists, they would struggle to differentiate between the meanings of individual words, to employ those words communicatively, and to retain the vocabulary.

So far, figurative language teaching research has been confined to aware-ness-raising activities involving conceptual metaphor, which according to Boers (2004), do not guarantee that learners will be capable of producing the metaphoric expressions in natural contexts. Boers (2004) also noted that due to a lack of longitudinal investigation, it is not clear whether conceptual metaphor awareness would provide long-term mnemonic benefits. Figurative language teaching research is also limited in that it can view the language classroom as a static environment. In her dynamic system view of the language classroom, MacArthur (2010: 158) argued that language learning should be viewed as a com-plex phenomenon in which the replication of results of controlled classroom ex-perimental research would be "variable, and no one method or technique will work for all learners; initial states, cognitive styles, mood swings, the L1 of the learners, group dynamics, and a host of other variables will be working together to affect the developing system". Thus, even explicit teaching of metaphoric ex-pressions may not offer satisfactory results without considerable attention to the learners' needs and abilities.

3 Awareness of the Embodied Nature of Metaphors through Actions

The sensorimotor experiences that we use to interact with the world provide grounding for our language and thought. Grady (1997) and Gibbs (2006) viewed conceptual metaphors as being rooted in bodily and sensorimotor experiences through primary metaphors. For example, Grady (1997) classified the concep-tual metaphor LIFE IS A JOURNEY as a complex metaphor that inherits its map-pings from primary metaphors such as PURPOSES ARE DESTINATIONS and CIRCUMSTANCES ARE SURROUNDINGS which are grounded in physical reality. Gibbs (2006) noted that since many metaphoric expressions are also rooted in bodily experiences, they can be understood through awareness of their sensori-motor links. To learn metaphoric expressions such as *to take a step forward* and *to climb a career ladder*, learners may be asked to stand up and take steps with their feet and gesture with their hands as if they were climbing a ladder.

While figurative language teaching research is yet to explore the extent of enactment-based metaphor awareness, research carried out in the fields of psy-chology, neuroscience, and cognitive linguistics has enhanced our understand-ing of the potential of embodied metaphors. In behavioural psychology, research has employed embodied metaphors to modulate suspicion (Lee and Schwarz 2012) and influence social proximity (IJzerman and Semin 2009). For example,

Lee and Schwarz' (2012) experiments on the olfactory experience of fishy smells and social suspicion indicated that exposing participants to fishy smells provokes suspicion and influences financial distrust. At the same time, the findings of this study indicated that encouraging participants to be suspicious heightens their ability to identify fishy smells. This bi-directionality of metaphor can be beneficial in the teaching of L2 metaphors, where the embodied sensorimotor motivations of primary metaphors can be manipulated to promote awareness of abstract target domains.

In neuro-cognition research, Desai et al. (2011) and De Grauwe et al. (2014) suggested dual linguistic and motor processing of action metaphors in L1 and L2. As to L1, Desai et al. (2011) compared the mental activation of literal, abstract, and metaphoric sentences through the use of functional magnetic resonance imaging (fMRI). Participants were instructed to think of the meanings of sentences as they read them. Metaphoric sentences with action metaphors (e.g. *the jury grasped the idea*) were processed similarly to physical action words (e.g. *the daughter grasped the flowers*). fMRI results indicated that both literal and metaphoric sentences activated the left anterior inferior partial lobule, which is an area of the brain generally activated when planning concrete actions. In addition, metaphoric sentences also activated the left superior temporal regions, which are activated with abstract sentences. Regarding metaphor processing in L2, Xue et al. (2014) compared Chinese-English bilinguals' understanding of spatial-time metaphors. Results indicated that the mental processing of L1 and L2 time metaphors involved different sensorimotor simulations for each language, suggesting that even in their L2, bilinguals processed metaphors through embodied grounding.

In the cognitive linguistic paradigm, studies that have investigated enactment of the embodied nature of metaphors were conducted in L1 (e.g. Gibbs and Perlman 2006; Wilson and Gibbs 2007; Gibbs 2013). Studies that investigate enactment-based metaphor awareness in L2 are scarce. Concerning L1, Gibbs (2013) examined the understanding of two groups of participants with regards to the metaphor LOVE IS A JOURNEY through actions. Gibbs asked participants to walk across a field blindfolded after they had listened to successful and failing relationship stories. Those who listened to the successful love story walked faster and further than those who had heard the failing love narrative. Gibbs' findings suggest that employing the embodied nature of metaphor influences related actions. Regarding enactment-based metaphor awareness in L2, Lindstromberg and Boers (2005) employed enactment and mime to teach English action verbs to Dutch university learners who were divided into enactment groups and comparison groups. Participants in the enactment groups played charades by miming metaphoric action verbs, such as *leap* and *pounce*, and the other students guessed the verbs. Participants in the comparison groups prompted guesses using only verbal paraphrases of the verbs. The learners in the enactment groups performed better in immediate post-tests which required students to supply the missing verbs in gapped sentences than the learners who had learned the vocabulary items through verbal representations. One week later, the students were given a new test in which the same action verbs were presented in contexts where they were used metaphorically. Accompanying these metaphorical uses were L1 translations, many of which did not fully capture the precise meaning of the verbs. The students' task was to evaluate these translations. Also, on this test the students who had learned the literal meanings of the verbs through enactment performed better than their peers who had learned the verbs only through verbal representations. Lindstromberg and Boers (2005) concluded that actions and motoric imagery benefited not only the students' retention of the literal meanings of the action verbs, but also helped them to more fully appreciate their meaning when used metaphorically. While Lindstromberg and Boers' study highlighted the benefits of enactment-based metaphor awareness, the study did not investigate the impact of this teaching technique beyond a one-week delayed test.

Employing enactment-based metaphor awareness to teach metaphoric expressions in L2 thus offers possible mnemonic benefits. Cognition research (Kelly et al. 2009; Macedonia et al. 2011) in support of Engelkamp and Krumnacker's (1980) enactment effect hypothesis indicated that enacting abstract words promotes retention for longer periods than verbal or auditory modalities in L2. For example, Macedonia and Klimesch (2014) performed a longitudinal 14-month study testing participants' ability to commit artificial abstract vocabulary to their long-term memory after a lesson that involved gesture and enactment. Memory performance was assessed at five time points. At each time point, enacted vocabulary items were remembered significantly more often than vocabulary items explained through audio-visual modalities. Since metaphoric vocabulary describes abstract concepts, cognition research serves as further support of the usefulness of enactment in figurative language teaching. Together, the findings of cognitive psychology, neuro-cognition, cognitive linguistics and cognition research are valuable starting points for an investigation of enactment-based metaphor awareness in language learning.

4 Production of Metaphoric Expressions

Only a handful of studies have investigated interventional methods in promoting production of metaphoric expressions. Boers (2004) noted that this lack of focus is partly due to a consensus amongst cognitive linguists that metaphor awareness-raising activities, while useful as tools for helping learners comprehend and retain expressions they are presented with, are limited as generative methods. MacArthur (2010) suggested promoting the production of metaphor through the use of written and spoken texts, dictionaries, and corpora, which could be employed both inside and outside the classroom. However, studies investigating such techniques are scarce.

Boers (2000) performed one of the few studies that have investigated learners' production of metaphoric expressions in writing. In his study, he taught 73 French business students vocabulary items on 'upward' and 'downward' economic trends. The experimental group was made aware of the nature of conceptual metaphors, whereas the control group was not. The learners were then encouraged to use the vocabulary items they had been taught in a short essay to describe graphs on economic growth. The experimental group produced more of the targeted vocabulary items than the control group (7.1 versus 4.9 in average). However, Boers (2013) advised that his early (2000) study should be viewed with caution because no pre-test was administered.

Viewing the topic of vocabulary production in Second Language Acquisition (SLA) research helps in clarifying difficulties faced in promoting metaphor production. Nation ([2001] 2013) viewed vocabulary acquisition in terms of the receptive-productive lexical knowledge continuum, where understanding of vocabulary items is placed at one end of the continuum and production of the items is at the other end. In most models of vocabulary acquisition (Laufer 1998; Nation 2013), lexical knowledge begins with receptive knowledge, or the ability to understand a word when it is heard or read (passive vocabulary), and ends with productive knowledge, or the ability to use the word in writing or speaking (active vocabulary). Passive vocabulary knowledge develops at a faster and more systematic rate than the much more limited active knowledge. Placing metaphoric vocabulary on the active-passive vocabulary continuum can explain why promoting the production of taught metaphoric expressions is so difficult.

In summary, although a gap exists in empirical classroom testing, the research conducted suggests that exploiting the embodied nature of metaphors through actions in the teaching of L2 metaphor can lead to longer-term retention. Promoting awareness of the bodily motivations behind a conceptual metaphor may not only clarify the metaphor's perceptual elements but also help learners retain associated metaphoric expressions. Thus, by shifting the focus from metaphor understanding to retention and from conceptual metaphor awareness to enactment-based metaphor awareness, we can broaden the scope of figurative language teaching research. In addition, MacArthur's (2010) dynamic system view is considered in the experimental design of this study so that it is closer to authentic classroom teaching. Instead of taking a standalone teaching approach to metaphor, the teaching of metaphor is embedded in teaching methodologies adopted as frames for the interventional teaching sessions. The teaching methodologies are Asher's (2012) TPR, Ray and Sealy's (2004) TPR storytelling and Presentation – Practice – Production (PPP) teaching approach. Also, the metaphoric expressions, teaching materials and tests were chosen and developed from authentic sources and online corpora. Moreover, since the difficulties of promoting the production of taught metaphoric expressions have not been thoroughly investigated in cognitive linguistics, this study also explores this difficulty in a classroom-based environment to further support the notion that metaphor awareness-raising activities may not BE sufficient to promote metaphor production.

5 Research Question and Aim

The experimental study seeks to answer the research question: How do 60 female Saudi EFL learners respond to awareness-raising activities in the teaching of metaphoric expressions when these activities are based on enactment-based metaphor awareness, conceptual metaphor awareness, and semantic clustering? This study investigates the use of bodily actions to make EFL learners aware of the embodied nature of the conceptual metaphor LIFE IS A JOURNEY and to help these learners understand the sensorimotor motivations of metaphoric expressions.

6 Method

The 5-week experimental study involved 60 female Saudi EFL students. The students were divided into an enactment metaphor group, a conceptual metaphor group, and a control group. Data collection involved metaphor comprehension tests and metaphor production tests.

6.1 Participants

The participants of this study were female Saudi university students aged 18 to 20 years old whose first language is Arabic. All participants were in their foundation year at a Saudi university studying at the university's English Language Institute. The courses at the English Language Institute teach students who are placed at A1, A2, B1, B2 levels as described by the Common European Framework of Reference (CEFR) for Languages. These courses are intensive 7-week courses that require students to take EFL classes for 18 hours per week. Two weeks prior to the EFL course, students undertook the Oxford Online Placement Test and were placed at the B2 upper-intermediate level. Three B2 level classes, which ranged from 31 to 32 students each, were chosen at random. Participants signed consent forms that ensured privacy and anonymity. Participants were then assigned as the enactment metaphor group (31 students), the conceptual metaphor group (32 students), and the control group (31 students). As some students were absent in some of the sessions, their data were excluded from the study. In the 5-week period of the study, 25 participants remained in the enactment metaphor group (mean age= 18.36), 18 participants remained in the conceptual metaphor group (mean age= 18.47), and 17 participants (mean age= 19.52) remained in the control group.

6.2 Selection of Metaphoric Expressions

The target metaphoric expressions for this study are 11 metaphoric expressions that have metaphoric and literal relations to the conceptual metaphor LIFE IS A JOURNEY. These metaphoric expressions include verbs, nouns, multi-word units, and collocations. I narrowed the number of vocabulary items to 11 metaphoric expressions because the teaching methodology TPR (Asher [1977] 2012) is a teaching methodology that focuses on the quality of vocabulary taught instead of the quantity. Asher ([1977] 2012) recommends that the target vocabulary in a TPR lesson should be kept fairly small in order to make sure that students participate in the actions and gestures, so that every vocabulary item is thoroughly practised by every student during class time.

I chose the metaphoric expressions according to three criteria. First, I adopted some of Boers and Lindstromberg's (2008) criteria for choosing metaphoric expressions for teaching. Namely, I selected the metaphoric expressions according to their relevance to students in their foundation year and how useful the metaphoric expressions can be to them. I also selected metaphoric expressions based on coverage and chose items whose meanings are more general (e.g. *a path*). I selected items based on how wide the range of the expression is in the discourse of life experiences (e.g. *a step in the right direction*). In addition, I selected collocations of different levels of difficulty and frequency to expose the participants to different frequencies of vocabulary. I asked participants in the piloting stage to rate the difficulty of the piloted metaphoric expressions and I chose items with varied difficulty ratings.

Second, I consulted Macmillan and Collins Online dictionaries to ensure authentic use of the chosen metaphoric expressions and that both the metaphoric and literal meanings of metaphoric expressions are documented uses. Third, I collected the list of metaphoric expressions from Lazar's (2003) *Meanings and Metaphors* textbook and from websites that discussed life experiences. I cross-checked the initial set of metaphoric expressions with the British National Corpus (the BNC) for frequency and kept only those expressions with a statistically significant occurrence rate (i.e. above 2.00 frequency band T-score). This technique for the selection of metaphoric expressions is based on the methodology outlined by Walker (2008), who explains that when the collocate has a T-score of 2.00 or above, the combination of words is statistically significant and did not occur by chance. With multi-word expressions such as *to take a step forward*, the T-score is extracted for the entire expression; and if the expression contained a verb, different verb forms are taken into consideration.

The initial list of metaphoric expressions included 15 metaphoric expressions. Piloting was performed with 18 language learners and 7 British speakers, and based on its results, the most frequently answered 11 vocabulary items were chosen. As stated earlier, different levels of difficulty were taken into consideration as well. Table 1 provides the final set of metaphoric expressions taught per teaching week and their frequency collocations in the BNC:

Table 1: Metaphoric expressions and their frequencies in the BNC.

Week 2 metaphoric expressions	BNC T-score	Week 3 metaphoric expressions	BNC T-score
to take a step forward	2.22	to climb	6.47
to overcome an obstacle	3.43	in the fast lane	8.15
to follow in someone's footsteps	7.15	a step in the right direction	17.44
a path	6.64	to stumble into	2.86
at a crossroads	10.66	a dead-end job	3.45
		up the career ladder	2.76

6.3 Experiment Time Frame

The study was designed as a 5-week experimental study to run alongside a 7-week teaching programme at the Saudi university. I coordinated with the teachers of the participant groups to spend 6 teaching-hours with the students during week 2 and week 3 (three 1-hour sessions per week). Table 2 presents the timeframe for each group, which is detailed in the following section.

Table 2: Experiment time frame for participant groups.

	Control group	Conceptual metaphor group	Enactment metaphor group
Week 1	Consent form Metaphor comprehension pre-test Metaphor production pre-test		
Week 2	Semantic clustering Reading a metaphoric short story	Conceptual metaphor awareness Reading metaphoric and literal short stories	Enactment-based metaphor awareness TPR Storytelling of metaphoric and literal short stories
Week 3	Semantic clustering Reading a metaphoric short story	Conceptual metaphor awareness Reading metaphoric and literal short stories	Enactment-based metaphor awareness TPR Storytelling of metaphoric and literal short stories
	Metaphor comprehension post-test		
Week 4	Metaphor production post-test		
Week 5	Metaphor comprehension 2-week delayed test		

6.4 Interventional Teaching

I designed teaching materials describing 'the journey of life' to teach the 11 metaphoric expressions surrounding LIFE IS A JOURNEY. Week 2 focused on teaching five metaphoric expressions, and week 3 focused on teaching six metaphoric expressions. The following subsections detail the interventional teaching for participant groups.

6.4.1 Enactment Metaphor Group

The enactment metaphor group learned the literal and figurative senses of the expressions through enactment and mime. Day one of each week was spent introducing the literal and metaphoric meanings of the metaphoric expressions which were obtained from Macmillan and Collins Online dictionaries. Students also elaborated on the relationships between the metaphoric expressions and the LIFE IS A JOURNEY metaphor. For example, I explained 'to climb' in both its metaphoric and literal senses and then asked the students to guess the similarities between climbing social ranks and physical journeys. Students brainstormed ideas about hiking and mountain climbing and related them to overcoming difficulties in one's career or education. Students were then asked to enact each vocabulary item in its literal sense and follow simple TPR commands. For example, to enact the phrase to overcome an obstacle, a group of learners were instructed to stand together and form an obstacle to prevent others from passing through. Another student would then attempt to overcome the obstacle. Then, day two followed Ray and Seely's ([1998] 2004) TPR Storytelling. The students read and acted out a literal journey story and a figurative journey story. Snapshots of the stories are presented in Figures 1 and 2 below. Finally, students spent Day three of every week repeating the commands and TPR stories. They also created and acted out their own TPR stories employing the taught metaphoric expressions.

Directions to the Grocery Store

When we moved to our new house, my mom wanted me to go to the grocery store to get us some food and supplies. I did not know the area yet, so she gave me some simple directions. She said to **take my first step forward** out of the house then to avoid the busy street by taking the green **footpath** to the left instead. **At the crossroads,** I should turn left again. She warned me to watch out for a small stream along the **path.**

Figure 1: A sample of the literal story.

Sarah's Career Path

I'd like to tell you the story of how I became a painter. After I finished high school, I started to go down the **path** of earning my medical degree. This wasn't what I wanted, but I felt like I had to follow **in my parents' footsteps.** The first step in medical school was to take a science placement exam. I failed it miserably! My instructors told me that medicine may not be the right path for me, but they still offered to allow me to retake the test in a week.

Figure 2: A sample of the figurative story.

6.4.2 Conceptual Metaphor Group

Students in the conceptual metaphor group learned the same 11 metaphoric expressions in the framework of conceptual metaphor awareness through the PPP teaching methodology. The three one-hour teaching sessions followed the phases of PPP across the two teaching weeks. On day one (Presentation Phase), the literal and figurative meanings of the first five metaphoric items were demonstrated through conceptual metaphor awareness. Similar to the enactment metaphor group, learners in the conceptual metaphor group learned the dictionary definitions of the metaphoric expressions. They were also encouraged to guess and create links between the source and target domains beyond the literal meanings of the metaphoric expressions. However, they were not asked to enact the metaphoric expressions as the intervention for the conceptual metaphor group targets only verbal explanations of the conceptual metaphor. For instance, '*a path*' was explained as a way from one place to another that people can walk along' as well as 'the way that someone's life develops'. Students were also encouraged to come up with ideas on how literal and figurative paths relate to each other and how a path can be a part of one's life journey. On day two (Practice Phase), the students read the two short stories and they were given worksheets to practice the learned materials. Students then extracted the metaphoric expressions from the two stories and compared the use of their literal and metaphoric meanings. On day three (Production Phase), the students practiced integrating the taught metaphoric expressions in their own speech by creating their own stories.

6.4.3 Control Group

Participants in the control group dealt with the metaphoric expressions only as figurative expressions according to the theme 'travelling through life'. The aim of the control group was not to remove the metaphor entirely, but to focus the students' attention on the metaphoric expressions without their conceptual motivations. As a control measure, the teaching of the control group did not involve referencing conceptual metaphor awareness, the source domain JOURNEY, or enactment; it only involved semantic clustering of the 11 metaphoric expressions. The PPP teaching methodology was employed as parallel to the intervention given to the conceptual metaphor group. On day one (Presentation Phase), the figurative meanings of the metaphoric expressions, which were extracted from Macmillan and Collins Online dictionaries, were introduced within the domain of life. On day two (Practice Phase), students read the figurative story, did the practice worksheets, extracted the metaphoric expressions from the text, and discussed use of the expressions within the context of life experiences. The literal stories did not constitute a part of the control group's treatment as the comparison between the two stories might have led the students to notice the source domain JOURNEY. Day three (Production Phase) was a revision day of the metaphoric expressions and figurative stories in which the students practiced using the metaphoric expressions in their own stories.

In relation to treatment design, the quality of teaching received by the two experimental groups and the control group was kept as similar as possible except for the variables tested. The three groups received the same amount of training time (six 1-hour sessions) and the same teaching materials (11 vocabulary items and two figurative short stories). The only differences between the groups were that they underwent different types of treatment according to the aims of the study. Only the experimental groups were given literal short stories, as the experimental groups' training required awareness of the source domain JOURNEY, and only the enactment metaphor group enacted the metaphoric expressions. This difference of treatment between the three groups could raise some questions with regards to the different variables introduced to each group. There was a concern about the higher cognitive effort exerted by the enactment metaphor group, who used actions and gestures to internalize the metaphoric senses of the vocabulary, as opposed to the effort required of the control group and the conceptual metaphor group whose teaching was mainly teacher-centered. To this we can say that requiring this cognitive effort on the part of the enactment metaphor group was intentional and gives more support to the hypothesis that employing enactment-based metaphor awareness leads to better understanding and retention. In addition, since two teaching methodologies (TPR and PPP) were employed across the participant groups, these methods are considered as variables for participant groups along with the metaphor awareness-raising activities.

Following the experiment completion and to ensure that all groups were treated in an ethical manner, I went back to the control group and the conceptual metaphor group and gave them a taste of the teaching of metaphoric expressions through enactment-based metaphor awareness. As to the control group, I introduced the conceptual metaphor LIFE IS A JOURNEY and reconnected the 11 vocabulary items to their source and target domains as well as their literal senses. Then, I had the learners enact the vocabulary and stories. As to the conceptual metaphor group, I had them enact the 11 vocabulary items and the four stories since they already learned them through conceptual metaphor awareness.

6.5 Metaphor Comprehension Tests

I designed the metaphor comprehension tests as multiple-choice questions that measured the students' understanding of the different meanings of the taught metaphoric expressions. Each question in the pre-test, the post-test, and the 2-

week delayed test consisted of a statement that used the vocabulary in either its metaphoric or literal sense. Each test included 11 questions; half of the tested items were presented in their metaphoric sense while the other half were presented in their literal sense totalling in five literal items and six metaphoric items or vice versa. For example, the following two sentences from the pre-test and the post-test use the term *crosswords* both literally and metaphorically:

- Metaphoric: After she had finished her master's degree, she was *at a crossroads*. She could pursue a PhD degree or find a job to establish her career.
- Literal: To get to the Children's Hospital, drive down Second Street until you are *at the crossroads*, then turn left.

I selected the metaphoric and literal statements in the tests using the BNC and simplified them to suit learners' language levels. I also selected the possible literal and metaphoric answers using Macmillan and Collins online dictionaries. Figure 3 shows that the multiple-choice answers comprised an incorrect answer, a literal sense, a metaphoric sense, an option for other possible meanings, and an option for a lack of knowledge.

---

10. Hoping to take over the family business one day, Mary **followed in her father's footseps** and became a lawyer. The problem is that she does not like being a lawyer at all.

    A. To carry a heavy object for a long period of time
    B. To walk or drive behind someone or to go in the same direction as them
    C. To do the same work or achieve the same success as someone else before you
    D. It means something else: _____
    E. I do not know

Figure 3: A sample of the metaphor comprehension post-test.

During data coding, multiple-choice options A, B, C, and E were easily coded. As to option D, students filled it in 21 instances in total. Because the students' answers were open to interpretation, an inter-rater reliability procedure was used by which two raters coded option D answers for correctness of meaning independently, and the rating scores were analysed through Cohen's Kappa. The test revealed that agreement between the scores of the two raters in the pre-test was 96%, with a Kappa score of 0.89 at (p= .000), while in the post-test, this agreement level was 97%, with a Kappa score of .95 at (p= .000). This result indicates that the agreement between the two raters on the pre-test and the post-test is almost perfect (Landis and Koch 1977). The raters then discussed the different answers until they agreed on the correctness of 11 cases in the pre-test and 6 cases in the post-test.

A statistical analysis of the metaphor comprehension tests was performed using SPSS Version 22. Since the number of participants in each of the three participant groups was below 30, the Kruskal-Wallis Test, which is the non-parametric equivalent of One-Way ANOVA, was used to compare their performances in the pre-test, the post-test and the 2-week delayed test. As only similarity of distribution of data was expected in the Kruskal-Wallis Test, the test results appeared to follow similar distribution shapes in histogram plots.

6.6 Metaphor Production Tests

The metaphor production pre-test and post-test consisted of free-writing assessments that were designed to measure free production of the 11 taught metaphoric expressions. Due to conflicts with university exams, the production post-test was postponed to Week 4 8 days after the metaphor comprehension post-test. The amount of time between the two posttests may not be enough to avoid test-taking effects, but it was the best option available at the time. The writing instructions are presented in Figures 4 and 5:

Have you ever been in a situation where you had to make a decision between two alternative choices? Write about this situation. Explain how you were undecided between the two choices and what made you make this life-changing decision. What factors influenced you to reach this decision? What would have happened if you had taken the alternative choice?

Figure 4: Instructions for the metaphor production pre-test.

Think of two alternative careers that you would like to pursue in the future. Write about these two jobs. Which career would you enjoy more and why? Which career do you think you will finally choose? Are there any external or internal factors that might influence your decision to pursue one rather than the other? How will you reach your final decision?

Figure 5: Instructions for the metaphor production post-test.

The writing topics were chosen because they revolved around life experiences, but there was no guarantee that the topics would promote productive use of the metaphoric expressions. Participants were given 60 minutes to answer each test and were instructed to write a 200-word paragraph without thinking about spelling, as this concern may hinder the writing process.

As this study aims to provide awareness-raising activities for the teaching of metaphors rather than measuring language learners' metaphor use, an overall metaphor identification procedure (e.g. MIP or MIPVU) capable of scanning the texts for each metaphoric instance was not needed. Instead, scanning the participants' writing samples was limited to the 11 taught metaphoric expressions. I read each writing sample twice to familiarise myself with the styles of writing. Following this process, I counted the number of words in each sample because the students' written samples varied in length considerably. Shortened uses (e.g. *I'll*) were counted as separate individual words (i.e. *I will*) to maintain conformity in the number of words per student. In the case where a metaphoric expression was used, I treated errors in spelling, verb tense, and singular versus plural forms as irrelevant errors and therefore counted the uses as correctly used metaphoric expressions. However, if the metaphoric expression consisted of a multiword unit, I verified that the entire unit had been used correctly and considered errors in the use of prepositions that constituted a part of the multiword-unit and/or phrasal verb as incorrect uses (i.e. *in the fast-lane*). Moreover, if a participant used a taught metaphoric expression on two different occasions, I counted this as two single uses of metaphoric expressions and two points were awarded for each use. The use of taught metaphoric expressions in writing by the three participant groups was then compared using the Kruskal-Wallis Test in SPSS.

7 Results

This study investigates how teaching metaphoric expressions through enactment-based metaphor awareness of the metaphor LIFE IS A JOURNEY could influence Saudi learners' comprehension, retention and production of taught metaphoric expressions in comparison with conceptual metaphor awareness and semantic clustering. Results are presented in terms of metaphor comprehension tests and metaphor production tests.

7.1 The Results of the Metaphor Comprehension Tests

To measure the differences in improvement between the control group, the conceptual metaphor group, and the enactment metaphor group, the Kruskal-Wallis Test was used twice. It was used first to study the differences between the metaphor understanding in the post-test and the pre-test and then to explore the differences between the 2-week delayed test and the pre-test. Table 3 presents the average scores of the metaphor comprehension pretest, posttest, and 2-week delayed test received by the control group, the conceptual metaphor group, and the enactment metaphor group. Table 4 presents a summary of the means, medians, standard deviations, and the 2-tailed significance of both:

Table 3: Average results of the metaphor comprehension tests.

	n.	Pretest avg.	Posttest avg.	2-week delayed test avg.
Control group	17	3.82	5.47	3.29
Conceptual metaphor group	18	4.33	9.38	7.05
Enactment metaphor group	25	4.52	9.36	9.68

Table 4: The differences of improvement between the post-test and the pre-test, and between the 2-week delayed test and the pre-test.

	n	Post-test/pre-test difference	Delayed test/pre-test difference
Control group	17	M= 1.65 Md= 2.00 SD= 2.57	M= -0.53 Md= -1.00 SD= 2.15
Conceptual metaphor group	18	M= 5.06 Md= 5.00 SD= 2.94	M= 2.72 Md= 3.00 SD= 2.96
Enactment metaphor group	25	M= 4.84 Md= 5.00 SD= 2.42	M= 5.16 Md= 5.00 SD= 2.37
2-tailed significance		p= .001	p= .000

The Kruskal-Wallis Test reveals that the difference in improvement between the post-test and the pre-test between the medians of the control group (M= 1.65, Md= 2.00, SD= 2.57), the conceptual metaphor group (M= 5.06, Md= 5.00, SD= 2.94), and the enactment metaphor group (M= 4.84, Md= 5.00, SD= 2.42) is highly significant (p= .001). A highly significant difference (p= .000) is also found regarding the differences in improvement between the 2-week delayed test and the pre-test between the medians of the control group (M= -0.53, Md= -1.00, SD= 2.15), the conceptual metaphor group (M= 2.72, Md= 3.00, SD= 2.96), and the enactment metaphor group (M= 5.16, Md= 5.00, SD= 2.37). Post-hoc tests in the form of a series of Mann-Whitney U Tests reveal the specific differences between the control group, the conceptual metaphor group, and the enactment metaphor group. Applying the Bonferroni adjustment to the alpha level, significance in the post-hoc analyses is judged at (p<.017). Table 5 presents the significant comparisons between the individual groups and their effect sizes:

Table 5: Post-hoc test results for differences in improvement with the effect sizes.

	Difference between the post-test and pre-test significance	Difference between the delayed test and pre-test significance
Control group and conceptual metaphor group	$p = .001 - r = .4$	$p = .001 - r = 0.41$
Control group and enactment metaphor group	$p = .000 - r = .45$	$p = .000 - r = 0.64$
Conceptual metaphor group and enactment metaphor group	NA	$p = .008 - r = 0.34$

The individual Mann-Whitney U-Tests in Table 5 indicate that the only significant differences in improvement between the post-test and the pre-test are between the control group and the conceptual metaphor group (p= .001) with a medium effect size (r= .4), and between the control group and the enactment metaphor group (p= .000) with a medium effect size (r = .45) (Cohen 1988). This finding suggests that by being made aware of the metaphoric motivations of the metaphoric expressions, the experimental groups have understood the taught metaphoric expressions more accurately than the control group.

In addition, the post-hoc tests reveal that there are significant differences in improvement between the 2-week delayed test and the pre-test between the control group and the conceptual metaphor group (p= .001) with a medium effect size (r= .41), the control group and the enactment metaphor group (p= .000) with a large effect size (r= .64), and between the conceptual metaphor group and the enactment metaphor group (p= .008) with a medium effect size (r= .34) (Cohen 1988). These findings suggest that learning metaphoric expressions through actions has aided the enactment metaphor group's retention of metaphoric expressions up to a period of two weeks in comparison to the control and conceptual metaphor groups. In addition, the results show that longer-term retention seems to have also happened in the conceptual metaphor group, but not as pronounced as in the enactment metaphor group. This indicates that enactment-based metaphor awareness is more effective in terms of retention than the teacher-centred conceptual metaphor awareness. In addition, employing conceptual metaphor awareness appears to aid longer-term retention of the senses of the metaphoric expressions, just not as much as learning the metaphoric expressions through enactment and mime.

7.2 The Results of the Metaphor Production Tests

As none of the participant groups used the target metaphoric expressions in the metaphor production pre-test, only the results of the metaphor production post-test are statistically analysed using the Kruskal-Wallis test. The Kruskal-Wallis test indicates that the difference in numbers of taught metaphoric expressions in the control group (M= .31, Md= .00, SD= .1), the conceptual metaphor group (M= .64, Md= .00, SD= .19) and the enactment metaphor group (M= .85, Md= .00, SD= .25) is not significant. The 2-week interventional teaching sessions did not yield a significant difference in the productive use of the taught metaphoric expressions between the three groups.

These results suggest that enactment-based metaphor awareness, conceptual metaphor awareness, and semantic clustering may be unsuitable teaching methods for the production of metaphoric expressions. There is also the possibility that the testing measure that consisted of a free-writing assessment played a role in the less than encouraging results. Comparing pre- and post-intervention production in the form of free-writing assessments which may contain opportunities for metaphor production, may not be the most appropriate method to test for metaphor production.

8 Discussion

The results of this study support the notion that adopting enactment for the teaching of the conceptual metaphor LIFE IS A JOURNEY aids the understanding and retention of metaphoric expressions than that of conceptual metaphor awareness alone. This finding is important, as Boers (2004) has pointed out the shortcomings of conceptual metaphor awareness as a technique limited to the understanding and retention of taught metaphoric expressions. By associating metaphoric expressions with their embodied nature through actions, longer-term retention, in this case in terms of two weeks, is achieved. However, a number of issues should be acknowledged when discussing the results of this study.

First, in terms of the results of the metaphor comprehension tests, there appears to be a dual advantage that can be gained from enactment-based metaphor awareness: one for the awareness of embodied meanings of the metaphoric expressions, and one for the enactment effect on memory. First, enactment-based metaphor awareness familiarised the learners with the sensorimotor motivations behind LIFE IS A JOURNEY and its metaphoric expressions, which was also observed in Lindstromberg and Boers' (2005) study on action verbs. The important addition provided by the current study is that the learners acted out not only action verbs but also complex constructions like nouns, collocations, lexical phrases, etc. Second, while Lindstromberg and Boers (2005) did not explore beyond 1-week retention of vocabulary, the current study has found that enactment-based awareness of metaphor has had stronger mnemonic benefits than conceptual metaphor awareness and semantic clustering two weeks after teaching. The results of this study also align with those of Macedonia and Klimesch's (2014) longitudinal study, which show highly significant results in 2-week delayed tests for enacted vocabulary compared to vocabulary items explained using audio-visual modalities. It is important to note that the difference between the three groups is based on a combination of variables including their respective teaching methodologies (PPP for the control group and the conceptual metaphor group and TPR for the enactment metaphor group), the amount of input for each group, the time spent by each group on the items along with the different metaphor awareness-raising activities. While it is not clear if the results of the enactment metaphor group are due to one of these variables or all, it appears that employing enactment-based awareness of metaphor through TPR aids the comprehension and retention of taught metaphoric expressions for learners.

In terms of the results of the metaphor production tests, the 60 learners provided writing samples ranging from 28 words to 199 words in the pre-test (M= 98.13, SD= 40.83) and from 20 words to 184 words in the posttest (M= 73.1, SD= 34.33) and appeared to be able to express themselves well without using taught metaphoric expressions. The results were also rather surprising especially that the students were reminded yet again of the metaphoric expressions in the metaphor comprehension test which was administered 8 days prior to the metaphor production test. As discussed in Section 4, Nation ([2001] 2013) details how productive vocabulary progresses at a slower rate than passive vocabulary, which could explain the delayed use of the taught metaphoric expressions. Further cognitive linguistic research should investigate the fostering of productive knowledge of metaphoric expressions in EFL learners focusing on the development of testing measures for metaphor production in L2.

In conclusion, since the current study was unable to test for the impact of enactment-based metaphor awareness for more than two weeks after the interventional teaching sessions, its results can be interpreted as indicative rather than conclusive. More longitudinal classroom-based experimental research is crucial to gain an accurate picture of the impact of enactment-based metaphor awareness-raising activities in L2.

References

Asher, James. 2012 [1977]. *Learning another language through actions: The complete teacher's guidebook*, 7th edn. Los Gatos: Sky Oaks.

Barsalou, Lawrence. 2009. Simulation, situated conceptualization, and prediction. *Philosophical Transactions of the Royal Society* 364. 1281–1289.

Boers, Frank. 2000. Metaphor awareness and vocabulary retention. *Applied Linguistics* 21. 553–571.

Boers, Frank. 2004. Expanding learners' vocabulary through metaphor awareness: What expansion, what learners, what vocabulary? In Susanne Niemeier & Michel Achard (eds.), *Cognitive linguistics, second language acquisition, and foreign language teaching*, 211–234. Berlin: Mouton de Gruyter.

Boers, Frank. 2013. Cognitive linguistic approaches to teaching vocabulary: Assessment and integration. *Language Teaching* 46(2). 208–224.

Boers, Frank & Seth Lindstromberg. 2008. How cognitive linguistics can foster effective vocabulary teaching. In Frank Boers & Seth Lindstromberg (eds.), *Cognitive linguistic approaches to teaching vocabulary and phraseology*, 1–65. Berlin: Mouton de Gruyter.

Boers, Frank, Seth Lindstromberg, Jeannette Littlemore, Hélène Stengers & June Eyckmans. 2008. Variables in the mnemonic effectiveness of pictorial elucidation. In Frank Boers & Seth Lindstromberg (eds.), *Cognitive linguistic approaches to teaching vocabulary and phraseology*, 189–116. Berlin: Mouton de Gruyter.

Boers, Frank, Murielle Demecheleer & June Eyckmans. 2004. Cross-cultural variation as a variable in comprehending and remembering figurative idioms. *European Journal of English Studies* 8(3). 375–388.

Boers, Frank, June Eyckmans & Hélène Stengers. 2007. Presenting figurative idioms with a touch of etymology: More than mere mnemonics? *Language Teaching Research* 11(1). 43–62.

Boers, Frank, Ana Piquer Píriz, Hélène Stengers & June Eyckmans. 2009. Does pictorial elucidation foster recollection of figurative idioms? *Language Teaching Research*, 13(4). 367–388.

Cohen, Jacob. 1988. *Statistical power analysis for the behavioral sciences*. Hillsdale: Lawrence Erlbaum.

De Grauwe, Sophie, Roel Willems, Shirley-Ann Rueschemeyer, Kristin Lemhöfer & Herbert Schriefers. 2014. Embodied language in first- and second-language speakers: Neural correlates of processing motor verbs. *Neuropsychologia* 56. 334–349.

Desai, Rutvik H., Jeffrey R. Binder, Lisa L. Conant, Quintino R. Mano & Mark S. Seidenberg. 2011. The neural career of sensorimotor metaphors. *Journal of Cognitive Neuroscience* 23(9). 2376–2386.

Engelkamp, Johannes. & Horst Krumnacker. 1980. Imaginale und motorische Prozesse beim Behalten verbalen Materials. *Zeitschrift für experimentelle und angewandte Psychologie*, 27, 511–533.

Gibbs, Raymond. 2006. *Embodiment and cognitive science*. New York: Cambridge University Press.

Gibbs, Raymond. 2013. Walking the walk while thinking about the talk: Embodied interpretation of metaphorical narratives. *Journal of Psycholinguistic Research*. 42(4). 363–378.

Gibbs, Raymond. 2014. Embodied metaphor. In Jeannette Littlemore & John Taylor (eds.), *Bloomsbury companion to cognitive linguistics*, 167–184. London: Bloomsbury.

Gibbs, Raymond & Marcus Perlman. 2006. The contested impact of cognitive linguistic research on the psycholinguistics of metaphor understanding. In Gitte Kristiansen, Michel Achard, René Dirven & Francisco Ruiz de Mendoza Ibáñez (eds.), *Cognitive linguistics: Current applications and future perspectives*. 211–228. Berlin & New York: Mouton de Gruyter.

Grady, Joseph. 1997. *Foundations of meaning: Primary metaphors and primary scenes*. Berkeley: University of California Berkeley PhD Dissertation

IJzerman, Hans & Gün R. Semin. 2009. The thermometer of social relations: Mapping social proximity on temperature. *Psychological Science* 20(10). 1214–1220.

Kelly, Spencer D., Tara Mcdevitt & Megan Esch. 2009. Brief training with co-speech gesture lends a hand to word learning in a foreign language. *Language Cognitive Processes* 24. 313–334.

Landis, J. Richard & Gary Koch. 1977. The measurement of observer agreement for categorical data. *Biometrics* 33. 159–174.

Laufer, Batia. 1998. The development of passive and active vocabulary in a second language: Same or different? *Applied Linguistics* 19. 255–271.

Lazar, Gillian. 2003. *Meanings and metaphors: Activities to practice figurative language*. Cambridge: Cambridge University Press.

Lee, Spike W. S. & Norbert Schwarz. 2012. Bidirectionality, mediation, and moderation of metaphorical effects: The embodiment of social suspicion and fishy smells. *Journal of Personality and Social Psychology*. 103(5). 737–749.

Lindstromberg, Seth & Frank Boers. 2005. From movement to metaphor with manner-of-movement verbs. *Applied Linguistics* 26(2). 241–261.

MacArthur, Fiona. 2010. Metaphorical competence in EFL: Where are we and where should we be going? A view from the language classroom. *AILA Review* 23. 155–173.

Macedonia, Manuela & Wolfgang Klimesch. 2014. Long-term effects of gestures on memory for foreign language words trained in the classroom. *Mind, Brain and Education* 8(2),74–88.

Macedonia, Manuela, Karsten Müller & Angela D. Friederici. 2011. The impact of iconic gestures on foreign language word learning and its neural substrate. *Human Brain Mapping*. 32. 982–988.

Nation, Paul. 2013 [2001]. *Learning vocabulary in another language*, 2nd edn. Cambridge: Cambridge University Press.

Ray, Blaine & Contee Seely. 2004 [1998]. *Fluency through TPR storytelling: Achieving real language acquisition in school*, 4th edn. Berkley: Command Performance Language Institute.

Skoufaki, Sophia. 2008. Conceptual metaphoric meaning clues in two idiom presentation methods. In Seth Lindstromberg & Frank Boers (eds.), *Cognitive linguistic approaches to teaching vocabulary and phraseology*, 101–132. Berlin: Mouton de Gruyter.

Tinkham, Thomas. 1993. The effect of semantic clustering on the learning of second language vocabulary. *System* 21(3). 371–380.

Walker, Crayton. 2008. Factors which influence the process of collocation. In Frank Boers & Seth Lindstromberg (eds.), *Cognitive linguistic approaches to teaching vocabulary and phraseology*. Berlin & New York: Mouton de Gruyter.

Wilcox, Amanda & Almitra Medina. 2013. Effects of semantic and phonological clustering on L2 vocabulary acquisition among novice learners. *System* 41. 1056–1069.

Wilson, Nicole L. & Raymond Gibbs. 2007. Real and imagined body movement primes metaphor comprehension. *Cognitive Science* 31. 721–731.

Xue, Jin, Jie Yang & Qian Zhao. 2014. Chinese–English bilinguals processing temporal–spatial metaphor. *Cognitive Processing* 15(3). 269–281.

Subject Index

https://doi.org/10.1515/9783110630367-014